Memories of Poland

Lessons From Growing Up Under Communism

PAYLIE ROBERTS

This book is for informational purposes only. The author and publisher are not offering it as legal, accounting, or other professional advice. The content of this book is the sole expression and opinion of its author, and not necessarily that of the publisher. While best efforts have been used in preparing this book, the author and publisher make no representations or warranties of any kind and assume no liabilities of any kind with respect to the accuracy or completeness of the contents and specifically disclaim any implied warranties of merchantability or fitness of use for a particular purpose. Neither the author nor the publisher shall be held liable or responsible to any person or entity with respect to any loss or incidental or consequential damages caused, or alleged to have been caused, directly or indirectly, by the information contained herein. Neither the publisher nor the individual author shall be liable for any physical, psychological, emotional, financial, or commercial damages, including, but not limited to, special, incidental, consequential or other damages. Our views and rights are the same: You are responsible for your own choices, actions, and results.

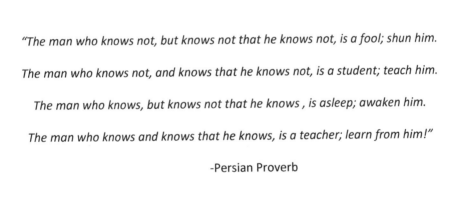

"The man who knows not, but knows not that he knows not, is a fool; shun him.

The man who knows not, and knows that he knows not, is a student; teach him.

The man who knows, but knows not that he knows , is asleep; awaken him.

The man who knows and knows that he knows, is a teacher; learn from him!"

-Persian Proverb

CONTENTS

ACKNOWLEDGMENTS

I first want to thank my husband for helping me write this book. His assistance was invaluable in reading my poorly constructed paragraphs, being able to understand what I was trying to say, and "translating" the meaning of my written words in a way that is not only clear and makes sense, but does so elegantly. Although I took English courses in college, my sentence structure was developed using grammar from a different language. Although I think I make sense, I sometimes need a bit of help to make certain. My husband was kind enough to help disguise my writing style, which would otherwise clearly show that English is my second language. He also expanded on numerous topics in this work of which I had only scratched the surface.

I want to say thank you to the two people that gave me life: my mother and father. Without their courageous actions when I was a child, and without their support of sending me recordings of answers to my numerous questions about life in Poland (recordings which often revealed weakened and cracked voices that told me it was painful for them to revisit certain memories), I might have never had the opportunity to put the pieces of this puzzle together into words on paper. My parents were never revolutionaries: I think they were just ordinary people who were trying to create a better life for themselves and their family. And I think they were trying to do what they thought was right. I hope you learn from this story, and recognize their courage — and the courage of other members of Polish Solidarity — as a courage that all people should have against any tyranny or oppression that may be lurking during their own lives.

I want to thank all the people who graciously provided feedback on the early drafts of this work, for being supportive friends, and for understanding that working full time while writing a book makes for one tired, cranky individual. Regardless, they have remained my friends throughout my endeavor, and offered honest feedback on a work in progress.

Similarly, I would like to thank Lisa Egan for her editorial feedback and assistance.

I would especially like to thank two authors that I have never met, nor will I likely ever meet: Jack M. Bloom and Shana Penn. Jack M. Bloom wrote *Seeing Through the Eyes of the Polish Revolution*, and Shana Penn wrote *Solidarity's Secret: The Women Who Defeated Communism in Poland.* These two works were major contributors to helping me connect the dots of the history of Poland that was intentionally concealed by the people in power at that time. The combination of these two works provide a compilation of facts that should be included in any historical account that covers that era of Polish history. They are also excellent resources for anyone who has further interest in learning about what it was like to live under communist rule in Poland, and how the people in the opposition found creative ways around challenges which led to the fall of communism.

Finally, I want to thank many people whom I have never met and who have never met me. I refer to many of the journalists from the alternative media and news bloggers who share my concern for the American way of life, and who see many of the same concerning trends that I point out in this book. There are so many people and web sites now that it would be too many to list individually. To those from this group who are reading this I want to say: realize that your information and real news does get out to the general public, and that you are making a bigger difference for all of us than may be immediately obvious. Keep up the good fight, and continue to find ways to disseminate the truth well into the future — regardless of whatever hardships or challenges you may face. If history is any guide, you will unfortunately face many.

INTRODUCTION

"Do remember, though, that sometimes the people you oppress become mightier than you would like."

-Veronica Roth, *Insurgent*

This was a very difficult book for me to write. I love writing, and I enjoy sharing stories of my life, but my life in Poland and the transition of coming to the United States is a very personal story. It's not something I share often, and until this book, never with strangers. It is a period from my life — and my parents' lives — that we would like to be able to put behind us, as it was not an easy or pleasant period.

So why write a book about these very personal experiences which I would rather keep private? Because I see a potential (or perhaps even a likely) future in America that may put my bleak and atrocious tale of living under communist rule to shame. I see cultural, political, and economic trends and patterns that I feel need to be presented to all Americans so they can choose for themselves what type of future they want to live, and what type of life they want for their children and grandchildren.

I wrote this book in the hope that it will become a "self-defeating prophecy." This term was invented by Robert K. Merton, a sociology professor at Columbia University. A self-defeating prophecy occurs when by making a prediction, you help it *not* come true.[1] By sounding a warning, based on the disturbing trends that are ongoing today, it helps people take actions that collectively will help move us in the right direction to correct the problems. By alerting people to the risks, they can behave in ways that make those risks not come true. And that is the desired outcome I hope to achieve with this book.

I love the US, and I am proud to be an American (naturalized, but very Americanized). I have proudly served in our military, and I proudly continue to serve my country by living by America's founding principles. Most importantly, I want to be able to continue to live by those principles in the future, and I have great concern that will not be possible if we continue on our current course.

Finally, I wrote this book with the hope of showing Americans a different view or perspective of the country in which they live. Like looking from the outside in on yourself, it is a perspective that many people would otherwise not be able to step outside to see. I hope you enjoy this story — my story — but more importantly I hope this book makes you think. I hope it gets you to look at your life and your country in a different way and perhaps motivates you to become more proactive in choosing what you want your life and the future of your country to be. Just like you, I didn't get to choose where I was born, but all people are free in what choices they make and what actions they take as adults.

This book was written and is intended to be read in a sequential manner. The story follows a chronological and historical path from the late 1970s to the present time. I have written this to include my personal story to make it interesting to those who would not otherwise wade through a book containing only facts and analysis. But there are plenty of facts and analysis for those who have that as their primary interest. The first few chapters provide a great deal of background about communist Poland and also compare and contrast Poland with the US today based upon my personal experiences, as well as historical research. However, each chapter does have certain topics that are emphasized more than others, and those topics are further built upon with each subsequent chapter.

Chapter One primarily discusses civil rights. Chapter Two covers economics and shortages. Chapter Three focuses on health care. Chapter Four is primarily autobiographical and discusses the challenges that immigrants face. Chapter Five covers several topics including public education, culture, and to a lesser extent, parenting. Chapter Six briefly mentions the US military, then discusses the police (law enforcement) and the historical role of terrorism. Chapter Seven discusses the philosophy of freedom and historical trends from America's past that are repeating today. Chapter Eight analyzes the US political system, propaganda, and the media's role in these. Chapter Nine provides a summary indictment of concerning trends and problems occurring in the US today. Chapter Ten provides suggestions for Americans, including the lessons provided by the Polish people and Solidarity.

I sincerely hope you enjoy reading this book, and if nothing else I hope you thoughtfully consider the information and ideas it contains.

"Great spirits have always found violent opposition from mediocre minds. The latter cannot understand it when a man does not thoughtlessly submit to hereditary prejudices but honestly and courageously uses his intelligence."

-Albert Einstein

CHAPTER 1: MY MOST IMPORTANT MEMORY: DISAPPEARING ACTS

"The ultimate tragedy is not the oppression and cruelty by the bad people, but the silence over that by the good people."

-Martin Luther King, Jr.

The knocking on the door from the messenger, who was delivering a telegram to my mother, is one of the most important memories I have from my childhood. I recall the knocking was loud and intentional, enough to get my mother's attention. My mother slowly walked to the door and asked with a voice that was firm, but poorly disguised her fear: "Who is it?"

The response of "Telegram" was terse but confident. My mother seemed surprised, and opened the door cautiously and slowly. I don't remember the exact wording of the telegram that was read to my mother, brother, and me. I can tell you that it was around June of 1983, and I was five years old at that time. I remember the excitement in my mother's voice when she discovered that my father was still alive, safe, and in Austria.

For three months prior to that she had no idea where he disappeared to — none of us did. One day, he just never came home. At my age and level of understanding, I couldn't fathom what it meant. I'm not sure how much I even noticed that my father was gone, as we were used to our parents working long hours, and often seven days a week. However, my mother must have been thinking of worst case scenarios. Yet she held strong and went on with life, raising her children and working, as she had no other choice.

As the expression goes, "you can't judge a book by its cover". Most people I've met don't know I'm not a US-born citizen, as my accent is only detectable to the most trained ear. I keep most of my childhood private, as I've learned over time that most peoples' opinion of history doesn't match my experiences. I certainly don't readily share the fact that my father was literally exiled from the country of Poland for being part of Polish Solidarity (*Solidarność*), which was a huge trade organization intent on improving working conditions in Poland, and which was illegal at the time. Specifically, he was arrested and ultimately exiled because he was distributing anti-communist flyers that had been produced by the Solidarity movement. So he was treated in that manner simply for exercising his right to free speech. Many members of Solidarity were arrested or exiled — or both — for similar reasons or similar types of activities.

At the time we received the telegram, we had no idea what my father had been through. It wasn't until I was older that I learned of what happened. At the time of his disappearance, he and many others were rounded up after being arrested at a Solidarity meeting. Those who refused to sign a "loyalty document" produced by the Communist Polish government were threatened with being sent to internment camps. The loyalty document basically stated that the activists would cease all activity that the communist government thought was a threat to their control. Some people signed the document as their circumstances offered them little choice, but many did not, as they didn't want to violate their principles or compromise on their cause. Signing such a document would essentially make them traitors to the Solidarity union, and to the true country of Poland. My father was rounded up with about fifty-five other Solidarity members who refused

2

to sign. They were put on a bus with no windows, and shipped off in the middle of the night.

He knew many of the people that were being "disappeared" with him, but he didn't know what would happen to himself or the others, or if he would even live. They were not allowed off the bus during the travel, and only upon daylight were they allowed off the bus. The handcuffs and shackles were removed when they arrived at the Austrian interment camp designated for anyone who was accused of opposing the Polish state. They were separated, interviewed, and badged.

After almost three months in the interment camp, my father was finally given the option to go to either the US, Australia, Canada, or South Africa. He chose the US as he felt that was the best free country (and to this day he still believes that.) He was then informed that he and the other exiles at the camp would never be allowed to return to Poland. That was their punishment for being activists against the socialist state: exiled forever from the very country he was born in. He was also finally allowed to contact us via telegram to inform us that he was being shipped off to America. He did not know the fates of most of the others at the camp, although he did know that some were not so lucky to be allowed to leave.

Once he arrived in America, he spent the next two years trying to both build a life here and bring over his immediate family to join him. Neither was an easy task for someone who did not speak a word of English, and literally started off with one dollar in his pocket.

That telegram didn't change much at first for my mother, brother, and I, other than let us know that my father was still alive. My mother was already used to struggling on only one income, as she had for the three months prior to the telegram. She was used to tending to everything herself: taking care of the kids, cooking, and standing in long lines for many hours in hopes of being able to buy some groceries. That was in addition to working long hours — often six or seven days a week.

We did receive more communication from my father at a later time once he arrived in the US. But it wasn't until my father was able to establish himself in the US that things really began to change for us back in Poland. Perhaps the biggest change was that it gave my mother hope that one day we would get to live in America as well. But that really didn't mean much to a five or six year old, who didn't know any different.

The life I lived in Poland was the only life I knew. Product shortages and price hikes were something everyone there, including my family, were used to. Stocking up and hoarding food and supplies when you could get them was a way of life. You never knew when the next shipment would come in, how much the price would skyrocket the next day, or how much your ration cards would "allow" you to buy next month. When that's all you know, you can't even imagine what grocery stores must be like that not only have the product you want all the time, but several varieties to choose from.

In 1983 television was still something that not every household in Poland had. Any television programs that were allowed to be broadcast were controlled by the oppressive government. Seeing a different and better way of life on television was not like it is today, where we have amazing special effects that can make you feel like you are experiencing what it's like to be on Mars. So when discussions surrounded our family and people would ask "Aren't you excited that you're going to go to America?" I just shrugged my shoulders. To me, at such a young age, that idea was only a cloud of confusion in my developing brain.

One thing I think is important to point out is that at five (almost six) years old, experiencing my father disappear was not a traumatic event for me. It was "normal" at that time in Poland for people to be "disappeared," especially if they were part of the Solidarity union, and therefore considered "anti-socialist".

It is important to note that Solidarity leadership never *officially* suggested that bringing down communism was one of the organization's goals, but most members must have been concerned in the back of their minds that that was a possibility. However, this was never discussed, as the walls had ears. The "official" Solidarity line was that the organization was an independent (non-government run) "trade union" whose many goals included fighting for improved working conditions for workers. Those who joined Solidarity typically joined to improve working and living conditions, and to be part of an independent trade union that offered a real voice into how things were run in the country — not to bring down the existing government. But given the repressive conditions in Poland at that time, those two goals often became muddled and confused in action if not intent.

When a tyrannical or oppressive rogue "government" is threatened by "its" own people, it will take whatever steps necessary to protect itself and get rid of those people who threaten it. Shipping Solidarity members to other countries was the solution at the time. Either that or prison terms, or worse yet: death. While this information was not something that was widely spread via the government-controlled news, it was something that most Polish people (Poles) just knew. *Common knowledge*, if you will. The Poles had seen what the Nazis had done to the Jews, and what the governments of other Soviet bloc countries (both eastern European and the USSR itself) had done to their own people (politicide or democide). With these events fresh in the minds of the Poles it was widely recognized that "it could happen here too". This was one advantage that the Poles had when formulating their strategies: most of them were well aware of the dire reality of their circumstances, and few had misconceptions that their government was functioning as it should.

For those three months before the telegram, my mother searched for my father in all the usual criminal prisons, but didn't find him. So she had a suspicion that perhaps he had become a political detainee; that my father was rounded up and shipped off somewhere, imprisoned, or even killed. She didn't know if he was alive, or if she would ever hear from him again. Since my mother too had been a member of Solidarity, when the knocking on the door came, she told me her first thought was, "They've come for me too!" This was a way of life for those in the Solidarity union, and my family was one of many that had worked hard to fight a supposedly "communist" way of life.

I should probably make a clarification here. Yes, Poland was theoretically communist then. But it was really more like a mutant hybrid of socialism and fascism. The idea of communism is a theory that some people find appealing, and that has been unsuccessfully tried over and over. But it typically depends on coercion, which almost always leads to totalitarianism. This is one reason why it doesn't work and never will. In order for communism to work, you would have to have *everyone* (no exceptions) be willing, *voluntary* contributing participants, with everyone *actually* being treated equally, and essentially *no* corruption from those willing to scratch each others backs. Instead, it actually turns out that a small group of insider elitists end up controlling a large portion of the resources while everyone else lives in relative poverty. Force and propaganda are then used to keep it that way. The French political philosopher Frederic Bastiat explains in his book *Economic Sophisms*: "*When plunder becomes a way of life for a group of men in a society, over the course of time they create for themselves a legal system that authorizes it and a moral code that glorifies it.*"[1]

Thus, in practice, communism turns out totalitarian, with the many serving the few. I am not talking about idealist theory here, I am talking about practical reality, and the two often turn out quite differently. My parents and I, along with most of the people living in Poland at that time, can tell you from experience that this is the case. Interestingly, history teaches us that under "fascism," which many people argue is the polar opposite of communism, the exact same thing ends up happening: it leads to oppressive tyranny with a small group of elitists in power controlling the majority of economic resources, and using force and propaganda to keep it that way.

The Austrian economist Friedrich von Hayek, in my opinion, correctly argued in his book *The Road to Serfdom* that *"Fascism and socialism have common roots in central economic planning and empowering the state over the individual."*[2] In other words, the descriptive labels may be different, but the practical end result is quite similar. I provide real world examples of these themes throughout this book as I describe some of my life experiences and lessons.

While the theory of socialism or communism may sound great to some, especially to those not as financially well off, the reality of how communism is implemented never comes close to the imagined fairy tale. According to the theory, everyone has what they need, everyone is nearly equal, everyone contributes roughly equally, and everyone lives happily ever after. It's an idyllic concept, particularly for those who are not satisfied with their current circumstances. But concept, or theory, or whatever you want to call the idea of communism, it is not reality. In reality, socialism, communism, or any other type of utopian thinking is unlikely to work. Utopian ideals have been tried — repeatedly — and never have they been successful. Whether you have religious beliefs or view evolution as being more accurate, or find yourself somewhere in between, human nature does not lend itself to such fairytale ideals. Many books have been written about human nature, both scientific and philosophical, so I will not spend time on that topic here. Suffice it to say that in practice, these utopian ideals have been demonstrated to not work as imagined by most people. This is particularly true given that these supposedly utopian ideal scenarios are almost always ultimately enforced through coercion and violence via the barrel of a gun, once the fairy tale propaganda wears off. The way in which the Poles were indoctrinated into communism and treated under communism are perfect examples of this. It is just unfortunate that humans seem to not learn from history what works and what doesn't to create a functional, civil, and prosperous society, and instead, continue to repeat the mistakes of the past.

Most Poles who have lived through that era as an adult will tell you that they never got to experience the promised idyllic socialism in Poland. In their minds, socialism equaled a profound democracy, education for all, no foreign debt, agricultural reform, availability of consumer goods, and the like. But in reality, *socialism* during that time in Poland was a system where the state owned the people (as in slavery), instead of the idealistic state owned *by* the people. Socialism and Communism at that time were merely marketing images. The factory workers were made to look like they had a say in the factory work they did, but it was only a façade to keep them compliant. The real decisions came from the top. And thus, the "communism" experiment was doomed to fail.

There are many researched and well-studied reasons for this failure, but as stated earlier, I will not delve into those here. Instead, I will share what I experienced myself. There is a huge difference between taking a large number of people and organizing them into groups of statistics and actually having been there as an individual, and experiencing firsthand why something failed.

People's memories are sometimes skewed, mine included. If you watch an old video of an important event in your life, like a birthday party or a vacation, you'll always be reminded of things that you didn't even know you forgot. The human mind just works that way. But it isn't necessarily the memory itself that is most important. I don't think a person always needs to recount exactly how something occurred. What is often more important is the *impression* that's left on the person. My memories of living in communist Poland and the transition coming to the free US are important because I now see a different pattern in what is happening in America than most Americans see. I have a different frame of reference, one in which certain liberties can not be taken for granted and certain assumptions about civil rights can not be made.

At the same time, records that were historically locked away are now becoming available to the general public, which allows historians and other scholars to paint a more accurate picture of what occurred during communist rule in Poland. Living in Poland we were not privy to the private discussions of leaders of many countries about which actions to take regarding the Polish Solidarity uprising. To this day there are still sealed records that prevent us from being able to see all the facts.[3] But some records have been released, which have been helpful in determining why things went in the direction that they did. As a child living in Poland, I only saw the country from within. Looking back, and studying about the very history in which I lived, I now see Poland from an outside view as well. I also see America from both inside and outside perspectives.

It is certainly important to study history, if only so that we don't repeat the mistakes of the past. But to study history and to actually experience it up close (and painfully) are two very different things. I experienced history, and I see patterns that I feel are important enough to share with you. Sure, it's partially based on a child's memories, but it is those memories that made me the person that I am today. It is those memories that help me recognize things that many others might not see going on around them. Even though I consider myself an American, I am still able to put myself on the outside and look in. The view of America from an outsider's perspective is very different from the view of someone who has only seen it from within. In addition to my memories, I have deeply researched scholarly works on Polish history from World War II to the present day. Finally, I have drawn material from interviewing family members, primarily my parents, who were adults at the time.

The memory of my father disappearing is and always will be an important one, even though I'm sure I don't remember it exactly as it happened. But now I recognize that governments sometimes need to be feared, and governments can go rogue and do things to their own people that some might think unimaginable. That's the kind of realization that a person can have when experiencing such life changing events.

Some might wonder why my family didn't try harder to find my father when he disappeared, as it would make sense to organize a search and bring a community together to find an innocent man. As mentioned, my mother did look for him in the criminal prisons, but did not find him in any of them. But there are many reasons why we didn't search more than just that. First, my mother knew that he didn't disappear because he got lost or injured. She knew he was at a Solidarity meeting, which was illegal at the time. She knew these meetings were dangerous places to be — if caught attending. By the Polish government's standards, because he was attending such a meeting — because he was a Solidarity member — he was by definition not an innocent man. So when he didn't come home that day, the only logical conclusion was that his disappearance was arranged by the totalitarian communist government, like so many others before and after.

Second, my mother had no idea where to even look for him. This was very common for family members whose spouses or relatives disappeared. Here in the US we have certain assumptions about things like due process, habeas corpus, and knowledge of the locations of county, state, and federal prisons. We even know about the Guantanamo Bay prison in Cuba, and we know that alleged terrorists are often taken there. So if a family member or friend was alleged or accused of being involved with a terrorist organization, it would be safe to assume that perhaps, when they were arrested and they disappeared, that they would be taken to one of those known US prisons or Guantanamo Bay. A US citizen would therefore have places to start looking. This was not the case in Poland. We had no idea where people were being taken if they were not found in the regular prisons. We had no idea where they were tortured if that's what was done to them, or if they were shipped off to working camps in Siberia. Nor did we have any idea where they would be buried if killed, as most bodies were buried in unmarked locations at night when no one would be able to witness the occurrence. There was literally no place that one could even consider to start looking. In addition, Poland was surrounded by many other countries, including the USSR, (East) Germany, Czechoslovakia (now the Czech Republic and Slovakia), Ukraine and Belarus. If my father had been taken out of the country, not only would my mother have to be able to get through the borders, but she would have to pick a country to go to. It just wasn't that simple. And, we didn't have the internet or cell phones back then to help us.

Third, there was the issue of finances. Before my father was expelled from Poland, money was not too much of an issue for our family. My mother was a teacher and had a reasonable income — until martial law was implemented and the schools were closed, and like many other teachers, she was banned from her profession. My father had many skills, including plumbing, welding, and construction, and worked as a plumber by trade. We were not poor by any means, nor where we rich. Despite popular misconceptions, communism did not mean that everyone had the same amount of income. There were still differences in income based on skill level, and women were still paid less than men in the same fields with the same levels of education. Women might have started off equally, but men were promoted much faster than women, and thus their pay increased. Regardless, as a family with two incomes, we weren't struggling financially.

But when my father was disappeared, our income dropped drastically, though our bills were the same. My mother now had to feed her family on a third of the income she used to have. After she was banned from her profession, she worked as an accountant, but such jobs were hard to find at the time. Thus her income was near nil for a while. She also lost one of her jobs because of her political (Solidarity union) involvement, and had to find two other full time jobs to make up for losing the one. Eventually she ended up working *three* menial jobs.

So she had to work more, and then had to raise her children on her own, including spending time standing in long lines in hopes of buying food.

My mother had very little time for herself. Between raising her children and struggling to survive, plus getting some rest in there somewhere (as people *do* have to sleep), there was just no time for unrealistic ideas of looking for a man (my father) who left no trail. At that time, as my mother put it, "We just existed, there was no life."

Lastly, if she had found him imprisoned somewhere, what could she have done? Let's say she found out through some means his whereabouts, was able to leave the children with family, and managed to have enough money and proper documents to travel to that location — then what? Charge the prison guards with her steak knife? It was not legal for anyone in Poland other than the military and police to own firearms at the time. (This is still largely true today in Poland. For an individual to own a weapon such as a firearm or even a crossbow requires a difficult-to-obtain permit which includes a psychological evaluation.[4]) At the same time, the Polish culture has generally been a peaceful one. In Polish culture to own a firearm implies ill intent. This is very different from America where owning a firearm is just part of the American culture.

Even if it had been legal for her to own a firearm, she would have had to acquire one by importing, which was also not realistic, as imports were rare. We couldn't even import necessities such as medication, let alone guns. To try to fight through the legal system was a joke. The law was whatever the communist government said it was, and they would be unlikely to even acknowledge that my father was at a particular prison or camp or even that he existed, let alone be willing to debate his legal status.

So for my mother, it was not like in the Hollywood movies where a lone person can take out an entire evil prison with a sniper rifle, nor was there a scenario where a lone legal activist could free an innocent man. In Poland, such ideas were akin to Hollywood fantasy. My mother was facing a cold, hard, large, blatant, and oppressive tyranny — up close and personal.

Martial law can be defined as "temporary rule by military authorities [via force] imposed upon a civilian population in time of war or when civil authority has ceased to function."[5] You can look up any dictionary definition of martial law you like, but living under such oppression first hand is as good of an explanation as you can get: absolute arbitrary rule by the government with a gun potentially pointed at you at all times, food used against you as a weapon, and being under surveillance at any or all times. It is a rare occasion today that my mother will recount this history, as she is happy today, and revisiting the evils of the past is painful for her.

So the idea of looking for my father was completely out of the question. It was not possible, nor practical, and we were not alone in that matter. Anyone who had a loved one disappeared was stuck in the very same circumstance we were. You had to work to eat, and you had to eat to live. With my father confirmed as a Solidarity member, the rest of my family was now at risk as well. Thus, our life in communist Poland became very difficult. We struggled to survive, while quietly and secretly organizing to improve our impoverished lives. It just so happened that we were fortunate that my father, and eventually the rest of my immediate family, ended up in America. Many other families weren't anywhere near as lucky.

There is a lot of history to be found on communist Poland, but there are few people actually asking this question: How did Poland end up in such a mess to begin with? I again feel the need to clarify some things before I go on, such as how Poland ended up being communist in the first place, and what relationship communism had with the way of life in Poland during those years. I don't intend for a long history lesson, so I will keep it as brief as possible, but hopefully I will provide enough information to allow for a good background understanding.

The ideology of communism, or socialism, can not alone be blamed for the shortages and living conditions that occurred in Poland during the 1970s and 1980s. As with everything else, it was a combination of factors.

After World War II, the country of Poland was destroyed, literally: it was bombed to smithereens. Most of the cities were completely devastated along with their industries, roads, and railways.[6] Many Jewish (and non-Jewish) Poles had been shipped off to and killed in concentration camps. The people of Poland were left with very little to rebuild their country. So when a new regime came along and promised to re-build the country and provide equality among people (including education to all, healthcare to all, and many other utopian socialist ideals), dishonest marketing triumphed over reality.

The new regime was rumored to be welcomed by most of the Polish citizenry as a result of these promises. However, it has been noted that Stalin himself "adjusted" the Polish vote, allowing the Soviet Bloc to claim a victory with 80% of the vote.[7]

Although there were a large number of Poles who supported the new regime, to say that the Poles wanted Soviet style communism is twisting the history. The Poles didn't want communism, but they wanted to rebuild their country. The only opportunity that some of the Poles saw to do so was to accept the new communist regime on their doorstep that promised these great things under the guise of socialism.

There were also many Poles who tried to fight Soviet rule and tried to warn other Poles about the dangers of accepting the oppressive Soviet regime. But they were far outnumbered by those who believed the promises from those in favored political positions. As a result, the people sounding the alarm about the dangers of Soviet allegiance were disregarded as kooks. There was also the issue of a rigged vote to go along with all the confusion. Apparently during the 1947 election, thousands of peasant party members, along with over a 100 candidates, were simply arrested[8] and thus unable to vote. Intimidation tactics and violence were also used against voters. Candidates and activists alike were arrested or murdered, and results were massively falsified. The real results will never be known, as ballots were destroyed without ever being counted.[9] So while my grandparents hoped for a better life for their future children, they, along with most other Poles, never wanted communism — especially one ruled by the Soviet Union.

After the falsified vote, the Polish citizens (including my grandparents) under the new communist government went to work to rebuild their beautiful cities. But it was barely a decade later that they found themselves under the watchful eye of an authoritarian regime — certainly not the dream they were trying to accomplish for their children. All of a sudden there was no freedom to live — everything had to have a permit. You wanted to start a book club? You needed a permit. You wanted to start a gardening club? You needed a permit. You want to do just about anything? You needed a permit. And if the lack of freedoms wasn't enough to anger the public, the lack of food in the stores along with price hikes just added fuel to the fire. These consequences were recognized quickly, and in 1956 the first strike against the communist regime occurred. The workers began protesting against the food shortages and the overall handling of the Polish economy. After many injuries and several deaths during the protests, Władysław Gomułka was placed into power by the communist party.[10] Although trusted at first by the Poles due to his history as a political activist, the Soviet government was the final deciding authority whether he could be placed into power, and they wanted him to be politically "rehabilitated" (more in line with Soviet communism).[11] Once Gomułka assured the Soviets that he could be trusted as an ally in bringing Poland to socialism, they did agree to his position in power.[12]

Gomułka, like most politicians, made many promises. He ruled for 14 years before he was removed from office. Even though I wasn't yet born during his rule, my parents and grandparents often commented during nightly discussions of politics about what was wrong with their country, and how no one listened to Gomułka as he only made promises but never acted or delivered. This is not to say that this politician did nothing. During his reign, many industries managed to get rebuilt, but it wasn't enough. The people stopped listening to or believing him.

When the Polish government raised food prices by 20-40 percent in 1970 (depending on which source you reference) to try to relieve some of the economic problems, the workers went on strike again. Because the workers were generally ignored, and elections were rigged, striking was really the only power the workers had. If workers weren't working, things weren't getting produced to be shipped off and sold to other countries or used by the Soviet Union. This time the strike turned into a massive upheaval that resulted in Gomułka being driven from office[13] and Edward Gierek became the new party leader.

Gierek also made promises to the people, and he tried to fix the problems of Poland by investing. His theory was that Poland would strengthen with the right investments. But since the country was destroyed during the wars, Poland had nothing to start investing with. So Poland borrowed money from western banks to invest.[14]

Unfortunately, the foreign debts added up quickly as Poland transitioned from an agricultural to industrial economy. Gierek's idea that the debts would be paid with the products created and sold by the Poles didn't pan out very well. The theory was flawed because production did not end up going as planned, and Poland ended up owing the US (depending on which history resource you reference) between $20 and $35 billion, which wasn't paid off until the year 2012.[15]

Accordingly, Gierek's wasteful investments resulted from a lack of planning and because heavy industry received a disproportionately large share of that investment. Lighter industries, considered more consumer-oriented, held less economic power than heavy industries. As admitted by the party, "various departmental and regional pressure groups had a decisive influence over investment policy," which meant higher wages for those who had the power to vote for such for themselves.[16] In other words, the money borrowed from western banks lined the pockets of corrupt individuals and politicians, and the workers toiled to produce enough to pay off that debt.

The large debt to the US resulted in western governments putting a stop to the lending of money to Poland, and to the forcing of Poland to pay back its debt. The leaders of Poland attempted to fix the issue by exporting everything Poland had, including basic necessities such as food and coal.

This would be similar to what would happen in the US if the Federal Reserve and all large foreign creditors to the US, like China and Japan, not only cut off the never-ending "credit card" to the US Treasury, but demanded repayment of the existing debt. In such a situation the US government would have to find another way to pay its bills, including balancing its budget through reduced spending and increased taxes and exports. This could result in a decision to export everything it possibly could to try and make ends meet. That would mean the store shelves would be fairly empty in the US, as nothing would be imported, and anything made in America would be immediately shipped off and sold to consumers of other countries.

At that time, Poland was one of the top five largest producers of coal in the world,[17] and yet most families, who often lived together due to housing shortages, couldn't heat their homes because they had no coal. To clarify, in those days you didn't get to go to your thermostat and turn on the heat; it didn't work that way. Instead, the flat assigned to you and your family was heated from a central location in the building. The centrally-located furnace would be fed coal to heat water that would run through the pipes. This water would heat all the flats, and also served as your hot water source. So with the coal shortages, due to all the coal being sent out of Poland to pay the country's debts, many flats went unheated. I saw my mother on many occasions arguing with the landlord about not having any heat coming out of the pipes, and no hot water. It was an argument that many tenants had with their landlords.

There wasn't just a scarcity of products, but dysfunctional prices as well. At one point, prices of staple foods, transportation (such as the bus system), and municipal services, were all set by price controls. Prices were set so low that farmers lost money selling food at the government dictated price. As a result, often farmers either stopped producing food entirely,[18] or would only sell enough to the government at prices set by the government to meet their basic requirements, and then sell the rest on the black market in order to try to make something of a profit.[19] In a nutshell, price controls didn't work — they never do. Price controls led to shortages — they always do. Like the law of gravity, the fundamental principles of economics don't cease to operate because the government legislates them out of existence. The principles of economics are still in operation, even if they are ignored. If it costs a farmer six months of ten hours-a-day labor to raise the crops or livestock, and the farmers' compensation would result in a net loss, there is no incentive to produce any food.

These shortages contributed to Poland not being able to pay back its debts to the Western world, and so the western banks told Poland to raise the price controls so they would be able to pay more money. Of course, the banks didn't then (nor really ever) have interest in the little people — they just wanted their money. The Poles could not afford the higher prices for staple goods and services based on what they were paid, so rebellion of the populace became larger and more widespread.

This economic disaster was what led to empty store shelves and long working hours for the average Polish citizen. The residents of Poland essentially worked non-stop to pay off their government's debts, with no hope for their future other than empty promises from the party leaders.

An even bigger problem for the people of Poland was that the government had no transparency. People were frustrated as they didn't know what the country's real debt level or economic status was, thus no knowledge of when it would end. The party leaders would always make promises, but nothing ever changed nor improved.

Though Gierek's investments did temporarily improve the quality of life of the average Pole in the early 1970s, this was short lived, and was followed by worsening economic conditions and continued increased price hikes. People were expected to work longer hours — without breaks — in dangerous working conditions for little pay. The more they produced and exported, the less they received in exchange for their labor. It was this lifestyle that resulted in the workers coming together and forming the Solidarity union to try to improve their situation.

It wasn't just living conditions and working conditions that led to the development of the Solidarity union. It was the fact that what the Poles hoped would become a socialist country turned out to be a tyrannical country. The people of Poland put in long days, had no food in their homes or stores, were cold, could not buy appropriate clothing such as coats, and then were spied on constantly on top of all the hardships. They were also continually lied to with censored media, and their children were brainwashed with censored education. The lines for bread never got shorter, the empty stores shelves never filled up with food nor products, and the threat of government force never seemed to cease. This was the world I was born into in 1977. This was the world my father was trying to change.

Solidarity was, in essence, an independent self-governing trade union.[20] To the Poles it was a unique and massive social movement which could be described as a "civil crusade for national regeneration."[21] What made this union different was that it wasn't a pretend union controlled by the party (government) leaders. Solidarity was a true union for the people by the people, and it empowered the working class, who up to that point had felt quite powerless. There were other organizations that were formed prior to the Solidarity union and laid the foundation leading up to it, but it was the Solidarity movement that finally broke through the enslavement by the country's elites and put pressures on those who insisted on controlling the Poles. What made this organization work so well was the number of people that were members: literally a third of the Polish population was involved at the time.[22] It also helped that Solidarity was organized — or more accurately *emerged spontaneously* — as a decentralized, fluid, "bottom up" organization without a great deal of vertical hierarchy. Its members happened to share common values, and therefore were able to work toward common goals with only moderate amounts of hierarchical and lateral organization. This contrasted greatly with the "top down" rigid structure of the communist government at the time.

I believe there were many contributing factors that catalyzed Solidarity. Of the many opinions and researched studies that have been published on the subject, one view I tend to agree with is that the events of December 1970, when food prices were raised by 35 percent, resulted in widespread protests – or a proto-Solidarity. The shooting by the government of several workers in the Lenin shipyard in Gdańsk also resulted in increased strikes, which led to the replacement of Gomułka with Edward Gierek. This was the most important precursor in the development of Solidarity.[23-24] The Poles did not expect Gierek to improve anything, as a common response to his appointment was "their musical chairs don't mean anything to us".[25] But that event empowered people and made them realize that their actions could bring about results.

As Solidarity grew in numbers, so did the possibility of the Soviet Union reacting with military action if control over Poland could not be maintained by the Polish government. A letter prepared for President Carter to be sent to NATO requested that Moscow be made aware of the repercussions of such Soviet military intervention in Poland,[26] implying that the US would get involved in some way if the Soviets did interfere. This memo circulated through Radio Free Europe and the BBC and caused the Poles to think that a Soviet invasion was a real threat.[27] This constant threat of attack by the Soviets was common knowledge, and was often referred to as "geopolitical reality," which was a code word for the threat of Soviet invasion.[28] This phrase was used almost too often as a means of perpetrating fear in an effort to get Poles to compromise and act against their true values. However, this constant threat of Soviet intervention did not prevent the Solidarity movement from growing.

Thankfully, the Soviets never invaded and the US never intervened, and the Solidarity momentum kept growing. When price increases where implemented yet again in August of 1980, the workers went on strike again. This was especially relevant this time as this general strike was estimated to have as many as 700,000 participants.[29] This strike resulted in Gierek being replaced by Stanislaw Kania (who barely lasted a year in power), and the legalization of Solidarity as an independent trade union in September of 1980.

The time from September of 1980 through December of 1981 at first appeared to have been a joyous period for the Poles. Under the surface, it actually involved various struggles of different sorts between Solidarity members and the communist government. Unknown to most Poles, the Soviet leaders only agreed to Solidarity's demands to buy themselves more time until they could figure out how to obliterate Solidarity completely.[30] Unfortunately, the actions of the Solidarity members trying to create a better life for their countrymen are now referred to as a long and bumpy road to martial law.[31]

Kania was replaced by General Wojciech Jaruzelski in October of 1981. He was trusted by the Poles until he declared a state of emergency in December of 1981, which resulted in martial law.

When martial law was imposed and the Solidarity union was no longer legal, the Poles suddenly found themselves even more oppressed and enslaved than before, and this just after having experienced a hint of possible freedom. Meetings other than church services were banned in an effort to prevent people from organizing. Almost all of the major leading activists in Solidarity were arrested, or the government attempted to arrest them and they escaped into hiding.

Even though initially most of the Solidarity leaders were arrested when martial law was forced upon the people, the Solidarity spirit continued on with many people (like my father) and underground newspapers that told truthful, non-propaganda news. My father wasn't caught until March of 1983. His consequence was an interment camp for three months, then banishment from his country. It could have been much worse.

Despite these realities, the Solidarity movement continued until 1989, when communism was finally brought down by an incredibly peaceful populace.

But it wasn't nearly as simple as it sounds. It took a large number of people, *to take risks; to stand up for the values they believed were humane and moral; to fight the system that oppressed them in whatever peaceful (and occasionally non-peaceful) ways they could think of; and to take the risk of losing their own lives knowing that activists were imprisoned, shipped off, and murdered for being part of such an organization.*

I am proud that my family and so many other Poles took such risks. Many of them will never be recognized for their achievements. Many died without proper (or any) recognition for what they did for their country or for other Poles. The freedoms that are enjoyed in Poland now exist largely because of those people, and they should never be forgotten. Similarly the people who fought for America, such as the Founding Fathers, should never be forgotten, and should always be accurately included in every history book.

Lesson 1: In a free country you can not be "disappeared" without a trial. The corollary is, if you can be "disappeared" without a trial, you do not live in a free country.

"What you cannot do is accept injustice. You must make the injustice visible and be prepared to die like a soldier in doing so."

-Mahatma Gandhi

CHAPTER 2: THE SHORTAGES THAT LED TO MARTIAL LAW

"When a man is denied the right to live the life he believes in, he has no choice but to become an outlaw."
-Nelson Mandela

So called "black markets" have a bad name and reputation. The name itself — *black market* — sounds like it is evil or immoral and should be illegal. Another name for black market is "underground economy". That still sounds not quite legal, but like less of an evil thing. When you're just a child, these words don't have any meaning to you. You see something such as food as a necessity. When you see your mother purchase that food for you, you don't question where it came from, or if it was "legal" to purchase it that way.

My understanding of black markets developed from the fact that purchasing items via the underground economy was sometimes the only way to get something that you needed. If you got caught, a little extra cash to bribe the corrupt policeman fixed the problem. So to me, as a child in communist Poland, the so-called "black market" didn't exist in that sense: it was just a perfectly acceptable way to get what you needed.

Shopping for food was often referred to as "hunting", and the phrase did not refer to shooting Bambi for dinner. Since severe shortages of consumer goods (including food) were common during this time, "hunting" for food involved going to many different stores in an attempt to find one with food, hoping there was food left by the time your turn to shop came, and then only being allowed to acquire a little (as the ration cards allocated). It was called "hunting" because you never knew if you would bring anything home.

Sometimes these shortages were due to actual scarcity of supplies, but other times food shortages were engineered by the government and were used as a method to control the people, or to place blame on the Solidarity union for striking.[1] During some of these "shortages" there were rumors of shiploads of food bound for the Soviet Union from Poland,[2] and there were verified reports of warehouses full of hidden food. Rather than distributing it to the Polish stores, it was left to rot, and authorities claimed it was for export.[3]

In Poland during these shortages in the 1980s, we referred to the underground economy as the "private market". It was a private market in the sense that no government interference was involved in regulating who was able to purchase items, how much was paid for items, and how much was earned from the sale of items. In the US today this system would be called something like the "true free market" rather than the "private market".

I remember one time when I was around seven years old, the phone rang, and my mother answered. She was only on the phone for about 15 seconds, but that 15 second call prompted her to ring a bell that she had. My brother and I knew what the ringing bell meant: get your shoes on, put on your coats, and get ready to go. As my brother and I were rushing to get our coats, my mother ran to our entryway closet and looked for any rope, string, bags: anything she could think of that might be helpful to us. Before I knew it, we were rushing very quickly to a small business. Once inside, we were piling up the toilet paper in our bags, stringing it across the rope we had, and wrapping that "toilet paper rope" around our necks as many times as we could, hurrying in an effort to beat the rush of families that we knew were on their way to do the same.

Toilet paper was rare. We had a bidet in our bathroom, and that's what we generally used when we had running water — which wasn't always reliable either. But this phone call informed us of a large supply of toilet paper that came in, and we took advantage and stocked up. We didn't know when it would be available again, or how much it would cost if it was. So we bought all that we could.

That was normal life for us. We usually followed the rules and used our ration cards to buy basic food items and supplies. My mother became very creative in cooking with potatoes. She could make three different meals a day every day for a full week, all with overcooked potatoes. Sometimes that's all we had to eat, and we didn't complain; potatoes were better than starving. We managed that way, as did most other Poles. But we also took advantage of the underground economy when opportunities arose.

Poland's economy during the years of communism was terrible. Price controls and import limitations did little to help. Many food items — especially sugar — were often too expensive to include in one's daily diet. Some products simply weren't available, so naturally an underground economy for such goods developed. This is not because the people of Poland were "fighting the system" and thus protesting by purchasing goods this way; it was simply done out of necessity.

Ration cards also contributed to the black market. Ration cards were issued again from 1976 to 1985.[4] We, like all other Poles, were issued ration cards for staples such as milk, butter, eggs, flour, and meat. To get ration cards, you had to register where you lived and how many people were in your family. If you moved, you had to register immediately, or no ration cards for you. And without ration cards you couldn't officially purchase food.

The purpose of the ration cards was to help keep prices low, but not in the way you might think. As anyone familiar with market economies knows, an increase in demand usually causes an increase in prices. The limitations placed on ration card purchases essentially intended to limit demand. People were not allowed to purchase more than what they had been allotted on their ration cards. In other words, because the ration cards only allowed a person to purchase a limited amount of a certain item, that would limit demand, and therefore would also control prices — or at least that was the theory.

The idea that a government could tell a family how much food they can purchase with their own hard earned money may seem foreign and even ridiculous to some. But having experienced it, and now as an adult understanding what contributed to the problem, I realize it could potentially happen again, and not just in Poland, but anywhere. There was even a time in the US that rationing occurred during the World Wars.[5]

But all ration cards did for the people of Poland was contribute to the hunger. When people are hungry, they will react. They will do what they think is necessary to calm the hunger pains of their stomach and their children's stomachs. There was a common slogan that every Polish family knew, "We all have equal stomachs."

In Poland during those shortages, many Poles protested peacefully by holding hunger demonstrations, and some started bringing people together and placing them into organizations such as the Solidarity trade union. Some accused the Polish government of intentionally causing the shortages, as they read in the underground papers about how food was "mis-managed" and therefore would spoil, but they were often referred to as conspiracy theorists.[6] Some people became corrupt themselves, receiving special favors in exchange for doing as they were told, including becoming informants. [7]

The ZOMO (special motorized riot police) were often used in riot control[8], and were much hated and distrusted by most Poles. As children, the ZOMO were our boogeymen that caused us to say "Shh...they might hear you."

Before September of 1981, the Solidarity trade union had up to a third of the working age population as members.[9] That means that at least one of every three Polish citizens were unhappy enough with their way of life that they joined forces to change it. That is one out of every three people that clearly stated "communism doesn't work." And those were just the people that were willing to admit that they were part of this organization; those that were willing to take the risk of being "disappeared" or mysteriously killed[10]. The number of supporters was likely much higher as many people supported Solidarity without becoming official members.

I can assure you that ration cards, while supposedly designed around family size, did not allow for enough food to be purchased to feed a family. You could have money, and there could be products available, but you still could not get enough of what you needed because the government dictated how much your family would eat. Or worse yet, you could have the money, and you could have the ration cards, but there were no products on the shelves, as I experienced was more often the case. If that wasn't bad enough, you still had to work six days a week, usually in jobs that were physically demanding, so you needed more calories in order to keep working.

Solidarity became a trusted organization because it was run by the very workers that sat next to each other six days a week. While the Solidarity leadership did not buy into the conspiracy theories about connected government officials hoarding quality food for themselves, they did insist on having access to the government stores. Only if a Solidarity leader could verify that the stores were empty — witnessed with his or her own eyes — would the people believe the government.[11]

These shortages were not just in basic foods, but also goods such as bus tires, soap, chocolate, alcohol, clothing, shoes, and other necessities and items that generally made our lives easier and more comfortable. To make matters worse, while most Poles (my family included) had their consumption of products controlled with ration cards, there were plenty of us who witnessed certain groups of people being favored and given more rations than others. These people included politicians and police. There were even special stores for these people that "common" Poles were not allowed to enter. There were many times that we would spend days waiting in line for a product that was not available, only to find that certain favored Poles (or foreigners, as were many of the police) who happened to be in a job that benefited the government (nomenklatura), would receive the very items for which we were waiting in line. While common Poles could not get many goods, corrupt officials received bounties for themselves and their families — all in a supposedly "equal" and "communist" country. Situations like this remind me of the famous line from George Orwell's book *Animal Farm*: "All animals are equal, but some are more equal than others."[12] How ironic it is that George Orwell's writing was *illegal* in communist Poland at that time, when it so accurately described the way things were.

The *nomenklatura* was a Soviet term for lists of positions to be filled by their people. These positions included local government officials, managers in industry and commerce, media editors, senior military officers, judges, and so on. The people who filled these roles were usually selected by the ruling party, on the basis of who would most likely remain loyal to the new regime. By 1980 it was estimated there were probably some 200,000 to 300,000 nomenklatura jobs. This became a type of informal ruling class, whose members and their offspring enjoyed status and special privileges. "The owners of People's Poland" were rewarded for their obedience and nepotistic connections to the party rather than individual initiative or competence.[13] Those who had the means to challenge this system were usually invited to join the inner circle as a way to buy them off. Among the nomenklatura it was commonly thought that whoever didn't steal was stupid.[14]

According to Jack Bloom, "Corruption became a means for people to obtain what was otherwise unobtainable."[15] And according to Jan Uchanski, a Polish coal minor, the problem with the Polish economy was as much moral as it was economic, because the cultural mindset became one of corruption, nepotism, and favoritism rather than hard work, competence, and merit.[16]

This was how people were divided and turned against each other, and is a tactic still used by governments today. How else would you get Polish secret service agents to treat their fellow citizens — who they are supposed to serve — as criminals by spying on them, locking them away in prison, and disappearing them? The government would simply bribe some corruptible common people with items that they generally could not get but needed, such as food, and those people would perform crimes against their countrymen as they were instructed. Similarly, politicians (then and now) pass laws that empower the government and disempower the people. This was the root of many of the problems at that time, and it remains a major problem throughout the world today. Of course, often the politicians participated so they too could get favored treatment in the form of receiving bribes of items or privileges they wanted.

In comparison, in America today we don't have food shortages, but we do bribe our politicians. It is actually a very complex system of bribery. In America, we have large corporations, banks, and all sorts of special interests that fund certain politicians so their campaigns can afford to play commercials on TV and lie to unsuspecting Americans about how great they are. In return for the campaign funding received, they help push laws through that benefit those special interests and not the people.[17] It's similar to the situation that occurred in Poland, just by a slightly different means. Here we have special interests collecting "donations" for politicians, and in turn, the politicians vote for regulations that will favor the donors, thus they get their money back — a return on their investment.

In Poland, the corrupt police and politicians would receive an abundance of products in exchange for keeping the Poles under control and in poverty, while they enjoyed wealth that they didn't work to earn — or at least didn't earn honestly. Here in America today, politicians pass laws and regulations that gradually take our freedoms away, gradually increase control over all aspects of life via regulations, and force us to pay ever more in taxes.

Things did change for us in Poland once my father became established in the US. Once he was finally making ends meet for himself and had a little extra income, we started to receive gifts, which were really supplies that we needed, things that we couldn't afford, or items that weren't generally available in Poland.

I remember once my father called and told my mother to get an outline of all of our footprints on paper and mail it to him. He wanted to get us shoes, but Poland's metric system didn't correlate with the American shoe size system, and the internet didn't exist yet to be able to convert Polish shoe sizes to American shoe sizes. So my mother got out paper and pencil, and we placed our feet on the paper and traced an outline of all our feet. We didn't have much paper so we traced our outlines all on one page. She then folded up the paper and mailed it to my father in the US.

The next box that arrived had boots that we never could have imagined: they were beautiful and fit us well. Upon putting my foot in the first boot there was a bit of discomfort, and we quickly realized that there was something in the boot. My father didn't tell us he was going to hide things like watches in the boots, because he was afraid that the government agents would hear it on the phone, and the corrupt customs officers would know where to look to steal them. This was after he had sent us several packages, half of which never made it to us, and half of which had clearly been opened and searched, with many items missing.

When the first box with disguised items arrived (and actually contained most of what he had sent), that became my father's new way of sending things. He would call my mother and tell her there was a package of socks on the way, as that was all he could afford this paycheck. He would send us socks, shoes, and other clothing, and would hide American dollars inside, along with vitamins (which we desperately needed due to enforced poor nutrition) and other goodies that were impossible to get in Poland. The customs agents still occasionally found an item or two they felt was worth stealing. But once my father started hiding things, and stopped discussing items over the phone, we generally got more of what he sent than the customs agents did.

My parents knew all along the phones were tapped; it was common knowledge among all Poles. The state's definition of socialism was allegedly Marxism, but ask any Pole who lived as an adult during those times, and they will tell you that socialism meant censorship, lies, prison, arrests, state sanctioned murder, and absolutely no human rights. The state owned *everything* from the economy right down to each human life. By that definition, we were essentially slaves. At first my parents were careless in exchanging information over the phone. But after many missing items, they figured out our phones were not only tapped, but our conversations actively listened to. Some might argue that this is not altogether different than things today in the "free" US, with the NSA recording all phone calls and internet communication. Perhaps because Americans' packages don't get searched, and things don't go missing, few people are concerned about it. But just imagine what it would be like with the NSA continually spying on us if sending a watch overseas was illegal. Even more frightening is contemplating what it would be like if it were made illegal to talk badly about the government, as it technically was in communist Poland. At that time, to talk badly of the Polish government was considered "anti-socialist."

I suppose it could have just been multiple coincidences that the packages containing expensive items that were rare in Poland were the ones that disappeared or were "inspected" and thus opened with half the contents taken. But then that would mean it was also a coincidence that once we stopped sharing this information over the phone, the searches and missing packages decreased. Our packages were still often inspected, as they arrived to us re-taped and often barely held together. But money was hidden in soles of shoes, and stuffed animals could hide larger items such as jewelry. Sometimes my mother would stare at something my father had sent and wonder if anything was hidden within, since my father had no way of telling her if he hid something in it without the authorities finding out. Such information would give them clues about future package contents.

Now, you might wonder why he didn't wait for us to come to America to give us these items, and I have two answers for that. First, we didn't know when we would be able to emigrate, if ever. We had to wait for permission, which required a lot of paperwork from both the US and from Poland. We didn't know if we would ever get to leave or see our father again, so it was best to send us items we needed to make our lives more bearable. Second, the gifts and hidden items he sent made us financially more stable and supplemented my mother's income. We were able to trade the items my father sent in the underground economy for food — something other than potatoes, and sometimes, to get potatoes we would otherwise not be able to get. We had essentially become the "haves" instead of the "have-nots."

Just by simply being able to receive items from another country, we were now richer than ever by Polish standards because we had things. The things we received were things that most Poles couldn't get; things that everyone needed or wanted, things that usually only those who were in the right status positions such as police and politicians could get. We could sell these hard-to-get items in the "private market" and still pay our bills with my mother's reduced income. Living in communist Poland became more tolerable and easier that way. At that time you could have never convinced me that trading our American stuff for food in the underground economy was illegal.

Looking back as an adult at the things I experienced as a child makes me realize how clearly ridiculous the ideas are that a government can place laws upon people that restrict them in how much they can eat, what they can purchase, or even how much money they can earn. All of that was supposedly for the common good? Even more absurd is the idea that the people living under these sanctions would willingly fully cooperate. Sure, we cooperated, but only enough to get us through so we could survive. But we also participated in "illegal" activities, at least by the government's standards. I don't think my mother was a bad person for purchasing items in the underground economy with American dollars to feed her children, which was also illegal at the time. If anything, her bravery for taking risks for such actions to care for her children should be recognized.

There comes a point where your survival and that of your family is at odds with following rules that are only there to oppress or control you. There comes a point when a person is desperate enough that they have no choice but to live outside of the (immoral) laws forced upon them, just in order to live. Not to live comfortably, but to literally just *survive*. You cannot live if you do not eat.

It is even more difficult and repugnant to follow laws that apply only to you and certain other people, but not to all people, such as those receiving special legal privileges like the nomenklatura. Double standards of laws and selective enforcement of laws were very common in Poland then. It is much like that in America today, where a huge number of laws apply to common citizens, yet politicians, Wall Street bankers, and those with elitist connections can get away with nearly anything they choose. In Poland at that time, there was no equal justice before the law, and sadly it has become that way in the US. I tried to research how many Wall Street executives and Washington politicians have been prosecuted for the fraud and corruption they committed during the 2008 financial crisis and was astounded that there were so few. One financial example is John Corzine of MF Global and formerly of Goldman Sachs. He made a billion dollars of customers' money disappear and has never been held accountable, other than a sham investigation by Congress that could barely be called a slap on the wrist.[18-19]

A political example is Attorney General Eric Holder, who has never been properly investigated — let alone prosecuted — for the "Fast and Furious" scandal where honest law enforcement personnel were killed as part of a politicized BATFE (Bureau of Alcohol, Tobacco, Firearms and Explosives) anti-gun "sting operation" that could arguably be considered entrapment.[20-21]

There are many more reference sources available online for these two examples alone, if one cares to look. These specific events are not my focus here, and are merely used as examples. More to my point is that there are many, many more examples that I could cite that show that in America today there are two sets of rules. The first set of rules involves the innumerable laws and regulations for us plebeians that we commonly think of. The second is for elitists with "special legal privilege" and involves only one rule: do whatever *you can get away with.*

As a brief aside I think it is important to point out this very issue is why the US Founding Fathers wrote the phrase "all men are created equal" in the Declaration of Independence. A brief study of history will reveal that they did not mean that all people are born with the same types or quantities of abilities as that is obviously not true, nor did they mean that there should be an equality of outcome as socialists advocate because the Founding Fathers clearly favored economic freedom. No, what Thomas Jefferson et al. were referring to with that statement was *equality before the law.* In other words, he meant that all laws should be applied to all people equally by the state, and that all people should be treated equally before the law by the state. With that phrase, the Founders also intended to imply that *no one* gets special privilege, because that was also a major problem they faced in their time. The US Founding Fathers were faced with British royalty receiving special legal privileges, just as the nomenklatura received in Poland, and just as elitists in America receive today. In America today we just don't have a catchy name for them like "royalty" or "nomenklatura" — yet.

In Poland, seeing politicians spend large amounts of money on grandiose parties — and knowing it was our hard work that funded these activities — resulted in hatred toward the very people who oppressed us. Poles hated all the nomenklatura politicians and police that kept us living in the impoverished lifestyle that was forced upon us, while they enjoyed the benefits of their position and drank expensive vodka and wore clothes that we could never afford, not even with our American packages.

At this point you might be asking yourself why you never heard about any of this in all the history of Poland that you have been able to read about, or have seen in images from old Polish newspapers. The answer goes back to the government censorship. When the legal newspaper was printed, the photographs on the front page (or any other page) were censored through several censorship committees. Journalists were not allowed to print a photo that showed empty store shelves, that implied police violence, or any image that would show what life was really like. Even photos of certain political figures talking together that were not supposed to be friends were disallowed. Only boring photos that would imply a happy and content life went to print. All others were either archived, or their negatives destroyed, depending on the image. Just as the photographs were censored, so was the writing in the paper, and the news broadcasts on the television and radio. Even when Solidarity held its first session of congress, the Polish government denied a visa to the head of the US AFL-CIO because the Polish government insisted that it be allowed to edit the broadcast.[22] This massive censorship of the true history of Poland led to many "gaps" in the formal academic history of Poland, and the Polish people refer to these gaps as "blank spots" or "white spots" (as in whited out paper) in Polish history.[23] To this day, scholars and historians are still trying to piece back together the history of Poland during communist rule, which becomes evident if you read through many of the works I cite in the references.

Such media restriction resulted not only in sparse news within Poland, but also prevented information from flowing out of Poland about the internal power struggle the people were experiencing. Thus only part of the story emerged, a disconnect occurred with the outside world, and misconceptions arose in the west regarding the true intentions of Solidarity.[24]

Fortunately, some of these historical photos were retained in archives, and eventually were allowed to be released to the public once communism fell. Unfortunately, much of the history of this period is only recorded in the memories of those people that lived in Poland during those times, and in the Polish underground press such as the KARTA center.[25] This is why it is still important to this day to record true first-hand historical accounts from people who lived through it, like my parents.

The many forms of the underground press were the only real uncensored news at that time in Poland. Also, the truthful (non-propaganda) books written either during Solidarity or right after communism fell helped to explain the events of those times. This means that Poland's history could be re-written many ways over, and that is unfortunate, because when history books are written after the fact, they are usually skewed one way or another, often according to the agenda of the book's authors and editors.

Interestingly, I was listening to a political talk radio show the other day. I do not promote any radio show hosts; I just happened to be scanning through the radio to see if there was anything interesting on. There was a discussion on a particular show about President Obama's $170 million (the most expensive in history) inauguration party.[26-27] The descriptions of the party, the dress of the first lady, the food, and all the other amenities that I have never experienced, even after moving to America, brought me back to memories of when I lived in Poland and reminded me of my family's hatred towards the politicians who took from us "peasants" to enrich their own lifestyles. I just kept thinking about how many hungry people I could feed or how many homeless shelters I could build with a 170 million dollars.

The parallels of history are happening all around us. The well-connected are living rich off of the hard labor of average Americans. They flaunt it right in front of you to show you that you better work harder, because their next event is going to cost you even more money. Think of your tax money, which they automatically take out of your paycheck, and you have to patiently wait for a refund once a year if they take too much or send them more if they didn't take enough. Consider for a moment if you would voluntarily pay for all the "services" the government provides, if the money was not automatically taken from you. This is not to say that America is communist or socialist per se. The labels change, but the reality that small elitist groups steal from and take advantage of average people through politics is a historical pattern that is repeating itself once again, now in the US. I think the difference is that these processes have been introduced slowly, through gradualism, to the American population, and it almost seems that things like the income tax have always existed, unlike the dramatic lifestyle change the Polish people experienced when the Soviet regime took over the country.

If you study true Polish history, you will read that the shortages described continued for many years. There were many demonstrations and strikes to change policy. People needed to eat, and they needed to feed their children. The problem was that the working class could not deviate from the system forced upon them. Most people lived in urban areas, and few people lived on land where they could grow food for themselves. So self-empowered, outside-of-the-box solutions were not typically practical for most. Many will also argue that the Poles perceived good qualities in the regime at that time, such as equality between men and women, with opportunities for women to be equal. But it was all a façade. In reality, people were so spied on that they feared the government, so they went along with the façade simply to stay alive and not be fired for political opinions, or worse yet, disappeared.

But there came a breaking point for many Poles. For a long time, people of Poland were scared of the government and were compliant because they hoped that change would finally take place with better policies, and they feared fighting the giant that could make their lives even more miserable. But when better policies never developed as the politicians promised, people started to come together and get organized.

The Solidarity movement, along with the underground press, were not only huge, but were effective. Like the internet, the so-called "alternative media", and the "liberty movement" today, the people organized themselves with real news and real information, not what was printed in the censored newspaper or shown on the censored television. Solidarity was the first union in Poland that was truly on the side of the workers and found an effective means to fight back, which was through truthful information and strikes. Previous unions were actually controlled by the Polish and Soviet ruling elite. These controlled unions functioned as a type of controlled opposition to make the common people think they had someone representing their interests, when in reality they did not. This is another parallel to America today, where people think their elected politicians represent their interests, when in reality it is likely that they do not.

During the period in which Solidarity was legal, the Polish people demanded reforms on information, especially information on economic status. Up to this point the Polish government had largely kept the Polish people in the dark about the country's economic status by withholding all economic data. This is another parallel with the US today. The main difference is that in Poland the data was withheld, while in the US the data coming from the Federal government and Federal Reserve is so manipulated and distorted that it may as well be propaganda.

Today in the US, some of the methods that are used in calculating the inflation data include "substitution", "geometric weighting", and "hedonic adjustment." I learned about these concepts in my macroeconomics class in college, but it wasn't until I studied on my own how they had been used that I realized their significance in the reporting of economic statistics.[28] When I looked further into the application of these concepts, I realized it all came to mean one thing: number manipulation, with the intent to deceive. These statistical methods result in underrated inflation and an illusion of economic recovery.[29] The methods used to calculate the unemployment rate are also very questionable. [30-31]

So while the US government makes it look like the data is available and therefore they are transparent, the numbers are so skewed that half the time you're scratching your head trying to figure out how in the world they came to such an analysis. To me, this is not much different than just plain old withholding the numbers, as was done in Poland during communist rule. Obviously to the politicians and financial elitists there are benefits. I'll leave it to you to determine what those are.

Pressure from the Polish people in early 1980 forced the Polish government to at least recognize that the people would not be subdued. Due to the large number of participants, the government initially refrained from attempting arrests. However, in the background, Jaruzelski (who ended up being the last party leader of communist Poland) was pressured by Soviet leaders to institute martial law. Jaruzelski was able to postpone martial law for a short time with the simple argument that he could not depend on the Polish military to fight Poles, and that if the Soviet military enforced martial law, it would be considered an invasion by the Poles, and would result in bloodshed.[32]

So rather than respond to the Poles with fair reform and honest information, the Polish government first spread many lies and disinformation via the controlled media about the ill intentions of the Solidarity union, and spread lies about the Solidarity leaders' involvement in other organizations. Activists were labeled as traitors to Poland, and others as anti-Semitics.[33] Rumors where also spread about a possible attack by outside forces, which was not completely a lie, as the Soviet Union could have invaded. This was largely because the Polish government was under pressure from the Soviet leaders who denounced the Solidarity union because it was a union over which they had no control. The goal of this propaganda/disinformation campaign was to get the union to lose creditability and therefore lose the support of the Polish people. This was a "divide and conquer" strategy, and would also confuse the general public about what was happening at that time (to distract the people from the real problems). Once the union started to become weaker and people were distracted, martial law was instituted by Jaruzelski, who was in power at the time.

According to my parents, martial law was implemented on Sunday, December 13, 1981. I was barely four years old, so my story is based not on memory but what my parents and other family members have told me (coupled with some historical research). That day, the phone lines were cut off, and television broadcasting was shut down. Most everyone at first thought that the communication cutoff was from an attack originating outside of the Polish borders. They thought this because of the previous disinformation/propaganda spread by the Polish government about a possible invasion from an external threat. Shortly before this event, there were news reports on television that talked of possible foreign threats, and Poles had always lived in fear of a Soviet attack. So when the lines were cut, it was natural for people to think that it was an outside attack.

It didn't take long for people to figure out it was their own government, especially since threats of martial law had been hinted at for almost two years. It was particularly threatened in the months leading up to this event, as Solidarity had become a threat to Soviet control. The Solidarity union had an agreement that if such an event occurred, they would strike. The National Strike Committee had developed and distributed instructions on what to do in case of a general strike, in case of a state of emergency, and in case of a foreign intervention.[34] Since they could not communicate via the telephone, they printed their own news pamphlets and spread them around.

However, the government was ready for such an event, and arrested Solidarity members and leaders prior to announcing martial law.

Little did the Poles know that the Soviet-controlled secret police had ramped up their spying operations on Solidarity members just a few months prior. Specifically, they focused on leaders, and had collected any information they could on the habits and lifestyles of those people in order to use it against them during the arrests.[35] Of the many who were rounded up and arrested was Lech Wałęsa, who was a very prominent Solidarity union leader. Over 10,000 Solidarity members were rounded up, arrested, and taken to prison. Some political party members were detained as well, including Gierek.[36]

Civil war broke out, and what shocked the Polish citizens most of all was the use of the Polish military against its own people during martial law. The Polish military had always been highly regarded by the Polish people, and no one would have ever predicted that their own military would turn against them. Yet, the unwritten law that *a Pole doesn't kill a Pole* was broken. Morale dropped quickly.

All meetings except for religious purposes were banned by the government. Mail was to be censored, roads to major cities were blocked, six day work weeks were reinstated, schools were closed, public transportation stalled, and the underground press was to be arrested if caught.[37] The people were forced to continue living the façade, and to continue living in the poor conditions they were in.

The US government knew ahead of time about the upcoming martial law that was imposed on the people of Poland, but did not warn the Solidarity leaders. The US CIA claimed it was surprised by the move of the Polish Government as they too were expecting an attack on Poland by outside Soviet forces, and thus didn't forewarn the Solidarity leaders or the Polish people about the upcoming event. However, this has proven to be untrue as many unclassified documents are now stating otherwise. Not only did the US know about the coming martial law, but Jaruzelski apparently knew the US knew, and the US did nothing to deter it.[38] Accordingly, Jaruzelski stated that the US's silence on the matter meant endorsement of his internal solution, which was a measure used to prevent an inevitable Soviet invasion.[39] Furthermore, then Secretary of State Haig had stated that he didn't want to warn Solidarity because it would risk violent resistance, which the US had no intention of assisting in that manner.[40]

As a matter of fact, not only did the American CIA know about the upcoming martial law, but they had been getting reports that Jaruzelski — while putting in writing agreements with the farmers unions and the students unions, making it look like the people were finally getting what they were demanding — was simultaneously covertly stepping up plans for the upcoming martial law.[41] While the Solidarity members thought that they were winning, it was merely a distraction to get them to stop striking until martial law preparations could be completed and implemented. Another lesson learned: If it seems too good to be true, ask yourself *what if it isn't real*? Land ownership does not belong in Marxist theory, so when the farmers union was allowed to register as an association, and promises of land ownership and the ability to buy/sell land, along with inheriting the land was agreed upon by Jaruzelski, this should have been a red flag that the accommodations were just a red herring.

While I don't care to bore you with too many details of my family member's passing away, I think it's important to point out that even during times of crisis, life goes on...or doesn't go on. It was during this time that my maternal grandmother suffered a second stroke, and my maternal grandfather died of cancer. We didn't know about the cancer, because often times doctors didn't like to give bad news when there was nothing they could do about it. So they just didn't tell my grandfather he was dying from cancer, and we thought he was just ill. The death of my grandmother during this time, coupled with my dying grandfather, only added to the stress of having martial law imposed upon us and everyone we knew. It just goes to show you that death and illness will strike at the worst of times. There is never a convenient time to die. Life keeps going regardless of the circumstances.

With the onset of martial law the government managed to temporarily control the people, forced the strikes to stop, and significantly slowed down the underground press. Yet the idealism of freedom never died among the Poles. The members of the Solidarity union began to meet privately in each others' homes, but in smaller groups to prevent being caught. The underground papers continued despite over the 10,000 Solidarity leaders being arrested and imprisoned. The spirit to live free can never be squashed with force from a determined people. The government failed to stop the people from working towards freedom.

To this day, Jaruzelski is spoken ill of in many Polish families, including mine. He is the one that as my mother would say (don't mind her lack of English writing skills) "Jaruzelski, he is no good, he make a curfew and people start the revolution". Martial law wasn't lifted until July of 1983, shortly after my father's disappearance in March of 1983. It was around the same time that my father finally arrived in the US.

There were additional events during that era that are historically relevant to the US today. Between 1976 and 1980, the Polish economy had been on an economic downhill slope.[42] By 1980, the Western banks had put together a syndicated loan of $550 million with the requirement that stricter economic reform measures be applied in order to qualify for the loan, which is when Gierek suppressed wage increases. By April of 1981, Poland was technically in default to its creditors (although the Poles knew nothing of this due to the government's lack of transparency), and yet, you would have never read about any of it in the papers. Instead, the US government decided to pay off Poland's debt to the US banks, even though Poland was not a member of the IMF at that time. This protected Poland, but more importantly to the US government, it protected the US banks.[43]

So yes, the US government bailed out Poland and the US banks. But why? This is a question I cannot answer, as I simply don't know for certain, and any answer I could come up with would be strictly speculation. In trying to get these answers, all I came up with is that the US government felt they should not interfere, and should allow the Poles to resolve their financial issues on their own by undertaking a systemic reform in their banking system.[44] But the timing of these statements didn't coincide with the Polish bailouts. The bailout didn't help the common Poles, nor the Polish politicians: it only helped the US banks. Among Poles, there were still shortages, still price controls, and still hunger.

There is a lesson that can be learned here. This is a perfect example of how history repeats itself. Back then the US government bailed out the US banks at the expense of US citizen taxpayers. More recently, the same thing happened: the US government bailed out the US banks in 2008 — again at the expense of US citizen taxpayers. In both cases the general population did not benefit, but US banks were rewarded for engaging in risky behavior. This is known by economists as "moral hazard" and is also an example of how elitism works: risks and costs are socialized, while profits are privatized. In other words, if the banks had made money on their risky loans, they would have retained those profits. But when the loans went bad, the taxpayers were the ones paying the bill. Thus there was little incentive for banks to care about the risk of the loans. Whether you prefer to label this elitism as "fascism" (corporatism) or "socialism" makes little difference. The result is the same: a small number of corrupt insiders benefit at the expense of everyone else. While perhaps not identical circumstances, to me, the parallels of history are striking. As Mark Twain is attributed to have said: "History does not repeat itself, but it rhymes."

When I look back at history and what I experienced growing up in a communist country, I realize more and more that America is repeating many of the same patterns that history shows us don't end well. There are national behavior patterns that inevitably lead to failure, whether it was the Roman Empire, the British Empire, communist countries like the USSR and Poland, or even the United States. Clearly these countries all had or have different ideologies, but the dysfunctional patterns were similar: excessive debt, a devaluing currency, imperial overreach, massive corruption among an elitist oligarch class, and differential enforcement of laws between the political elitist class and everyone else. In addition, dubious "news" information and propaganda passed for truth and reality, excessive bureaucracy and regulations stifled the ability of common people to be productive, and in most cases (Poland being the notable exception here), a largely distracted, disinterested, and disengaged public. The fact that the Polish people were so involved at the time makes them not only the exception, but exceptional.

There is something that makes America today very different from these historical patterns, and that is that technology has helped allow our problems to be stretched further without notice. The phrase that is commonly used to describe this is "kick the can down the road." In other words, putting off dealing with problems now, but they will have to be dealt with in the future — often with greater difficulty.

The economic and political problems of today are actually being exacerbated by the fact that we have factors that are supporting the US economy and political institutions which encourages us to "kick the can down the road" and delay the ultimate day of reckoning. Relatively new technologies such as powerful computers and networks, petroleum fracking, and certain political circumstances, particularly the petrodollar reserve currency status of the US Dollar, are helping to keep the American economy afloat. Just barely, but still afloat.

To partially explain how technology is stretching the road for the can to be kicked, consider the following: when other countries have historically experienced financial crisis such as hyperinflation, it got to a point where the cost and logistics for the paper to print the money was too much to be able to continue printing, even when using very large denominations. We no longer rely on paper for most financial transactions. Most of our money is digitized now, so we no longer have the logistics of paper limiting things. Instead, it's just numbers on computers that have little correlation to anything in reality, as these numbers are not backed by anything real or substantial. Up until 1971, the US Dollar was linked to gold, which provided a anchor between the Dollar and something tangible of actual value.[45-46]

Currently, the digitized money is linked to and backed by nothing but thin air. This would not be possible without technology that is available and used today. The only meaningful backing for the US Dollar is that it is "required" in order to buy petroleum (oil) from most (but not all) oil producing countries. But that requirement is slowly fading away as well. The significance of this can not be understated, because when or if the US Dollar is no longer needed to buy oil, the demand, and therefore the value of the currency, will rapidly drop. Everyone holding US Dollars will become poor quickly, just as has happened in other countries that have had significant currency devaluations.

The US federal government also continues to raise the debt ceiling. That is like continuously raising a credit card limit. Just look at what happens when there was a threat of *not* raising the debt ceiling in fall of 2013. Panic ensued, and the economy suffered.

Rather than allowing the US economy to fall in the short term and ultimately self correct and self repair by *not* raising the debt ceiling, the US government and Federal Reserve keep printing/digitizing more money, borrowing more money, and spending more money they don't have. It is to the point now that when the economy finally does come crashing down, it is going to be far worse than it would have been if it had been handled responsibly. It is certainly going to hurt the US more than it hurt Poland for several reasons, one of which is that the US standard of living has much further to fall. I am not sure that it is even theoretically possible for the US to get out of debt at this point. It is certainly not practically possible: not with all the promised future benefits (promised health care, retirement, pensions, and the like) and the hollowed out manufacturing industry. Not to mention that there is no other country in the world that has the financial means to bail out America when the time comes. Only an international bailout by the IMF (International Monetary Fund) or BIS (Bank of International Settlements) would be possible, and that would be far, far worse for the American people than simply defaulting on US debt obligations. As can be observed in other countries such as Greece, Argentina, and many others, when the IMF and BIS get involved in a country's economy, the cure is often worse than the disease. One aspect that will be very similar between Poland, the US, and other deeply indebted countries such as Greece, is that the common citizen pays the price of austerity for the decisions elitists have made.

I can't say that America's economic problems are only on the macro scale. Here in America, among individuals, saving is discouraged and debt is encouraged — the exact opposite of what supports a healthy, prosperous economy and financial system. Strictly from a common sense and folk wisdom perspective it is easy to see how personal savings equals prosperity and financial freedom, and personal debt equals poverty and financial slavery. But Americans have not lived by those rules of thumb for some time.

Culturally, people who behave responsibly by owning physical gold and silver or storing some supplies and food are called "hoarders", or crazy "doomsday kooks", or "preppers", and they are often exaggerated in some manner in the media to give them a negative persona. However, given the current economic circumstances, such behaviors are both logical and prudent. If nothing else, buying more consumable goods than you need is a good inflation hedge in a time when government inflation statistics are lies.[47-48]

It is interesting that "preppers" have been portrayed or propagandized by the mainstream media in such a negative light. In reality, everyone should be prepared for hard times or disruptive events. In a state of nature, there are cycles of scarcity and abundance, and scarcity is quite common. Modern society only has abundance because we have created it artificially using man made energy and technology, and there are no guarantees that will always be sustained. The Polish people intuitively understood this and were much more prepared to deal with it, if for no other reason than the dysfunctional communist economy forced them to always be prepared for shortages.

In addition, modern just in time delivery is unnatural, as is our current method of delivering goods to the grocery stores, and will be a killer to many people when a major economic crash or other disaster or disruption occurs (natural or man made). People who have suffered through hurricanes Katrina and Sandy can attest to this. The reality that people typically do not recognize is that while just in time delivery may be more efficient, it is also less resilient and more fragile. As a matter of fact, most people are not even familiar with just-in-time delivery, and have no idea that their grocery store is restocked based on purchases made, and there is no extra product in the back of the store like there used to be decades ago. Additional product is now delivered daily or every few days, based on actual demand. Many stores no longer have three days worth of goods (including food) stocked. So if a disruption occurs, what is on the shelf is it until the trucks are able to deliver again.

There is a trade-off between efficiency and resiliency. If stores keep more inventory on hand it is less efficient (and therefore less profitable) but more resilient against disruption. If stores keep less inventory on hand it is more efficient, and because stores make money on turnover, it is therefore more profitable. But that increased profitability comes at the cost of reduced resiliency. So if stores will not be resilient in our economy due to the incentives involved, it is up to us as individuals to provide that resiliency for ourselves. We are the ones with the incentive to do so, and if we don't the results could be unpleasant.

The point is that while living in a communist country we created our own resiliency by always trying to store more than we would immediately need, because it was never certain when more would be available, and as mentioned, shortages were common. The store owners in Poland never had to worry about keeping extra stock of product, as there simply wasn't any, nor did they have an opportunity to consider just-in-time delivery. As it was, the lines were always out the door the minute the doors opened, so such a concept couldn't even develop. Stores "functioned" on the basis of if product arrived, within hours product was back out, and there were still people waiting in lines. The thought of fully stocked shelves from floor to ceiling was only a dream.

While this scenario may seem like an unlikely distant memory from someone who used to live in a communist country, I can't help but point out how many times store shelves have been emptied when a disaster took place here in the US in recent years. Whether it was a hurricane, a widespread utility outage, or just an inch of snow in an area that normally did not experience it, disruptions have occurred.

I find it very unusual and unhealthy that most Americans want to be forewarned of an emergency, but then wait for the event to occur before they rush to the store to get supplies. Or worse yet, wait for the government to come help them; help that may not arrive on time, or at all. This whole process seems completely upside down to me. I try to understand this seemingly irrational behavior. But the only conclusion I can come to is that if a person has grown up all their life never once experiencing a shortage, as in *they have never experienced hunger pains*, then they do not believe that such a thing could ever occur. Thus, there is no perceived need to store extra. This is extremely unfortunate, as there are many potential threats that are lingering upon our once wonderful country. The possibilities range from natural disasters to terrorism, war, electrical grid failure, and economic collapse.

In the area where I currently reside, there are public service announcements on the radio regularly about the threat of a big earthquake hitting. The radio announcement states that one major earthquake occurs every 300 to 350 years, and we're just over 300 years since the last one, so we're due any day now. The voice on the radio continues to say that certain areas could be disabled for as long as six months, which would likely trickle over to surrounding areas. This sounds like a serious announcement, until you hear the ending of it, when they recommend that you keep one weeks worth of food and water on hand in case this emergency occurs. Really? One week? But didn't they just say it could knock out services for up to six months? Should you not stock up at least six months' worth of supplies? And perhaps even more if there are many aftershocks? To me this seems like a logical disconnect. But to everyone else? Nah, that makes you a crazy doomsday prepper kook. One week of food and water is plenty to survive for six months.

This is exactly the problem with the attitude in America today. Most seem to miss this concept that a major event could knock out services for an extended period of time, but as long as they have a week's worth of supplies they are safe. After all, "the government is going to save them," or so they think. Living in Poland, when crises occurred, which was usually either empty store shelves or increased food prices, the people fought the government by organizing strikes and refusing to work, rather than waiting for government to rescue them. Never would any Pole sit around and wait for help to come from the government. Such an idea would be, to put it bluntly and honestly, laughed at.

I was even more baffled once when talking with a good friend of mine, who knows of my "lifestyle," and also knows my history and has heard many of my stories. When I asked her if she had any supplies for emergencies, she answered me by saying that she generally has a great deal of food in the cupboards that she never eats, and so if an emergency occurred, all the food in her cupboards would be more than a weeks' worth. "At least two weeks," she said. When I asked her further what she would do if the emergency lasted longer, she said she would come to my house. Worse yet, when a major earthquake hit another country and aid was needed, she joked with me about how all those people should come to my house. I didn't know how to respond. But when I moved to a different area, I didn't give her my new address.

I hate to be the one to break the news to anyone with this type of belief, but if you believe that a weeks worth of supplies will be enough to get through a disaster until the government comes to help, answer me this one question: Do you think that our current President, who spends millions of our tax dollars on golfing adventures, trips to Hawaii, and extravagant birthday parties where the media is not allowed so that the minions don't see how well the king lives, do you truly think that our fearless leader really cares enough to get you help in a week? Even if he did, do you think that FEMA is even competent enough to do so, after the demonstrated failures of competency with Katrina and Sandy?

Alternately, if you think you can go visit Uncle Joe out in the woods because he has a cabin and mentioned putting some MREs aside, do you not think that if he wanted you there he may have given you an invite? Otherwise you might be met with a shotgun pointed at you, especially if you show up empty handed. Depending on your relationship with Uncle Joe, his attitude may be that "failure to plan on your part does not constitute an emergency on my part." Irresponsibility seems to rule the day in America, but that will eventually be a self-correcting problem. While in Poland families did live together out of necessity due to housing shortages, all family members, children included, contributed to the workload (in the home and outside the home), to the investments of food and supplies, and to saving money. Never did the burden fall on one family member who dared to plan ahead.

Setting all that aside, I want to really stress the lesson from formerly living under communism that saving and storing in times of plenty is like an insurance policy for times of scarcity. Much of our food preservation was developed for this very reason. Preserve the excess so you have it in times of shortages. We did that in Poland, whether it was extra cabbage that was available and we made sauerkraut to preserve the extra that we were able to purchase or grow, or just stocking up on toilet paper. Food preservation was born from the idea that we need to be able to store the excess food for times when crops failed.

So why in America people are laughed at for being prepared for emergencies is beyond me. Saving for a rainy day is not something that should be laughed at, frowned upon, or even made illegal. It was made illegal in communist countries such as Poland, and it could very well be made illegal anywhere else where an economy results in food shortages, including if it were to happen in the US. That scenario may seem implausible to many people, but be aware of the phenomenon of "normalcy bias." Wikipedia defines normalcy bias as "A mental state people enter when facing a disaster. It causes people to underestimate both the possibility of a disaster and its possible effects. The assumption that is made in the case of the normalcy bias is that since a disaster never has occurred then it never will occur. It can result in the inability of people to cope with a disaster once it occurs. People with a normalcy bias have difficulties reacting to something they have not experienced before. People also tend to interpret warnings in the most optimistic way possible, seizing on any ambiguities to infer a less serious situation." [49] I fear because most recent generations of Americans have not experienced true hardships and almost none have experienced long term food shortages, the majority of Americans are affected by normalcy bias to varying degrees. The last Americans I know of to experience such hardships are those who lived through the Great Depression, and there aren't many of them still around.

Even after communism fell and Poland was technically a free country, the shortages and price problems didn't stop there. Just because communist rule ended didn't mean that everything fixed itself right away. Price adjustments (normalization without subsidies) in January of 1990 resulted in 80% inflation (imagine the cost of everything you buy almost doubling in a week). This was due to the price controls, which caused price information that lacked validity or utility in a free market. In other words, prices have little meaning in a controlled economy. But in a free economy, accurate prices play a very important informational role in determining supply and demand, and how much of a good or service should be produced.

If you think 80% inflation can't happen in America, just ask yourself how much the Federal Government actually subsidizes in our country. Ask yourself what would happen if those subsidies all of a sudden ended because they could no longer be afforded. To make this exercise really fun, research for yourself about how the petrodollar reserve currency status of the US dollar also subsidizes the US economy. The topic is too lengthy to cover in depth here. But in brief, because most petroleum/oil is bought and sold in US Dollars, that creates artificial demand for those dollars, artificially increases the value of the US dollar, and thus allows Americans to buy goods from around the world very inexpensively by world standards.

The petrodollar program creates an artificial demand for the US dollar, and thus is a subsidy to the value or purchasing power of the currency. When the US Dollar eventually loses reserve currency status and ceases to be a requirement for petroleum transactions or international commerce, 80% inflation could look "not so bad." Note that at the time of this writing, many countries and institutions around the world, including China, Russia, Iran, India, Brazil, South Africa, and others (not to mention the IMF and the BIS), are already working on plans to end the petrodollar reserve currency status of the US Dollar. So it just might be a good idea to prepare for such an event.[50-51]

In Poland during my childhood, we didn't really use banks. We always had cash on hand because you never knew when something would be available, and so you would have cash on the ready if a shipment of food came in. You also didn't trust your money unless it was hidden somewhere where only you knew where it was. This was common practice among most Poles.

When my mother had extra cash to spend because we received a very nice package from my father, but there was no food to buy with it, she would buy gold and have it melted into jewelry. This was her savings account for the expected future rainy days. The Polish currency then, known as złoty, actually translates to the word "gold" or "golden". Gold was very valued in Poland, and could always be traded as money among the people. The little gold my mother was able to acquire was easily worn on our ears and fingers. We didn't have to worry about closed banks, looking suspicious for having a large amount of cash, or market losses. Gold almost always could get you goods.

In America right now, most people who have excess money for whatever reason invest it in either the stock market or bonds, keep it in an interest-earning money market account/savings account, or purchase elaborate homes — or worse yet, spend it on items that are completely superfluous for living.

Money in the stock markets tends to enrich bankers and politicians who engage in insider trading more than it does the typical American. Money in bonds can easily be defaulted on. And what happens to money in the bank when the bank doesn't open? FDIC? That plan didn't work out so well for Argentineans. "This is America," you say? Fact: The FDIC has less than 1% of what is needed to cover all bank deposits.[52-53] Not to mention that during the Great depression right here in America, the banks closed and never re-opened. What was once in bank accounts was gone, and what was in safety deposit boxes was no longer accessible.[54]

When the economy crashes again (such as in 2008 except much

worse), the very same middle class people will lose much of their hard earned savings, they may no longer be able to afford their overpriced mortgages, and they may end up homeless or living with their relatives (if they are lucky). To think that people could have better used that money to pay off their home if they bought something less extravagant, and could have stocked up on food for times of emergencies, and kept extra cash under their mattress, or even invested in physical silver or gold, so they can get through the difficult period of being jobless, is never suggested; it is even actively discouraged in our culture. After all, that is what unemployment is for, right?

Some might argue that the American dream never really existed as anything more than an idea or ideal. I'm not sure I agree with that, but I am pretty sure it is on the operating table with the shock paddles attached. The picture in most peoples' minds of a happy couple with 2.3 children, a nice house with a white picket fence with a little yard, and a nice car or two is sold to Americans through commercials, television shows, and movies. Rather than buying small and affordable items, most people buy too much on credit and become debt slaves for the rest of their lives, trying to pay for their American dream.

As someone who has lived in poverty and shortages, I find this "dream" a ridiculous way of life. The concept of taking on all that debt and living in unsustainable extravagance at the expense of financial and food security would again seem irrational to someone who lived through communism, or anyone who has lived through true hardship.

When we (Poles in Poland) looked to America during those times — the land of the free — we envisioned a dream of starting a business, offering skills such as construction, or owning a store to sell an abundance of products. We especially envisioned land ownership, not a mortgage. As in owning free and clear — something that was impossible or at least very difficult to accomplish in Poland during that time. We envisioned acreage, dirt, gardens, and livestock all our own, to manage as we please. This contrasted with the reality of serving as slaves to politicians and bankers who prevented us from ever being able to buy ourselves out of indentured servitude; where we worked the farms for their benefit, or worked in factories while living in cold flats (apartments) in the cities. We envisioned passing on to our children the fruits of our labor, so they could have more opportunity for education, prosperity, and overall better lives, rather than the slavery in which we found ourselves.

But if you suggest to the average American that they should buy a small home that they can pay for with cash rather than having a mortgage, they laugh at you. When you suggest that they should store six months' of food or more instead of three days' worth for that time when the big earthquake or other emergency hits, they look at you as if you were from another planet.

Since I believe in personal liberty and responsibility, I would never try to dictate to anyone how they should live their life. But in my mind, planning for times of hardship would seem like common sense, or at least a survival trait. Yet, a majority of the American population is unprepared for any kind of large scale disaster; natural, economic, or otherwise. More dangerously, they are also in denial that such an event could ever even occur here (normalcy bias).

It is, however, very easy to fall into that trap. My personal experience of coming to America from a country of poverty helped me become similar to every other American. I wanted the Madison Avenue version of the American Dream, at least temporarily. That was until I realized that dream was becoming a nightmare, and then I woke up.

Lesson 2a: In a free country the government provides transparency and truth. The corollary is, in a country where the government is constantly espousing lies and propaganda, you do not live in a free country.

Lesson 2b: In a free country people should be free to buy, sell and

trade (barter) goods with other freely willing participants, without government interference, repression, and prohibition. The corollary is, in a country where the government regularly interferes with, represses, and prohibits commerce between freely willing participants, you do not live in a free country.

Lesson 2c: In a free country everyone is held to the same governmental standards and no one gets special privileges before the law. The corollary is, in country where particular groups or individuals receive special privileges from the government or before the law, you do not live in a free country.

"When morality and the law contradict one another, the citizen has the cruel alternative of either losing his sense of morality or losing his respect for the law."

-Frederic Bastiat

THE SHORTAGES

CHAPTER 3: MY SECOND MOST IMPORTANT MEMORY: SLEDDING INTO COMMUNIST HEALTHCARE

"The State is the great fiction through which everyone endeavors to live at the expense of everyone else."

- Frédéric Bastiat

It seemed living in Poland was always cold. Perhaps I remember it as such because the flats were never heated, or perhaps because it really *is* cold there most of the year. Or, maybe it's because an important event occurred in my life when there was snow on the ground.

In the building where we lived, there was a neighbor kid about my age that I used to play with, and when the snow fell, we both wanted to go sledding. Here in America, children under ten (or even older) require that they have some type of babysitter or adult oversight. It is assumed they should have someone to watch over them to protect them; to keep them out of trouble and from harming themselves. That was not at all what it was like growing up in Poland.

Children in Poland (and much of Europe at the time) were —

and in some places still are — very independent. Sitters were not common, and there were no laws to state that your child must be accompanied by an adult until a certain age. I often went places by myself as a child, including riding the city bus by myself, even at age six. So going sledding without parental supervision wasn't exactly a big deal, though I do remember my mother distinctly telling me not to go down the "big kid hill," as it was too dangerous. I waved her off as if I had no intention of sledding down the big kid hill.

Indeed, I had no intention...until we got there. My little hill seemed so boring on my sled, and my neighbor friend ran off somewhere. As I watched the big kids sled down the big hill, I thought to myself that it wasn't that dangerous. So I took my sled by the rope, walked up the hill, got on my sled, and went down that big kid hill.

Everything was great until I realized that I didn't know how to turn or stop, and there was a building I was approaching very rapidly. I remember that I managed to turn my sled just a bit to the right as I hit the building with extreme force. At first the shock kept me from realizing what had just happened, and I pretended that nothing had. I grabbed the rope of my sled with my right hand and started to head back up hill. It was only after a few steps that I started to feel something on my left arm, the pain increased gradually until I couldn't handle it anymore as the shock wore off. That's when I started to scream and cry at the same time.

The severity of that impact could have resulted in serious brain trauma or even death. I think back to that event and sometimes wonder in awe about how not only lucky, but resourceful we were at the time. The mere fact that my arm is straight and I have full arm functionality is not a fate that every child living in Poland in 1984 would have been fortunate enough to experience had they been riding my sled.

That day I went down the big kid hill changed my life. I was lucky that I somehow managed to turn my sled just enough and I didn't hit the building head on. Instead, my arm broke the impact. I was fortunate to come out of that incident with only a broken arm and some scratches on my left cheek. I was also lucky that another parent was there that day with her children. She recognized me, placed me on the sled, and dragged me home to my mother as I was screaming the entire time.

We didn't have a car then — walking, city bus, and train were our methods of transportation. Mostly you would take the city bus, and on rare occasions, a cab. So my mother took me to the "cab stop" while yelling at me the entire time for going down the big kid kill. A cab stop is kind of like a bus stop, but instead you wait in line for the next cab that is available. There was a long line of people waiting for a cab, but I was screaming pretty loudly from the pain, so everyone graciously offered to us the next cab that pulled up.

One x-ray later it was determined that both the bones in my left arm were broken but no other problems were seen, and I needed surgery. Ironically, in order to perform the x-ray, my jacket sleeve needed to be removed. The nurses tried to gently remove the sleeve so as not to harm the coat as they knew that coats were hard to find, but my mother insisted they cut the sleeve to make it easier and faster. At that time, she didn't tell them that my father could just send me a new one. But I saw the surprised look between the nurses as they insisted they could save the coat, since kids' coats didn't come around easily. I remember being told to count down from 10, but I think I only got to seven before I was out, then I woke up in the recovery room with a cast.

There were plenty of other kids in the recovery room with me. But the time I spent in the hospital is mostly a blur, other than I made lots of friends with my roommates, and I got ill from the poor food. My mother took me out of the hospital as soon as she found out I wasn't feeling well. However, that wasn't the end of that plight. My mother was told that my arm would be crooked for the rest of my life, and I would probably not regain full use of it.

I give my mother all the credit she deserves for thinking fast and getting a letter from my violin instructor stating that I was extremely talented, and I needed a straight arm that would provide full functionality so I could continue to play the violin. You see, while Poland's constitution of 1952 guaranteed healthcare for all, communist, or socialized healthcare is not the best healthcare. It means that you receive services, but you do not get to choose the quality of care, unless you were very rich of course, or one of the nomenklatura. But we were only middle class by Polish standards, and my mother hadn't sold her soul to become one of them. The nomenklatura had access not only to extra goods we weren't privy to, but also special healthcare benefits.[1]

Without that letter, the powers that be that made decisions for that hospital would have never fixed my arm. It took a lot of work to convince them that they were denying an incredibly talented genius violinist kid a straight arm. Although my mother never discussed it, I'm pretty sure there was also a generous gift provided to the doctor who repaired my arm. I noticed months later that my mother no longer had one of her favorite gold rings given to her by her mother, but to this day she has never confirmed my suspicion. So back into the hospital I went for another surgery. This time I woke up with another cast, and a pin sticking out of my wrist.

The next few months were terrible. In America, when a child has an injury, you spoil them rotten to make them feel better. That was not the case in Poland. I still had to do all the things I used to do by myself. This included riding the city bus to school, cooking my own breakfast on days that my mother had to leave early for work, and fending for myself against my older brother who wanted to do nothing but torture me in my cast.

I got used to having a cast and learned to work with it. The real pain came later. Though it was only short lived, it's a memory that I will never forget. Even after the cast was removed, I still had the pin near my wrist in place, which was left sticking out after the cast was removed, and had to remain in place a little longer to make sure my arm bones healed properly. I don't remember exactly how long, but I do remember the day that I stood in line waiting to get the pin removed.

It was a long line of people, and they all had some pin or something that had to be removed from whatever part of their body. They all screamed in pain, or at least I think they all did. The line moved along rather quickly, considering the circumstances. When it was my turn, I was given no anesthetic, no analgesic, no lollipop, and no warning; nothing. The pin was ripped out of my wrist with a pair of pliers while a large hand held the rest of my arm down. I couldn't control the scream that came out of my mouth. The pain was excruciating. It was worse than the actual pain I experienced when I originally broke my arm. Perhaps the initial shock of when I broke my arm kept me from hurting as much. But this pin, even though the removal of it only took a few seconds, was excruciatingly painful.

I couldn't imagine American kids going to the doctor's office to have a pin (that had tissue growing all around it) quickly ripped out of their arms without the use of some kind of anesthetic or analgesic. I can't imagine that any parent in America would even stand for that. But that's how life was in Poland in 1984. That was what was provided as the "guaranteed healthcare" promised to all. But we didn't have many options for healthcare, so you dealt with what you had. I suppose it was better than no healthcare, but having lived in the US, I would never voluntarily want to go back to the socialist healthcare we had in Poland.

Thanks to a violin teacher willing to lie and an unknown (to me) gift to the doctor, my arm is straight with full functionality, and has a very big scar. To clarify: outside of some simple children's tunes, I don't play the violin well, and prior to coming to America, we didn't even own a violin. I certainly lacked the amazing talent that my violin teacher bragged about. But that is what you had to do if you wanted good healthcare: healthcare that was beyond "average", healthcare that actually took care of you and your needs. But that's also how socialist healthcare works. Why work harder at something, such as being a doctor, when you will be paid the same regardless? Why strive to be better than your college roommate when you will receive the same rewards in the end? When there is no incentive to be better, few people strive to do better than the next person.

It was also not just a lack of motivation, as there were great doctors and nurses out there who *did* try to provide the best care they could, regardless of the financial rewards, because they believed that providing the best care they could was the right thing to do. But when they didn't have the specialty equipment that they needed to keep a broken arm straight, there was nothing they could do. If they didn't have the analgesic or the pain killers to provide, then all they could do was provide the best care they knew how, knowing it was sub-standard. That's the reality that many people don't grasp when it comes to communism, or even socialism. Even if an individual wants to provide a quality product or service, if the infrastructure is not in place or is not allowed: it is impossible for them to do so. The "system" itself gets in the way and prevents it.

This is a very unfortunate result from a good intention. Sure, we all want healthcare. We all want to be able to afford to go to the emergency room when something happens. We all want to be able to receive the best treatment available if we are diagnosed with something potentially terminal. We also want the best care available at the time. But when you have de-motivated educated professionals who have no reason to do any better, they likely won't. And when motivated professionals lacked instruments, equipment, and supplies that are crucial for that excellent healthcare, they could only provide the services that the tools they did have allowed. This is why my grandfather never knew he was dying from cancer. There were no medical treatments for cancer at that time in Poland. He died at home because the hospitals were already overcrowded, and there was no room for anyone who did not have a good prognosis. And when there was a shortage of doctors and nurses, then people took whatever care they could get, because other options did not exist.

There is yet another caveat to this equation. While there will always be providers who care enough for their patients that they will try to do their best, just as there were many of them in Poland, they often had restrictions placed upon them that prevented them from being able to do what they wanted. An example is if a quota had to be met, and they had a long line of people waiting for services. If the broken arm surgery was a difference of 20 minutes to fix quickly versus two hours to fix correctly, these professionals will start making choices they might not want to make. But they had to make such choices to keep their jobs, because they had a quota to meet. Otherwise they would lose their jobs, or wouldn't get paid. And if they didn't get paid, their family wouldn't eat.

You might think that such history is tragic, and that it would never or could never happen in America. I disagree; it is already happening. Just look at some of the healthcare that is already being provided such as Medicare, Medicaid, or even Veteran's Health Administration (VHA) care, commonly referred to as the VA. Sure, you can be seen for an emergency, and you can get your free flu shot. But ask for something more serious that is perhaps not critical, such as an allergy test, physical therapy, or a joint replacement, and payment is not guaranteed. You might have to pay out of your own pocket for those treatments. Ask for Lasik eye surgery, or preventative care and again, payment is not guaranteed. If you forget to dot your i's or cross your t's on the paperwork, you might be footing the bill. Worse yet, if you're a veteran who is dependent on VA healthcare, you are placed in a priority group based on your eligibility, not based on need.

Interestingly, until recently, insurance would often pay for Viagra but not for birth control pills. This is a case where you pay insurance premiums but have to pay additionally out of your pocket for services that are not deemed necessary. If your income is good, paying out of pocket for these services may be easy. But if your premiums are based on income, and you are already paying more, then you will not have money left over for these extra services that are not covered.

These variables make you really wonder who makes these decisions. So with the current direction of American healthcare, in the near future — when, not if — America gets to the point where a surgeon has to meet a quota and has to make a quick decision about how much time to spend on a broken extremity, he or she might just choose to fix it enough to make it work, but won't have time to make it truly right. Not because he or she is a bad or ill intended doctor, but because they have to. The patient is not going to die from a crooked arm, so technically the Hippocratic Oath is still being honored.

When I think of the Affordable Care Act (also known as Obamacare), I fear what will come of it in the longer term. It has to be funded somehow. For those who say "let the government pay for it," I hate to break it to them, but the government takes money out of everyone's pockets to pay for these things. That's what taxes are. The insurance premiums under this plan will be nowhere near enough to pay for the program. I also doubt there will be enough revenue from taxes in our current economy to cover the gigantic healthcare costs that will quickly develop under this act. We already have a gigantic budget deficit, and now we'll be adding more to it.

This act will also dictate how much doctors are permitted to charge for services which could result in fewer students choosing to go into the medical profession, and ultimately lead to shortages of doctors. What person will spend hundreds of thousands of dollars for education when their returns will not make that expense worthwhile? When there is no money to pay for something, or when there are not enough doctors or nurses, services are reduced. It's only a matter of time before it trickles down to all of us, except for America's elitist "nomenklatura".

What I find interesting is that people compare other countries' socialist healthcare to the Affordable Care Act, but they don't consider differences in lifestyle. Many Americans are overweight and have no desire to change their lifestyles. Obesity results in many different disease processes that can be avoided, such as diabetes, sleep apnea, and heart problems. These diseases can result in very expensive healthcare costs.

In contrast, in Poland during that time, because food was scarce, and because most people got more exercise because of the type of work they performed and lifestyle they led, most Poles were underweight and did not suffer the same health problems that people do in America today. As a result, most of the healthcare was emergency care, maternity care, etc. But the care was not care for lifestyle diseases as in America today. Don't get me wrong: a large majority of Poles smoked, and cancer rates were extremely high. But treatments for such were unavailable and therefore not performed, and treatments that are unavailable and not performed don't cost anything. This was the case with my grandfather, as the doctors figured there was no point in giving him the diagnosis without being able to offer a solution. Of course, the Poles are famous for being able to handle their Vodka, and alcoholism became a national disease when the shortages occurred.[2] But once again, services or treatment for such a disease were unavailable, and therefore cost nothing.

Here in America you have a multitude of unhealthy habits, including smoking, drinking, and lack of exercise, combined with unhealthy food choices, which result in obesity. In America today, people not only expect these problems to be treated, but they are so commonly treated that this epidemic of "lifestyle diseases" are bankrupting governments and the healthcare industry.

This is important to point out because it makes a huge difference to the economics of a healthcare system. It is unrealistic to think that a person can choose to live a self-destructive lifestyle and not have an effect on the rest of the population that is forced to pay for the consequences of that lifestyle, whether it is someone who chooses to be a daredevil and performs dangerous stunts, or someone who chooses to eat unhealthy foods that result in a variety of diseases. So comparing a socialist healthcare system in America today to socialist healthcare in any other country whose citizens choose to eat healthier diets and/or exercise (or were forced to do so), is like comparing the cost of a mechanic working on a car that has had regular tune ups and maintenance, and a car run on poor quality gasoline and never having the oil changed.

The reality is that freedom and consequences necessarily have to go together. If people want to choose their own lifestyle, then they have to accept responsibility for the consequences of that lifestyle. Someone can't choose to live however makes them happiest and not take responsibility for the consequences of that lifestyle. It is immoral to force someone else to take responsibility for those consequences. So people can't have it both ways; it doesn't work that way.

If certain individuals want other people to take financial responsibility for their lifestyle consequences, such as in healthcare, then those individuals have to be willing to be told how to live by those people who are paying the medical bills. And being told how to live inevitably leads to loss of freedom, and ultimately to tyranny. I fear this is exactly where we are headed with the "Affordable" Care Act: government bureaucrats and politicians will necessarily be controlling every aspect of how people live their lives because it will impact health care costs. The recent ban on large soft drinks in New York City[3] is a perfect example of one of the first steps in that direction. Some politicians have threatened gun ownership as being next because owning a gun is allegedly more dangerous than not (although I have seen no data to back that up), and therefore supposedly increases healthcare costs.

Here is an example. Imagine that someone you know, maybe even a friend, chooses to skydive regularly. Then you are told that this person had an incident and broke every bone in his or her body, but lived. Now you are told that you have to pay — out of your own pocket — the cost of treating this individual, even though you told them over and over how dangerous sky diving is. But because it's socialist healthcare, they can choose to skydive, and you have to pay the medical bills. That works for any other choice an individual makes, whether it's smoking, drinking, using drugs, consuming unhealthy food, not exercising, or whatever your own example of an activity is that you like to do but of which someone else does not approve.

So here we have a tax on healthcare that says we have to pay to treat these people, but there's no incentive for people to change their lifestyles and improve their health so that they don't need these services. I myself have a problem with the idea of paying for someone's lung cancer treatment when they chose to smoke three packs of cigarettes a day. I have a problem paying for someone's stents because they ate unhealthy fattening food six times a day. And I have a problem paying for Viagra pills. No one will pay for these things for me, because I choose a healthy lifestyle, so I will not need them. I certainly don't expect others to pay for my healthy organic food, nutritional supplements, and gym membership. You might argue that there is a balance, as I might get hit by a car and need emergency services. But I disagree — that's what car insurance is for. If I get injured at work, we have workers' compensation coverage. There is always risk of cancer or another major disease process, but with my healthy lifestyle it's less likely. I suppose I could be walking down the street and trip and fall and need emergency services, but by then, there will be no money left in the pool of socialist healthcare, as the lung cancer treatments and cardiac stent surgeries will have wiped out the health care finances, and I'll end up with a crooked arm after all.

"Pessimist" you might say about me. But I'm not, nor am I an optimist. This is a silly American way to identify people. Reality is not about pessimism or optimism, and thus I'm a realist. Reality is what it is, not how you wish it to be, nor even necessarily how you perceive it to be. This is where my memories of communist Poland become crucial. I have lived through socialized healthcare, I have experienced socialized healthcare, and I know for a fact that it doesn't work (well, if at all); it never has, and it never will — at least not even close to the way that many people envision it.

When I think of freedom and America, I think of being able to make my own choices about what type of healthcare I receive. I imagine that if I want a surgical procedure, I either pay for it out of pocket, or freely invest in insurance that would cover it. I imagine being able to control what is put into my body or how my body is treated in case of emergency. As a matter of fact, I have experienced this in America and for the time being, am still able to make some of these types of choices for myself, to a certain degree. But I see the signs of socialist healthcare creeping in with the Affordable Care Act, and I see history repeating itself, only on a different continent, in a different year.

Some might argue that the Affordable Care Act was necessary to provide care for people who had pre-existing conditions or were too old and were denied coverage by insurance companies. I agree that those examples are extremely unfortunate situations, and I agree as a society we should try to develop solutions to problems like these. However, the Affordable Care Act is not the solution. The Affordable Care Act, which is really the UN-Affordable Care Act, is a complicated system of laws and regulations that just happens to also include the pre-existing condition clause. However, it also includes a large number of other regulations and unconstitutional laws that most people haven't even read and have no idea they exist within this law. Why create such a complicated document when all that was needed was a solution for the pre-existing condition issue? Wouldn't addressing just that one issue have been much simpler than a 906 page document of laws and regulations?[4]

I have painfully attempted on various occasions to read through all 906 pages, and the vast amount of rules, regulations, restrictions, and requirements — you name it — is enough to make someone want to rip all their hair out, let alone try to understand exactly what this bill is saying. Here I am a few years later still trying to understand everything in this law, and wonder how Congress could pass such a huge law in such a short amount of time. There is no way they have read through all of it. And, of course there is the famous line, "You have to pass the bill to find out what is in it" stated by Nancy Pelosi.[5-6]

What I did catch was the fact that states can receive grants if they provide support of the act (Sec 2793). The preexisting condition clause has a bunch of rules and regulations that somehow involved the tax code from 1986[7] (Sec 1101). This act goes as far as to regulate what vending machines disclose[8] (Sec 4205). For some reason homeland security has to be involved in communications[9] (Sec 5101), and Sec 1555 discusses how "no individual, company, business, nonprofit entity or health insurance coverage shall be required to participate in any Federal health insurance program created under this act...and there shall be no penalty or fine imposed upon any such issuer for choosing not to participate in such programs."[10] Yet, we are told we must pay a fine (via the IRS) if we don't have health insurance.

My memories of Poland have helped to shape how I think and how I view the world, and also serve as a reminder to be wary of government. It has been my experience that the government is not here to help me or you. As George Washington is attributed to writing: "Government is not reason; it is not eloquent; it is force. Like fire, it is a dangerous servant and a fearful master." Thus it is important to be *very* careful what duties you assign to government, as it is going to be executed with the threat of violence looming in the background, and potentially with very little rationality or morality. Perhaps Americans need to mindfully reevaluate what roles and responsibilities are appropriate for their government(s) to perform.

Lastly on this topic, I want to talk about our already government run healthcare: the Department of Veterans Affairs, also known as the VA. There are two sides to this department of government. There is the benefits side, the VBA, that decides which veteran qualifies for disability benefits as a result of military injury, and there is the healthcare side, the VHA, which many veterans are able to utilize to receive "free" healthcare. This is a fully government run healthcare entity, and it is very much on the path that the rest of our healthcare is following.

This is not to say that VA healthcare is completely bad: VA healthcare is neither bad nor good. That is too simple of an explanation.

Many veterans have special circumstances due to war injuries or physical and mental conditions, and this is the only healthcare that they are able to afford, as it is free for them. Also, many veterans have no war injuries, but are human and develop regular diseases like everyone else. Based on their level of service connection or their income, they too receive VA healthcare for free or at reduced cost. For some of our veterans, VA is all they have for healthcare, and they are very happy with it. Meanwhile, other veterans won't step foot in a VA because they are convinced that the VA is trying to kill them.

Many Vietnam veterans have a huge distrust of the government, and thus the VA because it is government run. This is not the place to debate the quality of care provided by the VA. I will say however, that the VA is very much like socialized healthcare. First, veterans don't have doctors, they have "providers". They are assigned a team, and that team tends to their medical needs. Every VA is different, but when you look at the VA as a whole, they all have quotas to meet; the providers have to see a certain number of patients a day. My point here is that there is already evidence that we are moving to a healthcare system like I experienced in Poland. And as I described, this does not bode well for quality of care in general.

The wait time to receive care from the VA can also be quite long, as recent scandals in the news headlines have illuminated.[11-12]

Providers are scheduled out months in advance to meet the needs of their patients. According to a VA provider I know, on average, a veteran has to wait for three months to see their provider for a full physical exam. If they are able to get in to see their provider for a half-hour visit (not a full physical), they are typically only allowed to bring up *one* issue they have, even if they have more than one issue, because of the time constraints on that provider. This is not because the provider doesn't care, but because they have a quota to meet: they have to show they saw x number of patients. The *system* in place *prevents* them from providing quality care.

I have seen providers work seven days a week from five o'clock in the morning until eight o'clock at night to get caught up on the work and demands of the VA on those providers. This is a caveat that many are unaware of. There is a misconception that doctors are overpaid, especially those working in government. In reality, if you were to break down the number of hours these providers put in because they care but are bound by so many rules and regulations, they don't make much more per hour than the average person.

In addition, the veteran's choice of medications is often unavailable and the VA has to substitute what is in their formulary. If the veteran is allergic to that drug, the VA has to make an exception and the veteran has to hope some bureaucrat approves it so they can get the medication they need. On top of that, they have to conform to certain regulations. If they need opiods for their pain, they have to submit to a drug test anytime the VA wants (not all VAs require this at the time of this writing), or they don't get their pain medication. If a veteran finds that medical marijuana (which is legal in some states but is not VA approved) helps them, they are not able to get any other pain medication as long as they choose to medicate with the medical marijuana. I understand this is to "protect" the patient and keep them from overdosing and mixing medications. But I also understand that this requirement prevents the patient from choosing how to manage their illness and they are forced to accept treatment as the government sees fit, not how *they* see fit. This is very much un-free, and un-American, which is ironically the type of care that our patriots who fight for our very freedoms receive.

I can foresee the Un-Affordable Care Act turning most of our healthcare into government run healthcare similar to the VA, and so I can foresee America repeating the very history I already learned from. If things keep going the way they are in this country, you might want to consider putting aside some expensive special gift items, like real gold jewelry, to keep as emergency payment for that time that your child needs their broken leg fixed *properly*.

Recent news reports of long waiting lists for veterans to receive care — with some veterans dying while waiting to be seen — only serves to underscore the stark reality of the type of healthcare we are heading toward.

Lesson 3: In a free country you can choose whatever healthcare you want. The corollary is, if your healthcare choices are dictated to you, you do not live in a free country.

"Americans are so enamored of equality that they would rather be equal in slavery than unequal in freedom."

-Alex de Tocqueville

CHAPTER 4: COMING TO AMERICA

"Power concedes nothing without a demand. It never has and it never will. Find out just what any people will quietly submit to and you have found out the exact measure of injustice and wrong which will be imposed upon them, and these will continue till they are resisted with either words or blows, or both. The limits of tyrants are prescribed by the endurance of those whom they oppress."

-Frederick Douglas

When you're at the government's whim to decide when you get to fly out of a country that your father was exiled from, you follow all the proper paperwork rules that they throw at you. You are careful what you say on the telephone, or write in a letter, for fear of being denied the ability to leave. We did that on both sides: my father on American soil, doing everything he could to maintain his green card since he was a legal alien, and my mother on Polish soil, jumping through every hoop put in front of her in order for us to get permission to leave Poland.

As a child, it made no difference to me. I simply wasn't aware of the better life out there. The packages that came from my father already made my life better, so anything even better than that, I only heard about. I didn't understand why people envied me and my family because we would one day get to go to America. I didn't understand it, and I don't think any child who has never experienced anything different really could.

While life was improved for us overall because of the items my father was able to send us, we still had to live in Poland. We still had food shortages, we still had a cold flat, and we still had our daily lives of my mother going to work and us kids going to school. We just had the extra work of filling out paperwork and being interviewed and the like, and pretended to be doing everything right so that there would be no reason to deny us permission to leave.

One major change we made was to leave the Solidarity union. Well, at least my mother did: my brother and I had no say in the matter. It wasn't that she didn't want to be a part of that organization — it was that we had to be very careful what we did, or we might never see my father again. Or worse yet, we would be disappeared ourselves. We were already a target, and giving the Polish government any more reasons to get rid of us was not a good idea. There was also the time factor. My mother had to raise her kids by herself on her meager income. She just didn't have time for politics. That is one way the ruling class kept common people out of politics then, and it is a method still used today: keep people so busy just surviving that they don't even have time to pay attention to politics, let alone do anything about it.

Dropping the political involvement was not an easy task to do, as the Solidarity movement had its own dynamic. As Jozef Tischner wrote in his book *The Spirit of Solidarity*, "Solidarity does not need to be imposed from the outside by force. The virtue is born of itself, spontaneously, from the heart".[1] It was a movement of moral and ethical protest. It was about *truth*, and unlike what the censored papers and television said, it was not against the Polish constitution, or against the Warsaw pact. The meetings of Solidarity union members had changed to smaller groups in fear of being caught by the Polish Police, or even the Polish military. Still, our family had to be careful, as union association was a risk that could cause us to be stuck in Poland. We played the game of good and obedient Polish citizens while we patiently waited for permission to leave. We spent over two years waiting for that permission, so when it was finally granted in late 1985, we acted quickly.

First, we had to decide what to take and what to leave behind. When moving from one continent to another you can't exactly rent a U-Haul and pack all your stuff. We had some major decisions to make. What made it more difficult for my mother was that even though things were available in the US, there were items she would never be able to replace. Deciding which precious family heirlooms and photos to take with her to America, and which to leave with our extended family, was a difficult task.

We did ship much of our stuff via mail to our father, but this was tricky because we knew that our packages would be opened and things would be stolen, just as they were with packages that were coming in. It is a great irony that they were searching for goods being shipped *out* of a country experiencing shortages.

Then we had to find bags that were large enough for our stuff to fit in, but small enough to be able to take with us as luggage on the plane. This was more difficult than anything. In a country full of shortages, finding such items was almost impossible. This was where the unregulated market came in handy. My mother was able to hire someone that could sew us a quality set of bags out of leftover materials they already had.

These bags were nothing fancy, and I distinctly remember they were light blue, but not an attractive blue. They were sewn very strangely, probably due to the leather-like material and shapes of the material available, and they had one zipper on top. They were large enough that as a child I could fit inside them. We were able to get three of the bags. These would be our check-in luggage, and some of our most valuable and prized items would be carried in them (nothing expensive and worth stealing, of course, but valuable and prized in that the items belonged to our family and were not replaceable). For all we knew, we would never see our extended family again.

During this time, we also had to say goodbye to all of our extended family; our grandparents, aunts, uncles, and cousins. We left them many of the items that were not practical to take with us. We took the train across Poland to visit, stay a few nights, and say our goodbyes. This was another difficult task, as we had no idea if we would ever see them again. The state of Poland was still communist, and travel back to Poland would likely not be an option. My mother made the conscious decision to give up ties to all our family to be with my father, and of course, to live in a free country.

I never got to have a say in her decision to give up all my future relationships with an extended family that I would never get to know. International phone calls were expensive, and my future family communication would be left to writing handwritten letters (at that time, personal computers and email were unheard of). There were many consequences that resulted from leaving Poland, but it was all worth it to move to a free country.

The overall decision was a no-brainer. The future was much brighter for my immediate family than any of my extended family. Anywhere seemed better than where we were. My mother made promises that once we were established, she would try to find ways to bring the rest of our extended family over as well. Our goodbyes were all hopeful. There was also still hope that one day communist rule would end, and life would be better for everyone, on all continents.

Looking back, I find it absolutely fascinating how many names and addresses were given to me in school by those who wanted me to write to them regularly. I suspect they were hopeful I would send them stuff here and there. I was already quite popular because as a child, I had more things than most Polish children my age, and it wasn't a secret that my father was in America. Of course I don't remember any of those kids now, as I lost contact with them a long time ago. Looking back, I realize that they didn't want me to keep in touch because I was such a great person, but because I was a connection to a better life. Or I was at least a connection to the *hope* of a better life, which for someone in those conditions is perhaps almost as good as the real thing.

We tried to learn a few words in English, but that wasn't practical, as there were few teachers or translators available that could help us. And Polish-English dictionaries weren't as readily available as they are now. In our current time you can learn another language simply by the use of the internet, or take just about any foreign language course you want in school. But in Poland during those times, it was Polish and Russian or nothing. This has of course changed, and most Poles can speak English as well as Polish today. Our phone conversations with our father were limited as well, since international calling was very expensive back then, so that option for learning English was out as well.

Here in America, you can choose to travel to almost any country using your American passport. The freedom to see the world has been taken for granted. Sure, some countries restrict visitors, but that's not because of American laws. However, those freedoms are now eroding as well. The Transportation Security Agency (TSA) has expanded to the point that if you want to fly you have to be x-rayed or groped, and you can't bring anything with you on board. Furthermore, various aspects of American foreign policy have made it more dangerous for Americans to travel abroad, as those policies now tend to make many foreigners hate Americans. In addition, the Internal Revenue Service Fair and Accurate Credit Transactions Act *(*IRS FACTA) has turned Americans into pariahs if they want to do anything more than be a tourist while traveling abroad. The FACTA rules require *foreign* banks to provide extensive invasive reporting on American customers, even if the banks have no connection to the US whatsoever. These onerous requirements greatly discourage banks from doing business with US citizens, and therefore conducting business (particularly banking) outside of the US as an American is very difficult and problematic these days. Multinational corporations seem to have no problem doing so, however — another double standard. It may seem unlikely now, but just as it was in Poland, in America's near future it is possible that travel restrictions will become even greater — even to the point of restricting the ability of Americans to leave the US.

I have been on a personal boycott against these TSA regulations and airlines, and have refused to fly. This limits my travel options, but that is the price I pay for my personal choice. However, I fear that as things continue to get more difficult, the TSA will become even more invasive into our daily lives. This will become a very real possibility in 2016 when the national ID program known as RealID becomes fully implemented. At that point, you will no longer be able to fly or take a train without a federally sanctioned biometric ID.[2] The history I have lived and experienced in Poland tells me this will likely become the "new normal." Travel restrictions were common and pervasive under communism in Poland. Sadly, America is becoming another place where travel is being restricted and the demand for "papers please!" is once again occurring, regardless of the rationalizations or excuses used to justify it.

Fortunately, in 1985, TSA didn't exist, and the travel bureaucrats that did exist at the time, such as customs and immigration, were much more respectful and less abusive.

It was still a long flight for us. I don't remember much, other than being amazed at how big an airplane is in person in comparison to only seeing them in the sky. I also remember my confusion of having to have to switch planes in Switzerland, and not understanding why we couldn't just go straight there. As a child, you don't comprehend vast miles of ocean separating land, cultures, and lives.

My first night in America was spent in New York City. We had unfortunately missed our connecting flight to meet my father, and were at a loss. We did not speak English, and the signs in the airports were all in English, not like it is now where you have signs in several different languages. We got off the plane and found our connecting flight terminal. Then we stood there in awe trying to figure out what to do when the realization hit us that we missed the flight as we stood in the terminal by ourselves.

We didn't know what to do, and we weren't able to talk to anyone to find out what to do. So we sat in the seats and just waited. I think I was fortunate that I was barely eight years old and did not comprehend the reality of the situation. I think if I had been an adult with two children, in a strange country, in an airport that paid no mind to me, and no one with whom I could communicate, I would have panicked just a little. We had some American dollars thanks to my father, but how we used that money in Poland was very different than how you would use it in a country that you had never stepped foot in before.

In 1985 individual cell phones were unheard of, and none of us knew how to make a phone call on a pay phone, nor did we know what number we would even call. Fortunately, my father had planned ahead, and expected we might have a delay in connecting flights. He was living in Salt Lake City, Utah, at the time. When he found out we didn't make our flight, he was able to hire a man to come find us, a man he had made prior arrangements with should such a situation occur.

My mother was standoffish at first when this strange man approached us and started speaking to us in a foreign language. He finally whipped out pictures of us that my father had given him, and my mother relaxed enough to try to communicate. Our lack of English got us nowhere, and it was only after a time that the man attempted to communicate in Russian. I didn't speak Russian as I wasn't old enough yet to start learning it in school, but my mother and father both spoke Russian, as did many other Poles. This man's Russian was quite poor according to my mother, but it was enough.

The communication began, and we were able to go to a restaurant and get some American food for the first time. My brother and I looked at the menus in confusion and had no idea what they said, or what it was that we were looking at. We had never eaten at a restaurant or seen a menu before, so the very concept was foreign to us. We were also completely exhausted. The eight hour time difference is not something you adjust to immediately. The hired helper ordered for us, and although he meant well ordering salads, my brother and I both looked in confusion at our plates. Fresh greens were not common fare for us, and we only heard of wonderful foods like burgers and pizza. We didn't touch our food, and instead went to a hotel room the man helped us attain. I don't remember much about that hotel except for what happened the next morning.

My mother woke my brother and me up early for our new flight. As she was washing up, she was in awe at hot water coming out of the faucet without any effort and no arguing with anyone. My brother had turned on the television. I don't know what made him do it, as we didn't generally watch television in the mornings. Perhaps he had an insight to what was going to be on TV. The second he turned it on, I was immediately glued to it. I was in disbelief. Cartoons at six o'clock in the morning! Sure, I didn't understand a word of what Scooby Doo was saying, but it was cartoons! In Poland, we had a half an hour cartoon once in the evening, if that. The realization of what a different life I was about to begin finally started to make sense. All those people were envious of me because I would get to watch cartoons at six o'clock in the morning!

The arrival in Salt Lake City filled me with excitement. All I could think about was the cartoons I would get to watch. Little did I know of the rest of wonderful America I had yet to discover!

My father met us at the airport, and we were detained by security because we were immigrants and required certain vaccines before we could go to our new home. Fortunately, my father was there this time to help us translate. His English, while still very poor, was much better than the complete lack of ours.

We were processed in by suits, and all I really remember is that everyone was continually trying to impress us, whether it was intellectually or with cool things — they just had to show off. We were of course awed and mesmerized by everything. My father couldn't wait to show off America himself. Once we got most of our luggage (and I say most because one of our ugly blue bags seemed to have gotten lost), he drove us to see our apartment and drop off our stuff. Then we headed out to go shopping.

The shopping experience was a shock in itself. First, we had never been in a store where you walk around with a cart and choose products. Actually, I had never been in a store that had shelves stocked full of products. I had only experienced stores where you had to stand in line for a pound of butter. Once you got to the front of the line, you'd say "Half a pound please," and they would slap some butter on wax paper on a scale. Then you would pay for it, they'd cut out your ration card, and you would go to the next store to stand in line for bread.

A regular grocery store was stimulation overload enough for someone like me at that time, but when you walk into the equivalent of Costco, you don't know what to make of the abundance of food — not just food, but breads, meats, cheeses, fruits, vegetables, and things I had never even heard of or seen before. And the clothing! I only got a taste of things with the packages my father sent. There we were, picking out clothes, belts, shoes, and other items. I don't even remember everything we bought, but I do recall our cart was overflowing, and I felt like the most fortunate kid on earth.

I remember when we first walked into the store, the size of it was mind boggling to me. As my father grabbed the shopping cart to lead the way, my mother's only question was "How do you pay?" as he put the first items in the cart. He explained to us that you load up your cart, and when you have everything you need, you go to a register and pay. This concept made sense, but was overwhelming at the same time: getting everything you needed in one place, standing in only one line, paying for everything all at once, and no ration cards!

Little did I realize that I would be placed in school the very next day and part of that shopping trip was oriented around having appropriate clothes to wear to school. At the time I didn't care about anything; I was overwhelmed by the complexity of the new world I had entered. And all I could think about was that cartoon with the dog that ate sandwiches.

The next day my brother and I were taken to the school we would attend. This was an interesting time, as we were immediately placed to take tests to evaluate our education levels. I suppose that an eight-year-old who speaks not a word of the English language should perhaps be placed in the second grade. But after taking my test, because of my math skills, I was put in the third grade.

It was a strange experience to go to school and sit in class and only listen in the hope that the language would start to make sense. As it turned out, math class was the only class I understood, as the numbers and methods were the same as those I had learned in Poland. But other than adding and subtracting numbers, I understood nothing.

I understood even less when Halloween came around. Most kids were dressed up as demons and cartoon characters, and bats and witches were hanging on the walls. To make matters worse, those dressed-up kids came knocking at your door at night wanting something. It was a very confusing time indeed.

When you are young, you learn very quickly, and my brother and I adjusted quickly to the American way of life. Eating became a delicious activity rather than a survival necessity. My father was quick to introduce us to the big hamburgers found in fast food chains, and a variety of foods like tacos, pizza, and fish sticks. In fact, I got spoiled so quickly that when I was home one evening and asked for something to drink and was given a glass of clear liquid, I was immediately disappointed. I said, with a clearly unhappy tone in the Polish language, "Water?" I was laughed at by my parents, who told me to try it. I then tried to redeem myself, yet still sounding unhappy, and said, "Water with sugar?" It was as if to say, "We're in America, I should get better than this." It wasn't quite water with sugar, but close. It was 7Up.

We adjusted to the spoils very quickly. We adopted the American way of life even more quickly. As a child, I had no concept of the struggles that my parents were going through. Even though we had moved to the land of opportunity — the melting pot — employment was difficult for my parents.

There was the language barrier. Mispronouncing words and not understanding half of what someone is saying to you will result in reduced communication, and lack of employment. There was also the issue that any accreditation that my parents had in Poland did not transfer to America. My mother certainly was not able to teach if she didn't speak the language, and my father's contracting and plumbing skills were limited because everything was done differently in America, and his licenses were not recognized.

We were only in Salt Lake City for a year before we moved to Oregon. Portland was "the place to be," we were told. Jobs were available there. My parents had considered moving to Chicago, where there was a huge Polish emigrant community. But Portland seemed more promising as far as work, so that's where we went.

At this point, I was used to moving. During our year in Salt Lake City, we moved several times because we couldn't afford the apartments from month to month. My father took on whatever jobs he could find, but supporting a family of four was much harder than just supporting himself and sending a package every now and then. There was great irony in the fact that when we were living in Poland we had money but empty store shelves, and then living in the US with an abundance of products in the stores but no money to buy them with. This was quietly obvious to my whole family. Our lives were drastically different in America.

Once we moved to Portland, we were actually helped by the state and we received a notable amount of assistance. Interestingly, we met a lot of other foreign families in the offices waiting for assistance, but not many were Polish, so the language barrier continued to be a problem.

My father went through several construction and plumbing jobs that were only temporary, and continued to look for work everywhere. Fortunately, we were used to being hungry, so when these hard times hit, it wasn't a shock to us. At the same time, we never changed our "prepper" way of life. So when my father did have work, and we had extra cash, it was extremely easy to stock up on food, and have it for when times were tough.

There was also the interesting culture difference of how sales were conducted. My mother would often comment on the idiocy of American businesses to lower prices and offer sales on items that were more popular during certain seasons, such as eggs on Easter, and turkey on Thanksgiving. She would take full advantage of these sales and stock up on these foods to home can them, or would buy extra cans of pumpkin and green beans. The concept of abundance never quite sank in with her, although that may have turned out to be a good thing.

Things actually turned around for us rather quickly after we moved to Portland. My mother got a job working in a factory. It was a bit of a step down from her previous career, but it was a job. Sure, it paid minimum wage, but it was a job that included two fifteen-minute breaks, a half-hour lunch, only an eight hour work day, and working only five days a week. That was a significant improvement over the working conditions in Poland. Plus, if she had to work more than that, they paid her extra. It was a good deal as far as she was concerned.

Thanks to the extra income, my father was able to acquire all of his proper licensing and permits, and open his own construction business. As our finances improved, so did our spending habits. It wasn't long before we fell into the same trap as every other American. We paid for things like cable so we could watch more cartoons. We bought fancy clothes that we wore to take pictures to send to family in Poland so we could show off our great life.

Eventually my parents purchased an old run-down house that needed a lot of work, and we lived our spoiled American life there. My English was almost proficient by the time I was 10 years old. I went to public schools and grew up as an American kid, with the exception of my accent of course, which I largely lost by the time I turned 13.

I do have an interesting memory of school, however, and how quickly I accepted my fate as an American. While in elementary school for my 5th grade year, I didn't know anyone yet because we had just moved to that area of Portland. I stood out in the crowd because I was the foreign kid with an accent that wore funny clothes. At the beginning of the school year, the gym teacher was talking to us during class. I don't recall exactly about what, but he was demonstrating how to climb a rope. The goal was to climb the rope to the ceiling and ring the bell. He asked for volunteers and wanted to know if anyone could do it, and no one raised their hand.

I volunteered. I knew I could climb that rope, and I did. I got to the top, rang the bell, and then climbed down. I impressed all the kids, made friends, and went on with the rest of the school year. I enjoyed school because they had a delicious breakfast program that I received for free due to my parents' low income, and an even better lunch program that was free for me as well. The best part was that the school sold ice cream bars after school for 30 cents a bar. Somehow I always managed to scrape up 30 cents, and had one of these ice cream bars almost every day. But at the end of the school year, when all the kids were climbing ropes to the top and I was called upon, I couldn't do it. I couldn't even get halfway to the top. The gym teacher scolded me, and asked me why I couldn't do it now, since I could do it when school started. Truth be told, at that time, I had no idea why. I didn't really care either. As far as I was concerned, life was good.

Looking back, I know exactly why I couldn't climb that rope at the end of the school year. It was my new American diet of hamburgers, French fries, apple pies, ice cream, and other wonderfully tasting junk food never available in Poland. We fell right into the American trap. Both of my parents worked full-time and were too busy to cook healthy meals during the week. Fast food was cheap, easy, and convenient, and often we kids were left on our own without our parents watching over what we put into our bodies. We glued ourselves to the couch and ate junk food as we watched TV before and after school: what a good life for a child (end sarcasm). On the weekends my mom would still cook healthier meals, and do all her home canning with the items she found on sale. But that was only two out of seven days a week — not frequently enough to remain healthy.

In Poland, children were raised by the state. In America, children are raised by television. I'm not sure which is worse. In neither case were the parents actually raising their children the way they should, because *they were too busy trying to survive*. This is another parallel between Poland and the US: keep the parents busy so the children can be indoctrinated. The only differences are *who* is doing the indoctrination and *how* it is done.

Regardless, what an unhealthy way for a child to live! With our language barrier, we had no idea what ingredients were in our food. We were also not used to processed food, and had no idea how it was made. We just knew it was cheap and easy, and it tasted good. There is something appealing, when you're a kid, about an all-American hot dog with all the trimmings. There was another caveat to this as well. When we lived in Poland, my parents never had to worry about us kids overeating because we simply didn't even have enough food as a minimum to eat. So how would they know that my school sold ice cream sandwiches at the end of the day? I'm not sure which was worse: being undernourished with an inadequate *quantity* of food in Poland, or being malnourished with nutritionally devoid poor *quality* "food" in the US. The concept of substituting *poor quality but high quantity food* for *higher quality but lower quantity food* to placate the people I guess never occurred to the Polish leadership.

My parents also became unhealthy and began to put on weight. They too ate cheap (monetarily as well as qualitatively) fast food and no longer walked to the bus stop since they owned a car. Often the only cooking my mother did was on weekends when she was canning the peaches she found on sale. While we never changed our "prepper" way of life, we did change our immediate way of life, and became very Americanized. If only we had known what it *really* meant to be American.

But like most other Americans, we blindly followed the belief that we now lived in a free country. We could say what we wanted. We could DO what we wanted: all it took was a little elbow grease. The goal of my parents was to start their own business and own their own home with a little land.

Since we were in Portland, acreage wasn't really an option. So the old house my parents bought had a little lot with it, and that had to do. My mother immediately began gardening. Self sufficiency just never left us. Unlike living in Poland, the opportunities were supposed to be there. We just had to work hard for them. In Poland, having your own business was unrealistic, as you had to work so hard just to survive that becoming an entrepreneur required you put in time that you didn't have. Food had to come first. There was no way to save up and take a leap: you just worked.

So my parents took the leap in America quickly, and my father started his construction business. But all was not well. First, the business struggled because of the language barrier. Proving quotes was not easy for my father, and oftentimes he misunderstood what the customer wanted, and built something wrong. Second, customers were already getting used to cheap pre-made materials. My father only knew how to work with quality raw materials, so he couldn't match prices.

When the construction business failed, my father opened a plumbing business. That worked a little better at first, but again, the language barrier was a problem. In addition, his plumbing skills were quickly becoming outdated as new and better technologies were becoming available. My mother had to continue working at her factory job in order to make ends meet.

My parents tried to network to get more business by going to different churches. That was a very interesting time in my life, as I was dragged to churches of different denominations almost every weekend. My parents would never give up their Roman Catholic faith, but they were willing to give other religions a chance as a way to network.

Don't misunderstand me here, as I know this is a very sensitive topic for many people. When we lived in Poland, the Polish culture was only found at home and at church. We were ruled by Soviet communist dictate, and after most of the Polish Jews were killed in concentration camps, many Poles converted their religion to Roman Catholic or became atheist in an effort to survive. So Roman Catholic Poles dominated the country because that was really the only religious option the Soviets allowed.

I want to briefly further comment about the high rate of Roman Catholicism among Poles because as someone who grew up listening to "dumb Polack" jokes, I like to take every opportunity to correct any pre-conceived biases. I don't know for certain why so many Poles are part of the Roman Catholic Church, because at one time there were many Jewish Poles as well. While I don't know the exact numbers, I do know that one contributing factor for such a significant shift in religion was due to the majority of Jewish Poles being murdered in Nazi concentration camps. Another contributing factor could be that Catholicism was the only religion permitted by the communist government while under Soviet rule. I bring this topic up only because I want to make it clear that not all Poles are Roman Catholic. There is also the fact that many families claimed they were either atheist or Roman Catholic as a means to hide their Jewish heritage, for fear of being sent to concentration camps. To this day, many Poles don't know that they are of Jewish heritage. Even when I inquired if there was any possible Jewish background in my family, all my mother could say was that she had no idea for certain. "If there is Jewish in our family, then it's a deep secret, and it's likely we will never know the truth," she told me.

I will say, however, that the Roman Catholic Poles took their religion very seriously, as it was one of the very few things that remained "Polish" to them through all their tribulations. Since Poland under the communist regime was dominated by Soviet influence, much of Polish life for the average Pole was foreign. So Poles held on dearly to their Polish traditions (including church) so much that when the Pope came to Poland, the Poles turned out en masse. When Pope John Paul II, who was head of the Catholic Church at the time, openly admitted his views to be anti-communist, the Poles rallied together and thus further increased the strength of the Solidarity union. There are even many who believe that without the Pope bringing the people of Poland together, there would not have been such huge support for Solidarity or other similar groups, and therefore freedom would have not evolved as it did without him.

Religion was something that was held dear by many Polish families, as it was truly one of the few cultural relics that we were permitted to hold on to. My parents would have never converted to another religion: they were too loyal to the Catholic Church. But they were also smart enough to know that if you want to sell your business, you must be open minded with everyone, including those of other religions.

So when my parents met people and advertised their business

in an effort to get more customers, and the invitations to a church came, we went. We accepted the gifts of Protestant bibles along with other representative paraphernalia from other religions. We went to the churches and listened to the sermons, but we continued to go to our Polish Catholic church, and my parents never changed their beliefs. However, the different Sunday schools I attended did change how I started to look at religion. I learned that in every religion there was a common theme: there is a God, and you should be a good person. Why in the world people squabble over labels of what type of God they believe in is beyond me. While there are certainly different religious doctrines, when you break it down to the simplest of equations, most people actually have similar religious beliefs. Putting a label on people's beliefs only separates and divides us. Except in cases where there are very significant material differences in doctrines between religions, squabbling over trivial or superficial details of doctrine or tradition seems lacking in psychological maturity and grace — two things that all religious traditions aspire to.

Perhaps because my parents didn't convert to another religion, or perhaps due to the language barrier, or perhaps even due to my father's quality of work, or some combination of these factors, contributed to his various business failures. Regardless, my father gave up on his dream of having his own business, and got his commercial driver's license. This made life difficult again, as he would drive across the continent and be gone for months at a time, while my mother still worked at the factory. This was not dissimilar to when we were living in Poland and my father was in the US, but at least the paychecks were reliable most of the year. Again, my mother's persistence in stocking up on foods that were on sale helped us get through the difficult times.

But our dream of living the American life the way we saw it on television was quickly failing to come to fruition. No matter how hard we worked, something always prevented us from being able to own our own land outright and live a completely self-sufficient lifestyle. It was still much better than living in Communist Poland, but it was not the dream we had envisioned.

Lesson 4a: Just because life has improved and is easier to live, doesn't mean that your journey is over, or that life couldn't improve even more.

Lesson 4b: Just because there is a calm respite from the storm, doesn't mean that the storm is over.

"It is often easier to become outraged by injustice half a world away than by oppression and discrimination half a block from home."

-Carl T. Rowan

*My school
ID in Poland
in 1985.*

*My kindergarten picture when I was four years old wearing hand sewn
dresses as tradition for the Christmas Holiday (1981).*

Photo taken in Wałbrzych, Poland to send to my father in the US.

First Day in America in Salt Lake City, Utah airport. (October of 1985).

CHAPTER 5: GROWING UP IN A WORLD WHERE YOU DON'T FIT IN

"When a well-packaged web of lies has been sold gradually to the masses over generations, the truth will seem utterly preposterous and its speaker a raving lunatic."

-Dresden James

With the exception of the Native Americans, all US residents have some ties to their distant family as a foreigner. One of the many things that made America great was the amazing amount of foreigners that moved here to better their lives. The "melting pot," it was once called, and the greatness of that was most people accepted a certain minimal shared set of values and principles in regards to economics and politics. Not that everyone agreed on everything, or lost their native cultures, but all accepted certain basic principles.

It did not matter where you were from, as long as you were a hard worker and you believed in freedom. It didn't matter what language you spoke, as long as your views were in line with what the US was founded upon, which was basically to live and let live; to allow people the opportunity of freedom to be left alone so that they can build better lives for themselves. It was certainly *not* about having prosperity handed to them — it was about the opportunity to *earn* it, with minimal government interference. A personal example of this is how my husband's grandparents immigrated to the US from Germany and England in the nineteen-teens in search of better lives for themselves and their families.

This is not to say that America and its citizens have always been perfect and without flaws. Certainly there were struggles for different groups such as slaves and horrible periods of racism, not to mention the original takeover of a country from its native people. Many foreigners and natives were treated as second class citizens, and even women struggled with gaining their rights to vote and work. But in the big picture, America certainly developed into a beautiful country full of diverse, hardworking people with integrity. People used to build businesses and sell products that they proudly made in America. People were entrepreneurs and created amazing things that helped to advance our society. People came from all walks of life and had common goals in mind: freedom and prosperity.

But somewhere in America's history that has changed. I don't know if it was before or during my generation, but somewhere along the line these important values and principles have not only changed, but changed the people growing up and living in America.

America was supposed to be a place of opportunity for me, as well as for the rest of my family. But as the economy went through its cycles, and during the low times, our family didn't fare very well. It certainly didn't help that our language skills were in need of improvement, and that our overall skills were pretty much useless in a society where many things could be bought for much less at major "box" stores. So with abundance all around us, but little money, life was a different type of difficult for us.

Before my personal (soon-to-be teenaged) troubles started in the 6th grade, I had one more life-changing event in elementary school. It was during lunch one random day that some ladies came down to the cafeteria with pictures of cute little rabbits with their sides exposed as flesh. They were teaching us about cruelty to animals and animal testing. Their goal was to convince us to become vegetarian and to not buy products unless they weren't tested on animals.

Their little plan worked. I was traumatized by the images, and so were the other kids. No offense intended to anyone who has good reason to choose to be vegetarian, but this is how propagandists often operate: go after the impressionable minds of young children who have not yet developed their critical thinking skills. I use this as an example because in hindsight I suppose I never really fully escaped propaganda and indoctrination when I left communist Poland and came to America. In certain aspects, it seems like I simply traded one set of propaganda — communist indoctrination — for another, such as corporate commercials. It was perhaps not nearly as destructive, but the takeaway lesson from this is to *never* let down the guard of your critical thinking skills. I try to keep my "bovine excrement filter" in the "on" position all the time, because those times when you think you don't need it can often turn out to be times that you need it the most.

That day, the lunch lady serving our gruel was frustrated to no end because all of a sudden we were all asking for vegetarian food. She had nothing of the sort, and finally found bagels and cream cheese for us. Not long after the animal rights ladies left, our desire to "go vegetarian" faded, and our choice of products was limited to either what our parents decided to buy for us, or what the commercials convinced us to tell our parents to get us. Although, in the back of my young and impressionable mind, the images of the cute little bunnies stayed with me.

I was young enough when I left Poland that at the time I couldn't have understood the politics of what made Poland the way it was. All I knew was that we were in America, and things were better. In my mind, I was an American, and I should live like an American. So I didn't understand why my parents got upset when I told them I didn't want to eat meat. To them, they couldn't fathom why in the world I would refuse to eat something that they used to have such a difficult time getting when we lived in Poland. I didn't realize it then, but a generational schism between me and my parents was already beginning. And that schism was largely created by environmental influences (including media, school, and culture) to which neither my parents nor I were really paying too much attention.

When middle school came, I had to switch schools. Most of the friends I made in elementary school went to a different middle school than I did due to zoning. I think sixth grade was the time that I started to really notice my peers, and they also noticed — and judged — me. I didn't realize until that time that my clothes were never cool. They were not brand names, but rather generic, or sewn by my mother. Some of my clothes were even hand-me-downs from my older brother. They were what my family could afford. Most of this didn't phase me until I was surrounded by so many peers that had "better" clothes who were not bashful about pointing it out to me. Peer pressure can be used as a powerful tool to influence opinion, not just in children, but in people of all ages.

So I struggled, because although I wanted to be like the other American kids, I couldn't. We were very poor in comparison to most of my classmates' families. We also had a different culture, and when I showed my mother a school bag that I wanted, she laughed at the price tag and told me she could sew me one that looked just like the one at the store. She did sew me one, but it was out of old scraps of material that she had, and when she couldn't figure out how to make the straps strong enough to hold all my books, she used rope. I was initially actually very fond of this homemade bag and proudly took it to school with me.

It didn't take long for me to become disillusioned with what was truly important. Actually, it only took one person to make a comment about my bag, who asked in a tone of disbelief, "Are the straps made out of rope?" I immediately hid the straps inside the bag and carried it to my locker and left it there. I proceeded to carry all of my books in my arms for the rest of the school year.

I think my actions and reactions were completely normal for a kid my age at the time. Most everyone wants to fit in, and when you already have several unique characteristics (such as an accent), you want to eliminate any other things that make you stand out. This is a problem when your parents cannot afford to buy all the stuff all the other kids have, and a huge disconnect develops between the generations. My parents couldn't understand why I wanted all the latest fads, when only a few years prior I had nothing. And I couldn't understand why my parents didn't want me to fit in. I was sure they could find a way to buy me things. All the other parents could do so; why couldn't mine? I was embarrassed to show up after Christmas break when all the kids were showing off their new toys and sweaters, and I had nothing. I certainly wasn't going to show them my mother's knitted scarf. No — I would be made fun of. That stayed in my locker as well. How little did I actually understand back then what it meant to live in America. But then again, I was only an impressionable kid.

This may seem like just another story about an adolescent trying to fit in, but I'm using another personal example from my past to elucidate methods by which people are controlled, often without even knowing it. Social pressure and ridicule are often used to control people, and enforce conformity and groupthink. While some people mature and outgrow the influence of social pressure on their behaviors and thoughts, many people do not. Many adults still live their lives based on what other people think of them, whether it is regarding their consumer habits or their views on politics and economics. In fact, in modern America, conformity with pop culture and political correctness has become more pervasive than ever, as if we've had a mandated national reduction in maturity level. Americans seem to have become so distracted with pop culture, consumerism, and political correctness, that other than superficial tribute they have forgotten the values and principles by which they achieved their success and prosperity in the first place. That Americans seem to be so easily distracted that they lose sight of what is truly important is concerning in itself. But that they have allowed their views about economics and politics to be manipulated by media propaganda and peer pressure does not bode well for the future of a free American Republic.

What I didn't realize back then was that in choosing to "fit in" as an American consumer child, I had not only chosen to give up my native culture completely, but I also completely missed what it meant to be American and what was truly important about America. My brother and I both changed our names to more American-sounding names. I even refused to speak Polish at home. I told my parents that we were in America, and they should only speak English too. It would help them to practice by speaking English at home. While I don't believe there is necessarily anything wrong with giving up a culture, especially if you find its values do not fit your own, I do think there is something wrong with someone else pushing their values onto you, and you giving up your culture or values because someone else told you how to live. That is not the American way; that is the communist way.

A true problem for me at that time was that what I thought was independent thinking or decisions on my part. My dislike of the Polish culture because it was "outdated" was really what television told me to think, along with the influence of my peers in public school. My views were not based on any rational reasoning or values. So in a sense those decisions weren't truly my own or of my own free will, because at the time I was not conscious of the forces that had influenced me. I had been brainwashed.

Another problem at that time was that my family and I all had developed a great misconception about what it meant to be an American. The culture in which I grew up in America was not the same culture that emigrated here when the Founding Fathers wrote the Bill of Rights and the Constitution, nor even the culture of the American people in the early 1900s. The Founding Fathers wrote exceptional documents that truly *acknowledged* (not granted) that the people are sovereign and have the right to live freely.[1-2] They acknowledged that people inherently have the natural right to free speech,[3] the right to bear arms (the right to defend oneself),[4] the right to practice any religion of their choice,[5] and most importantly in my view and my family's view, the right to own property.[6-7]

In fact, James Madison went so far as to state that individual civil rights and property rights are inseparably connected when he stated the following at the Virginia Ratifying Convention: "It is sufficiently obvious, that persons and property are the two great subjects on which Governments are to act; and that the rights of persons, and the rights of property, are the objects, for the protection of which Government was instituted. These rights cannot well be separated. The personal right to acquire property, which is a natural right, gives to property, when acquired, a right to protection, as a social right."[8]

What makes a person American is not junk trinkets that you can buy at the dollar store that were made by slave labor in a foreign land. What makes a person American is, at a minimum, reading the Constitution, the Bill of Rights, and the Declaration of Independence, and actually living by the principles, values, and spirit of those documents.

But how could I, or any child growing up in the US in the 1990s, have known that? Certainly no teacher ever announced to the class that wearing brand names doesn't make a person an American. My parents were unable to teach me these things, though they did make fun of me for advertising brands for free by wearing the labels largely printed on my shirts. And the television only taught me exactly the opposite. I actually learned more about the Constitution and American history when I was studying for my naturalization citizenship test than I ever did in public school, which means that if I wasn't taught it in school, then neither were the hundreds of other kids who also attended my school. As it turns out, even as far back as the 1980s when I was still living in Poland, most students in America had never even heard of the Declaration of Independence, and this was the minimal requisite for a person to be considered an informed US citizen.[9] This concept will probably be argued by many, and my goal is not to debate the purpose of school. I will merely say this: if an adult has never heard of the Declaration of Independence, or the Constitution, then the vote they place in the ballot box may just as well be against what this country was founded upon. Worse yet, that very same citizen may be called upon for civic duty to serve on a jury for a case that may involve the actions of an individual who would require the protections of the Bill of Rights to keep him or her free. If you were sitting on the stand waiting to be judged by twelve peers, would you not hope that sometime in their lives, those people were taught the founding principles of this country?

I certainly did learn important things in school, such as the English language, reading, writing, mathematics, and other topics such as basic science and certain pieces of history. It was also during my middle school years that personal computers were becoming more common and they started to teach us those skills as well. While I appreciate most of my public education, there were some moments in my life when I realized that I was very much misled in the topics I was taught, specifically in history and economics. There were several things in history that were taught in an incomplete or misleading way. I was taught that Columbus "discovered" America, but not the harm it caused to the Natives. I was taught that the Founding Fathers wrote the Declaration of Independence to free America from an oppressive government in another country, but not what was in the Constitution or the Bill of Rights. I learned to memorize important dates, but not to think critically about any of the topics we were studying. I learned to memorize specific events, but not look at the whole picture, or what any of it actually meant.

I don't want to make it sound like my education in the public school system was terrible. But in reality, it wasn't great. Very few teachers taught me to think: instead, I was just told to memorize and regurgitate. I was also often treated as a second-class student by many of the teachers because of my poor English language skills. While there were some great teachers in my life that took the extra time to explain things to me in a different way because English was my second language, there were more teachers that clearly didn't care, and used my foreignness as an excuse to not teach me. But despite the good and bad teachers, and despite the skewed history and economics textbooks, I still benefited greatly from my education. I am a believer that real education, including civics, critical thinking, and practical philosophy, along with the more typical subjects, is key to a free society.

When you grow up in the public school system, you are exposed to certain things in life that perhaps your parents were not, and which they would not consider normal. Let's take current computer technology as an example. There are still many older people out there who do not own a computer, let alone know how to use one. Yet their children or grandchildren are proficient with computers and even smartphones. The older generation has a choice at this point. They can either ask their children (or someone else) to teach them, or they can continue living the way they always have, and never invest in a computer. After all, if they survived this long without one, why bother getting one now? That choice is completely up to them.

However, the younger generation doesn't really have that choice. Our world has become so computerized that you have to be computer literate in order to maintain almost any type of employment. The next generation will require this even more. Actually, any child that goes to public school and doesn't live in the boonies in an isolated environment is exposed to computer technology and learns about computers from a very young age. Computer technology is now a fact of American life. This is an example of the process of *gradualism* at work in our culture and society.

With things like income taxes, some people among the older generations still tried to refuse to pay federal income taxes because they found them unconstitutional and would fight with the IRS to no end. (Yes, I do realize that the 16th Amendment technically authorized the income tax; this is serving as another example.) However, the younger generations grew up with federal income taxes, accepting them as a fact of life. They usually don't even consider the constitutionality or legality of something so commonly accepted, unless someone introduces them to the idea that they perhaps shouldn't be forced to pay an income tax, or they happen to really become interested in history, laws, or taxes. This is another example of gradualism.

One generation may not be willing to do something, but the next generation is indoctrinated into those behaviors, so it doesn't even phase them. And the generation after that is indoctrinated into something else new, which they don't bother questioning at all. Thus, a continuous march further away from America's founding principles and values occurs, and simultaneously, the population is directed toward something very different. This is sometimes also referred to as "social engineering."

The parable of the boiling frog is often used to describe this process. If you put a frog in a pot of boiling water it will obviously jump right out. But if you put a frog in a pot of cool water, it won't jump out, because it's comfortable. And if you turn on the burner, the frog still doesn't jump, because the increase in temperature of the water is gradual, and the frog doesn't realize that eventually the water will get too hot. The frog only realizes that it is being cooked after it is too late, at which point it can no longer jump out.

This is gradualism in action. When you grow up and you don't know any different, then how would you know something is wrong? A good example of this occurred when I lived in Poland. I was used to the shortages and standing in line for hours on end, and I was used to the oppression that I lived under because that's how life always was. I literally didn't know anything different until I came to the US. I didn't really have anything to compare it to. There was no baseline to serve as a point of reference.

Is being educated in how to use a computer a bad thing? Of course not. But if you are only taught how to use a calculator rather than how to do a math problem manually, then is that omitting something important in education? If you've only been taught to use a calculator, and had no idea that you could do such math in your head, would you know to question the teacher instructing you on the use of the calculator?

For example, if you don't have a point of reference on what it means to have civil liberties, then how would you know if you really have them? If the NSA monitors all of your communications, do you have civil liberties? If you grow up not knowing anything different, you might think that the NSA monitoring all your communications is normal and that you do still have civil liberties. It is like when I lived in Poland and I knew that our phones were tapped. It was common knowledge, and it had always been that way. I never knew a life where our phones were not tapped. The NSA invasion of privacy is a perfect example, as many communist places had massive surveillance programs. These were most well known in the Soviet Union and East Germany, but communist Poland had them as well. When my family came to America, we considered it a great relief to not have to worry about being spied on constantly. Sadly, the US is now going down that very same oppressive path. Frighteningly, most Americans I talk to don't see it the way I see it. In their mind, they don't care if they are spied on because they feel they are not doing anything wrong. To them, being spied on is irrelevant. Thus, the next generation will be so accustomed to the idea of the NSA that they will likely not grasp the concept of a world without it, just as I didn't until I came to the US.

Gradualism in loss of civil liberties has actually already occurred in the US. If it were possible to use a time machine to bring a well-informed US citizen from one hundred years ago to have them live in the US today, such an individual would be enclosed by laws, regulations, and restrictions when it comes to civil rights and all types liberties that they likely could not have imagined. They would be in disbelief of the number of laws and regulations imposing on their right to live freely. They would probably be in shock to learn that not only is the American government spying on its own people, but that the American people purchase, of their own volition, the very gadgets that the American government uses to spy on them ("smartphones"). Of course the technology would be much more advanced than that of one hundred years ago, but that actually is a completely separate issue. Principles don't change because technology does; only the implementation of principles changes.

So due to gradualism, there is clearly a shift in culture with the American people when it comes to the understanding and respecting of their civil rights and liberties, just as what my parents understood about freedom having lived in communist Poland as adults was different from what my brother and I were taught in the American public school system. Thus, we grew up to have a different understanding of what it means to be free. That same process of gradualism is also how we went from having a monetary and banking system based on honest money with intrinsic value that benefits everyone, to a system of fiat currency that is backed by nothing and primarily benefits those who control the counterfeit production of that currency.

Returning to the topic of our public school system, and further tying that in with gradualism, let's ask some questions: How many parents actually get involved in their children's education? How many parents have time to do that? How many go to PTA meetings, read the school books the kids are reading, and review the material that will be covered during that school year? Very few. This is not because the parents are bad, but because reality warrants they have a full time job (or two), and often parents have more than one child to look after.

So what is to stop a bad teacher from instilling objectionable ideas or principles in unsuspecting children that their parents wouldn't generally agree with? Or, what is to stop someone from teaching a child that it is proper to spy on their parents and to report something silly like excessive alcohol consumption, or maybe even excessive water usage? Or, what is to stop a teacher from pushing their religious views onto someone else's children? Or, what is to stop a government from requiring the use of books that teach children things that parents never even imagined?

This is where gradualism is key. Looking at this from an outside perspective, hypothetically consider if the books that the Federal Government required schools to use were published by McGraw-Hill. And what if the major authors of these books didn't believe in the Second Amendment, so they changed the wording a bit in the history books to reflect the idea that the Second Amendment only applies to military, and not the people? Consequently, the children who use those books will grow up believing that guns are bad, unless you are in the military. "After all," they are taught, "look at all the school shootings." Yes, these "gun free" zones are clearly working (end sarcasm). The parents of these kids understood the Constitution and Second Amendment rights. When they questioned their children, the kids sounded like they knew what they were talking about, so the parents didn't delve any deeper into what was actually being taught.

Now, hypothetically consider the following: A generation has now passed, and the new McGraw-Hill textbook even further changes the description of the Second Amendment. The grandchild is now taught that all guns are bad and people shouldn't own them. This grandchild is also taught that anyone who owns such guns is a domestic terrorist and needs to be reported. So now what happens to grandpa? He goes to prison for being a domestic terrorist. His weapons are confiscated as evidence, and because it is now acceptable for people to be disappeared, he is never seen again.

It is easy to be a busy parent, but if a parent is trusting their child to a school system outside of the home, it is imperative to not blindly trust the strangers who pick up your child on a school bus or a host of teachers that you've never met. Meet the staff of your school, interview them, talk to them, and get to know their values, principles, beliefs and views. Most importantly, hold them accountable for their actions and what they are teaching. Also, don't forget to inquire about any uninvited guests who offer fifteen minute presentations to the students during lunch. Better yet, if possible, home school your children or send them to a private school.

Białe plamy is a very well known term by most Poles who lived through the communist era of Polish history. "Blank spots" is basically what it means. It refers to the re-written history by the Polish communist party, which was ruled by the Soviets. History was re-written and much of Polish history was omitted in an effort to brainwash the Poles into believing that the Soviets had saved them from the Nazi Germans.[10] This re-written history was used to gain compliance among the Poles. Gradualism was used so Polish children grew up learning the re-written history, and thus thinking the Soviets were allies. If it hadn't been for their parents taking an interest in their children's education, they might have never known anything different. Teaching the true history of Poland that was not approved by the communist state was forbidden. So in order to circumvent these restrictions, parents and teachers created "floating schools," which were basically secret classes taught in people's homes on a variable basis where children were taught the true history of Poland without the "blank spots". They wanted to make sure the next generation of Poles would know the true history of who they were and what their country had been through.

I think there is a fascinating history about the public school system. I grew up with the understanding that every child in America went to either public or private school, and the concept of alternate education such as home schooling never occurred to me, because I had never heard of it. As far as my world was concerned, both in Poland and in America, kids always went to school, whether private or public. It wasn't until several years ago when my husband suggested to me that our public school system is out of control and needs to be reformed, that I really learned about alternative schooling options. I was dumbfounded by his statement, and simply asked, "Well, who is going to teach the children?" My husband encouraged me to research the history of the public school system, and loving to always prove him wrong, I delved right into the research.

But I never got to use my famous "I told you so" line. I was shocked to learn that the history of public education was originally based on teaching religion and civics, not the three Rs of reading, writing, and arithmetic. It was definitely different.

In 18th century America, schools started out as a 12-week elementary school for boys, whose parents paid for the schooling.[11] This education was supplemented by learning at churches and from neighbors. It was not considered important, and it was definitely not free. More importantly, it was not controlled by the government. This also meant that what determined if a child received education was the family's societal status.[12] It was not until the 1860s that the property owners were charged a property tax to pay for public education that was to be available to all, including those that did not own land at the time.[13] The dynamic changed and no longer did a parent need to be in a position of status in order for their child to attend school. However, only reading and religion were taught in these schools, and only older males were privy to more astute subjects such as grammar, math, Latin, and philosophy; and still only the most privileged were able to attend college.[14] The education system continued to evolve as funding came into question by those who did not want their children to be educated by those who had different religious beliefs, thus altering the child's beliefs originally taught by the parents. This is what resulted in private Catholic schools.[15]

Segregation then came into play, and then shortly after that, it was determined that children would not only learn to read, but also learn morality that would be considered common to society.[16] By the late 1800s, although education was offered to more people in the US than in any other country, white people were still favored, segregation was prominent, and even the Native Americans were forced to move away from their families and culture in order to attend special separate schools.[17]

What was first intended as a place to teach family, religion, and community, morphed incredibly over generations. While civic duty was a key educational topic in the 1700s and 1800s, reading and writing became emphasized shortly thereafter as a means to an ends. But parents were still expected to teach their children most of the skills that adults were expected to have. Farmers taught their children to farm, and blacksmiths taught their children to work with metal. If a parent didn't have a particular skill to pass on, then it was possible to arrange for a child to be an apprentice under a particular tradesman, providing free labor (and sometimes monetary compensation) in exchange for the tradesman's instruction. Although today we still sometimes refer to an apprenticeship as such, that method of learning has fallen out of favor in our modern society, replaced by formal college or university education. Much of what parents did back then would today be called "home schooling." Amazingly, I had never even heard of the term "home schooling" until I was an adult. Worse yet, it seems in our culture today, the idea of a parent teaching his or her own children (as in home schooling), is frowned upon by much of our society. Cui bono? Who benefits from this? I am inclined to think it is not the children.

As Andrew Coulson, author of *Market Education: The Unknown History* writes, "Public schooling arose in response to an influx of immigrants who had different religions or cultures. Its primary focus was to establish social order and mainstream vast numbers of immigrant children into a common school setting."[18] The American school system has come a long way since the 1700s, including who was to be educated, as higher education was still for the more privileged in the mid-1800s.[19] But as our society improved and allowed almost everyone to receive public education, what is being taught in our classrooms has also changed dramatically.

When martial law first occurred in Poland, schools were closed. Teachers were unable to work and children were unable to get an education. While there were a myriad of other shutdowns, including public transportation, the shutting down of public education was a hard hit to the parents who only wanted a better life for their children.

One of the promises made by the Soviet ruled Polish regime was that of education for all. Many Poles did benefit, my parents included. My parents were able to break free from hard-working farm life and receive an education that taught them skills that they were able to utilize and live in the city. Thus, life should have improved by education, as current and future generations should have been able to utilize the education system as well, and learn even more advanced skills. Instead, the regime that controlled the education system decided the curriculum. There we were, Polish people, with Polish culture, living in Poland — yet learning the Russian language was a requirement. The Polish history taught in schools was changed to alter children's minds to develop distrust toward Germans, while the Soviets who ruled over us were our friends, and Polish culture was completely left out of the schools. Those teachers who chose to teach the truth were expelled from the profession. And when education reforms failed to fully brainwash the Polish children, schools were closed under martial law.

Schools did eventually re-open, as did the public transportation system. I remember getting to school by riding the city bus by myself. The school shutdown didn't affect me at first, because I was too young at that time to be in school, but it did affect me upon re-opening.

We were fed in school in Poland, as I was also in America. But our Polish school meal was more of a gruel consisting of overcooked spinach mixed with potatoes, and the portion was so small that students were required by administrators to drink a glass of water prior to eating to help us feel full. I recall having to have to stand among my fellow students to await my dose of vitamin C. These were not Flintstones vitamins by any means, but rather a slice of lemon that we were to put in our mouths and sink into with our teeth. My parents didn't argue with these tactics as they knew this was the only way for my brother and me to get our vitamin C at that time. So they were more than happy to allow the public school system to manage my intake of vitamins. Perhaps that's where their trust of American public school system came from. Maybe they thought that if the schools in Poland were offering vitamins (in whatever source), then the American school system must be offering something even better. At the same time, my parents' lack of English skills and lack of knowledge of American history prevented them from being able to home school their children even if they had wanted to. As immigrants, they had no choice but to trust the American public school system to educate their children while they worked.

Since we were now living in a free country, my parents thought they had no reason to believe that our education would be skewed in any way, at least not like it was in Poland, where after the schools re-opened, many of the classes failed to include certain parts of history. We actually did receive some history education in Poland, but certain subjects of Polish history were obliterated or altered, and other subjects of politics were off limits completely. Somehow, all Polish children knew that certain things were never questioned. This may have been due to witnessing their favorite teachers being fired for teaching the truth. This was an eye-opener to many: children and parents alike. Or perhaps children knew what topics were verboten because they were taught by their parents that certain topics were off limits, or the "glina" would get them ("glina" translates to "mud", which is what we nicknamed the corrupt police because they were as pliant as clay in following orders to oppress the Polish people). Regardless of the method by which this knowledge was impressed into our minds, the reality was that as long as certain topics were not discussed, certain questions were not asked, all was well.

This resulted in many children, myself included, not learning true Polish history until an older age. Many children grew up without the "proper" accepted knowledge (by communist government standards), and upon beginning their required two-year conscription into the military, they were further indoctrinated into believing in the "wrong" enemies. This indoctrination contributed to the Polish military being willing to attack their fellow Polish citizens when the time came. Gradualism had become a work of art and a tool of tyranny in the communist Polish education system.

But we were in America now, the land of the free. My parents had absolutely no reason to even consider the possibility that what we were being taught in school was in any way skewed. If anything, their faith in the public education system was almost a belief that it was exactly how it should be. Their inability to speak the English language fluently prevented them from being able to know what it was we were really being taught, and also prevented them from being involved in things like PTA meetings. They essentially had no choice but to leave my brother and me to be educated by the state.

I believe that my parents have a valid but rare excuse for their lack of involvement. Our situation was somewhat unique in America. Not everyone can use a language barrier as an excuse, especially now, with many people being bilingual or fluent in Spanish. Unfortunately, not enough parents are involved in what the public education is teaching to their children.

Involvement of parents in their children's education can be traced all the way back to the city of ancient Athens, which turned out a culture of human liberty, art, and science that can be considered one of the greatest advances in human history relative to what came before it. However, this only occurred partially because the parents of the Athenian children had control over what their children were taught, and how.[20] This is in contrast to the Spartan civilization, where the government controlled what the children were taught, and parents had absolutely no say. What the Spartan system produced was nothing but illiterate soldiers who were willing to die for their country. Spartans were denied exposure to theater and arts, and unlike Athenians, they did not have the freedom to travel outside of Sparta, nor purchase any comforts in life.[21]

If you look back at the history of education, including Athens, Sparta, and the Roman Empire, education was either used to promote the success of students in life, or to control students and mold them into the military apparatus. When education was left for the government to decide, it never chose for students to succeed in their personal endeavors. Even Julian Augustus, the Roman emperor in 362 A.D., required that teachers be "certified," and any "dissenter" who did not teach what was "approved" was denied the certification. He went so far as to deport anyone caught teaching without a license. Those teachers loyal to the government were rewarded with special benefits and funds, so much that more funds and rewards were received by those teachers who were most willing to teach distorted facts that were in favor of the emperor.[22] Such a lack of real education as a result of bureaucracy, combined with dependence on slave labor, resulted in significantly fewer technological and scientific advancements during the 800 year period following the 200 years the Athenians advanced just prior.[23] Clearly, education matters, and *what* is taught in public schools certainly influences how much a society advances.

Learning from history can turn hindsight into foresight. Yet, instead, history keeps repeating itself over and over again. In Poland in the 1970s and 1980s, just as in Rome under Augustus, teachers were not able to choose what to teach without repercussions. Those teachers that passed the certification tests were rewarded with pay and food.

While not as obvious at first, here too in America, history is repeating itself. US government-mandated programs such as "Common Core" claim to offer "standardized" education in a rapidly advancing society,[24] regardless of a student's learning ability or lack thereof. For those not familiar with it, Common Core is basically a set of educational content and standards shared nationally to ensure that students are taught the same things and are held to the same expectations across the country. These standards are supposedly comparable to those of students in other countries that are considered the highest performing. Common Core also claims to offer students success in achieving higher education, and success across the globe.[25] It sure *sounds* wonderful.

Yet it is worth pointing out that many have argued that the Common Core curriculum is at odds with the US Constitution, national sovereignty, individual rights, and individual liberty, and instead emphasizes collectivism, centralized planning, so-called "sustainability" and "global citizenship."[26-27]

Today we have a standardized, structured system of education that has a set schedule of children heading to school on a school bus, reading all the same textbooks, and taking all the same tests as children on the other side of the US. That may seem great, but there is a lesson to be learned here. While schools have certainly improved the literacy rate in America, they have also dumbed down much of the American population in critical thinking skills. I'm going to go out on a limb here and state that it's not the teachers' faults for such dumbing down, but rather is due to federal and state government involvement in and creation of standardized programs such as No Child Left Behind, or now today, Common Core.

So here we are with the onset of Common Core, which is regulated by the centralized Federal Government (not individual states), and certainly with no input from parents, most teachers, or local communities. As per the General Education Provisions Act, the Department of Education Organization Act, and the Elementary and Secondary Education Act of 1979, the Federal Government is supposed to refrain from involvement in K-12 public education and leave that responsibility to local and state governments.[28] However, the way power-hungry and agenda-driven federal bureaucrats circumvent restrictions like this is always with money: they offer educational funding bribes to states and local municipalities, but only if they "voluntarily" adopt these "national standards" developed by federal bureaucrats.

Among the minority of parents who are familiar with Common Core, there has been a great deal of skepticism regarding the content of and true motivation for the initiative. However, most parents aren't completely aware of what Common Core means for their children. What was initially intended as a package of content standards along with standardized tests turned out to also contain a curriculum enforcer.[29] Students are assessed on the Common Core standards, and these assessments determine the sequence of the upcoming instruction.[30] All students are to be taught exactly the same way from coast to coast and take exactly the same tests. *Common Core also calls for massive data collection and monitoring of children.* The alleged justification for all this data collection and monitoring is supposedly to help students by personalizing the learning process.[31] That sounds great until you ask these questions: What actually happens to all the data that is collected? Could it be used for a mass social engineering project?[32] Who is privy to this information and why? What else will they do with this information? And shouldn't the parents of these children have a right to choose whether or not data about their children is collected, stored, monitored and shared? Finally, who is paying for all this?

Common Core mandates that a national student database be created.[33] The National Center for Education Statistics (NCES), which is a part of the US Department of Education, together with state officials, created a standard coding system so that information from all fifty states would be standardized and therefore transferable as the child moves from state to state. However, it was not just the student's learning skills that were being tracked, but also sensitive statistics such as the student's religion, health problems, behaviors such as whether or not they were a bully, *who their parents voted for, and what the family income was.*[34] Why? This was followed by a change to the Educational

Rights and Privacy Act in 2011 that now allows schools to release student records to third party organizations, and the family does not have to consent, nor can they opt out.[35] So parents have no way of knowing where these statistics about their children will end up. So who is getting all this information and for what purposes? Why do parents not have the choice to opt their child out of this program?

With Common Core not only do parents not get a say in what is taught in the classroom, nor what textbooks are used to teach their children about "history" and other topics such as math, but with the changes in teaching methodology present in Common Core, many parents will not even be able to help their children with their homework. I was fortunate that when I came to the US, the math taught in my American elementary school used the same principles that were taught to me in Poland, and thus I had a common language I could understand: numbers. But I recently helped a friend's daughter with her homework, and I could not figure out how in the world they were doing their multiplication. It made no sense to me at first, and I'm pretty sure that my "A" in college calculus implies that I'm not a dummy when it comes to math. I could, of course, calculate the correct answers to these simple multiplication problems. Yet, at first I couldn't replicate the *process* that her daughter was trying to use, as she had been taught to perform the calculations in a strange way. Once I did finally figure out the procedure she was taught, I couldn't understand why it was being taught in such an unnecessarily complicated manner. I still don't.

How schools are funded has also changed, and who benefits from this funding change is an important subject to visit. Common Core requires standardized tests and specific books, which the schools have to pay for. But who profits from these testing and study materials? In her book *ConversationED*, which was not published yet at the time of this writing (I was fortunate to receive a short excerpt in my email box), Kathleen Jasper discusses what the problems are with programs such as Common Core. Specifically, large sums of money are paid to the book publishers and test creators and administrators, and those who decided upon these standards are the same groups who produce the textbooks and create the tests. The marketing ploy these educational authors and publishers used was arguing that not standardizing all children's abilities would be "racist" as some children would not be able to compete in the adult world against those with higher testing standards. Regardless, instead of getting all students to an equally educated level, these standards have negatively affected those with disabilities, including those with poor test-taking skills (despite their real-world classroom skills). As it turns out, Common Core has only lined the pockets of those that created its curriculum: people who never stepped foot in our current classrooms. Furthermore, while the states agreed to implement Common Core because they would receive federal funding awards, that money never benefited the students, and instead went right back to line the pockets of those selling the testing materials and textbooks.[36]

To me, some of the arguments in favor of Common Core are really saying that rather than emphasizing the individual abilities of students, they should all be dumbed down equally. That result is not in the interest of any students.

What about other educational authors and publishers who do not subserviently acquiesce to the Federal Government's new standards of Common Core? They will not be part of the immense education marketplace, as that market will no longer be open or competitive for those that do not align themselves with the "official party line."[37] The power of the teachers to choose textbooks that they find useful in educating their students has been taken away. This will certainly have the effect of greatly reducing the marketplace for alternative educational materials. Meanwhile, the authors of "approved" books receive the title of "exemplar authors" due to the Federal Government's endorsement.[38] Just as in Poland, I suspect this will also result in the elimination of most criticism of or descent toward the Federal Government in the curriculum, and will instill in the curriculum whatever perspectives the federal bureaucrats dictate.

So, what does all of this mean to the parents and children of this generation? It means that what is taught in schools is not intended to benefit the students and their parents, but rather, the publishers and creators of the textbooks and standardized tests. We sure have come a long way from basic civics and morality teachings. Most American parents want for their children the same thing that my parents wanted for my brother and me, which according to polls dating back to the 1970s is mainly to improve career prospects in order to be able to lead better lives that are both richer and more satisfying.[39]

Standardized education across all of the US may seem like the answer at first, as everyone would receive equal education and everyone would have the same opportunities for getting into colleges or attaining jobs. But it is not the answer. It is not possible to successfully approach the process of educating humans, particularly children, like they are standardized widgets being produced on a factory assembly line. The human mind simply doesn't work that way. Each individual is different, with different abilities, interests, strengths, and weaknesses. Forcing one standard across the board will not recognize the talents of those who are gifted, and forcing a standard of education upon those who learn better through other means (such as "hands on" learning) will not be effective.

From a career perspective, networking has constructively played a role and nepotism has destructively played a role in many of the jobs and careers in which I have worked, including in education. Corruption will unfortunately always exist, so opportunity will unlikely be equal for everyone regardless of how good someone's education is. Standardizing education only results in giving the centralized Federal Government the power to make decisions for all schools and all students. This might not be ideal for small-town schools, where the needs of the children are likely different than those of major cities. There is a similar issue for towns that have specific industries or trades and may need the local population to concentrate education more on those industries rather than on only generalized academic skills. There is already a problem in our public education system with students graduating with only academic skills but without real world practical skills. Common Core standardization will only make that situation worse.

I myself am an example of someone who would have been harmed by "one size fits all" educational standards. I benefited from programs intended for those who learned English as a second language, and I would have been at a disadvantage if I were forced to learn at the same pace as my fellow classmates whose first language was English. Similarly, my classmates would have been at a disadvantage to have their education dumbed down to the level of someone else's needs, such as mine at the time. My lack of English proficiency was only a temporary hindrance, but it did not stop me from educational development, nor did my late start with the English language prevent me from leading a productive life as an adult in America. Not all sixth graders wear the same size shoe, and thus, a standard shoe size should not be forced upon them.

There also has to be, at a minimum, a balance between what the school system teaches your children, and what you, as your children's parent, are responsible for teaching them. There must be proper prioritization of who benefits from that child's public education. It should be the child, not a publisher, and certainly not politicians and bureaucrats.

Another important consideration for children in public schools is that parents no longer have control over what their children eat. The schools carry lunches that entice students to toss their nutritious homemade meal from mom and dad and have a slice of pizza, or to run to the vending machine for a soda pop and a bag of chips. As someone who utilized the school's free lunch program when I was growing up, as we were extremely poor, I have a difficult time stating that perhaps such programs are not the best idea. The nutritional quality offered by these programs is usually quite poor, and parents should ultimately be deciding what their children eat. At the same time, when I was in school, pizza wasn't a common food in the lunch line until I reached my senior year in high school. I still had healthier choices as I was growing up. Today it is not always common for truly healthy nutritional choices to be available as part of school lunch programs. And quality nutrition is perhaps one of the more important ingredients for developing healthy children, both physically and mentally.

As well-educated and experienced as my parents were in dealing with a communist government, they completely missed what was happening to their children in the US public school system. They were relieved that the school was educating me (something my parents couldn't do in the English language) and feeding me breakfast and lunch. But what really happened is they had unintentionally allowed the state to raise me, and so I grew up to be a "typical American teenager." Unfortunately that included disinterest in education in general (especially math), skipping school to do fun things, and not caring about my grades, because I didn't recognize that there would ever be any long-term negative consequences for my actions. All I cared about was fitting in with my peers. While my parents thought about how fortunate they were to have a child receiving free education, the generation gap was widening.

Another environment that was difficult for me to fit into was church. We were Roman Catholic, and as with many other Poles, Roman Catholicism was strongly ingrained in my parents. This actually played a huge role in the early Polish emigrants' lives way before our time.

Earlier generations of Poles who immigrated to the US found that language was a barrier, and it was no different for my family. The affordable land they dreamed of was not so affordable when the Poles finally got to the US, so they moved to the suburbs or cities for work. They bonded with other Poles, with religion and language being common denominators. Thus, Polish families were able to better maintain their culture, which included a patriarchal relationship among the family. However, this resulted in generational conflict as the children grew up in a very different culture from their parents. So history repeated itself with my family as well. However, religion was something my family still held on to. But, it was another one of those things that made us stand out.

As I mentioned earlier, most people my family met who tried to help my parents find work also wanted to convert us to their religion. My parents would agree to attend their churches in hopes of employment opportunities, and so I was dragged to every type of church imaginable. Sunday school became very confusing for me. My language skills were already superior to those of both my parents, including my father who had a two-year head start. As I moved from church to church, I could never figure out why the teachings were so different when to me it was all one God. So I became a snotty kid who questioned the Sunday school teacher with difficult and impossible questions about why there are so many different religious beliefs about one God. I argued constantly that we all believed in the same God — just differently. My questions were never answered to my satisfaction, and I came to despise organized religion: any organized religion. My parents would get upset and tell me to just sit and not say a word. They needed the connections to the employment opportunities.

Looking back, I realize how difficult it had been for them. My parents never gave up on their religion, they were just open to other religions in order to survive. Once both my parents were employed, we stopped going to all churches but our original Polish Catholic church.

I bring this up because to this day, people push their religious beliefs on me, and often ask me what religion I am. I have learned to refrain from answering such questions partly because my views do not fit into any one "box," and partly because when I used to tell people "Roman Catholic," I was given the "Oh" as if to say, "You're one of those."

The First Amendment to the US Constitution states:

Congress shall make no law respecting an establishment of religion, or prohibiting the free exercise thereof; or abridging the freedom of speech, or of the press; or the right of the people peaceably to assemble, and to petition the Government for a redress of grievances.

I think that the First Amendment sets a good precedent for us all: I feel that all people should respect religious freedom and not push their religious beliefs on others, nor discriminate against others based on their religious beliefs. Regardless of that personal philosophy, people should, at a minimum, respect the religious freedom of other people. I think it's unfortunate that my memories of wonderful America include such confusion over religion, where I was supposed to be free to practice any religion I chose, yet instead, I was constantly judged by it. Though, at least religion was one thing that was not forced on me in public school.

In a perfect world, which I often dreamed America to be, people would tolerate the differing views of others around them, from all walks of life, so long as those views and individuals are not harming anyone else or violating anyone else's rights. "Live and let live" was the American motto. Rather than laugh at a culture that is different from our own, we should instead learn the best traits from one other, while overlooking those that may seem peculiar. In every culture there are certain practices that work well and others that may not work so well. By adopting the best practices from different traditions, we can create a society that works well for most people. To me, that was the greatness of the "melting pot": incorporating the best traits from different cultures and backgrounds within the context of individual liberty. I believe the US Founding Fathers definitely had one thing right in that liberty is the universal context in which almost everyone can live together peaceably. But somewhere along the way, Americans forgot this principle and instead various groups developed the hallucination that they had the right to dictate their particular views to everyone else — using the threat of government force and violence to do so. To me, that is not American. To me, that is little different than the tyranny and oppression that was forced upon people by Communist and Nazi governments of the past, and which is unfortunately still being forced on people in some religious fundamentalist countries.

We should especially teach our children to learn from each other, respect other people's rights to their personal beliefs, and to refrain from laughing at other cultures. Freedom of religion is one of our most important founding principles, and we should strive to maintain this principle by tolerating others and their religious beliefs, without trying to convert them to ours.

More importantly, in order to have a functional society we need to return to having a base-level shared set of values and principles about economic and personal liberty. With economic disaster remaining a very real possibility in the US (the 2008 financial crisis was merely a practice run), the country could easily descend into a state of civil war without a basic level of shared values, regarding personal and economic liberty. If we *fail* to reestablish *any* common values or principles, our country will likely tear itself apart, particularly under the stress of another economic crisis. If we *succeed* in reestablishing liberty and the Constitution as our most fundamental values or principles, we stand a good chance of being able to put the pieces back together again, because we will have a functional foundation that most Americans could agree to from which to build.

The Constitution used to be known and understood by most Americans, regardless of if they were born in the US or immigrated here. Nowadays, if you ask any student what the 4th or 8th Amendments are, they likely will not know. Their parents might not know either. The more we isolate ourselves from each other based on our differences, the more divided we become. And an America divided against itself will inevitably fall. There is a reason for the expression "divide and conquer."

I experienced a very interesting psychological dichotomy as a teenager. First, I and my immediate family were still envied by all my family members back in Poland. They all wanted to live in America. It was the land of opportunity and it was the land of stocked shelves. Our extended family back in Poland envisioned my immediate family as full of riches, our stomachs full of delicious food, and an overall comfortable life on our way to retirement. There was no such thing as retirement in communist Poland; you worked until the day you died.

The truth was, that while we struggled living in America trying to make it, we never let our family back in Poland know. I don't really know the true reason behind that, nor would I dare insult my parents by asking them. But I imagine that it had to do with their pride of being in America. It was not an easy task to emigrate, nor was it easy to become citizens. I also imagine that admitting that there were some struggles would be to admit that the place that was providing hope to people back in Poland wasn't always what it was cracked up to be. Perhaps my parents maintained the mythology of America to continue to inspire hope for the people they knew back in Poland. Despite the drawbacks of America, it was still far better than communist Poland.

Sometimes dreams are all people have left to hope or live for, and to shatter those dreams with reality would be to shatter any hope someone may have left. It's a harsh act, though sometimes a necessary one. But my parents chose not to shatter anyone's hopes back in Poland. My parents often described living in Poland as not at all enjoyable as you only lived to work, and worked to live. There was no purpose and no passion.

Unlike our extended family and others back in Poland, we were not hungry by any means, so we were still much better off. To tell our extended family that life was difficult for us would be to forget where we came from. We were used to having it rough.

Regardless, I wasn't very involved with my extended family or any of my Polish friends anymore. Somewhere in those few years I had figured out that those people in Poland only wanted to stay in touch with me because I might send them stuff or even bring them to America. At the same time, I wanted to desperately disconnect from my background, as being a teenager in a world dominated by brand names on television was tough when you were just a poor dumb Polack.

I was a teenager after all, and all my friends had the latest trinkets and clothes. They had the latest fashions, my mother would sew my clothes in hopes to copy the latest styles. They had parents that bought them balloons and chocolates on Valentine's Day, and my parents would make fun of Americans for wasting money on needless purchases for silly fake holidays. It was a hard and difficult life as a teenager in America, and while I felt fully American, I lacked the typical American parents that everyone else had.

The real problem was again a combination of things. First, my parents allowed me to be raised by television. They put absolutely no restrictions on what I watched on television, or how much of it I watched. They were busy working, so the television and public school system raised my brother and me. This is never a good combination. Second, I was a very independent child. Again, my parents were busy working, and with a school bus to take me to a school that fed me, they had little to worry about. Third, I felt very American. I went to American schools, I watched American TV, I had an American diet, and American friends. Indeed, I was American, except for the funny homemade clothes and the accent. I had even acquired some of the bad American traits. The combination of these things resulted in the generation gap between my parents and myself becoming wider and wider. Little did I know that none of that truly made me American, nor did I, at that age, have any idea what it really meant to be American.

There was also the commercial aspect of television. Commercials are designed to get children to want things so badly that they convince their parents to buy them. My brother and I were terrors to our parents, because we could never really afford these things, but we wanted them. While my parents tried to buy us stuff we wanted, they really couldn't, and they ignored us most of the time as they were busy trying to make ends meet in the land of opportunity. Even though the store shelves were full of stuff, none of that helped them attain the independent life that they were hoping to build.

So here I was, an American teenager who felt isolated from the world. I wanted nothing to do with my parents because they were Polish and couldn't hide their accents. I was so wrapped up on teenage superficialities that I took absolutely no notice of the world around me, or that this new way of life could one day be compromised. No, to me, America was how it was, and I didn't have to pay attention because it would always be there for me.

When communism fell in 1989, there was a lot of excitement in my house. I was not even a teenager yet at twelve years old, and I didn't pay too much attention at that time. After all, I was American; what did I care about what happens in Poland? But my parents were thrilled, and they immediately started saving money so they could visit family in Poland, as the restrictions no longer applied to my father. They even talked about the possibility of moving back. While they enjoyed their freedoms here, they missed their family, and they missed their culture.

A year later they were able to visit Poland for a month to see their families. They returned to America with a much more appreciative perspective on our life here. My brother and I did not get to go, as we had school obligations, and my parents couldn't afford the extra airfare. But when they returned, they told us that even though it wasn't communist in Poland anymore, that life was still better in America. Jobs were easier to find, and finding a house with a lot of land was much more practical here. They said that Poland had a long way to go before it would be as strong as America. They were also overwhelmed by the cost of everything. A million zloty didn't buy much.

I immediately felt like I was right and they were wrong. Clearly, they had just admitted that America was better. But I was confused about a couple of things. First, I was confused about what it meant to be an American, and second, I was confused about what it meant to live in America.

Lesson 5: A person is very impressionable at a young age, and those impressions can last a lifetime. Therefore, whoever controls the education and cultural influences of the young has the potential to control the future direction of a people.

"If a nation expects to be ignorant and free, in a state of civilization, it expects what never was and never will be."

-Thomas Jefferson

CHAPTER 6: WHAT WE THOUGHT IT MEANT TO BE AN AMERICAN

"If Tyranny and Oppression come to this land, it will be in the guise of fighting a foreign enemy."

-James Madison

I joined the military at age seventeen. I took an oath on my seventeenth birthday to protect and uphold the Constitution. I had little understanding of the Constitution then: I basically took an oath to uphold a document that I, at that time, had never fully read, and even if I had, I'm not sure I would have understood it. I was in the delayed entry program for the Navy, as I had yet to graduate high school. I had four months left and I would leave for boot camp upon my graduation.

I joined the military for several reasons. One reason was that I wanted to follow in my grandfather's footsteps. He served in the Polish Army. I was now an American, so I wanted to serve my country too. I also wanted to travel the world, and at the same time, I hadn't figured out what I wanted to be when I grew up. I knew college was out of the question, as my family was poor.

At that time, I had it in my mind that I would serve twenty years and retire at age thirty-seven. The retirement check after serving twenty years looked really good to me at seventeen years old. I also had no concept of inflation or the devaluation of the US dollar back then. But the biggest reason I joined the military was because I wanted to escape from my Polish culture, which was, as previously mentioned, very prominent in my home.

I was happy to graduate from high school early and have that over with. No matter how much I tried, I just never fit in. No matter what group I joined, no matter what sport I took on, I just never felt I belonged there. My accent was long gone at age seventeen, so only those with a trained ear knew I wasn't born in America. I was relieved to no longer hear that hated question "Where are you from?" with the requisite dumb Polack joke that would follow.

Even though I was raised by the state (practically if not technically) and American consumer culture, I was still not fully American. I was still different. I just could never put my finger on exactly what it was that made me different. I thought I was like everyone else. When I got my first job and earned my first paycheck, I spent my hard earned money on clothes, music CDs, and other unnecessary junk I didn't need, just like everyone else. I bought overpriced brand name items and went to the movies, and did all the teenage things that teenagers do, but I had a knack for always saying something awkward. I always managed to make myself stand out, no matter how much I wanted to fit in.

So after not fitting in at any grade level, I was hopeful the military would allow me to turn things around. I couldn't wait to step foot in Great Lakes, Illinois, for boot camp. I was even more excited to learn that I would be one of the first groups of women to train in co-ed boot camp. Not completely co-ed, as we still had separate housing, but we had a brother company that we challenged in competitions and that we marched with.

Rather than being supported by my fellow senior classmates,

again I was viewed as different. I received a lot of negative comments about "supporting war" because I joined the military, even though at the time women weren't yet allowed in actual combat. Regardless, I was proud to have joined and excited to serve my country. To me, serving in the military meant I was doing something good for my country, and I felt that those who accused me of supporting war were just misguided about what it means to serve. Life was just starting for me as far as I was concerned. My plan was to stay in for twenty years, retire, and live happily ever after.

Boot camp was not at all what I thought it would be. Actually, the entire military experience was a bummer. It was all politics. I tried to be a good sailor and follow orders, but my mind was constantly in awe of what I was experiencing. My first shocking moment in boot camp was not the petty officer yelling at me with the worst dragon breath you could possibly imagine; I expected that. But what did surprise me was the large number of women in my company that didn't know how to swim. *In the NAVY!* One of the exercises we had to complete was intended to mimic jumping off a flight deck in the event you had to abandon ship, and then you had to tread water for ten minutes to be considered successful. To me, that was a simple exercise, like the one I completed in elementary school of climbing a rope to the top. But I also knew how to swim from a very young age. I had just assumed that in America, every child would be taught how to swim. I had lived in Poland which was oppressed, and I was taught how to swim; why aren't children in America?

Worse yet, no one taught these girls how to swim. They were given instructions on how to tread water, and as they barely made the ten minute mark they were helped out of the water and rescued. My sheer disappointment for these women who were going to serve on ships sailing the oceans is beyond words. The rest of my training followed the same pattern. I thought I would leave boot camp fully ready for any chaotic events that may occur, but instead, I was shown how to "half-ass" just about everything you could imagine. Surprisingly, our company beat our brother company in almost every single competition we had, with the exception of the 1.5 mile run, and push ups. I also left boot camp twenty pounds fatter than what I weighed when I joined. Officers argued that it was muscle I gained. But I assure you the fattening food of green eggs and what they called ham that they fed us to help build our muscle only turned into fat, as we failed to exercise as much as one would imagine the recruits in boot camp should.

My next three years in the service were as much of a disappointment as boot camp. Eventually the fear tactic of threatening any behavior with Article 134, the general article in the Uniform Code of Military Justice (UCMJ), had no affect on me. The general article in the UCMJ basically states that any conduct that discredits the armed forces, but is not listed in any other article, is still punishable. It was a catch-all article that was always thrown at you for any action that a superior didn't like. Little did I know back then that the Constitution supersedes the UCMJ. Regardless of the extra rules, I mostly managed to stay out of trouble. I wondered if I would have fared better if had I joined the Army, or maybe the Marines. But what was done was done. So after three years of ridiculous politics that only resulted in me landing in Captain's Mast (a Navy term for Non-Judicial Punishment [NJP]) for a behavior that I still to this day disagree was wrong, I gave up on the idea of retiring at age thirty-seven and chose not to re-enlist. Overall though, the military was the first place I did finally *mostly* fit in.

Starting my life after the military was easy, as the economy in 1998 was decent and jobs were plentiful. I was used to a small paycheck since the military didn't really pay much, so I wasn't picky about just being an office worker.

I also never forgot the propaganda of those tortured cute bunny pictures from fifth grade, and had made the conscious decision to eat a vegetarian diet, now that I was on my own and finally able to make my own food purchasing decisions. I didn't have a public school, my parents, or the military telling me what to eat. Little did I realize then that I was unconsciously allowing some animal rights activists from my childhood influence my thinking this entire time – without ever having researched for myself the subjects of human nutrition or animal cruelty.

So I lived my "American" life the best I knew how by working a low wage job, renting an apartment, buying a car on credit, and spending any leftover money on fast food and trinkets that I didn't need. I tried to hide my Polish culture as much as possible by distancing myself from anything European and anything that was related to family. I thought I was living a happy American life.

The irony here is that while most of my family members back in Poland were envious of me, I was envious of the typical American who lived on credit and didn't truly own their own home. I was envious of things that the television told me to be envious of, and I certainly voiced my opinion to my parents, who often only laughed at me. They referred to me as a "typical stupid American." If I'd known then what I know now, I would have realized how insulting that was, especially coming from them.

Another life-changing event occurred, not just for me, but for all Americans on September 11, 2001. I went to work like usual, only to learn that the World Trade Center was attacked. My boss had brought in a little TV so we could all be glued to it and watch the events unfold. I had so many questions: Where was the military? Why didn't someone see that the planes were off-course? Why didn't the people in the planes fight back? Box cutters? Really? Even with my limited Navy boot camp training I could take on a person with a box cutter: couldn't hundreds of passengers take on a few terrorists? And the buildings...weren't American buildings built more durably than that? Many of Poland's buildings were completely bombed during WWII and they didn't fall like that. Things just didn't add up for me.

Over the next few days I was as glued to the TV as everyone else. I watched the planes hit the towers over and over. My questions remained unanswered. Later that week, my boss told me about a candlelight vigil that was being held, and I agreed to go with another co-worker. We met in a parking garage after taking separate vehicles, and as we started to walk down the stairs together, my co-worker told me of another possible threat that he heard about on the radio. I felt my stomach drop, and I felt fear for the first time as an American.

In all my experience in America, I had never felt fear before, not like the fear I had experienced living in Poland, which I was almost too young to comprehend at the time. That was the constant fear of attack by the Soviets, an underlying feeling that never went away. There was always a threat. My parents often talked about it. It was a catch-22 situation: if you wanted a better life, you joined the Solidarity union and went on strike, yet you feared that if Solidarity went too far and won too many freedoms, the Soviets would invade, or martial law would be put in place. It was always a fine line that Poles walked, knowing they might never truly be free.

In Communist Poland, this was a way of life, but in free America it was supposed to be different. Fear. I didn't like how it felt as a child, and I especially didn't like how it felt as an adult. It was a fear of understanding my limits as a human being. The fear of being relatively weak and defenseless. The fear of always being on guard. This was not the life that was promised to me in America. I never expected to constantly live in fear of terrorists who hate us so much that they would attack us with violence and kill innocent human beings. And why would they hate us? Because of our freedoms? That didn't make any sense. Living in Poland we were never hateful of the Americans; we were envious, we wanted their way of life. The mindset of a terrorist made little sense to me. Who would attack a country that everyone else wants to escape to otherwise?

That evening after the vigil, I went home and turned on the news to hear more about this possible threat. I stared at the news anchor repeating the words that they had been saying all week, and as the word "terror" came out of her mouth with every sentence, I decided I had enough. I turned off the television — permanently. If I was going to live with the knowledge of possible threats in the back of my mind, I was willing to accept that. But I was not going to let the media exacerbate my fears without accomplishing anything.

In Poland, the fear of a Soviet attack was used against us so much that we lived our lives *ruled* by this fear. Our lives were *controlled* by this threat, by this *fear* so much that we *accepted the oppression* placed upon us, over the *potential* of a Soviet attack. There was never an actual Soviet attack. The *potential* was enough to keep us reserved in our resistance to oppression.

The Soviets were, in reality, our enemy and our conquerors. They wanted to rule us, and they did. They had the manpower and military equipment to start a war we were sure to lose. That fear of constant attack resulted in a great deal of acceptance of oppression by the Poles that I would have never thought would be tolerated by the American people. Yet, with every mention of the word *terror* that I heard on the news, the more compliant Americans seemed willing to be because of that same type of fear. Except, this enemy did not have the ability to inflict the type of harm on the US that the Soviets did to Poland. Their terror strategy was aided and abetted by the media magnifying the small threat that was real into something much larger that was illusory. I was no longer living in Poland, I was in America. But people were succumbing to the same tactics that were used in Poland. I considered succumbing to those types of fear tactics to be *un-American*. Americans were stronger than that, better than that, I thought. Weren't they?

As I stared at the silent black television my mind raced. The longer the TV was turned off, the more my fears began to subside. I was right: the TV was making my fear worse. That's not how I wanted to live

— not in constant fear. That would only let the terrorists win. I was not going to let them win.

I kept the television off and I changed my life. I refused to have conversations with anyone about 9/11 unless they were questioning the issues, or talking about how it could actually be prevented in the future, rather than just being scared of it. I also isolated myself from many of my so-called peers. I had decided that I no longer wanted acceptance if it meant living in fear, and giving in to anything the media told people.

As I continued my isolation from most people, I started to really see what was happening. The further I distanced myself from the situation, the better I could see the picture from the outside perspective: fear was intentionally being promoted by the government and by the media, just like it had been in communist Poland. I knew we were going to go to war. I had signed up for eight years in the military as required, but only served three on active duty. I knew I could be recalled at any time. I still had two years left to go on my obligation.

The longer the television stayed off, the more I really started to question the events of 9/11. I kept thinking back to when my parents told me the story of martial law in Poland, and how all the Poles thought it was from an outside attack. But instead it was our own Polish government that knocked out communications and killed their own people, all to maintain control and stop the Solidarity movement from continuing to strike. Yet, when I asked my parents what they thought of 9/11, they didn't question the mainstream narrative. This surprised me, so I continued to isolate myself even more.

With my television turned off (and kept off), I started to read more books. I spent more time educating myself on different topics of interest, and started to volunteer many of my hours to keep myself busy and away from the TV. Before I knew it, I was being different again. But this time I recognized what made me different. This time, I recognized that I didn't *want* to be like everyone else. I didn't want to live my life in fear. *I didn't want to live my life the way that television told me to live it.*

I made my own *conscious* choices for the first time, instead of what others or TV told me to choose; except for that whole vegetarian thing. It's amazing how much an event in the fifth grade will lock your mind into certain beliefs.

The more I isolated myself from the world, the more questions I had about what was going on in the world around me, and the more doubts I had about the choices that Americans were making. All these excessive and oppressive new laws came into place after 9/11 like The Patriot Act, which gave power to law enforcement to conduct searches without a warrant, to monitor banking activities of everyday Americans without justification, and wiretapping. Worst of all, law enforcement began to detain and deport those who were suspected of terrorists connection, *but in secret*,[1] just like they disappeared my father in Poland. Our very liberties were being taken away one by one. Our liberties had been compromised in the name of security. It made me think of this famous quote attributed to Benjamin Franklin: "Those who would give up Essential Liberty, to purchase a little Temporary safety, deserve neither and will lose both."

The Patriot Act wasn't all: more and more laws were put into place against the American people. The Department of Homeland Security Act of 2002 allowed for foreigners charged with terrorism to be classified as enemy combatants and tried by military tribunals.[2-3] In 2004, the US Supreme Court ruled that even US citizens could be held as "enemy combatants" with certain stipulations.[4]

All Americans are now familiar with the Guantanamo Bay detention camp. Prisoner abuse became common. The war in Iraq played out, which never did unveil weapons of mass destruction as claimed by former President George W. Bush. There were so many changes for America that I can't even list them all, and it hasn't stopped. The FISA Amendments Act of 2008 allows electronic surveillance of Americans by foreign intelligence. The Intelligence Reform and

Terrorism Prevention Act of 2004 allows DHS into airport security measures, and now the TSA uses scanners to invade people's privacy. Ethnic profiling is now allowed as per the FBI Domestic Investigations and Operations Guide of 2008.[5] And, ultimately, the National Defense Authorization Act (NDAA) of 2012, which codifies that it is legally permissible for the Federal Government to disappear American citizens with indefinite detention and without due process. Some have argued this is not the case because that would violate the US Constitution, but if you actually read the text it certainly seems that is the intent.[6-7]

Although I turned off the television and did not permit the language of fear to be pounded into my ears, I did pay more attention to what the American government was doing. As I watched these laws being put into place, I wondered in awe how the American public did not see what I saw.

During this time, another life-changing event occurred for me as I was flipping through the newspaper looking for volunteer opportunities. I had randomly noticed an ad in the local paper for volunteers for a "crisis call center." I really wasn't sure what they needed, but thought I would at least call and ask some questions.

The next thing I knew, I was answering calls from folks who were at the end of their rope in life. It was a very eye-opening experience for me. Here I was, in the greatest country on earth, and yet there was a huge need for volunteers to talk to people who called us as a last resort before attempting to end their lives. Why would someone want to end their own life? I volunteered as much as I could, as I value life very much, and the thought of suicide saddens me. For the record I would *never* commit such an act myself under any circumstance. I also decided to take the next step and volunteer as a sexual assault advocate, which is basically a person who meets a sexual assault victim at the hospital and guides them through the next steps of what to do, and holds their hand through their exam. This was a huge undertaking, as the training involved was very intense and emotional from a variety of perspectives; but of relevance here, it also forced me to go on a police ride-along.

The police ride-along was difficult for me. All my life, I had hated police because of my experiences in Poland. To me, police were always corrupt, and they had only one interest: themselves. I had been taught from experience and from my parents that you never talk to police, only to a lawyer. Yet there I was, required to spend the next eight hours riding around with what I thought was one of my worst enemies.

Sometimes things happen for a reason, and I think this was one of those events that I was meant to experience. There I was riding around as a passenger in a cop car, with two officers I was sure were corrupt, when we responded to a 911 hang-up call. What happened next changed my entire view of what a police force *can* be.

Three police cars in total responded to the 911 hang-up. The officers I rode with knocked on the door. Here I thought they were going to harass some innocent people, but instead, something different happened. When a lady answered, the officers were very professional and very nice to her. They explained that there was a 911 hang-up call from that residence, and they would like to make sure that everyone was safe.

The husband showed up at the door during this time with his toddler daughter, and immediately apologized. He said the toddler must have been playing with the phone again. But instead of walking away and leaving the family to be, the officers asked if they could speak to the wife and husband individually. They agreed, and I tagged along with the first officer and the wife. I was astounded by the questions the officers asked after we were out of the husband's earshot. The officer was actually concerned for her safety; he was asking her if she was truly safe, and if she was not to please tell him. He reassured her that there are ways to help her and her daughter if she was in danger. Meanwhile, I sneaked over to where the husband was being interviewed, expecting to hear prejudiced and harassing words from the officer. I was shocked even more by the questions there. The husband was not being accused, but rather, being asked the very same questions concerning his safety, in case she was the one abusing him!

Fortunately in this case, it really was just a toddler playing with the phone. But my view of the police changed completely. I no longer felt hatred for the uniform, but I was still confused because this was the first time I had ever experienced something positive from police. I had read about cases of police abusing their positions in the US, particularly since the Federal Government has been gaining more influence over local police departments by providing military equipment and funding.[8-9]

The trend of the militarization of state and local police was just getting underway at the time, and has gotten much worse since then. Despite that, it still reminded me too much of militarized police in Poland. Using such incentives and "gifts" of equipment and funding to influence local police also reminded me of the similar way the Federal Government has used funding to try to take over local school systems. All of that made me very skeptical of the idea that there are good officers out there.

I inquired about this behavior and line of questioning when I returned to the crisis call center, only to be informed that the reason that the officers are so professional and concerned about the welfare of these women *and* men was because the crisis call center had been working with the police department for several years on proper *training* of these officers. I was disappointed to learn that this wasn't standard practice in every county, but delighted to learn that a group of volunteers can make a difference.

Even more inspiring was the realization that ordinary people took the initiative to get involved with the county police and work together on issues affecting residents of that county, and cross-trained each other on how to properly handle various situations. This resulted in a police force that was truly on the level of the people, to protect them, and not above them, to oppress them.

So my attitude towards police changed. What I saw that night is what local police or Sherriff's forces *could* be with the help of community involvement. But I wondered why more communities didn't try to solve their problems with police abuses by having community members more involved in police training, or at least involved in police oversight. Regardless, I continued to volunteer for the crisis center. I also joined a gym; without television, I found I had a lot more time to do things for myself.

By 2006, I found myself in better shape than when I was in the military. I had more friends than I ever had in my life, and I met my husband just the year before. I still had a house filled with junk I didn't need, and I still thought I was eating healthy, but I was definitely different from most, and I embraced my different self.

Somehow in all my hours of volunteer work, and self discovery of who I was, I found self confidence. That was what made me different from earlier in my life. When I was younger I lacked confidence because I was a foreigner, and therefore I was afraid to be different. An amazing thing happens when you exude positive confidence about yourself: people like you and everyone wants to be your friend. I had gone from wanting to be like everyone else, to most everyone else wanting to be like me.

Once we were married, my husband and I decided to start a new journey in our lives by expanding our education and getting university degrees. So we started on our long and tiresome journey of continuing to work while going to school full time.

We had to make changes, as we were not able to maintain our lifestyle while paying for school and working our dead-end jobs. I was thrilled when my husband was supportive of cutting back on our purchases. Actually, he might have been more thrilled to see *me* want to cut back. It was during this time that my husband helped me fill in the blanks about a lot of the questions I had.

My husband introduced me to many alternative media news websites that offered news that wasn't designed to constantly scare or persuade you into giving up all of your Constitutional rights, or what he called "Natural Rights." At first, I thought some of them were a little over-the-top, but my husband asked me to give them a fair chance, so I did. The more I read, the more my questions were answered. All those holes in various topics started to get filled in and made more sense, whether they were related to politics, economics, or health.

One of my favorite college professors taught me (and the class) the most important question to ask in reference to any assertion being made: "Show me the data." As I learned how to better evaluate data in my science courses, I started applying that critical thinking, skepticism, and analysis to everything I read. Show me the data. I also learned in my biology courses how to look at raw data and evaluate it for myself, not to just take someone else's word for it, so I started doing so. I started asking others to show me the data; then I took that data and made my own evaluations and conclusions based on what the raw data said. I kept doing this over and over and over.

In addition to that, my husband taught me to start asking — of everything — the very important question of "Cui bono?" or "Who benefits?" Sometimes people also refer to this as "Follow the money."

Before I even finished college, I had come to the conclusion that the American people were being lied to about the events that occurred on 9/11. Now I just had to figure why. Why would our own government leaders lie about something so atrocious that happened to our own beautiful free country? Again, things didn't make sense.

But a bigger challenge came before me. Now I was *really* no longer like everyone else. Not only had I been weird because I didn't watch TV, ate healthy, and exercised, but now people thought I was a "conspiracy theorist" too. It seemed that just by simply asking critical, skeptical questions about things that didn't add up got you immediately branded as a kook, or a conspiracy theorist, or worse yet: being accused of being anti-America. This once again reminded me of living in Poland where anyone who dared to question the actions of the government was branded "anti-socialist" and an "enemy of the Polish state." These are all *ad hominem* attacks designed to silence dissent without actually addressing the topic(s) in question.

The difficulty of living a life where you feel like you have to keep your thoughts and beliefs to yourself for fear of being branded a so-called "conspiracy theorist" can only be understood by those who have lived through it. I had a huge dilemma before me. I felt I knew some information that needed to be shared with every American, but these Americans would not hear it. Why?

Had I become the same type of person that my grandparents met in Poland, who warned about the false promises made by the new Soviet-backed regime coming to power in Poland? The same regime who promised equality to all through socialism? And the Polish people chose to ignore those people providing that warning because they were just "kooks" and because they saw no other way to rebuild their country other than to accept the "offer" from the new regime? Yet, despite being suspicious, the Polish people believed the voting results that claimed that 90% of the population supported the new Soviet backed regime? I guess the Poles had never heard the quote from Stalin: "The people who *cast* the votes decide nothing. The people who *count* the votes decide everything." But now, decades later, *I* was the "kook" warning the masses about the government using deceptive tactics to trick the people into giving up their rights and freedoms? When I later watched the documentary *Hacking Democracy*, I wondered to myself if Americans would react to Bev Harris, the creator of the documentary, the same way the Poles reacted to those who tried to warn them that the Soviets rigged their voting.

There had to be a way to tell people and get them to open their minds; there had to be. I became politically active and tried to talk to people to bring attention to issues that I thought were vital, but to no avail. People didn't want to listen. Each president signed more and more executive orders, and each Congress passed more oppressive laws, all in name of our supposed "security." Most people unquestioningly and uncritically accepted these laws and believed they somehow magically made them safer.

I finally understood the famous quote "You can lead a horse to water, but you can't make him drink." As I continued to try to educate anyone that would seem open-minded enough to listen, I also continued to seek my own answers.

Before I knew it, I found myself looking back at my Polish roots. I noticed so many eerie similarities between Poland then and America now. I dove deeper into my research of Polish history, along with the history of other civilizations.

Almost everyone knows about the many Jews and those helping the Jews who were exterminated in concentration camps, and almost everyone is familiar with the atrocities that occurred. But few people have asked the question of why Hitler's troops went along with his heinous orders. Why did people willingly kill other innocent people en masse?

That question was partly answered when I discovered the psychological research known as the *Milgram experiments* conducted by Stanley Milgram of Yale University. I won't go into a long explanation of his experiments here, but I encourage people to learn about his research independently. The take away lesson from his research is that humans have an innate tendency to be blindly obedient to those they view as authority.[10]

The other piece of the puzzle about why Germans where willing to go along with Hitler's plans fell into place when I read about an important piece of history. It's something that I somehow already knew in the back of my mind, but which I never gave much thought before I started doing my historical research.

In February of 1933, the Reichstag building in Berlin Germany burned down. At the time, this was the building in which their parliament met. The person responsible was caught and executed, and this event was used as proof that the communists were plotting against Germany. Hitler, who was Chancellor of Germany for only a few weeks at the time, had requested an emergency decree to suspend civil liberties. This allowed for the mass arrests of communist leaders, which then led to the consolidation of power of the Germans. As it turned out, the Reichstag fire was actually started by the Nazis themselves. Such an event is considered a "false flag" event, meaning that the leaders made an attack on themselves in order to have an event to blame "the enemy" and have reason to go after that enemy, while receiving the support of the people. This is how Hitler came to power.[11] The reason they did this is obvious: to frighten the public into giving them power and into going along with their plans.

The origin of the term "false flag" comes from the history of early naval warfare where a ship flies a flag other than their own true flag before engaging their enemy. The trick is intended to deceive the enemy about the true nature and origin of the attack.[12]

Such false flag events have been very common throughout history. The Russo-Swedish War, the Second Sino-Japanese War, the Gleiwitz Incident, the Winter War, Kassa Attack, Operation Northwoods, the Reichstag Fire, Project TP AJAX, and the 2008 Kurcha Incident are some examples. These are just the ones listed in Wikipedia,[13] but there have been others throughout history. These false flag events serve two purposes. They provide a justification for going to war, and they convince the public to go along with it, for the "security" of the people, of course.

On a smaller scale, a false flag event almost occurred in Poland in March of 1981. When Jaruzelski took over the reins, he accommodated the demands of the Solidarity movement in exchange for ninety days of peacetime with no strikes. The Solidarity leaders agreed, but some strikes continued for various (good) reasons, including a four-hour strike, which was the largest in history. That four-hour strike was a precursor to a longer strike that led to an attack by the secret police on farmers and Solidarity members while they were meeting. This became known as the Bydgoszcz Incident.[14] Many were severely injured and some were hospitalized. The consensus by many was that Solidarity was being intentionally provoked by the secret police with the goal that Solidarity would turn violent, so that Jaruzelski could justify initiating martial law. Further investigation into the matter revealed this to be the case.[15] Fortunately for the Poles, they immediately recognized the Bydgoszcz incident as an intentional provocation, and didn't fall for this tactic and trap.

With that said, in hindsight, would it be so hard to imagine that 9/11 was perhaps also allowed to occur as another false flag event? After all, there were reports of a possible terrorist attack circulating in US intelligence months in advance of the attack.[16-17] Then, what occurred right after 9/11? Our freedoms were stripped away one by one, and the US went to war in the Middle East. Even after Osama Bin Laden was killed, the US remained at war. But with whom? For what? Now there are new alleged threats to scare Americans into compliance. There never seems to be an end to the alleged external threats. So why are the American people still going along with of all of this?

Perhaps it is all just coincidence. Perhaps it is also a coincidence that Military Industrial Complex (MIC) corporations (AKA defense contractors) that Dwight Eisenhower warned about make billions of dollars from supplying weapons for perpetual war.[18-19]

"Conspiracy theories" aside, I do not have all the answers to many of my own questions, but I do have a different perspective, one that doesn't align with the traditional mainstream media, or the traditional false divide of "left/right" politics. It is a perspective that questions the actions of our own Federal Government, regardless of the political affiliation of the politicians in office. From a longer-term perspective, it is interesting to note that while the political affiliation of the politicians in power may change, the march toward fewer individual liberties and more government restrictions seems to be the one constant trend in play.

What my family thought it meant to be an American (holding on to superficial traditions, pretending to go to church, buying as much consumer junk as we could acquire, and eating junk food,) is not at all what it is about. What it really means to be an American has nothing to do with all the distractions. It *IS* about the principles and values that once made America great, but are no longer present in America, or at best minimally so.

An American is someone who has read, understands, and lives by, the views in the Constitution, Bill of Rights, and the Declaration of Independence. Such an American would ideally also have had some exposure to other documents such as the philosophical works that inspired those documents. An American recognizes the propaganda when controlled media such as *Time* magazine puts on the front cover a suggestion that the Constitution is outdated, and refers to such advocates of it as a cult.[20]

I was appalled at that Time article titled *One Document, Under Siege,* as it blatantly changed wording (lied) to make the Constitution sound like something it was not. In addition, the article failed to mention both the reality of what it took to create such a system of government, as well as the rationales for why it was designed that way. The system of checks and balances was designed to prevent tyranny. It succeeded in this for quite some time, but perhaps no longer.

As a brief background: During the development of the

Constitution there was an impassioned debate among those who wanted to create a strong central government to bind together the States (known today as the Federalists), and those who preferred a weak central government, fearing that if they created too strong of a central government that it would ultimately end up becoming tyrannical itself (today this group is known as the Antifederalists). It is true that certain compromises were made between the Federalists and the Antifederalists, yet I think American history demonstrates that the Anti-Federalists were correct in their concerns. But the mere fact that the two groups were able to come together to a consensus enough so that they all signed their name to the Constitution shows the importance of the ideals intended in the document.

The fact that power-hungry megalomaniacs have found ways to circumvent all of the restrictions and checks and balances placed upon them by the Constitution doesn't mean that our current government has done so lawfully, nor does it imply that the Constitution itself is an outdated document. This merely tells us that the American people have not been adequately vigilant in maintaining our free Republic.

Freedom, liberty, the right to be a human free of shackles, and basically live a life free from being told how to live, are ideals that *never* become outdated. These ideas can never expire, not even with all the wonderful technology in the world that makes life more interesting, and more importantly, easier. Just because the Founding Fathers never heard of Facebook doesn't mean that they lacked an understanding of human nature or the philosophy of freedom. In fact, the evidence suggests that they had a better understanding of these topics than most people do today. Clearly the propaganda machine exists here in the US. To what end I do not know, other than there are those who do not believe in Natural Rights and liberties, and have every intention of oppressing them away.

"The price of liberty is eternal vigilance." –Thomas Jefferson

I think that while the US has been the land of the free, it is not so indefinitely. As Thomas Jefferson stated, *the people must always work to keep it so*. To do so, the people must always be aware of what is happening in their government. This is very difficult today as the Federal Government in particular, but also state governments, are greatly lacking in *transparency* in what they are doing and what their true values, interests, and intents are. That just means that the American people need to pay that much more attention. They need to assess if their government(s) has (have) been bought off by those who have ill intentions or just plain selfish, corrupt reasons. The American people must never give in to fear and give up their liberties and rights. They need to constantly be alert (vigilant) to what is happening all around them. If they do not, one day they might find themselves in a similar situation to what my grandparents found themselves in, where they handed over control to a government that lied to them and then relentlessly oppressed them. The next thing they knew, they were under the constant watchful eye of that government, with no freedoms in sight.

A true American does not sit idly by to let history repeat itself, and allow his or her country to become divided and inevitably fall. No, not on my watch.

Lesson 6: No one is exempt from those who try to oppress others. It can happen anywhere, and yes, even here in America.

"In a time of universal deceit, telling the truth is a revolutionary act."

-George Orwell

CHAPTER 7: RESEARCHING MY ROOTS, AND THE ROOTS OF MY FEARS

"The ideal tyranny is that which is ignorantly self-administered by its victims. The most perfect slaves are, therefore, those which blissfully and unawaredly enslave themselves."

-Dresden James

One of my biggest fears is of the dentist. It is not a fear like I felt shortly after 9/11, which was more of a fear for my life — for my very existence. No, the fear of the dentist is more of a fear of pain.

Growing up in Poland, I had only frightening experiences at the dentist, and many of them. In the early part of the 1980s, my next-door neighbor happened to be a receptionist for a dentist's office, and was also very good friends with my mother. Often my mother would be found at the dental office, chatting with this friend while waiting for her shift to end so they could go stand in long lines together. On days that I would arrive home from school and my mother and brother were not yet at home, I knew I needed to go to the dental office to find my mom.

On more than one occasion, I walked into the building where the dentist was and saw a long line of people waiting for their turn.

Many of them were holding the sides of their cheeks, clearly in pain. These people didn't bother me. It was the regular screaming that I heard from behind the walls that bothered me.

Novocain was almost unheard of for the lowly commoner in communist Poland. Only corrupt police, politicians, and people in power would have access to such spoils. With toothbrushes scarce, toothpaste even harder to find, and mouthwash and floss unheard of, tooth decay was rampant. Usually the only method of addressing the problem was removal of teeth.

I would walk toward the receptionist's desk, hearing people scream in agonizing pain, as their teeth would be pulled out without any form of anesthetic or analgesic. I did smell ethanol or alcohol on more than one occasion. But looking back, I don't blame them. If a person does not have the option to use any painkiller whatsoever while getting a tooth pulled out of his or her mouth, it is understandable that person might resort to using alcohol.

This memory is so ingrained in me that now when I step foot in the dentist's office and hear the buzzing of cleaning tools, I panic almost immediately. Although I never myself sat in a chair and had a tooth pulled in such a manner, the memory of hearing the screams of pain is enough to keep me from agreeing to too many dental procedures, and is a great motivator to floss every night.

Fortunately I'm not alone in my fears, and many solutions exist to the problem, including laughing gas (nitrous oxide), and various medications. While I understand completely the problem, I still require a good amount of self-convincing that it will not hurt — that I will not have to scream in pain.

Just as the animal rights activist left enough of an impression on me in the fifth grade for me to spend a good portion of my life looking for products that are cruelty free and/or vegetarian, so had the dentist experience affected me at such a young age. As an adult, I struggle to sit in a dentist's chair. Similarly, my experiences living under a communist government have taught me that governments can not be trusted, and anyone who suggests you should trade your rights and liberties for security and handouts should most definitely not be trusted.

My understanding of the world is one I would never give up, and I believe it's due to my experiences as a child living in a communist country, and then moving to a free country. I experienced firsthand the transition from controlled markets to free markets, from empty store shelves to overstocked shelves, from fear of saying the wrong words out loud to the freedom to be able to say anything. I have also experienced the slow and steady gradual transition taking me back to my communist roots. This circle of experience gives me a different perspective on things that I would not have understood otherwise.

Although I am no longer a vegetarian after doing my own research into nutrition, and I'm capable of mentally reassuring myself that all will be fine in the dentist's chair, I am still affected by these memories from my youth.

No one is exempt from being impressionable, especially at a young age. This is why advertising is a billion dollar industry. It makes me question our current American culture (which I have experienced) of allowing children to be raised by television, considering it is a major way children today often become desensitized to violence. It also makes me question allowing children to be raised by the state via our public school system (which I also experienced). While I never personally experienced that Polish method of tooth-pulling, I am affected as if I had. So if a child learns something is appropriate via television, such as that proactive violence is acceptable, would they not be either influenced or affected to a certain degree? Just as I never experienced treating animals in a cruel manner, I was still affected by a fifteen-minute presentation by a stranger that I had never met before, nor ever saw again.

I am certainly not suggesting that any television, marketing, or free speech be banned or limited. However, children's minds have not yet fully developed judgment, critical thinking, and moral assessment skills, or the ability to fully differentiate fiction from reality. What I am suggesting here is that it is the responsibility of parents to pay attention to and make decisions about what their children are exposed to, and not depend on MPAA ratings (unless they were involved in determining these ratings).

Of course, adults can also be manipulated and brainwashed as well if they do not have well-developed critical thinking and moral reasoning skills. But in theory, adults are capable of such skills and are therefore responsible for making decisions for themselves *and* their children. Children, however, are much more easily influenced and manipulated, and therefore greater care must be taken with what we expose them to. If a child is raised and taught well, he or she will develop into an adult that is well-reasoned and capable of making conscious decisions based on free will, rather than social or cultural programming, and will be able to withstand the onslaught of brainwashing in our society. If we are not careful as parents, that process is short circuited, and children can grow up into automatons programmed by whatever government or corporate entity can get inside their heads. And that is usually not in anyone's best interest. A free society requires free-thinking individuals capable of critical assessment and conscious decision-making. If that is the type of society we want, then we need to raise our children to exhibit those traits.

In Poland, children were taught in school and socialized by the media with the intent that they had to be subservient to the state and become obedient workers serving the collective. There was little mention of the unique abilities or desires of the individual. Certain stereotypes were reinforced to corral young minds into certain kinds of work (I can't even use the term "career") paths. And as people grew up, they "learned" that they were relatively "helpless" in directing their own lives and to accept their fate of being a cog in the big machine. I see similar trends — or at least certain stereotypes — being perpetuated in the US media today.

Let's use Disney as an example of how media influence can function as a type of brainwashing. Disney is a much-loved brand name of children's movies and also provides a network station. But if you look at their classic stories, you will see a pattern. There is always a beautiful damsel in distress who is rescued by a gorgeous prince. The ugly ogre is the evil villain, and the ugly woman is the evil witch. We (and I include myself in this, as I grew up with these characters) learn that the ugly man is evil; the ugly woman is evil. The gorgeous man is a prince, and the gorgeous woman will always be in need of rescue. So we learn to judge people based on how they look. Boys grow up learning that fighting is the answer and the good guy always wins, and girls grow up believing that a prince is always en route to rescue them.

Girls grow up wanting to wear makeup and color their hair as they try to look like a princess, while boys grow up believing they have to act macho and be tough, and kick the butts of anyone who stands in their way. We grow up with certain (often unrealistic) stereotypes and judgments of people. If a person has a mole on their nose or are born with a deformity, they must be evil; therefore we are distrustful of them. We also assume that if people are beautiful, they are naturally good.

Of course, this is a terrible way to learn to judge people. Although there has been improvement in television, the majority of our cartoons and movies still show a male to be the hero and a damsel in distress that is rescued. But this isn't the only issue with what our children watch. Our current television shows and movies rarely show the level of corruption that can occur in government, and if there is any, there's always a good guy who comes along to save the day. The unrealistic lives of characters on television can make it very confusing for someone without a fully developed brain to decipher real from artificial. This leaves people with unrealistic impressions of life.

Just as my dental office experience taught me to fear the

dentist, my experience with corrupt cops in Poland (while under Soviet rule) taught me to distrust the police uniform — until I learned otherwise. As mentioned earlier, my personal experience with working with civil servants who get to wear a badge and a gun has changed my perspective: now I know that not all police are bad. This is not to say, however, that all police officers are good either. My point is that impressions can change under the right circumstances.

There are countless stories in the news of police doing wrong by the people. There will likely continue to be countless more stories of police doing wrong by the people, particularly if the US continues trending in the current direction. But I learned not to judge all police as the same anymore. Even those cops who have done wrong to the people may not have been intending to do so. What it comes down to is what type of training have they received, what their beliefs about the Constitution are, the laws, the people, and where their personal breaking point is. These concepts apply to everyone, not just police officers, but also judges, lawyers, politicians, and teachers, etc.

As I learned at the crisis center, a small group of volunteers can make a big difference. Just as the volunteers at the crisis center created training materials and a presentation and received permission to present them to the local police (which made a difference in how the police treated a potential domestic violence dispute), so can a small group of volunteers get together and put together a presentation on what it means to take an oath to the Constitution. Organizations with this type of goal are already appearing, such as the Oath Keepers. It is time we supported their efforts however we can, including providing training about the Constitution to those who have already sworn an oath to it.

There are also many organizations that claim to represent we the people, but do not. They claim to support the working or middle class, but then stab them in the back and live their own lives as kings and queens via the wealth they have stolen from ordinary people. Politicians typically say whatever they feel like saying to claim their support of the "common man", but then vote for the passage of laws that benefit themselves at the expense of almost everyone else. Statements like, "We have to pass the bill so that you can find out what is in it,"[1-2] epitomize the problem.

This is no different than what occurred in Poland when all the unions claimed to represent the workers, but none of them actually did. In reality they were part of the nomenklatura and received benefits as such. Their job was to pretend to represent the people, to pretend to give them a voice, and to give them a useless outlet for their grievances. That's when the creation of independent unions became essential, and thus Solidarity was born.

One of the many attributes that made the Solidarity movement successful back in 1980s Poland was the many organizations that formed to help those that needed help. KOR is one I mentioned previously that helped families of political prisoners and published their own independent news. But there were many others that sprung up from ordinary groups of people that recognized a need for such organizations, especially after martial law was declared and there were many political prisoners, unemployed activists, and Solidarity leaders in need of assistance. Although they had to function underground after marital law, these organizations helped Solidarity grow. These organizations, along with Solidarity, also helped the Poles see that they were not alone.

Solidarity had many successes before martial law disrupted their efforts. One of these successes was when large organized strikes forced the Polish government to grant Solidarity legal recognition as a valid trade union. Thus the Poles gained some power and were not only able to succeed in their workplaces and prevent most workplace injuries, but most importantly they began to feel empowered in their struggle. This empowerment allowed them to shed their apathy, which was a result of their "learned" powerlessness.[3] Solidarity activist Aleksander Krystosiak told Jack Bloom in an interview regarding Solidarity's success: "With lightning speed, the society rebuilt itself morally."[4] This is an important lesson, but not in the sense of the specific political and economic details. What was important was the empowerment of the people. Much like a cocooned caterpillar turning into a butterfly, this sense of empowerment transformed people because they felt they could accomplish something and make a difference, including eliminating much of the corruption at the time.

However, with power comes responsibility. In creating an organization to help the people, Solidarity also took on significant responsibility, intentionally or otherwise. People had to get along and put petty differences aside. This is yet another important lesson from Solidarity: any social movement that hopes to effect great change must work to focus on core common ground issues between its constituents and be vigilant to not become divided against one another over less significant or trivial matters. "Divide and conquer" is a tried and proven strategy by elitists to distract and defeat people, and has been used quite effectively in the US with so-called "wedge issues." A wedge issue is basically using a controversial issue to create an intentional split among people and groups in an effort to weaken said groups.[5]

In Poland, the greatest threat to the communist government was the fact that they could no longer divide society.[6] Soviet power diminished when ordinary Poles no longer felt they had to continue to accept conditions that they initially felt were inescapable.[7] The workers took power into their own hands and changed their working conditions to better their lives, so much so that during the year that Solidarity had legal status and the workers had a voice, not a single miner was recorded to be fatally injured or killed.[8] In contrast, when people felt impoverished by the nomenklatura, they became divided against each other and treated each other with short tempers over the smallest of issues.[9]

Herein lies an apparent paradox: in order to achieve greater freedom for all individuals, people had to work together cooperatively in significant numbers. While each of these individuals may have had differing values in certain respects, they all held the shared value and shared vision of freedom or liberty for individuals. In reality, this apparent paradox is not a paradox at all. In reality, freedom allows individuals with differing values to co-exist peacefully and productively, rather than individuals or factional groups trying to use the force of the state to compel those with different values to comply with a particular doctrine. This is the "live and let live" attitude that the US was founded upon, but was lost somewhere along the way.

I have seen many groups form that held the same Constitutional or liberty-minded beliefs by all members, and yet split up when minor differences became apparent. I've heard the analogy used that getting liberty minded people to work together is like herding cats. But when one looks at society as a whole, while a tyrannical government is bearing down, people must set aside the smaller issues (even if they seem big). Again, this is the apparent paradox of the liberty movement: in order to defeat tyranny, people need group cohesiveness among individuals that value individuality, liberty, and independence. You cannot let minor differences divide you, and you must accept this "paradox" of group cohesiveness based on liberty and independence. This is not to say that all advocates of liberty have to believe all the same things, be carbon copies of each another, or suffer from groupthink. Quite the opposite applies, in fact: an acceptance of just a few common basic values allows for a great variety of difference in the details of opinions and perspectives of how a person should live. Some suggestions for these basic common values could include: Don't commit aggression against others or their property (non-aggression principle), do what you say you are going to do (contract law), and leave others alone to live their lives how they want as long as they are not harming anyone else (liberty).

To succeed in promoting liberty as cohesive groups may also involve putting one's own personal struggles aside temporarily. For example, the many underground newspaper writers in Poland chose not to fight for identity and/or position; rather, they humbly did their job of spreading truth as they had no time to worry about status or position.[10]

The lesson here is that a certain degree of group cohesiveness is needed among individuals in a society, something that brings people together and does not allow minor differences to divide them (or us). Historically in the US, this was freedom and the Constitution. In Poland it was freedom from communism, better working conditions, Polish language and culture, and to a certain degree, Catholicism.

Tyrannical leaders use "divide and conquer" strategies all too well, and I see them working in America to a degree I never thought imaginable — including using race as a means to divide people. The mainstream media fuels the problem by planting ideas into people's minds. An example of this is that perhaps a white cop shot an innocent unarmed black teenager for no good reason other than that the kid was black. The truths of the stories are often intentionally butchered and those that ask to "see the data" and get "just the facts" are up against media distortions and the people who believe them. Thus, a divide among the people begins, or is aggravated and exaggerated.

This was a well-used tactic by the Soviets in Poland. Shortly after Solidarity gained legal status, the propaganda came on strong. The government-controlled mainstream news blamed Solidarity for everything disadvantageous that occurred, including the food shortages. When the only perspective people were exposed to on television was that Solidarity was responsible, after seeing it enough times, people began to believe it.[11] Government politicians and bureaucrats will always make the bad guy be someone else — never the government itself — and will use their propaganda machine to back up their claims.

Putting together an organization is not easy, and reaching out to the community to help educate is a huge undertaking. But I have personally seen the results of such training, which resulted in police officers treating the victims in the correct manner, without prejudice or preconceived notions. I witnessed nothing but utmost respect for both husband and wife in a situation where one of them may have been abusive. Unfortunately, not every county offers such training, and not every police officer has had the opportunity to be properly educated on every topic. But that just provides the opportunity for people to come together, organize, and offer such training. If such training does not exist, then this provides a community the opportunity to develop such material.

The training that our police forces are now receiving is largely unknown to most of us. We have no idea if they are taught the Constitution, or if they are being taught to shoot at targets of pregnant woman and children due to civil disturbance training.[12] Just as no one informed me that the Constitution supersedes the UCMJ when I was active duty military, perhaps such important information is being left out in the training of other civil servants.

In Poland, the opinion of hating police has largely changed because the country is no longer under communist rule. The police and military are the ones that are trusted with protecting the Poles from violence, not the people themselves. In Poland today, gun laws are still extremely restrictive, unlike in America.

There are two different mindsets between Americans and Poles when it comes to owning weapons. As an American, our Constitution enumerates the right to bear arms so that we can protect ourselves against all enemies, foreign and domestic. However, that right is not mentioned in the Polish constitution, even though the Natural Right to defend oneself against aggressors is universal. But since the Poles are a peaceful people that would generally not be aggressive, the need for personal self defense is small, and the police and military are there to protect the people from the few violent criminals or foreign invasions. Even today the belief is ingrained in every Pole as they are growing up that the Polish military would never kill another Pole. While that is a noble ideal and belief, unfortunately the historical facts do not prove this to be true.

Recognizing this difference in mindset between Americans and Poles is important, because it stirs up many emotional thoughts when debating the need for legalization of guns in Poland. It is important to recognize that it was this very belief, that the Polish military would never strike against Poles ("a Pole doesn't kill a Pole") that allowed martial law in Poland to be implemented with such success. It took very little for the leaders of the military to confuse the infantry and have them at least start shooting at Poles.[13] However, it is also important to point out that when the Polish military figured out it was Poles they were shooting at, they began to refuse orders to shoot, and many units disbanded.[14]

This was a unique situation in Poland during Soviet rule, but it still provides a valuable lesson. Just because someone is shooting at you doesn't mean they know truthfully *why* they were given that order. But since military members are trained to react to orders while sleep deprived, hungry, and cold, the thought to question orders goes against their very military training. This is why it is important to get involved in what your own government is training police forces and the military to do. Other than the National Guard, it is currently extremely difficult to have an influence on how the military is trained. This may be something to try to change, or at a minimum, at least make certain that soldiers take their oath to the Constitution seriously, along with having read the Constitution with an understanding of what that oath means. Another minimum that should be required in military training, as the history of Solidarity demonstrates, is soldiers should be trained to not attack or fire upon citizens/civilians of their own country, except in the most extraordinary of circumstances, such as self defense.

I am not suggesting that people should stand down and allow a rogue military or rogue unit shoot them without trying to escape or fight back. What I am pointing out is that members of such a rogue military may or may not be aware of the true nature of the circumstances or why a particular order was given. By the nature of their training, soldiers are taught only to obey orders, not to question them or think about them. This is why approaches like what the Oath Keepers advocate are so important: to remind military personnel and police that they took an oath to the US Constitution, and that they have not only the right but the *duty* to disobey unconstitutional orders. The Oath Keepers' "Declaration of Orders We will NOT Obey"[15-16] is a good starting point for additions to military and police training programs.

The public has to get involved in what civil servants are trained, whether it regards those that wear a badge or hold a gavel, or even just upholding EPA regulations. The public needs to take control of what their government is demanding of their civil servants. Otherwise, we may end up with civil "servants" performing in ways that are contrary to the American public. Police abuse is only one example. EPA destruction of property rights is another. Just as Poland experienced oppression by required permits for everything one did, it has become the same in America. I just about choked on a sip of water when a Forest Service employee told me that I needed a permit to move rocks from my friend's house to my own. This did not even involve Forest Service land! ROCKS! Yes, in America, you need a permit to move rocks. Bet you didn't know you broke that law, huh?

For me, this question arose: How is it that Americans have permitted such government excesses to proliferate? I found one answer in the concept of normalcy bias. As stated in Chapter 2, normalcy bias is a type of mental state a person falls into during a disaster, which causes them to underestimate the possibility of said disaster and the effects. This can result in the failure to prepare for such a disaster and the inability to cope once the disaster occurs. Those with normalcy bias struggle with how to react to something they haven't seen before, and look for optimistic ways to interpret warnings, even if the optimism is unrealistic.[17]

Normalcy bias is very common, and even occurred in Poland despite the populace being quite alert to the problems. In Poland, martial law was always a threat, along with Soviet invasion. As martial law crept up on the Polish people, there were many that tried to warn not only the general public but also the Solidarity leaders that it was increasingly likely. Yet, they were disregarded as radicals.[18] When martial law finally took place, many people refused to believe that it actually happened.[19] The very same is occurring in the US today. It's almost as if history is repeating itself and the American people think that America is larger than life: it is too big too fail. The passengers on the Titanic were also convinced it was unsinkable. So Americans trust their government to manage their safety and their economy, and in return, they give up their personal liberties.

John Barnhill wrote (though this quote is often attributed to Thomas Jefferson), *"When government fears the people, there is liberty. When the people fear the government, there is tyranny."*

People shouldn't fear the government, including agencies such as the IRS, the EPA, or the FDA. Instead, those in government should fear the wrath of the people. Yet, I have many peers who fear the government — especially the IRS. It is like when I lived in Poland and we would always whisper, *"Shhh...you don't want them to hear you say that,"* after someone said something that we knew the authorities wouldn't like. We said that because if a "glina" or other authority figure heard you, you would be on their blacklist, and they would do to you as they pleased.

So here in America, while we don't say *"Shhh,"* we do say things like, "You better include that yard sale income on your taxes, just in case you get audited and they find out." Or, "Don't speed, you'll get a ticket or a police beating." Or, worse yet, "You can't carry a gun in public without a permit." Thus, we fear our government. But we're so used to having these laws on the books that they are natural to us; they have been there all our lives so we don't question them. Thus, we don't realize that gradualism has impacted our personal freedoms. We don't even realize we have *lost* so many freedoms.

Sometimes you have to take a step back, step into someone else's shoes, and look at America from a different perspective. This might provide a different understanding of who it is that hates our freedoms, and whether or not we really have much freedom left. As someone who grew up without those freedoms, and who grew up surrounded by government tyranny, I am perhaps more acutely aware than most Americans of how great it is (or was) to have those freedoms, and how long term creeping gradualism has greatly eroded American liberties. I'm even more painfully aware how few Americans realize this. If it weren't for the "alternative" uncensored, truthful media, I would perhaps feel quite alone in my thoughts.

When I was trying to figure out 9/11 and started to look back at my Polish roots, I realized that even though I'm full-blooded Polish, I knew little of my history. Even though I lived through martial law, oppression, and starvation, I still understood little of my roots and the world I was born into. Even with all the stories my family told me, I still only knew the history from one perspective.

It wasn't until I started to research and read about Polish history that an understanding began to form in my mind of what it meant to live in Poland during the 1970s and 1980s. I read the works of different authors of that time who described their experiences. I saw that their life experiences were so different from one another, yet the underlying causes and themes were similar. It wasn't until I learned about what caused the shortages, bad economy, oppression, martial law, and many other issues that I realized how two people can have such different experiences.

What I thought was a one-off event that I managed to escape was in reality a scenario that could repeat itself over and over anywhere. It doesn't matter where I was born. To see this, you have to study the history of other countries and societies along with your own history, and not just one book by one source, but several. It is also important to study who wrote that history and what intent or bias they may have had. You need to make sure that information is not skewed to benefit someone. Always remember to ask yourself: "Cui bono?" *Who benefits?* And when statistics are thrown at you to prove a point, always say, "Show me the data."

History will repeat itself because people do not learn from the mistakes of the past, and allow those same scenarios to play out again. I certainly see the parallels and repetition in motion here in America, and I suspect the Founding Fathers would as well if they were alive.

In reading the reasons the Founding Fathers wrote the Declaration of Independence, and the governmental actions described in their grievances, their complaints would sound eerily familiar in the US today.

Here are just six examples taken from the Declaration of Independence, which was adopted on July 4, 1776 (which is the reason for our 4th of July "Independence Day" holiday, which sadly most people view as the "fireworks holiday").

In the "Indictment" section of the document, which is the section that listed the King's "repeated injuries and usurpations," meaning complaints or grievances about actions by the King of England, it states:

> *"He has erected a multitude of New Offices, and sent hither swarms of Officers to harrass our people, and eat out their substance."*

In other words, the complaint here is that many new government agencies were created, and their officers endlessly harassed the people and stole their wealth. In those days, wealth was comprised largely of material goods like tools, land, farm animals, clothes, and food, rather than the paper and electronic "wealth" we have today. If you were to put the same grievance in today's terms, it would be equivalent to the IRS seizing your bank accounts or your business because they claimed you didn't follow some obscure regulation. Another example in today's terms would be if the EPA was a new regulatory agency that was created, and the agents employed under the EPA came on your property and took your farm animals because they were drinking from a river, and then seized your land because the river contained an endangered species, regardless of if the endangered species was anywhere near your property. We have a large number of new federal bureaucracies with absurd and unjustified regulations. We have ever-increasing taxation that impoverishes people of all income levels. While the path to getting here may be different between Colonial America, communist Poland, and the present-day US, the end result is looking disturbingly similar.

This next complaint against the King very clearly stated that he would not follow the same laws that were placed upon the people:

"He has refused his Assent to Laws, the most wholesome and necessary for the public good."

There are now two standards of justice in the US. Common Americans are subjected to so many laws and regulations that it is impossible to be aware of them all — let alone follow them all — and well-connected elitists can get away with just about anything.

This next grievance discusses how the King maintained the British military among the colonies without the consent of the American people and their local governments. Today this would be similar to the US Federal Government maintaining martial law throughout the US by deploying the US military inside the US — against the American people.

"He has kept among us, in times of peace, Standing Armies without the Consent of our legislatures."

While the US military has not yet itself been deployed to police America, partly because of the legal precedent known as Posse Comitatus which prohibited the use of military troops for law enforcement purposes within the US, there are other frightening similarities. Parallels here include the militarization of domestic police forces through a program known as the "1033" program, which authorizes the transfer of military equipment to all levels of police forces.[20-21] Furthermore, legal changes made in 2006, 2008, and 2012, have made it legally possible for the Federal Government to actually use the US military within the US, against Americans, because of changes to the Posse Comitatus precedent.[22-23]

The previously mentioned 1033 program has resulted in the US military handing out MRAP type vehicles (military armored personnel vehicles), weapons, body armor, and a long list of other military and combat items, to local police forces like candy to kids on Halloween. These programs have gotten so large that it has become impossible for their administrators to even keep track of how all the equipment is being used. Even a report for the Office of the President admits this.[24] The first question that comes to mind is why local police forces need equipment like MRAP vehicles, even if they are for SWAT teams. For that matter, why has our society degraded to the point where cities need to have SWAT teams at all?

A deeper consideration of this situation led me to wonder if the militarization of the police was a way to circumvent the use of the US military within the US. But this raises an obvious additional question: What is the Federal Government expecting or preparing for that they perceive the need to arm police forces across the nation as heavily as a war-ready military? Similarly, why did the people of Boston allow a practice run of martial law to occur and allow "authorities" to search homes without warrants after the Boston bombing?[25-26] Photos of this event which can be found with a simple internet search look eerily similar to the photos in this book of Polish martial law.

Returning to our theme of the similarities between the complaints against the King of England during the American Revolution and modern America, consider this passage. It was written in obscure terminology and will require some explaining.

"He has combined with others to subject us to a jurisdiction foreign to our constitution, and unacknowledged by our laws; giving his Assent to their Acts of pretended Legislation."

While this complaint may take extra effort to grasp, it is extremely important to our modern legal system and to holding on to our Constitutional laws and rights. This passage is stating that the King has worked with foreign interested parties, other than the colonials, to create laws that circumvent the legal system of the colonies without proper legal procedure, to the benefit of those foreign parties.

The similarity here is the US President or Secretary of State signing international treaties without proper ratification by the US Senate. For example, Secretary of State John Kerry signed the UN Small Arms treaty despite the fact that the US Senate rejected it, AND despite the fact that it is unconstitutional.[27-28]

This action is clearly unconstitutional in two ways. First, a US administration can not enter into international treaties without the ratification (approval) of the US Senate. Second, some would argue that this treaty will violate the Second Amendment. There has also been a great amount of opposition to this among the American people, which has clearly been ignored by Mr. Kerry and the Obama administration. So this example very much parallels the grievance against the King listed above.

International laws and treaties are a very dangerous tool that can be used to circumvent US Constitutional law and eliminate the rights of Americans, with little say from the House of Representatives, the courts, or the people. International treaties also pose a threat to Americans' health freedom in the form of Codex Alimentarius, which regulates food and nutritional supplements in international trade under the World Trade Organization (WTO) rules.[29] (More on Codex later.) If you were not already aware of the threat that international treaties pose to our Constitutional rights, liberties, and legal system, you may want to study this topic in greater detail.

This next grievance against the King states that people were being taxed on issues that not only did they not agree to be taxed for, but that they did not agree with in general, and were still forced to pay:

"For imposing Taxes on us without our Consent."

Many things could be written about taxation without consent in the US today. I will only mention two:

1. Polls show a majority of Americans do not support the Affordable Care Act (AKA Obamacare), and yet the Supreme Court and Federal Government are treating it as a supposed "tax".[30-31] It is worth pointing out that it seems rather odd that this "tax" is paid to private third parties rather than government for "insurance", which strikes me as resembling corporatism or fascism.[32]

2. According to Benjamin Franklin, "Democracy is two wolves and a lamb voting on what to eat for lunch." We now have a situation where a majority of people are voting to transfer payments in the form of entitlements from higher income earners to themselves via the Federal Government. Similarly, we have wealthy individuals receiving transfer payments from everyone else via the Federal Government through things like bank bailouts and essentially interest-free loans from the Federal Reserve. We now have a system where the government is used

as a system through which everyone tries to steal from everyone else, either through taxation, entitlements, bailouts, inflation (money printing and currency debasement), special legal or business "privileges" granted in statutory and regulatory law, and no-bid contracts. Just like both communist Poland and the colonies under the British Empire (and the latter stages of the Roman Empire), the current system in the US has become a cesspool of corruption and political rot.

The last example I would like to share of how complaints against King George of colonial England apply to modern America relates back to Chapter 1.

"For depriving us in many cases, of the benefits of Trial by Jury."

The National Defense Authorization Act (NDAA) of 2012 and every year since has included provisions for "disappearing" people without trial. This is not reserved only for foreigners, and can be applied to both foreigners as well as US citizens, both within the US and abroad.[33-34] Having lived through such an experience in Poland, I don't doubt one bit the ability, or even the intent, of the government disappearing American citizens who challenge their supposed "authority".

There are many additional parallels, such as the National Security Administration (NSA) spying on all electronic communications of Americans, but this list is sufficient to make my point. That point is there are many parallels in history, whether between colonial America and the US today or between communist Poland and the US today.

As generations pass, our children and grandchildren will be born into a world where they don't question their government's actions because it has "always" been that way. They will have also become normalized to accept certain things, like violence, as being commonplace because their brains were conditioned with it at a young age when watching television and/or the internet. Thus they may thoughtlessly join a cause to fight a public that is trying to save their freedoms, and may end up fighting you. In a situation like that, would you do?

Lesson 7a: Gradualism has historically frequently been used by tyrants to transform cultures and societies in adverse ways to achieve their objectives. The US today is not immune from this tactic.

Lesson 7b: Being passive and ignoring your surroundings is only a way to enslave yourself. Don't fall into the "it can't happen here" trap. Don't let normalcy bias allow you to deny to yourself what is blatantly in front of you. "It" already is happening.

Lesson 7c: There are many examples in history of peaceful civilizations collapsing. If you don't learn from the lessons of history and vigilantly work to prevent repeating the errors of the past, great loss of life and liberty could easily occur again.

"One of the saddest lessons of history is this: If we've been bamboozled long enough, we tend to reject any evidence of the bamboozle. We're no longer interested in finding out the truth. The bamboozle has captured us. It's simply too painful to acknowledge, even to ourselves, that we've been taken. Once you give a charlatan power over you, you almost never get it back."

-Carl Sagan

CHAPTER 8: THE AMERICAN POLITICAL-MEDIA ILLUSION

"Majority rule only works if you're also considering individual rights. Because you can't have five wolves and one sheep voting on what to have for supper."

-Larry Flynt

In my mind, coming to America was "it." It was the end of the quest for freedom. We were here, we could live life as we wanted, free — forever. And then I woke up.

At a certain point, I came to the realization that just because a person was in a car accident once, doesn't mean he or she never be in a car wreck again. Similarly, my mindset had been that I escaped tyranny and oppression once in Poland, so surely I wouldn't have to deal with it again, particularly in the US. But reality had a different plan for me.

Sometime in early 2007, my husband introduced me to then-presidential candidate Texas Congressman Dr. Ron Paul. It all started with some YouTube videos. At first, I wasn't interested in politics because I had such a negative experience in the military. But something about Dr. Paul — the honest way he spoke, and the things he was concerned about — made me change my mind rather quickly. I was also taking a political science course at the time as a college requirement, so I had to delve into politics just a little if for no other reason than to get a good grade.

The college course itself was a complete joke, which I realized as soon as I read my assigned political science textbook. It basically explained that getting elected is all about which candidate can be the most popular and raise the most money so they can advertise with fake commercials to manipulate people into voting for them. This book clearly pointed out that promises are made but are not required to be (and rarely are) kept, and that it is all a popularity contest based on public relations and marketing deceit. The more I studied, the more I realized how true this was, not only of current politicians, but past ones as well. This may be common knowledge to people born in America, but as an immigrant I still harbored a somewhat idealized view of American politics. After this class, I no longer did, as I realized that it was not the class that was the joke, but that our current American politics are the joke. And the joke is on us.

The more I read about Dr. Ron Paul and his principles, the more I wanted him to be our next president, as he was not like most of the others. But that meant I had to actually vote if I wanted to see that happen. So I decided that it was finally time to quit being lazy about my (legal) permanent resident status and get my US citizenship, if for no other reason than to be able to vote. I had become eligible for citizenship many years prior, and both of my parents and my brother were already citizens. I think I felt comfortable as a permanent resident, and never felt the need to spend the few hundred dollars to make it official. But I decided it was time. I felt like an American most of my life. I grew up here, I planned to stay here. I figured I better participate, or else I would have to face the unpleasant consequences of not actively participating. (By the way, you do not have to be a US citizen to serve in the US armed forces — think about that for just a minute.)

My husband warned me several times that voting probably wouldn't make any difference. Regardless, I got involved anyway. We both did. So during the time I waited for my citizenship paperwork to be completed, I studied about our state caucus process, and the national electoral process, and continued with college.

I will admit, I was completely baffled by the caucus system. Note that some states have a "primary" system, and some states have a "caucus" system for voters to choose the candidate for each political party. At the time, I happened to live in the state of Nevada, and it was the first year with a caucus system there. Before that time, I never really gave much thought to how presidential candidates ended up on the ballot. I always heard people talk about voting for the lesser of two evils. But again, I never considered how two evils got on the ballot in the first place.

This turned out to be an important lesson to learn. I always understood voting to be going to the ballot box and casting your vote for who you wanted to win. The votes were counted, and then you were done. Well, I learned that if I wanted to be able to cast my vote for a specific candidate, such as Ron Paul, then we first needed to get him on that presidential ballot, which was not as easy as it might seem. That was where the caucus came in — at least in the states that are caucus states. Explaining the whole political system is a bit much for the purpose of my story, and would require a book the size of an encyclopedia. For my purposes here, it is important to understand that I am referring specifically to the Nevada Republican caucus for the selection of the Republican presidential candidate by the state of Nevada.

We started off by becoming registered Republican voters and volunteering to be delegates to represent our local precinct. We then had to canvass our neighborhood and convince neighbors that they should vote for us to become local delegates to represent them, so that they could be properly represented at the county level caucus convention. Once at the county caucus convention, a straw poll was held. Many people think that voting in the straw poll made a difference, but in Nevada it actually didn't. However, in some states it does, but again, that is in issue too technical to get into now. Long story short, the straw poll vote was not enough.

During the county convention, delegates were elected to represent the county at the state convention. The winning delegates then moved on to the state convention. My husband and I moved on to represent our county at the state convention. It was at the state caucus convention that a small number of delegates were finally selected, out of all the delegates present, to represent Nevada at the Republican National Convention. Only those delegates who attended the national convention would have the opportunity to cast votes for which candidate would be on the ballot for that party in the national election. There are some rules that are included in this process, but in the end, it's all about playing the game and knowing how it works. So, often the candidates that end up on the ballot are not the ones that are desired by the voting public.

I completed my citizenship process just in time to canvass my neighborhood and ask my neighbors to vote for me and my husband in the local caucus. We both ended up participating in the state convention. We were, in a way, involved in a huge movement toward freedom, all brought together by one common denominator: Ron Paul.

Looking back, I imagine that's how my parents felt when Lech Wałęsa, who co-founded Solidarity, became a prominent figure in every Polish household. Lech Wałęsa won the Nobel Peace Prize in 1983, and was voted in as president of Poland in 1990. But before he could become president many things had to happen, including the Poles organizing to say "no more" to the tyranny that was running every Pole's life. Lech Wałęsa also had to earn his leadership role. He didn't do it by accepting bribes and marketing himself to become popular. He did it by staying true to his principles and never betraying the people he represented as a union leader. (He used bad judgment once, but that will be discussed later.)

During this time, there were several occasions where I looked back at my life in Poland, and remembered listening to my parents speak to each other and to friends about what life *should* be like, about Wałęsa and other prominent names, and about the great changes that were happening. It was surreal in a way. Back then, as a child, I didn't understand the importance of the conversations that I overheard, and the importance of the many people that were discussed. I often compared what was happening in the US in 2008 and what we were a part of to the historical figures of the past who helped shape this country and other countries.

Wałęsa is a distant comparison to Ron Paul. Dr. Paul, while a congressman for many years, is also a medical doctor who delivered thousands of babies. Lech Wałęsa was a typical blue-collar worker, like any other Pole. But what these two had in common was they were not career politicians. This actually makes a huge difference, as people who are not career politicians often have much less to gain in political office, and much less to fear if they lose an election or leave office. This allows them much more leeway to act upon upstanding principles rather than what will most benefit their own position in office. This could be argued as a reason for political term limits.

Regardless, Wałęsa was a figure who stood up and fought for people's rights and never sold out no matter how tempting the offers. His leadership and integrity were one of the common denominators among the Poles, particularly among Solidarity members. Honesty and support of a true free market economy are rare traits found in politicians these days. When you have a political figure that you can trust, and that tells the truth, then people can come together.

That is what happened at the Nevada State Republican Convention. We, the Ron Paul supporters, found common ground that we could all work together toward, for the same principles and beliefs that we believed in; mainly, the US Constitution and liberty. We came from different backgrounds, religions, and races, and had other different characteristics, yet we found common principles to agree upon. Who would best follow the Constitution and speak the truth about what was happening in our country? At that time, it was Ron Paul.

We met some of the most amazing people in our lives through our participation in this process: People who truly understood what it meant to be free. People who understood that all the laws and regulations being thrown our way were a sign of not-so-good things to come. People who had actually read the US Constitution. People who cared about their freedoms and rights as much as we cared about ours. At first I realized how much awareness I lacked in comparison to many of these amazing people, because of my pure ignorance growing up as an American. Yet, I ended up "growing up" to become the very same type of people that my parents were. My involvement was intense: talking late into the night with my husband about many different issues and philosophies, posting informational flyers about Ron Paul at the college campus, making and hanging signs around town, and meeting with people from around town to discuss politics and how much better this country would be if Ron Paul were to win. The thought did occur to me on several occasions, especially when passing out flyers, that these very activities were what resulted in my father's three month political imprisonment, followed by exile. The question always lurked in the back of my mind as to when the US would get as bad as Poland had been.

What really became obvious to me at that time was the amount of disinformation that was being disseminated in the media. I had done my homework, and while working my way toward a degree in research biology, I learned how to verify sources of information. I knew how to research candidates and compared them all. Ron Paul was a winner in every aspect. Sure, I didn't agree with *everything* he said, but I agreed with him on most of the issues that actually mattered. And when I read between the lines on certain issues that I initially disagreed with him on, I came to support him even more. Yet, there was so much negative media propaganda about what a horrible person he was. All of it was out of left field to anyone actually paying attention. There was no evidence whatsoever to back up the accusations. No one in the media actually mentioned his voting track record, nor the principles he advocated. It had become very obvious to me that the mainstream media was spewing nothing but lies about Ron Paul. If there was any news coverage, it was all negative, and they preferred to ignore his candidacy as much as possible.

Just as the Solidarity movement in Poland was attacked with untruthful accusations, so was Ron Paul. All the other candidates received free publicity on the networks, and Ron Paul was ignored. When a "Money Bomb" raised over six million dollars in one day for Dr. Paul's campaign, the media was silent about it. To me, watching these events unfold, it was so obvious. Yet even people like my own parents, who had lived through these very same types of lies in Poland, fell for the media hype. They disengaged from Ron Paul supporters as if they were from another planet.

It was during this time that I kept asking the question, "How are people so blind?" What was different about me that helped me see what was going on in plain sight that others couldn't? I realized it had to be television. Because I had mostly stopped watching television and instead received my news via the internet and the "alternative media" (non-propaganda media), I was seeing the picture from a different perspective.

It was then that I researched who owned the television networks that allowed such disinformation, and that investigating led me to discover that every single thing broadcast on television, radio, and major newspapers is owned by only six different companies. And who are they?

1. General Electric, which makes most people think of appliances, but it's much more than an appliance company. GE is a giant corporation that also owns some of the networks, including NBC and the History Channel.
2. Time Warner, which is the largest of the media companies, owns CNN along with several other stations, and co-owns the Cartoon Network.
3. The Walt Disney Company is not just about Disneyland, Disneyworld, and Disney movies. This company also owns ABC and ESPN, along with a host of other networks.
4. News Corporation, which owns Fox and National Geographic, along with Hulu on the internet in partnership with GE. It also owns MySpace.
5. Viacom, which owns MTV, along with several other entertainment stations.
6. Columbia Broadcasting System, better known as CBS.

It is also worth noting that both 5 and 6 above have the same owners.[1]

And that's it. When you look at the media closely you will realize that every single television channel available out there, most radio stations, and most non-independent newspapers, fall under one of these six companies. I will add that the Associated Press and Reuters also play a role in newspapers. With such concentration of media ownership, it doesn't take much for a few large owners to come together and agree on what content should and shouldn't be allowed to be shown to the American public, especially when there are large amounts of money and power involved. Interestingly, while doing my research, I discovered that there is actually a law that prevents how many stations a network can own. As per the FCC site itself:

> The rule does not limit the number of TV stations a single entity may own nationwide so long as the station group collectively reaches no more than 39 percent of all U.S. TV households. For the purposes of calculating the "national audience reach" under

this rule, TV stations on UHF channels (14 and above) count less than TV stations operating on VHF channels (13 and below), this is also known as the UHF Discount."[2]

I have no idea who came up with that number, but it goes to show you that there is a reason why real diversity in news media is required to maintain a free society. That reason is so that it is not possible for a limited and controlled narrative to be regurgitated over and over again on television, radio, and news, as if no perspectives existed outside of that narrative. Real diversity of news and opinion is required so that there is diversity of information and perspectives. The Founding Fathers of the US recognized this when they included freedom of the press in the First Amendment. Now, throughout most of the US, so-called "media diversity" consists of the opinions of five or six corporations, often working in collusion (or at least engaged in groupthink). Thus, the only truthful media or "free press" that still exists in the US is what has been dubbed the "alternative media," largely consisting of internet-based news websites. To provide just one example of how this has degraded the quality of news in the US, almost no true investigative journalism is performed by the big six news companies, and almost all true investigative journalism is now performed by reporters employed by this so-called "alternative media." This concentrated control over the American media also extends into the book publishing industry, which is one reason a book such as this would never be published by any of the large publishing companies. Thankfully, free press alternatives still currently exist in the US, just as underground publishers existed in Poland. Also just as in Poland, in the US we will likely be challenged to see how long the true free press and alternative media can hold out under increasing oppression of free speech by the government.

The realization that the media disinformation issue was much greater than I thought possible only made me fight harder. I put more bumper stickers on my car, and I then noticed I was followed by police more often, trying to find a reason to pull me over. The more people tried to get me to support Obama, the more vocal I was about his lack of real qualifications and his various drawbacks. The more people tried to get me to support McCain, the more vocal I was about his traitorous actions while a POW, not to mention his other drawbacks. The more people parroted the false information they heard about Ron Paul on TV, the more facts I threw at them to show them they need to think for themselves. If I could have given a copy of *Brave New World* to each and every one of them, I would have. The frustration I experienced trying to save the very country that saved me from starvation in another was beyond words. But instead, I remained hopeful and continued to volunteer for the Ron Paul movement. I even felt we had a slight chance when he received second place in the Nevada county caucus straw poll. The media, of course, didn't mention it; they mentioned Romney in first and McCain in third, almost as if second place didn't exist. I was sure we were going to win Nevada.

But it wasn't to be. Although the liberty movement gained huge momentum during Ron Paul's 2008 run for presidency, "the powers that be" didn't want it to happen. The media blocked Dr. Paul from many speaking opportunities in which other candidates were allowed to participate. Worse yet, mass media puppet "reporters" laughed at Dr. Paul for some of the truths he was speaking. They called him names, stooping to irrelevant ad hominem attacks, and referred to his followers as "kooks." None of what the major mainstream media was doing really slowed any of us down. The momentum was so great that we felt, even if just for a little while, that we could save this country yet.

The time for the Nevada Republican state caucus came. I brought my school books with me to study while I was waiting for the time to vote. The Ron Paul supporters were very organized and we heard reports of some shenanigans that could be committed by the state Republican Party, so we were ready.

When the state Republican Party leaders tried to send their pre-selected group of delegates to the National Convention, we challenged them, and made them obey their own convention rules. They first tried to ignore us, but we fought it with the very same rules they made us follow. They counted the yays and nays, and claimed the nays had it. We asked for "division of the house" (we asked that they count individual votes by raising hands, rather than the loudness of the yays and nays), which they tried to ignore. Then division of the house came, and the real vote counting occurred.

It was amazing what happened next. We were voting on the issue of sending pre-selected delegates to the National Convention, or voting to select those delegates at that moment. Having been heavily involved in the Ron Paul movement, I knew there were roughly 400 plus Ron Paul delegates out of roughly 1,200 delegates total at the state convention. And yet, during the vote count, more than 800 delegates voted to choose the delegates to go to the National Convention, rather than sending the pre-selected group. As it turned out, a majority of delegates present thought that we ought to actually get a say in who would be selected as delegates to the National Convention and thus who the Republican candidate would be. To do anything less seemed both corrupt and a waste of time and trust. What a concept! Wait a minute — wasn't that why we were there in the first place?

Finally, we received the opportunity to vote for the national delegates of our choice, and we felt like winners. The votes came in, and plenty of people volunteered to help count the votes. I did something mildly dishonest at that point. I had already dressed up in my best interview business outfit, so I placed a McCain sticker on my lapel. I then walked over to the party leaders and offered my help to count the votes. I was immediately let in.

As soon as I walked to the back where the vote counting was to take place, I ripped the sticker off. I felt ashamed for being dishonest, if only for a moment. But I also wanted an honest vote count. And considering what I had already witnessed in the past, and the fact that they tried to send their pre-selected delegates without our say-so, told me that I had to do something, because everyone's vote should be counted. After all, what was the point of having the State Convention at all if the delegates were already pre-selected by who-knows-who to represent the state of Nevada? What was the point of caucusing neighborhoods to become a delegate, if in the end you're just there for a dog and pony show? This was America after all, not Poland. I got to have a vote, as did all the other delegates.

During the vote count, the three delegates chosen by Ron Paul supporters were winning by a landslide. We all agreed in advance who we would vote on, and we all knew and trusted these people. It wasn't a list of names of people we had never heard of, or people who weren't even attending the convention (as was the case with the pre-selected delegates). So we organized and planned, and when the voting came, we all agreed to vote for the same three Ron Paul delegates.

Most scraps of paper that were grabbed held the same three names, those of *The Three Musketeers*, as they were nicknamed. Things were not going well for the Republican establishment. The next thing I knew, my cell phone was ringing, and my hubby was telling me that the convention was being shut down in the main hall. The lights had been turned off, and the vote count was going to be halted: we would not get to finish counting the votes. Before I hung up, sure enough, the leaders of the Nevada Republican party were coming in to the room to take charge, and to take the votes home with them, to "keep them safe," they claimed.

After much argument, and barely avoiding a fist-fight after some establishment Republican attendees discovered that I was a Ron Paul supporter, the votes were locked up in the casino's cashier cage (the convention was held at a casino). The convention was never re-opened. There was initially a story circulated that stated the casino had notified the Republican State Party that we had gone past our allotted time and that we would have to reconvene the next day. So we all returned the next day, only to learn that the casino had never given the state Republican Party such a time limit or notification. The person who held the key to the votes, the Nevada National Committee chairwoman never returned. At least, she did later announce her retirement.

Thus, we lost. Actually we didn't lose — we just had no voice.

The "news" disinformation that evening made things even worse. Lies told included, "The Ron Paul supporters took over the convention," and "They made a terrible rule change."[3]

It was a hard blow and a difficult lesson. I was there. The Ron Paul supporters didn't take over the convention and they didn't make the rule change. The votes were over 800 in favor of the change. That was 400 more than just the Paul supporters. That meant more than two thirds of the delegates wanted this change, not just the Dr. Paul supporters. The Dr. Paul supporters only represented a third, and it wasn't even a rule change, it was a requirement to follow the state Republican Party's own rules. So for the Republican leadership to claim they "weren't prepared," is an absurd lie. Shouldn't they have been prepared for something that was clearly expected and listed in the rules? It was interesting that they stated that this was the only State Convention that allowed Dr. Paul to speak. Really? What a concept: let's "allow" a popular presidential candidate to speak at a political convention. Seriously? Little more needs to be said to explain the mindset of the state Republican establishment. I'm sure this mindset is pervasive across the country throughout the establishments of both major political mafias, err... parties.

The pre-selected group of delegates, whom none of us ever met, nor did we vote for, got to attend the Republican National Convention. They cast their votes for the presidential nominee on our behalf, without any of the elected state delegates having a say. All that work, just to see my first vote in the "land of the free" locked up in a casino cashier cage, never to be counted. All that work for someone else to make the decision for me.

Worse yet, after the convention, when I tried to explain to people why Dr. Ron Paul wouldn't be on the ballot, no one understood. Not one person who wasn't involved with the convention process understood what delegates meant, what their vote meant, or even how a person got on the ballot from which you eventually selected.

The locked-up votes were eventually counted, but not until after Obama was already president and after a lot of arguing with the state Republican Party. At first, they tried to say that no one had the key, but I told them who had it: I saw her sign for it. Then they said that that there was no one left to get the votes opened, and I told them that was a lie too. I knew at least two people that signed for the votes. Finally, one day, the key mysteriously appeared, although the responsible person was nowhere to be found. We went to the casino to unlock the votes and count them.

When the votes were finally counted, the pre-selected delegates that represented Nevada at the National Convention had very few votes. One received zero votes. The other two had only a few votes each. The whole voting process was a sham, I realized. It was designed solely to make you *think* your vote counted, but you didn't really get to have an influence. Right here in America, in the "land of the free," you didn't really get to have a vote. It was all fake and pretend. You're allowed to vote for the lesser of two evils, but you don't have a way to prevent evil people from getting on the ballot in the first place. It reminded me a great deal of the "voting" process that my parents talked about in communist Poland.

It is ominous to think about how comparable the American caucus delegate and Electoral College systems are to that of the Polish system back in the 1980s. Starting sometime in 1980 in Poland, a political trend called the "horizontal movement" developed. Its primary goal was to enable the nomination of government leadership positions by the individual party units, rather than merely being an approving vote for pre-selected delegates from the top. Advocates thought that a fundamental overhaul of the party election statutes was needed. In April of 1981, the horizontal movement held a meeting that resulted in a package of proposals which were later watered down by the leadership. While free nomination of candidates was agreed upon, nominations that came from the top-down continued to be permitted.[4] Is our current American voting process so problematic that it resembles an oppressive communist regime? Or are the parallels just a coincidence? In a manner similar to how Ron Paul supporters have attempted to infiltrate the Republican Party in the US, the Solidarity movement actually succeeded in infiltrating the Polish system by voting in better people and better regulations, including term limits. Granted, this ultimately led to martial law. But the point is that unlike our "free" American system where the national and state level voting we do makes little to no difference in policy, the people of Poland were able to actually improve their lives, even if temporarily, while under Soviet communist rule.

You could not imagine the frustration that traveled through my veins the day I witnessed those votes getting locked up. I'm surprised they *ever* got counted, as I was sure I would never see them again as they were getting locked away. A year's worth of work of trying to be the voice of the people in my neighborhood was locked up in a lock box, completely ignored. What was the point of all that effort? The time that every delegate put into the convention, and the money spent for the convention, and for what? A dog and pony show to make you feel warm and fuzzy inside because you felt like you voted? An illusion to make you think you have a say in your government?

The combination of knowing the history of controlled voting, now in two countries, coupled with my own personal witnessing of the locked-up votes and the spewed propaganda on television, made me really question if any election — ever — was honest, or if it was all rigged, regardless of sides. Can an honest vote even be possible?

The pendulum started to swing the other way on the national level for Dr. Paul as well. He was falsely accused of being a racist as a smear tactic, and was not offered a fair chance to defend himself. The next thing I knew, the mere mention of Ron Paul resulted in being called a racist as well. The idea that I was a racist was absurd and very painful for me. The lies on television were blatant, yet no one saw them for what they were. A majority of people were clearly brainwashed zombies, lacking any independent or critical thinking ability whatsoever.

The accusation of racism wasn't the only problem. In March of 2009, a few months after the 2008 election was complete, the Missouri Information Analysis Center (MIAC) report was leaked via the alternative media. That report stated that domestic terrorists or members of "militias" would likely include Ron Paul supporters.[5] When I first read the report I laughed out loud, as the mere thought that I could be a militia member was ridiculous, let alone the absurdity of me having any connection to domestic terrorism. But the laughter soon faded, as I realized this was pure propaganda to brainwash our domestic police forces. Just as my father was sent to an internment camp for rebels for three months, then evicted from Poland because he was a member of Solidarity, now I too could be persecuted simply because I supported Dr. Ron Paul in an election.

Ever since that time period, I have observed ever-increasing parallels in history all around us. In Poland, shortly before martial law took place, the Polish party was issuing harsh public statements implying that Poland was at risk by those "who do not hide their counterrevolutionary plans" and by those who vowed "anarchy and chaos." The term "counterrevolutionary" was the equivalent of "enemy of the state."[6] The Solidarity members were being treated as counterrevolutionaries, just as the Ron Paul supporters were being treated as domestic terrorists. Same plot, different terminology.

So when it came time to vote for the president of the United States, Ron Paul wasn't on the ballot. I was in disbelief about how blind the American people were — at least those not actively participating in the promotion of liberty and the Constitution. Worse yet, when people discussed politics at my college, and I asked them to name all the presidential candidates, they could only name two: Obama and McCain. I would quietly and calmly say "an informed voter is one that can name all of the candidates," but they would look at me like I was speaking in another language. The political spectrum that rightfully ranged from A to Z had been narrowed to M to O for the majority of the American public. McDonalds or Burger King? How about something that is actually healthy?

It was from observing this complete voting sham that I realized I was in the same place where my grandparents were when they welcomed the communist regime and found themselves enslaved by the very people who promised to "help" them. By this I do not mean to refer to any one particular presidential administration, nor any particular political party. Instead, I refer to a corrupt, controlled, illusory "*Matrix*-like" political and media system, in which the people have no true say in the decisions that are made, and the majority of what is presented in the mainstream media is lies.

"We'll know our disinformation program is complete when everything the American public believes is false."[7]

-William Casey, CIA Director 1981-1987

The difference between the Soviet media propaganda in Poland and propaganda in America is that in Poland, everyone recognized it was all propaganda. Soviet propaganda was not effective, and in part that is why they failed to control the Polish people. One of the reasons it failed was because when they claimed food was aplenty, the reality was empty store shelves, and it was very blatantly obvious that it was a lie. This is starting to happen in America, as the news media reports that the economy has been improving, but people are clearly not seeing that in their personal financial situations. Contrary to what some propaganda and marketing pundits would like to believe, reality is not created by the consent of mass hallucination. Reality is what it is, and the more a person's mental map deviates from the actual landscape, the more that perceived map is incorrect, or the person is lying. Another reason Soviet propaganda was less effective was because the Poles knew that the government was not of their own origin, as in *not Polish*, but rather Soviet. It's much harder to pass convincing lies past someone who is different than you, especially when it is so blatantly obvious. I also think Soviet propaganda failed because it didn't adequately use gradualism. In America, gradualism has been expertly used, and only a minority of people realize most of the media they are exposed to is propaganda. Most people actually believe it is real news.

The political reality is that the public merely holds the illusion that they have any say in decisions — decisions which are actually made by elitists or oligarchs, people who were not elected. The politicians are merely puppet-whores high on their illusion of power. That realization was when I fully understood the current American reality. No way was I going to leave to my grandchildren the very same circumstances that the US Founding Fathers fought to free us from.

But even if the votes were properly counted and the properly elected set of delegates went to the National Convention, it wouldn't have mattered, as the shenanigans at the Republican National Convention were even worse than what occurred at our state level event. During both the 2008 and 2012 Republican National Conventions, delegates who supported Dr. Paul were cajoled, intimidated, and threatened with all sorts of tactics, up to and including threats of physical violence. In the end, all Ron Paul votes were turned over to McCain (2008) or Romney (2012), the gavel hit the podium, and the National Convention was over. Another sham dog-and-pony show.[8-9]

After the 2008 fiasco, Ron Paul supporters reassessed things and determined that to beat the system, we had to become more involved. The next four years were spent infiltrating the Nevada

Republican Party with Ron Paul supporters, with hopes of a fair vote, and the appropriate delegates being sent to the Republican National Convention. I was shocked by the change in the Party during the 2012 convention. This time, the speakers at the podium were mostly people I knew. The ballots were cast and everyone had a vote, and the Ron Paul slate of delegates won. But something in the back of my mind told me that the powers that be would once again not allow Ron Paul to be on the ballot.

Sure enough, when it came time for the National Convention, many of the delegates from various states that supported Dr. Ron Paul were denied seats. And the same shenanigans that occurred in 2008 were repeated in 2012. We may have won over the local or state parties by becoming the parties, but we didn't make a big enough dent to beat the corrupt system at the national level. The cards were stacked against us.[10-11]

The 2012 election came and went, but I hardly paid attention after the Republican National Convention. The lesser of two evils is still evil, and what was the point of voting when the options set before you were not real options, but rather a controlled and contrived popularity contest that provided no substantive difference? No politician is ever held to the campaign promises they make. And even that would be to assume that they made any clear and desirable policy statements, which they generally do not. I had come to the conclusion that to cast a vote for the lesser of two evils is to pretend that I get to have a say in policy. I don't believe in pretending, and came to the conclusion that to participate in a completely rigged (so-called) "election" process would only support and encourage a corrupt and controlled system. The thought that crossed my mind was "What if they held an 'election' and no one showed up to 'vote' because everyone knew the political system was a rigged sham?"

Although a feeling of loss blanketed over most Ron Paul

supporters, we had not really lost in the long run, just as the Solidarity movement in Poland did not lose even though the early strikes made little difference. The Solidarity members recognized that they were not alone and realized they could challenge a system that once seemed overwhelming.[12] Liberty advocates, Constitutionalists, and Ron Paul supporters may have lost those elections partly because the voting process turned out to be a rigged sham. But, what we won was a changed perspective among all who were involved with the liberty movement.

There was a realization not only of how many of us there really are, but that we could organize enough to effectively challenge the controlled establishment. We were not the "little guys" against a big government and corporate machine. We were the people, working against a small group of elitists who just happened to control the money (printing) and the media so they could make themselves appear powerful. In reality, the greatest power such people have is the deceit, brainwashing, and fear instilled in the public, and the consent via *apathy* of that public to continue supporting that which is evil. Such elitists occasionally have to back that propaganda up with financial power or firepower (physical violence) to make examples of people and maintain the fear (like the IRS, DHS, and NSA, etc. do). But that only works if it only has to be done occasionally. If that had to be done all the time, as was the case of martial law against Solidarity in Poland, it becomes financially unaffordable and logistically impractical. In Poland they had enough tanks to scare the people, but a shortage of enforcers in the security service made it impossible for them to arrest all the resistance members: there were simply too many.[13] In addition, the public wakes up to the obvious fact of who their oppressors truly are. It also becomes obvious that it is the people, and those advocating for liberty, that hold the moral high ground, and that it is the state and corporate apparatus that are the criminal element.

Despite Ron Paul's retirement, the "Ron Paul movement" is still going strong in the form of the much broader "Liberty Movement." This transformation has occurred under many different names over the last eight years, but all hold similar beliefs in individual liberty, personal responsibility, civil rights, property rights, free markets, and honest money. The common theme is a revival of freedom and adherence to the Constitution, both of which have been in decline in the US for at least a hundred years.

While I doubt that Ron Paul will ever run for political office again, there are other, new-to-the-scene, non-career politicians that are supporting the same principles that Ron Paul advocates. They are few and far between, but they are out there. We should support them as much as is practical, but the deck is stacked against them as well.

Therefore, trying to establish change through the political system at this point seems to me to be mostly a waste of time, money, and effort. Working within the political system when the rot of corruption is this far advanced is little more than a means of buying time to work on other approaches. These other approaches will be discussed later.

There is an important lesson to be learned here as well. Just as the Solidarity members were arrested by their own Polish military in December of 1981, and literally any meetings of large groups of people were made illegal, that didn't stop the members from continuing the fight. They had to fight it differently, but they continued, and they won nine years later when the communist government conceded power and Lech Wałęsa became President of Poland. Just because the media made Ron Paul supporters out to be kooks and crazy people (when in fact they may be the most sane and rational Americans out there), doesn't mean that supporters of liberty have lost. It just might take a long time for liberty activists and entrepreneurs to turn things around. Until such time, the people who believe in the Constitution must keep communicating, teaching, doing, and most importantly, developing outside-the-box approaches and strategies to "live free in an unfree world."

I do hope history repeats itself for us in America, in terms of a revival of liberty such as when the Founding Fathers defeated England, or as occurred when the Polish Solidarity freed themselves from communism. I hope even more that it doesn't take nine more years as it did in Poland, but I suspect that it could take even longer to truly reestablish liberty in the US. The lesson here, if you care about liberty, is that you cannot give up trying to live freely. I almost did give up in despair until I started to really look back at my past. I realized it's not in my blood to give up on the cause of a freer and better life. It's not in my blood to put down my arms and give up. And under no circumstance, will I ever live under, comply with, or accept tyrannical rule ever again.

The truth is that the battle for freedom will never end. There will always be someone trying to suppress the masses, either for economic reasons, or if for no other reason, than power-mad megalomania. This has been repeated over and over in history, and will likely not change, unless humans inherently change. As stated by Timothy Garton Ash, in his book *Magic Lantern: The Revolution of '89 Witnessed in Warsaw, Budapest, Berlin, and Prague*: "If 1989 was the end (in reference to communism ending in Poland), then what was the beginning of the end?"[14]

This realization is not easy to accept. But as stated by Andrzej Rozpłochowski in an interview with Jack Bloom, "being humble in front of a tyrant does not protect you; it only emboldens him."[15]

Lesson 8a: If your voting system is rigged, you don't live in a free country.

Lesson 8b: If your voting system is rigged, you must circumvent the political system and utilize alternative strategies and methods to create and live in freedom.

Lesson 8c: If the media is all highly controlled and propagandized, you don't live in a free country.

Lesson 8d: If the media is all highly controlled and propagandized, you must build a better, truthful media with which to spread real news and out-compete the controlled media.

"The difference between a democracy and a dictatorship is that in a democracy you vote first and take orders later; in a dictatorship you don't have to waste your time voting."

　　　　-Charles Bukowski

Store shelves so empty you can't help but laugh.. Photo by: Joanna Helander.
KARTA Foundation

"Queue for shopping" – Standing in line for toilet paper. This photograph is in the
public domain according to the copyright law of March 29, 1926 of the Republic of
Poland.

December 13, 1981. Imposition of martial law - the entry of riot police to the headquarters of Trade Union Solidarity. The image is an excerpt from a series of still pictures taken December 13, 1981 before the Regional Headquarters. The images were published by independent publishing houses. Photographer unknown. KARTA Foundation.

December 13, 1981, Warsaw. Imposition of martial law - armored personnel carriers at the Krakow suburb. Photographer unknown. KARTA Foundation.

*December 13, 1981, Warsaw. The first day of martial law, the riot police patrols.
Photo credit shared by: Ryszard Marszaek and Jerzy Boruc. KARTA Foundation*

December 15, 1981, Gdańsk, Poland. Sit-down strike in the Gdańsk
Shipyard. The crowd at the gate No. 2. Photo by: Stanislaw Składanowski.
KARTA Foundation.

Winter 1981-1982, Gdansk. Martial law – tanks and armored personnel
carriers in a school playground. Photographer unknown. KARTA Foundation.

March 5, 1982, Warsaw, Poland. Independent demonstration in the old town, organized by the underground structures of "Solidarity" in the anniversary of the adoption of the Constitution of 3 May. Photos by: Maciej Czarnocki, KARTA Foundation.

206

Although all of these photos were taken in communist Poland in the early 1980's, some of them look disturbingly similar to recent events in the US. If you are skeptical of this I encourage you to look up photos yourself of some of the US events mentioned below.

The empty store shelves and long lines remind me of the photos I have seem of the stores before hurricanes Katrina and Sandy, or even some of the less severe emergencies that have occurred over the last few years.

Several of these martial law photos remind me of photos I have seen of the lock downs that occurred in Watertown Massachusetts after the Boston Marathon bombing, or in New Orleans after hurricane Katrina.

Some of these martial law photos also remind me of the riot police that have been deployed for security at any number of protest demonstrations that have occurred in the US over the last fifteen years, including the 1999 Seattle WTO protests, the 2009 Pittsburgh WTO protests, and some of the more recent "Occupy" protests.

While I think that there are certainly much better, more effective ways to accomplish constructive change than protesting, I definitely do not think having militarized riot police abuse protestors is either justified or acceptable in an allegedly "free" society.

The parallels are an ominous sign.

It is true that America is not Poland and Poland is not America. However what is important to consider are the political and cultural trends of a country, as history rhymes. So you can look at the history of Poland, and look at the history of America, and learn from the mistakes and the success of the past. By studying the past one can draw extrapolations into the future, and the future direction of America is very concerning.

PHOTOGRAPHS II

CHAPTER 9: THE REALITY — WHAT IS HAPPENING TO AMERICA

"Individual rights are not subject to a public vote; a majority has no right to vote away the rights of a minority; the political function of rights is precisely to protect minorities from oppression by majorities (and the smallest minority on earth is the individual)."

-Ayn Rand

America with its current laws can be a very interesting place. Sometimes I get lost in the all the new laws and regulations, and sometimes I wonder if I am breaking any laws without even knowing it. It really doesn't take very many laws to have a functional, advanced society. So when a government body begins to create so many laws that the citizens can't even begin to keep track, it's a sign that things are going downhill quickly. Creation of such a vast amount of laws and regulations is never truly for the benefit of the people.

"The more corrupt the state, the more numerous the laws."

- Publius Cornelius Tacitus, a Roman historian, *The Annals of Imperial Rome*

I think that if I had never witnessed it myself, the idea of disappearing someone would be difficult to believe. But because I have personally experienced it through the disappearance of my father, and then hearing stories growing up of what it was like for him in an interment camp, the idea seems almost natural — especially because I have learned from experience to distrust government. When disappearing someone seems natural, so do other unlikely events.

When someone in Poland would say, "you can't say that or you will be disappeared," you didn't necessarily believe them due to normalcy bias. That was, until it happened to someone you knew, or yourself. At that point, it was usually too late. That person was gone, and your life was forever changed. It eventually got to the point, with so many activists jailed and killed, that it became just common knowledge. There was no doubt in anyone's mind that such an event could occur.

While my family specifically didn't deny that we were all under surveillance, or that being part of Solidarity was dangerous, there were plenty of Poles who wanted to believe that the party leaders actually cared about the people, that they intended change, and that the food shortages were just temporary. I think there will always be a large number of apologists who do not like conflict, fear the government, and accept their fate as it is.

The problem with accepting such things is that eventually, if you allow a small group of elitists or oligarchs to control things, they will eventually cross a boundary that you are not okay with. Everyone's boundary is different, and as Frederick Douglas pointed out in the quote at the beginning of Chapter 4, sometimes people will put up with a lot before they finally speak up or take action. The problem with waiting too long is that by that point, everyone else will have been imprisoned or killed, and there will be no one else left to speak up.

There is a famous quote by Martin Niemölle in reference to the Nazi German government and it goes something like this:

> First they came for the Socialists, and I
> did not speak out—
> Because I was not a Socialist.
>
> Then they came for the Trade Unionists,
> and I did not speak out—
> Because I was not a Trade Unionist.
>
> Then they came for the Jews, and I did
> not speak out—
> Because I was not a Jew.
>
> Then they came for me—and there was
> no one left to speak for me.

There is a timing issue involved here. If you speak up or take action too early, you make yourself an obvious target of those in power, and other people may not be adequately mentally prepared and will likely disregard your statements or actions as those of a "kook." If you wait too long to speak out and take action, it will be too late as the struggle will already be lost. As with most things in life, timing is crucial.

Some people will always prefer the perceived comfort of ignorance to actually knowing the reality of a situation. They are like the proverbial ostrich that sticks its head in the sand when a predator approaches. There is nothing that can be done for someone who doesn't want to know or see reality; they will be eaten by the predator. For everyone else, it is important to both characterize the problems, as well as suggest solutions, or at least actions that can help mitigate the situation. After all, how can we try to correct the problems if we don't understand the way things are? It's like trying to be a doctor and attempting to treat an illness without having any understanding of human physiology. This chapter is an attempt to further identify or clarify many of the oppressive political problems we face today.

Language barriers are, simply put, barriers in communication. Communication barriers can even occur between those who speak the same language. Often I will say something that is obvious to me, but someone else will take it very personally and in a way I hadn't intended. This is an important topic regarding confusion of language, and I discuss this more in-depth toward the end of Chapter 10.

When my parents were first learning to speak English, they had a lot of American friends who often struggled to understand them. There were times when my mother or father would be having a conversation, and they would point out something that was obvious to them, like their thoughts on buying items for a cheap price. The items fell apart, so in the long run people would end up spending more money on items that could only be used once or twice because they would have to keep purchasing new items to replace the broken items. My parents' friends would get angry and say, "If you don't like it here, go back to Poland." This would completely catch my parents by surprise, as they were not intending to be rude; they were just stating what was obvious to them, not realizing that their friends would take offense to such a statement. It also didn't mean that they didn't like America: they were just pointing out what to them seemed like a very logical observation. In Poland, obtaining items was hard, so you wanted the best quality because you would probably not have an opportunity to buy a replacement. Yet in America, getting items is easy, but Americans usually buy items of low quality based on price that don't last long and need to be replaced.

I bring up this issue about communication because there are a lot of problems in our country today, and I feel the need to warn or raise awareness about these issues. But I fear that I will come across the wrong way, and people will tell me to go back to Poland. For the record, I have no intention of going back to Poland; I am, after all, an American. But because I am an American, I want to preserve the Constitution and help reestablish this country as a place of liberty. The only way I know how to do that is to bring up the issues that are currently destroying our very freedoms and rights that this country was founded upon.

If there were no issues in this country, then we would not have a need for an alternative media. By "alternative media," I mean news outlets that cover topics and perspectives that are never covered in the mainstream controlled-mass-media news: in other words, truthful independent media that is not influenced by government and corporate propaganda. There are so many websites with "real news" that are not reported in the mainstream press that I can't even keep up with all of it every day. There are so many that there is great competition and diversity among them, which is great, because it guarantees that the most important stories are covered. It also demonstrates that if there is so much competition and diversity among the alternative media, then there is something clearly wrong with the popular mass media.

Among the mainstream media (television, newspapers, radio), where there is little real competition or diversity, and where they all seem to present the same information from the exact same perspective, they are trying to peddle the same narrative as if there are no differences in perspective. If there was truly diversity of coverage and perspectives in the mainstream media press, why would you have an alternative media that was so different and diverse? Something is clearly broken, and I don't think it is the alternative news media. That is why internet news usage is skyrocketing, and why newspapers and broadcast news are dying.

Similarly, the Polish underground press was huge. At one point, there were over one hundred independent publishers in Poland that sold books and news in the black market.[1] The mere fact that these had to be sold in the underground economy tells you that there was something wrong with the official media in Poland. And what was the Polish underground media writing about? Here's a statement about one of the main papers, *Tygodnik Mazowsze:* "It was a forum in which political opinions and declarations could be made. It was a link among people in finding sympathizers in a dangerous time when people were dispirited."[2] To many Poles, having access to underground news was an eye-opening experience because it allowed them to read *real* news.[3] While our current alternative media here in America isn't selling anything in the underground economy yet, if free speech on the internet ends up being controlled, or the internet is shut down or censored, the underground economy will be the only place where truthful news will be available. We would be going back to the old-fashioned underground press, as was taught in an Indiana university in 2010, with regards to how the Polish underground journalists operated. Journalists would have to engage in the modern equivalent with computer security of covering typewriters with fabric to muffle the noise in an effort to not be caught.[4]

Most American people are busy watching television shows, such as so-called "reality TV", or "news" that concentrates on inane subjects such as the latest music star's drunken episode. In Poland we had distractions too, but they were a different type of distraction. Here in America, things like legalization of marijuana are distracting a large percentage of the public, while in Poland, the distribution of vodka kept people drunkenly compliant. Yet, there are so many issues that do hit even the mainstream media that are easily ignored and rarely talked about except in the alternative media.

Ron Paul running for president was only one example. Another situation that should have been given more attention is the story of Edward Snowden, who leaked NSA insider information and basically let the American people know that they were being heavily spied on by their own government, proving what the alternative media had been warning about for some time. However, rather than put Mr. Snowden on a pedestal and thanking him, the mainstream press called him a "traitor." Fortunately, Mr. Snowden was smart enough to leave the country and seek refuge in Russia, of all places.[5] (The irony of this never ceases to amaze me: seeking refuge in the same country by which I and the rest of the Polish people were once oppressed? Ummm, something is wrong with this picture.)

The secrets that Mr. Snowden revealed should have never occurred in our once wonderful "free" country. Yet, more and more evidence has surfaced to show that we were, and continue to be, spied on. Most of my co-workers and friends would simply say, "I don't have to worry about anything, I'm not doing anything illegal." While this may be true for now, in a nation with diminishing respect for individual rights, liberties, and the Constitution, and an ever-growing body of repressive laws, what is legal or illegal can change instantly upon political whim. Before they know it, my friends and co-workers will indeed find themselves doing something illegal, even if they don't realize it is so. Several individuals argue that there are so many laws in place now that the average American commits several felonies a day without even knowing it.[6-7] This is where selective enforcement of the law comes into play. In such an environment a rogue government can prosecute people it deems as detractors, while ignoring many others who engage in the very same behavior.

"There's no way to rule innocent men. The only power government has is the power to crack down on criminals. Well, when there aren't enough criminals, one makes them. One declares so many things to be a crime that it becomes impossible for men to live without breaking laws."

-- Ayn Rand

I don't sleep soundly at night knowing that the NSA stores my every email and records each phone call. Everything I say and do may be legal now, but within the current US legal and political environment, that could change overnight based on mere opinion or perception. In the absence of solid philosophical principles and with the corruption of equal justice before the law, almost anyone can be turned into a "criminal" overnight. Will what I write or say today be used to prosecute me someday? Or, worse yet, cause me to be disappeared like my father? These questions unnerve me. But given that the NDAA of 2012 allows for US citizens to be detained indefinitely without trial simply on the basis of a politician saying so, and given that Constitutionalists and libertarians are now considered by some police forces to be potential domestic terrorists simply because of their political views,[8-9] these questions are not merely academic and could one day prove to be all too serious.

While the majority of people respond to the NSA spying on them as no big deal because they are not doing anything wrong, I must point out that neither were the Solidarity members and leaders in Poland in 1981 when Solidarity gained legal status. Most Solidarity members registered as required by law, including their home addresses, since it was a legal trade union. So Solidarity members were not doing anything illegal either, until martial law was forced upon the people and Solidarity was made illegal. Most of the *registered* leaders of Solidarity were rounded up and arrested: this happened to at least ten thousand of them. It was easy for the Polish government to round them up, because not only were they registered as Solidarity members, they had to register where they lived in order to receive ration cards for food. The government simply took that information and rounded them up, and off to jail they went. This is not unlike how US drivers today are required to provide their home address to get a drivers license, or gun owners are required to provide their home address to purchase a firearm through licensed dealers. Under tyrannical regimes, what is legal one day can be made illegal the next. It is not clear if the US is immune to this scenario; the jury is still out.

That would be like the president saying that the American economy has become too much of a problem, and deciding to force martial law upon the American people, and then having every single person that is registered politically as an independent, libertarian, or a constitutionalist (or even gun owners or any other group), rounded up and arrested because a particular activity was declared illegal by executive order.

The threat of such has already happened to a smaller degree, without the arrests (at least to my knowledge), when the Missouri

Information Analysis Center (MIAC) report was publicized through WikiLeaks. The report showed that folks who were described as Constitutionalists, libertarians, and Ron Paul supporters were considered potential domestic terrorists, simply for having a certain political view, or just by having a bumper sticker implying such a political view,[10] even though they never threatened anyone with anything. This is only one example. There are many others. The obliteration of civil rights and freedoms in the US has become quite serious, including frequent police abuses, and a great loss of privacy and economic freedom.

I could provide a very long list of individual rights and liberties that have been lost in the US. However, before I provide a summary of the most important ones, I want to make a very important point about liberty in America.

At some point in the history of the US, Americans became divided among themselves regarding what types of liberty or freedom are permissible and what types are not. Politicians and those who would benefit from keeping the American people distracted with internal division have only exacerbated and taken advantage of this situation by harping on so-called "wedge issues."[11]

The result is this: The so-called political "right" or "conservative" position is that economic liberty is acceptable and good, but personal and social liberty are not. And the so-called political "left" or "liberal" position is that personal and social liberty are acceptable and good, but economic liberty is not. As a person who has lived under true tyranny, where *all* types of liberty were non-existent and where the people were oppressed by tyrants on every level, I can say with certainty and authority that this is a absolutely a false division. This is a false choice or even a "straw man" fallacy used to distract the public and keep them busy arguing among themselves. There is only one liberty — one freedom — and the opposite of this, which is tyranny.

In America, over the last one hundred years in particular, both "sides" of this artificial divide have been very successful at *reducing or eliminating* the liberties they do not find acceptable, but neither side has been very successful in *increasing* the liberties that they do approve of. This has led the US down a gradual path of not only loss of many liberties and rights, but a massively expanded government presence and laws intruding into every aspect of our lives. In my assessment, and in the assessment of author Naomi Wolfe in her book *The End of America: Letter of Warning to a Young Patriot*,[12] and many other authors, analysts and activists, this situation has led us precariously close to tyranny in America. So a key first step to correcting the problems described herein is to move beyond this controlled false left/right political paradigm.

Who or why would people encourage internal division? Cui bono? Who benefits? In other words, follow the money, or follow the political power. I assure you that those who benefit from keeping the American people divided do not truly follow such artificial ideological divides. They focus on only getting power and money for themselves using whatever tactics they can, regardless of superficial ideology. If it is effective for such people to accomplish their ends using big businesses as tools, they will do so. Likewise, if it is effective for such people to accomplish their ends using big government, they will do so. And if they have to own and operate all the major media outlets to accomplish their goals, so be it. Their only ideology is power and money for themselves, and the means they use to accomplish that are fairly irrelevant to them.

Here is a *partial* list of liberties and rights lost over the course of the last century, with many of these changes occurring since I came to the US. This is far from a comprehensive list, but the following examples strike me as some of the more egregious examples of destruction of liberties and Constitutional rights. Note that some of these are federal, some state, and some are at the local or county level.

1. The right to free speech and public demonstration has been significantly restricted to "free speech zones." Free speech has also been greatly curtailed any time it involves a law enforcement officer being captured on video or audio engaging in unflattering behavior, when the law enforcement officer then tries to destroy the recording or prosecute or bully the person involved. In a country where citizens pride themselves on freedom, including the right to free speech and a free press, the US has fallen 13 places to number 46, right between Romania and Haiti in the World Press Freedom Index. This is a result of sacrificing freedoms in the name of so-called "national security needs," along with the prosecution of whistleblowers such as Private Bradley/Chelsea Manning, Julian Assange of WikiLeaks, and the continued hunt for Edward Snowden.[13]

Liberty Blitzkrieg comments: "As you might expect, the economic decline of a nation [America] into rule by a handful of corrupt oligarchs will have many other negative repercussions. One of these is a loss of civil rights and freedoms that many of us have taken for granted. Reporters Without Borders puts out their Press Freedom Index every year, and the 2014 ranking came out today. It was not a good showing for the USSA. Specifically, the US registered one of the steepest falls of all nations..."[14]

2. The right to defend oneself with firearms (and any other weapons consistent with self defense) has been greatly restricted. I realize that some people think that firearms are inherently "bad" because they are weapons. But this makes about as much sense as saying a hammer is inherently "bad." They are both just tools. Tools are not inherently good or evil, the morality is found within the use, and the user. I have never seen a gun get up and shoot someone by itself. As Colonial Jeff Cooper explained so well, "The rifle itself has no moral stature, since it has no will of its own. Naturally, it may be used by evil men for evil purposes, but there are more good men than evil, and while the latter cannot be persuaded to the path of righteousness by

propaganda, they can certainly be corrected by good men with rifles."[15]

Just as a hammer can be used to build someone a house or smash in their skull, likewise there are definitely morally good and legitimate reasons to own firearms. These legitimate reasons are not limited to merely hunting and target shooting. Self defense is certainly a legitimate reason, as only the most avowed pacifist would sit idly by while they are murdered, raped, assaulted, or robbed via force (and the assailant's force might not even involve a firearm). Firearms can be used to take a life, yes, but they can also be used to save lives, and they often do. It is "the rest of the story" that is rarely told by the propagandized mainstream media.

If statistics on the number of crimes committed with firearms are going to be used in policy debates, then *accurate* statistics should also be collected and used regarding the numbers of crimes *prevented* with firearms. The statistics that I have found on this have been debated by both those who advocate gun ownership and those who oppose gun ownership. Part of the problem here is that most of the people tasked with maintaining such statistics have an interest in advocating a particular position, most commonly biased toward disarming people. Qui bono? Who benefits? So, show me the real data. I don't trust any of the statistics on this topic, because everyone maintaining statistics has an interest in the outcome. There is no *objective* data. However, there *is* data supporting that the number of crimes prevented or stopped with firearms is many times greater than the number of crimes committed with them.

When looking at the available data, you'll see that home invasions are deterred approximately 498,000 times by Americans using firearms every year, and in 87% of these, the attacker used force or threatened force first, and in 91% of these self-defense incidents, not a single shot was fired.[16] As many as 60% of convicted felons admitted that if their target was known to be armed, they avoided that target.[17] Of note, of the attackers who ended up being gunshot victims, 71% had previous arrest records,[18] meaning that this wasn't their first rodeo in attempted crime.

Of course there is no discussion in the mainstream media about how many crimes have been prevented by the mere fact that someone was able to hold an attacker at gun point (or shoot if necessary) until police arrived, allowing for the arrest of said attacker and the prevention of future crimes this person may have planned on committing.[19] The problem with looking at mere statistics is, as mentioned earlier, that data can be skewed to make it appear to fit the analyst's pre-determined beliefs. This can be done simply by using language as a means to skew the data. One example is the use of the term "defensive gun use" in statistical data. Such terminology has been the subject of great controversy in statistical data.[20] Lastly, I found it interesting that a CDC study commissioned by the Obama administration found that firearms for self defense were an important crime deterrent.[21] Though, what you hear on the mainstream media is exactly the opposite of these results.

Regardless of how anyone makes the statistics appear, individuals have a human right to defend themselves against aggressors, and they have a right to own tools (weapons) that are consistent with defending life, liberty, and property. As far as I'm concerned, this RIGHT is non-negotiable. The practical matter is that police cannot be everywhere at all times, so it is ultimately the responsibility of individuals to protect themselves and their families. As the saying goes, "When seconds count, help is just minutes away." Or, in the case of rural residents, hours away.

There is another point that is equally true: if guns are made illegal, only criminals will have guns. This is self-evident logic, because by definition criminals do not follow laws, but law-abiding people do. It is certainly a valid goal to employ approaches that make it more difficult for *real* criminals to obtain firearms, but making it more difficult for law-abiding citizens to obtain and own firearms is not one of them.

There is even a philosophically legitimate place for the use of firearms as a *last resort* for throwing off political oppression and tyranny. For example, if the people of Chile had been permitted to own firearms in the 1970s, the atrocities that resulted from General Pinochet's military coup may have been prevented by an armed citizenry.[22] Yet our society has all but abandoned the philosophy of acquiring social change through methods such as physical rebellion, by changing the meaning of words like "revolution" to be less regarded and no longer recognized as they were when the Founding Fathers were around. We have turned into a culture where self-defense is correlated with violence, making self-defense immoral.[23] This is how the Polish culture still looks at guns to this day, and sadly, many Americans are starting to follow such a mindset as well.

Even Gandhi, who most consider a pacifist, accepted the potential for the use of force when he wrote, "He who cannot protect himself or his nearest and dearest or their honour by non-violently facing death, may and ought to do so by violently dealing with an oppressor."[24]

Historically, governments of free societies not only permit but encourage firearm (or weapon) ownership, and only tyrannical, oppressive, criminal governments fear and prohibit the ownership of firearms by law-abiding citizens. What does that say about most governments around the world today? Historically, firearms have been a great equalizer between those who have power and those who do not. Therefore, groups or individuals who advocate disarming other law-abiding people (note that I did say *"law-abiding,"* not real criminals), at best have a complete lack of understanding of the importance of firearms in the hands of average citizens in maintaining free societies, and at worst only do so because the former wants to have power over the latter. All of the other alleged justifications for "safety" and "crime prevention" are either ignorance based in fear or lies and excuses to disguise the *true* intent of disarming people: *to have coercive power over them — that is all.* History shows us that people who can't fight to defend themselves and their rights are frequently turned into slaves.

222

3. The Fourth Amendment right to be secure from searches without a warrant is now completely gone. Government agents now routinely stop and search people, in vehicles or otherwise, without a warrant. Phone calls and internet communications are all monitored without a warrant by the NSA. After the 1970s, when it was discovered that the US government was abusing its eavesdropping abilities, the Foreign Intelligence Surveillance Act (FISA) was enacted into law, which made such abuse a criminal offense.[25] The requirement of FISA court oversight is now used as a justification for allowing the continued spying on unknowing Americans. In practice, those are a joke and provide no limitation on electronic surveillance. An individual can't even challenge a FISA court ruling without significant evidence that their communications have indeed been under surveillance.[26]

It seems that what goes on behind the scenes often only comes to light when organizations intent on maintaining freedom perform due diligence in acquiring information through use of methods such as the Freedom of Information Act. When the American Civil Liberties Union (ACLU) reviewed a recent release of government documents, they discovered that the NSA has not been in compliance with court orders, including the NSA staff abusing powers and violating court mandated limits on spying on innocent people, such as their love interests. That's only one of the issues that has been reported. There are countless other reports of misuse/abuse, not to mention the events that have not been reported, and the fact that the FISA court has no way to determine who follows orders and who does not. Thus, the inadequacy of FISA courts as an oversight institution is clear.[27] The thought that an ex of mine who now works for the NSA may spy on all of my emails and phone conversations between my spouse and me makes my stomach churn.

Unfortunately, the ACLU and other advocacy groups have not been fully successful in acquiring all of the information needed to determine if there is a continued increasing threat to individual rights. Regardless of the number of requests to Congress that had been made by these advocacy groups, FISA courts' activities, including hearings and decisions, have been and continue to be conducted in the utmost secrecy.[28]

Clearly our Federal Government has no transparency. How can the American people claim they are free when they are spied on constantly, have little power to fight the wrongs done to them, and worse yet, have few options to even find out if wrongs have been done to them? Any desire by the American people to fight such an oppressive system has been ignored by their *public servants*, known as the Supreme Court. Monitoring and recording of telephone metadata (who called who and when) began with restrictions requiring warrants. For practical purposes, these have been bypassed by the NSA, ignoring the Constitutional rights of the people. And although the telephone metadata program was supposedly shut down by the Obama administration, it continues to collect massive amounts of data as justified by the USA Patriot Act.[29]

How many applications for searches did FISA deny? Apparently out of 1,789 electronic search requests, not a single one was denied.[30] Not a one: zero. All approved. Still trust FISA to keep the government's surveillance program in check? I don't.

Lastly, the Fourth Amendment has been completely thrown out any time the Transportations Security Administration (TSA) is involved, such as in airports. The naked body scanners and molestations that pass for searches do not truly improve security, they merely create the illusion of security while acclimating the populace to acquiescing completely to those who claim to have "authority." A simple search on the internet will reveal many documented cases of abuse by the TSA.

5. People are being deprived of property without due process of law through Racketeer Influenced and Corrupt Organizations Act (RICO) laws and other similar Asset Forfeiture laws. RICO, supposedly enacted

to be able to prosecute those who didn't commit a crime directly but ordered someone else to do it for them[31] (often used in illegal drug cases), is greatly abused in this country. There are various cases of innocent people having their assets seized ("forfeited") for crimes they did not commit, such as the case of Laura Dutton. She was stopped in the city of Memphis and was arrested as a result of police finding a large amount of cash in her purse after a drug dog gave a signal for drugs. Although no drugs were found, and Dutton's family confirmed a property sale earlier that day, Dutton was still arrested and her cash seized.[32] Or the case of Jennifer Boatright, who was threatened with charges of child endangerment simply because she had a large amount of cash in her center console while driving with her family to purchase a new car. She willingly signed an agreement to give up the cash after being accused of being a drug distributor even though no drugs were found.[33]

In any criminal cases involving illegal drugs, RICO, and asset forfeiture, people are often "guilty until proven innocent" with regards to seized property. This turns our entire justice system upside down. In our Common Law based justice system, people are *supposed to be* considered innocent until proven guilty, but RICO makes them guilty until proven innocent. In such cases, your assets are stolen until you can prove they are legitimate. What is even worse is that in many of these cases the assets are kept and used by the agency that seizes them, thus creating an incentive to continue this immoral and illegal practice.[34]

What is referred to as "civil forfeiture" has turned into a nice profit for various corrupt police agencies right here in the good 'ol US of A. "Civil forfeiture" allows for money to be seized without a court-ordered warrant. Furthermore, "interdiction" allows for other assets such as cars, boats, and cash to be confiscated without any proof that the person who likely worked hard all their life to acquire these assets even committed any crime. They then must spend thousands of dollars on attorney fees to try to get their money back, or give up all hope and move on. More importantly, 80% of the money seized goes right back to the agency that seized that money.[35] What a bonus one might receive for busting a particularly rich individual and seizing their assets without justification, all under RICO law.

An additional problem with asset forfeiture laws is that they result in a massive loss of financial privacy and they turn banks into spies for the federal government. Under these laws, banks are required to file "Suspicious Activity Reports" or "SARs" for most transactions involving cash over a few thousand dollars.[36] Thus, the Federal Government knows about all your financial transactions, even those you would rather be kept private.

6. On the topic of the war on drugs, in the form of the Drug Enforcement Administration (DEA), we now have prohibition for everything *except* alcohol and tobacco, and we have an entire agency dedicated to enforcing laws surrounding those: the Bureau of Alcohol, Tobacco, Firearms and Explosives (ATF, BATF, or BATFE).

There are many reasons the war on drugs is unworkable. I will only name three: practical considerations, economics, and morality.

From a practical perspective, the policy doesn't work. Federal, state, and local governments have been fighting this war for decades at a cost of many billions of dollars, yet drugs are still on the street, and people still want them. This is just as it was under alcohol prohibition, and we all know *that* worked out so well. At least the criminals thought so, because it raised the price of their product and made it much more profitable for them.

From an economic standpoint, the law enforcement cost is bankrupting governments at all levels. I would argue a person can not truly advocate economic freedom if he or she accepts taxing and spending huge amounts of money to fund the micromanaging of what people put into their bodies. The huge financial and budgetary demands necessary to implement such control is incompatible with economic freedom.

From a moral perspective, if people were truly free in America it would be acknowledged that people own their own bodies and can put in them what they choose. The problem with accepting the principle that the government has the right to dictate what we may or may not put into our bodies is that the premise or precedent then has no boundaries. Next they will dictate which medical drugs we put into our bodies, and then they will dictate which nutritional supplements and even food we may put into our bodies. (More on those items later.) Once the principle has been accepted that it is the role of government to dictate what we put into our bodies, there is no end to it, and ultimately they *own* our bodies. As a result, America abolished slavery in name only as apparently, the government owns our bodies. Instead of freedom to choose what is best for our own health, we have accepted a theme of allowing only those with special privilege and monopoly status to be granted "licenses" to dispense all medications.

7. On the related topic of health care, people were once free to choose whatever health care they liked. Today, people have their health care choices dictated and mandated under threat of "taxation." Simply put, people who make their own healthcare choices outside of government control will likely be coerced for non-compliance, and in certain cases may even face arrest.

8. There was no federal income tax prior to 1913, and people actually owned the products of their own labor. And up until that time the Federal Government managed to function just fine without it.[37-38]

The income tax today makes everyone a partial slave by requiring a certain percentage of one's labor be paid in taxes, often for services that people would not voluntarily pay for. Again, this is abolishing slavery in name only. The Sixteenth Amendment, which is the amendment used to authorize the collection of taxes based on an individual's income, fundamentally conflicts with the Thirteenth Amendment in my opinion. The Thirteenth Amendment is the amendment that theoretically abolished slavery, by the way.

9. Not only are you a slave, but in many states your children are as well, with mandatory public education requirements and vaccination requirements being forced upon them. Home schooling or private schooling is not permitted in some locales.

10. Recent IRS targeting of particular groups and individuals that just happen to be pro-liberty is another example of how freedoms are eroding away. In a free country, individuals should be free to form groups that educate the public about matters that are important, but instead, political groups with certain themes such as the Tea Party and Occupy movement groups are targeted.[39] At the time of this writing, the Obama administration still refuses to release over five hundred records in connection to the IRS targeting of these groups.[40] This is reminiscent of how the communist Polish government would target political dissidents and have no transparency.

11. The US now has the highest per capita prison population in the world. That means that the percentage of people (but not the absolute number) in prison is higher in the US than any other country. The prison population stands at seven hundred and seven prisoners per one hundred thousand people, which does not include inmates that are held in US territories, military facilities, US Marshal Service contracted facilities, juvenile, or Indian country facilities.[41] As a continent, America only has five percent of the world's population, and yet, has the highest prison population (with China being second, and Russia's number trailing only slightly behind). This is a result of incarceration for smaller

crimes for which many other countries would not place someone in prison, such as personal drug use, or something as desperate as writing a bad check, and also as a result of longer punishment times than many other nations.[42]

A country with that high of a percentage of people in prison does not indicate a country that values freedom, liberty, and individual rights. Maintaining such a large prison population is not compatible with a "free" society. It is true that having a large population of people living in poverty can lead to real crime. But instead of creating a prosperous environment to help Americans from impoverished backgrounds, we lock them up, mostly on nonviolent charges, and fail to offer any type of rehabilitation.[43]

Keeping that many people in prison is also a *very* expensive burden for taxpayers to bear. Perhaps the "land of the free" has way too many unnecessary laws? Perhaps the very idea of a "victimless crime" is oxymoronic? Or just plain moronic? It seems to me that the very definition of a "crime" indicates the involvement of a "victim" — someone who is actually harmed by the activity in question. Victimless crime inmates now constitute *86 percent* of the federal prison population,[44-45] with some prisons so overcrowded that they are running at 155 percent of capacity.[46]

Yet, when one of the "privileged elitists" commits a *real* crime, he or she not only doesn't go to prison, but suffers no repercussions at all. One example is Timothy Geithner, who owed over $34,000 in taxes from early 2001. Rather than going to jail, he was sworn in as Secretary of the Treasury.[47] In contrast, a non-privileged non-elitist, such as Wesley Snipes, serves three years in prison on misdemeanor charges of failing to file taxes.[48] So Mr. Geithner gets rewarded with a cushy job where he gets to write bailout checks for his kind, while Mr. Snipes serves time.

Let's look at another example of the privileged class. Jon Corzine (a former New Jersey Senator and New Jersey governor[49]) worked as CEO for Goldman Sachs, then as CEO of MF Global. When $1.6 billion of customer money went "missing" as a result of Mr. Corrine betting customers' money on European sovereign debt, he was not sentenced. Instead, he merely had to testify before Congress that he was "really sorry," and he was off the hook without any criminal consequences.[50-51] In this case it is important to note that MF Global did not own this money, nor did it even have authorization from its customers to use their money in this way. In contrast, look at Bernie Madoff, who was busted for operating a Ponzi scheme. He was not one of the privileged class, so he is now serving time.[52] Worse yet, Congress changed laws so that certain privileged groups (including members of Congress) can be exempt from certain insider trading rules while ordinary people are not,[53] and would serve jail time for insider trading, unlike those who are exempt.

If unfair and unequal punishment weren't enough, I haven't even covered the topic of the potential problems of the growth of private, for-profit prisons, and the "prison industrial complex." I was shocked to learn that a private prison system exists in the US. Basically, a private industry builds a prison or takes over an existing one, and then the government, which claims the right to imprison people, pays the private industry a per diem per prisoner[54] — all with taxpayer dollars. It is important to keep in mind that incentives almost always matter. So if there is an incentive to have *more* people in prison, then it is likely that more people will end up in prison. For-profit prisons create that incentive, as they typically make money based on the number of prisoners they house. This is absolutely the wrong incentive to create for prisons. Our goal should be to keep people *out* of prison, not to try to get more people placed *in* prison! But that's not all. The prison-industrial complex, which is a complex of private prison companies along with sellers of goods that are supplied to those prisons such as food, surveillance technology and medical supplies, have their own lobby groups, and are dependent on the expansion of the prison population.[55] The mere fact that a "prison-industrial complex" exists is problematic.

These prisons hold a disproportionate amount of people of color (blacks and Hispanics).[56] The final piece to this monstrosity is that the inmates are basically used as slave labor, paid only pennies for their work, to the benefit of corporations and investors on Wall Street. This inmate labor force then displaces and replaces higher cost, law abiding employees.[57] This prison labor force is perhaps as big of a threat to the law abiding American labor force as the outsourcing of labor to third world countries. As prisoners, these people have no rights to equal pay, choice of work, or even workers' compensation for injuries.[58] If this isn't a form of slave labor, I don't know what is. And it doesn't end there: When their sentencing is over, they leave the prisons with a record, no chance at a decent paying career, and no faith in America. Chances are, they will repeat their crimes for three hots and a cot. Thus, a vicious cycle of the well-connected elitists enslaving the poor and disadvantaged is perpetuated.

12. The right to trial by jury and being properly charged with a crime has been greatly diminished since the "war on terror" began. In some cases, this has started to border on "disappearing" people without proper charges or public trial.

In addition, the true nature and power of the jury has also been obscured to the American people. In criminal courts today, judges typically instruct jurors that they are solely "finders of fact" whose job it is to assess the accuracy and truthfulness of the facts presented, and then pass a judgment of guilt or innocence based upon those facts. However, there is another very important and legitimate role of a jury based in Common Law tradition, and that is to be a judge of the law itself, which is known as jury nullification. This means that if a jury finds a particular law to be unjust, immoral, or for some other reason unacceptable, they have the right to refuse to find the defendant guilty, even if the facts in the case support that ruling.[59] The organization known as the Fully Informed Jury Association provides a wealth of additional resources and information about jury nullification.[60]

This latter function has been intentionally and dishonestly hidden from the American people by a corrupt judiciary and court system. The US Founding Fathers absolutely intended for jurors to assess both the facts of a case AND the law itself when participating in a jury. They thought that trial by an informed jury was another important check on tyranny and an oppressive government. And they were right. Jury nullification is one of the last lines of defense against tyrannical and unjust laws perpetuated by an out-of-control and unresponsive legislature. Jury nullification also upholds the principle that the *people* are the ultimate *sovereigns* and ultimate decision makers when it comes to the validity of laws, rather than *any* court judge.

13. People used to be free to prepare for their own retirement, rather than being forced by law to pay into what has ultimately been turned into the giant Ponzi scheme known as "Social Security." Note that Social Security was originally designed to be a "trust" fund where the funds were kept separate from the general Federal Treasury. Politicians found it convenient to change this so they could confiscate those funds to be used for their own political ends.

It used to be that Social Security was intended to be enough to cover a retiree's expenses. However, we all know that a Social Security pension is often not enough to survive on. So additional retirement accounts, such as 401(k)s, have been an option to supplement one's retirement income. However, that will now be changing as well. The current administration has announced a "solution", which will probably be something that forces owners of American retirement accounts (such as 401(k)s and IRAs) to buy a certain amount of Federal Treasury bonds.[61-62]

This same measure was used in 2008 in Argentina when private pension assets were exchanged for government debt to improve the government's balance sheet. Similarly in 2013, Cypriots learned that their government was confiscating a portion of their savings to bail out the banks,[63-64] and shortly after, Poland's government announced that private pensions will be exchanged for government bonds over the next ten years to reduce their debt.[65-66]

I don't doubt that Americans could suffer the same fate by being forced to hold US Treasury bonds as a major part of their 401(k) or IRA holdings. There have already been discussions about this by federal politicians,[67] and America has quite the deficit to manage. The only money left is in the investment and retirement accounts of the American people.

14. Individual real property rights have been greatly curtailed regarding what property, *ahem*, "owners" can do with their property. County governments dictate how the property can be used based on "zoning" laws. The federal and state governments also dictate how real property can be used based on "environmental" laws. Both of the previous limitations are imposed without *just compensation* as mandated by the Fifth Amendment and eminent domain law. To clarify, I do not advocate environmental destruction, or irresponsibility toward the environment: far from it. However, I am opposed to using the environment as an *excuse* or justification for instituting programs of oppression and destroying property rights, particularly when the property is being put to legitimate productive use, and particularly when it involves individual (as opposed to large corporate) land owners. Unfortunately, in America today, these adverse applications of environmental laws are more common than actually protecting the environment. (It is worth noting that certain politically well-connected groups and corporate organizations manage to be exempt from such laws when they often cause far more environmental damage than any single individual property owner ever could.) While in the past perhaps

not enough attention was paid to environmental mindfulness, today the pendulum has swung too far in the other direction and environmental regulations are being used to oppress people and promote an agenda, rather than to actually protect the environment. Local county governments also act as though they own all real property, and the owners merely "rent" it by paying property taxes. In a free society, if people truly valued the services provided, they would be willing to pay for them voluntarily rather than being subject to this type of extortion.

15. Several US presidents have authorized (and the US military is engaging in) unconstitutional wars, repeatedly, without congressional authorization (proper declarations of war). As a US veteran myself, I have great respect for our US military personnel. However, I do think that our US military is being abused in terms of it being used for purposes for which it was never intended, and for which it should not be used. The purpose of the US military should not be to achieve foreign-policy goals, as Henry Kissinger would suggest,[68] but rather to defend the US and the American people from foreign aggressors. Period. My heart goes out to our military personnel.

16. Current judicial interpretations have turned the Constitution and the Tenth Amendment upside down in modern practice. The intent of the authors of the Constitution was to list all the powers that were *permitted* to the Federal Government, not to list what was *prohibited* to it. All powers not specifically described in the Constitution were *assumed to be prohibited* to the Federal Government and were specifically left to the state governments and the people, as described in the Tenth Amendment. However, in modern practice, this has been completely turned upside down. In our modern time, the legal interpretation is that if it is not explicitly *prohibited* in the Constitution, then the Federal Government is *permitted* to engage in the activity. This interpretation has allowed for a massive expansion of unconstitutional

and illegal overreach by the Federal Government, getting involved in many activities for which it was never granted any authority. I would bet that if federal politicians had to cite in their bills what part of the Constitution the authority for their bill relies upon, they would not be able to do so, as a significant percentage of the activities of the Federal Government has no authorization in the Constitution.

If the US Constitution is the supposed *social contract* by which we live in the US and from which the US Federal Government derives its authority, then the Federal Government is in breach of contract by greatly exceeding its legitimate authority (more on this shortly).

As a final component of this list, I am well aware that women and "minorities" were discriminated against throughout American history, and did not necessarily legally have all the same rights and liberties as others. The solution to that was to grant those rights and liberties to both women and minorities equally, not to strip everyone of their rights and liberties as has been done.

Similar to inverting the intended meaning and practice of the Tenth Amendment as described above, the role of the US citizen has also been turned upside down in modern practice. The intent of the US Founding Fathers was that individual citizens were the sovereigns, meaning the primary holder of power, and the federal and state governments were merely "public servants," meaning that they serve the sovereign citizens. Citizens only delegated certain authority to the governments for the purpose of protecting certain Natural Rights. This was a significant contrast to the monarchies that had existed up to that point, where the citizens were basically the property of the supposed "royalty." Today, these roles have in practice been reversed again. Politicians, bureaucrats, and other similar power-hungry megalomaniacs have done their best to turn these roles completely around, so that in practice our country is now operated more like a monarchy where the mentioned elitist politicians, bureaucrats, oligarchs, and bankers are the ruling "royalty" class, and the people, the citizens, now serve *them*. Rather than being "public servants" the public is now serving the "ruling class." I cannot put into words how disgusting, how upside down, and how philosophically and morally wrong this is.

Politically, socially, and economically, we have regressed in practice back to what is almost monarchic oppression. We have regressed back to the very practices that the US Founding Fathers rebelled against in the first place. The only reason that this has occurred is because we the people — we the sovereign citizens — have relinquished our rights and our liberties. We have handed over our political power to politicians and bureaucrats, put them on pedestals, and turned them into "kings and queens" who we expect to act like rulers instead of servants. So they do.

"Kings are not born; they are made, by a universal hallucination."

-George Bernard Shaw

One of the first steps to reclaiming our rights and liberties is to realize that we the people are the ones with the rights and freedoms, and that the reason we lost them is because we gave them away. The first step to getting back our rights and liberties in practice is to reclaim them philosophically, and to accept responsibility that we allowed this inversion of roles to occur. Remember: the PEOPLE are the sovereigns, and the representatives of the state are merely SERVANTS of the people. When people in government stop acting like servants and start trying to act like "masters," that is a sign that things have gone very wrong, and we need to either replace or get rid of those people, or that government.

It is also important to realize that "government" is nothing more than a representative of the people. Individuals have certain Natural

Rights, and they delegate some of that authority to government to carry out certain beneficial functions for them. This is one of the few reasons governments have any authority at all. The only "rights" the government has are those delegated to it by the people. And because those "rights" come from the people, the government does not in theory, and should not in practice, have any more or any different rights than individual people do. For example, as an individual, I do not have the "right" to steal from people at gun point. Why then do people consider it perfectly normal and acceptable that theft at gunpoint is committed in the name of "government"? In other words, if it's not acceptable for an individual to do x, then neither is it acceptable for "government" to do x, because the government is merely a representative of the people. Government has no rights that individuals do not. Any assertions that governments have rights that individuals do not are being made by either someone who is confused, ignorant, or un-educated, or is a tyrant who is trying to deceive, control, and oppress you.

As far as I can tell there are only a few possible reasons or justifications why government has any "authority" whatsoever. They are:

1. We the people consent to the state having authority, because we delegate some of our authority or our sovereignty to the state to carry out certain functions for us.

2. The supposed (so-called) "social contract" theory, which may or may not have validity, depending on how it is applied. More often that not this theory is applied in a way that is not valid. For a Common Law contract to be valid it must be voluntary and explicit, rather than coerced or implicit, and can not be changed on a whim, as politicians and bureaucrats tend to do. So the arguments for legitimate authority via social contract theory are certainly suspect.

3. "Political power grows out of the barrel of a gun," as China's Mao said,[69] meaning the government has authority because it is best capable of using violence or force against people. In reality this is no different than the mafia, and is certainly not a *legitimate* reason for having any "authority."

4. People are brainwashed into believing government has authority.

So if we withdraw our consent from the government/state, then number one no longer applies. And if number two is suspect or dubious, then what is left?

Since I have been writing quite a bit about "laws" it does seem appropriate to briefly discuss and define exactly what a "law" is. I realize that most people have certain concepts of what laws are, but in the context of what I have written thus far it is important to make certain to clarify why one's definition of "laws" are important. Unless I am referring to Common Law, when I refer to the word throughout this book, a "law" is a particular behavior that is either prohibited or a particular behavior that is required, either by a government or by a group of people comprising a "society" or "community." That prohibition of action or requirement of action *must be enforced with the use of violence or force*. The first part of this definition is usually clearly understood. For example, people are prohibited from committing murder and are required to pay taxes. But it is the second part of this definition that most people don't give too much thought. If a law is not enforced by violence or force, then it is nothing more than a social norm, much like saying "excuse me" if you bump into someone. There is no requirement to say "excuse me" because there is no enforcement. Force or violence is required for a law to actually be a law, because if someone simply ignores that behavior, such as not paying taxes, then there is nothing to make them do so; no consequences or repercussions. Therefore, it is important to realize that all "laws" are really descriptions of when it is acceptable to use violence. This is important. Laws are not guidelines, they are behaviors enforced by violence. If you don't want violence to be used, then you need to find another way to change people's behaviors, such as through persuasion, courtesy, and social norms.

Since laws are generally enforced by the police, or by the government or state, what this means in practice is that laws are descriptions of when it is acceptable for the state to use violence against individuals related to some particular behavior. So keep that in mind whenever someone says "There ought to be a law about..." What they are really saying is "The state ought to use violence in this situation." Since the state is theoretically a representative of the people, if you want to propose a new law, a good guideline to follow is this: Would you personally be willing to use violence to enforce this law? Because each time a law is created representing you, that is exactly what is happening through the intermediary of the state. People in government, or "the state," usually only know how to accomplish things through violence. That is why to the government everything is a "war on [fill in the blank]." Take, for example, the "war on poverty," which to me sounds like the government wants to kill all poor people. So is this government violence really the best way to approach solving most problems?

Now follow this logic: Is a society more or less civilized when it uses more violence? Most people would say more violence results in a less civilized society, and less violence in a more civilized society. We just previously established that laws are rules about when it is acceptable to use violence. And now we have established that a less violent society is a more civilized one. So here is a question to ponder: Do more laws (acceptable uses of violence) make for a more or less civilized society?

Returning to a theme from the beginning of this chapter, in terms of turning otherwise law abiding citizens into "criminals" through absurd "laws," another scenario to consider is during times when "resource allocation" (AKA rationing) goes into effect (such as in Communist Poland), and people are told how much food they may buy, or how much energy they may use. If there were to be a time in the US, such as during an economic collapse, or natural disaster, where resources may become even temporarily scarce, my friends and co-workers may find themselves in a position where they might have to break the law in order to have enough to eat, or to keep their homes warm. At that point, it will be too late, as the surveillance state will already be fully operational and they will not be able to get away from it. Even though they were not breaking any laws before the disaster because they were all good citizens, they may be breaking laws by simply trying to acquire enough food to feed their families during or after a disaster.

Unfortunately, people who have never experienced a government telling them what to do with their resources don't understand the necessary consequences of socialism. A controlled economy necessarily means having government agents dictating (via force) what you may do with "your" resources. My impression from living in the US for almost thirty years is that Americans do not really understand what hard tyranny is like, and do not perceive or recognize soft tyranny when it is right in front of their faces.

Currently in America, one of the few groups of people who are starting to truly understand this are farmers and ranchers who are being told by the federal Environmental Protection Agency (EPA), and the state equivalents, what they may or may not do with "their" land. Farmers have discovered that they are fighting for water against the EPA, and fear that these regulations are turning a conservation effort into a regulatory effort.[70] This is not a new battle; the water wars have been ongoing for quite a while. A huge loss to approximately 1,400 canal irrigated family farms occurred in April of 2001 in Southern Oregon, when the Endangered Species Act (ESA) was used as an excuse (there was only dubious evidence that the sucker fish were affected) and resulted in the Bureau of Reclamation (BOR) stopping water from reaching the family farms and ranches. The same ESA type of excuse was used to cut off water to other farmers in California, Colorado, Idaho, Arizona and others, including Montana.[71-72] No water means the crops dry up.[73] The economic consequences to such crop failure is often detrimental to small family businesses. Not to mention that, not paying the land owners eminent domain for the loss of their land use violates the Constitutional Fifth Amendment's "just compensation" clause.

But the water is not the only issue. EPA is overreaching its authority by attempting to regulate what land a land owner may continue to use, what land they must retire, and how they can use their land including how much fertilizer can be applied.[74] In Wyoming a man was fined $75,000 by the EPA for building a pond on his own property.[75] Back in Oregon, a man was fined over $1,500 and sentenced to thirty days in jail for collecting rain water on his property.[76]

When things like collecting roof rain water in a rain barrel or building a pond in your backyard become questionable under the law, one tends to wonder how far the EPA will go in oppressing people. Apparently, so far that even the mainstream media takes notice. I was surprised to read about the EPA's secret maps that were intended as a blueprint for controlling all waterways, including those on private land, and all under the auspice of "the clean water act."[77]

These instances of the EPA using "protection acts" to take people's rights away on their own land are just a few examples of dictatorial activity, but in reality, there are so many that it would be impossible to list them all.

Many doubt that our own American government would ever restrict what people can do in such a manner, but as the headlines reveal, agencies such as the EPA have recently been demonstrating significant overreach on residents, especially with the water regulation. Meanwhile, golf courses are not restricted on water usage, especially golf courses that politicians use. President Obama took a flight to California to discuss the water crisis, only to turn around and play golf on a very luscious green golf course, where the one hundred and twenty-four golf courses consume about 17 percent of the water.[78] And even in cases where lawsuits are brought fourth against ridiculous amounts of golf course water usage, such as the case in Washington State University (WSU) and their golf course that used nearly 45 million gallons of water a year, somehow the court ruled in favor of the golf course.[79] One might wonder if any interest groups were involved in this case, or if the judge himself perhaps enjoyed playing golf.

So golf courses can use as much water as they want, so that our kings and queens may play golf after working so hard curtailing *our* access to water. Meanwhile, the EPA has the authority to arbitrarily declare any land they so choose as wetlands under the clean water act,[80-81] making it clear that *they believe* we the people have no right to water, even if it's on our own private property.

The EPA apparently chooses which science fits them best, and uses that to steal land from private land owners based on this supposed "data." When the EPA requested jurisdiction over "intermittent, seasonal and rain-dependent" public *and* private streams, this was referred to as the biggest land grab.[82] And yet so far, the people are providing very little pushback to stop these abuses. I suspect this may change in the near future.

While not exactly the same scenario, a rancher did get a little reprieve when the Cliven Bundy Ranch near Bunkerville, Nevada, was threatened by the Bureau of Land Management (BLM). There was a standoff as many people, including members of Oath Keepers, had enough. They chose to drop everything to show up at the Bundy Ranch and help Mr. Bundy get his cattle back by facing the armed BLM personnel face to face. It was fortunate that no shots were fired, and this was a standoff like no other.[83]

But after the incident was over, the mainstream media once again played their propaganda card. They dishonestly made Mr. Bundy seem racist and claimed this was all about not paying grazing fees[84] in an attempt to try to discredit his rights and actions in response to their attempted land grab, even though the BLM would not back up their assertions that Bundy owed what they claimed.[85] The full video was released of what Bundy was stating, which was taken out of context to smear his image and make him sound like a racist.[86] None of the truth made it to the mainstream media. It was thanks to the independent uncensored media that this information was available to us.

Again, while most people were mesmerized by the lies, I again was astounded by the unbelievable blatant propaganda on the mainstream (state/corporate controlled) news that was intentionally trying to divide people against each other. Equally amazing about this situation was how quickly a Wikipedia page went up on this very topic that happens to be very one sided and also tries to make Mr. Bundy out to be a racist. There is no mention that the BLM never upheld their side of the contract and did not maintain the fences on the land as they were supposed to. This was what Mr. Bundy's grazing fees were supposed to pay for, and thus why Mr. Bundy refused to pay these fees, as he paid for the fence maintenance himself. Like most misquotes, his "racist comments" were taken completely out of context.

So while the news implies that Mr. Bundy doesn't have rights to range his cattle on BLM land in Nevada, Mr. Bundy states he doesn't recognize the US government as having rights to the Nevada land. The person who is correct is Mr. Bundy: Article I, Section 8, Clause 17, of the Constitution clearly states: "To exercise exclusive legislation in all cases whatsoever, over such district (not exceeding ten miles square) as may, by cession of particular states, and the acceptance of Congress, become the seat of the government of the United States, and to exercise like authority over all places purchased by the consent of the legislature of the state in which the same shall be for the erection of forts, magazines, arsenals, dockyards, and other needful buildings."[87] It is clear that the

US Founding Fathers and the US Constitution never intended for the US Federal Government to maintain massive amounts of land *within* the individual states.

That land was intended to be utilized or dispensed as the citizens of each individual state thought best. The massive amount of land held by the US Federal Government could be seen as in violation of the US Constitution. Some legal scholars would argue that Article 4, Section 3, Clause 2 gives the US Federal Government this authority, but the counterargument is that is an incorrect interpretation. This section actually states: "The Congress shall have Power to dispose of and make all needful Rules and Regulations respecting the Territory or other Property belonging to the United States; and nothing in this Constitution shall be so construed as to Prejudice any Claims of the United States, or of any particular State."[88] A common sense reading of this section does not seem to construe that the US Federal Government should retain ownership of large percentages of land in some States. Once again, we see gradualism in action, as most Americans grow up used to the idea that the US Federal Government owns vast amount of land within various individual states.

Much of this may relate back to policies laid out in Agenda 21. Agenda 21 is a three hundred-page document written for the United Nations (UN), as a non-binding, *theoretically* voluntary plan of action related to sustainable development.[89] This sustainability agenda has very detailed definitions and plans for local communities and development, which the UN re-named as "smart growth"[90] to make it more palatable for unsuspecting Americans. But what these "smart growth" plans enable includes the ability to change zoning laws, regulations to reduce property values, and other actions that avoid the eminent domain clause.[91] All under the guise of promoting "sustainable" land use, providing humans with shelter, better infrastructure for water and sanitation, better transport systems and construction systems, and many more.[92] But what all this so-called "sustainable development" would require is governmental control of all land, water, and all other resources to achieve its goals.[93-94] According to the Agenda 21 documents, that would mean that for everyone to have basic shelter, no one would be able to own their own residency or property — except the well-connected elitists, of course. Despite all the feel-good propaganda and rhetoric, this "agenda" would in practice essentially end ALL private property rights. I would say that is a pretty big deal, and people should be very clearly informed of the true consequences Agenda 21 any time and any place these policies are implemented, particularly when they are introduced under some alternative feel-good marketing nomenclature. Yet establishment-controlled media mouthpieces claim that this is no big deal and conceal both the true intent and the true consequences of these oppressive policies.

If land grabbing and water rights theft weren't issue enough, we also have to deal with insane applications of the Clean Air Act by the EPA. The EPA is systematically targeting homeowners who heat their homes with wood stoves with the alleged rationale that it will improve so-called "public health" by reducing particulate emissions. There are many flaws with this rationale. It would take much more space in this book than I would like to dedicate to this topic to adequately dissect the flaws of the EPA's current position on wood stoves. I will simply point out some basic facts. First, most homes that are heated by wood are in rural areas where population density is low, there are few people that are affected, and there is plenty of unpolluted air. In addition, particles larger than 50 micrometers (PM 50) tend to settle out of the air, while those smaller than 50 micrometers but bigger than 10 micrometers are too large to reach the respiratory tract. Particulate matter greater than 10 micrometers is filtered through the nose and throat without ever reaching the lungs. The EPA is allegedly concerned more about particles less than 10 micrometers, called PM 10, because of their ability to surpass the nose and throat and reach the lungs. PM smaller than 2.5

micrometers, called fine particles or PM 2.5, are of significant concern because they can penetrate deeper into the lungs and even get absorbed into the blood stream. The major sources of these particles are from dust roads, wood stoves, gases emitted from power plants, industrial facilities, automobiles, and commercial trucks.[95]

The EPA is making many brands and models of wood stoves "illegal" because of these emissions requirements, and is requiring homeowners to purchase newer "certified" stoves. The first problem with this is that there are several sources of these pollutants other than wood stoves, and the percentage of these pollutants that wood stoves contribute is relatively low. The next problem is that wood stove use reduces the need for power plant production (energy for heat), and by requiring people to switch from wood to other forms of heat they are increasing power plant demands. None of this even takes into consideration the economics or cost factors, which should also be considered. However, the biggest problem with this is that the new "certified" stoves do not eliminate the problem of the fine particulates (PM 2.5) that are the greatest health concern, they only marginally reduce it. Further, if you try to sell your home, and your wood stove is not "certified" then you must remove it, even if it is a brand new energy efficient stove. If it's not "certified" it's out. So either EPA officials have been bribed by executives from companies that make the "certified" wood stoves, or they are trying to eliminate the use of wood stoves altogether. The EPA continues to make wood stove pollution standards ever stricter, to the point that it will eventually become impossible to legally use wood stoves at all.[96]

Wood stoves provide an independent, decentralized source of heat and energy. They also provide a backup redundant source of heat during emergencies such as power grid outages, weather related emergencies, widespread economic turmoil, or even personal financial struggles. No individual or even small community can run their own fossil fuel power plant, so these are a dream for those who like centralized control, because they require large-scale centralization to function. While "green" energy alternatives like solar and wind power are great for providing an independent source of electricity, they are too cost prohibitive (at this time) to use for heating homes. Only a relatively small percentage of the population uses wood stoves for heat, mostly people in rural areas who are more independent from the rest of the socio-economic-political collective. It would normally strike me as an irrational fetish for the EPA to be so viciously focused on wood stoves if I hadn't experienced for myself (in communist Poland) how tyrannical governments rabidly hate anything that provides people with more independence from their collectivist and centralized control grid. Since the EPA's requirements regarding wood stoves provides only marginal improvement in pollution, it definitely seems to me a desperate attempt to control people who would rather remain independent. This reminds me of the centralized heating systems found in the Polish apartment buildings that rarely heated the flats, because all the coal had been shipped off to benefit others. This reminds me of oppression.

Yet, no one considers the fact that almost all county and state roads are being sprayed with toxic herbicides such as glyphosate to control weeds.[97] Simply perform an internet search for "noxious weed laws," your county or state, and "herbicide" and you will likely find that this is true. Since the EPA is so concerned about pollution, surely they must be concerned about the environmental impact from that, if they really are so concerned about our health and well-being. After all, no credible independent peer-reviewed scientific research can be found to show the safety of spraying such a heavy and widespread use of herbicide. There, is however, plenty of peer-reviewed scientific data on PubMed to support the argument that glyphosate exposure is not safe for a number of reasons.

Real unbiased scientific studies have shown that exposure to glyphosate can result in various medical pathologies including but not limited to kidney and liver impairment,[98] induce breast cancer cell growth,[99] disrupt hormone producing cells,[100] induce cell death of umbilical, embryonic, and placental human cells,[101] decrease testosterone in rats,[102] disrupt male reproduction in rats,[103] damage DNA of the cells found inside of your mouth,[104] and much more. These are only from the first page of a search that revealed hundreds of studies showing that glyphosate exposure is potentially harmful. Even the World Health Organization (WHO) has now publicly stated they believe that glyphosate is likely a carcinogen.[105-106]

Yet this widespread spraying is done on almost every county and state road in the US. Does that not reduce air quality? What about soil and water safety? What about the wildlife? And what about the children who stand along these roads waiting for the school bus? What is the environmental impact of widespread agriculture of genetically engineered organisms? The EPA has not the first clue as to how to answer such questions, because they have never been studied. The corporations bought off the EPA to make sure of that. We mere peasants can't afford to, or are too moral to pay off the EPA bureaucrats to keep our petty wood stoves.

The message from the EPA is clear. If a relatively harmless activity provides greater self reliance or independence it is bad and must be regulated to death. But if an activity poisons and kills you, and/or benefits big corporations, then it is ok; in both cases the environment is secondary, or an excuse. If a person sets up a water catchment for a vegetable garden, the EPA sues, while completely disregarding truly environmentally harmful activities committed by the politically well-connected, such as Nestlé depleting aquifers around the country.[107] It is hypocrisy in action. These types of examples demonstrate how the US is becoming, more and more, a corrupt, politically-controlled tyranny, like communist Poland was.

The EPA is only one government agency, but there are many others. The Food and Drug Administration (FDA) is attempting to regulate natural nutritional supplements as pharmaceuticals to protect the pharmaceutical-medical monopoly. On the other hand, many synthetic food additives and pharmaceuticals which are known to be harmful are approved by the FDA to benefit big business.[108] The FDA wants to regulate the supplement industry forcing them to limit dosages to inert levels, thus partly defeating the purpose of the nutrients to increase health.[109] The FDA is behaving more to protect the pharmaceutical interests than they are individuals' health.[110] Much of this is being conducted under the justification of the CODEX Alimentarius component or World Trade Organization (WTO) standards.[111] As mentioned previously, this is another instance of using international treaties to circumvent the US Constitution. US regulations implemented to "standardize" with CODEX rules would in effect fully destroy health freedom and almost completely eliminate Americans' ability to access nutritional supplements. This would likely have a significantly negative impact on the health of Americans, to the benefit of the pharmaceutical-medical complex.[112,-113] Meanwhile, the large number of deaths and disabilities that are reported as a result of drugs and vaccines seem like they are intentionally ignored, and SWAT teams are used to raid raw milk producers and whole foods businesses,[114] even though not a single complaint had been made against them.

Rather than embracing people's choices for healthy natural foods, bills are passed such as the *Food Safety Accountability Act* that would basically make criminals out of those who use scientific researched data to tell the truth about the supplements they sell.[115] This is also a violation of the right to free speech. The USDA has conducted SWAT raids with rifles ready, because otherwise law-abiding people were consuming raw milk. *RAW MILK!* Since these events have been unreported in the mainstream news media, one has to know where to look on the internet for real news, watch documentaries such as *Farmageddon*, or be a raw milk or organic food producer to experience first hand what controversy exists over raw milk.[116] Even the Amish are not exempt from FDA raids simply for selling eggs and milk to knowing consumers,[117] even though the evidence against raw milk is nil.

If it wasn't bad enough that our personal dietary choices are being dictated to us by a government bureaucracy, such a bureaucracy then takes it a step further and requests sub-machine guns.[118] I suppose when people decide that they've had enough of government alphabet agencies telling them how to live their lives, they're going to show resistance. But are submachine guns really necessary? Over the last several years many federal agencies have been making large purchases of ammunition, including the Department of Homeland Security (DHS), Immigration and Customs Enforcement (ICE), the US Postal Service (USPS), the Social Security Administration (SSA), the Department of Health and Human Services (HHS), the National Oceanic and Atmospheric Administration (NOAA), the EPA, the IRS, the Department of Agriculture (USDA), the Federal Bureau of Investigation (FBI), and others.[119-120] *Some* of these agencies, like the FBI and DHS, have legitimate reasons to purchase *some* ammunition, but not in the quantities they have been, and certainly not many of these agencies at all. Should we even tolerate all these federal agencies getting armed like they are preparing for a war? And exactly who are these *domestic* agencies preparing to fight?

Must we enslave people in private prison systems over raw milk? Must they come up with crazy tactics, such as adding new mental disorders to the never-ending list that call people who choose organic foods mentally ill because they suffer from *Orthoreixa Nervosa*?[121] At what point do people say enough is enough? Will it be when these alphabet agencies start pointing guns at them?

The abuses coming primarily from federal agencies, but also state agencies, have turned into a flood. Some apologists will try to explain away all these actions and all this evidence as being exceptions rather than the norm. But the available evidence is overwhelming: government and corporate oppression, tyranny, and abuse IS the new normal. It is just that it has occurred gradually, using the "boiling frog" approach, so *people have gotten so used to being oppressed and abused that they don't even realize that things aren't supposed to be this way.*

While it is certainly true that there are good, well-intentioned people working in the federal and state governments, good intentions do not always produce good results. This is partly due to unintended consequences, and particularly due to the fact that the very nature of the way governments currently operate is based on coercion or violence, not voluntary participation. To force someone to pay for something they find immoral, is itself immoral. Two examples are forcing a pacifist to pay for war, and forcing a strictly religious person to pay for state-sponsored abortion. I've heard people say that is just how democracy works. I would argue that is how tyranny works, not a free society. The sacred cow of unchecked democracy is not a value in itself, and can lead to as much tyranny as any other form of political oppression. This can be easily demonstrated with a simple example. Put four racist white people in a community with one darker skinned person and then hold a purely democratic vote to see gets to have rights and who doesn't. You could similarly substitute any majority and any minority group and use "democracy" to oppress the minority. Of course, this is a terrible way to do things, and was the entire reason the US Founding Fathers intended the US to be a *Republic*, albeit a democratic Republic. What they meant by a "Republic" is that individuals have certain unalienable rights that can not be taken away by the democratic vote of the majority. An individual's right to free speech or right to own property does not go away because a group of other people votes it so. But this is the very same principle at work when people are forced to participate in something which they would not voluntarily participate, support, or pay for. The American people, and US politicians in particular, seem to have forgotten the idea that individual people do have unalienable rights that can not be taken away through the ballot box. As the quote at the beginning of this chapter points out, and the quote at the beginning of Chapter 8 also suggests, the rights of minorities and individuals must be protected in a free society from any tyranny imposed by the majority. To accept that the majority can take away the rights of the individual via "democracy" is simply tyranny and oppression by a different mechanism. And unfortunately that is the point to which politics in America have degraded. If we are to restore or rebuild a free society, we have to recognize and change this. Perhaps if people want certain services to be provided, they can get people to pay for them *voluntarily*.

As if everything covered in this chapter so far wasn't enough, let's look once again at the US healthcare system. When it comes to health, there is little emphasis from the pharmaceutical-medical complex placed on preventive behavior (diet, exercise, stress management, and sleep), which will make us feel well, make us healthier, and which will help us think more clearly. Instead, we are given pills, and as stated earlier, our right to choose healthy foods is taken away. Our society is all about advertising pills in an effort to get you to run to your doctor, to repeat the symptoms you hear on television in hopes that your doctor prescribes the pill and solves a problem you never actually had to begin with. Eating organic healthy food is frowned upon, made fun of, or considered insane.[122]

Most people eat poor quality, genetically engineered and herbicide and pesticide laden "food" (so-called) that real independent scientific research has shown to cause cancer.[123] But instead of changing our lifestyles to promote health, we run to the doctor for that magic pill we saw on television to manage our sickness. If you follow the money here in the US, pharmaceutical companies don't make money unless they sell drugs, so we over medicate our population with drugs instead of promoting health. Huxley's soma anyone?

This is all made possible by more corrupt people and organizations that bribe your doctor with pharmaceutical parties where they pretend to teach your doctor all about their new drugs. Instead, during the presentation, they wine and dine them with surf and turf, and the thirty-year-old scotch of their choice. The pharmaceutical reps then give the doctors samples to give out to patients, to get them hooked, so that the insurance company pays for more drugs than is really necessary. At one point in my life I worked in fine dining, and oh my, could I tell you stories about corruption between pharmaceutical reps and doctors. There's nothing like an 18 percent gratuity on a $10,000 dining bill to introduce a new drug to twenty-five doctors, even after splitting the tips with three other people. It's a sick game, and I can't believe that the people of the United States have supported such a system for so long. Although interest has been rising in the US for different, better models of true "health care" to replace this "sickness management" model, government regulation, pharmaceutical companies, and insurance companies have now set the status quo in stone. So it will be very difficult to change approaches now, short of completely abandoning the mainstream system and creating a better one — paid for with cash.

A huge problem with our current healthcare system, whether it's for ourselves, or our families, is that people are not taught how to objectively look at medical and scientific evidence, or even nutrition labels. Neither average people nor doctors are taught to question what "has always been." Instead, they follow routine procedures, or "standards of care." If a patient brings in self-researched scientific literature, the doctor is usually too proud to admit that he or she is not familiar with such research, and questions the validity of it. Doctors try to stick with what they know, and in the process potentially deny patients treatment from which they may benefit. Yes, I have experienced this myself. I was told I'm not a doctor, and my degree and scientific background in research biology and biotechnology was completely disregarded as irrelevant.

If over-medication in adults who repeat symptoms they hear on television isn't bad enough, just look at what is done to American children. Look at the case of Justina Pelletier, who spent over fifteen months in state custody after being taken from her parents after they took her to a Children's hospital in hopes to add to her already well-established health care. The Children's hospital decided the previous doctor's diagnosis was wrong, and accused Justina of having unresolved psychological problems that caused her merely to act physically ill.[124] When Justina's parents denied any psychological condition existed, she was taken from their care, a gag order was placed on the parents, and Justina was basically kidnapped by the state of Massachusetts.

The state claimed the parents neglected their child, who was actually well taken care of by her parents. She was kidnapped and removed from her parents' custody by the Boston Children's hospital, who claimed that Justina's illness was "all in her head." Boston Children's hospital started to treat her accordingly, thus stopping her from receiving her previous treatment, which was working for her. For fifteen months, the family battled to get their daughter back as she struggled with her health condition.[125] Had it not been for her father, who broke a gag order and contacted a radio show, and for news radio publicity which resulted in a team of attorneys that volunteered their time, the parents may have never seen their daughter again. Fortunately, the court ended state custody of Justina.[126]

Only after Justina was able to return home was she able to tell the public what really occurred. She told the world that no one should ever have to go through such an ordeal. Not only was she restricted in how often and how long she could see her family, she and her family were treated poorly. No one at the hospital believed her, and instead they were mean and nasty to her.[127] Yet, the mainstream news that followed that case implied that the reason the judge let her go home was because the parents were now cooperative.[128]

The key point here is that it should never be up to the state to determine what regimen is given to someone's child; NEVER. If you believe that there was child abuse, and Justina was taken from her parents with good cause, then answer me this: Why was there a gag order placed on the family which prevented them from talking to the public? Why, when the father broke the gag order (because he refused to be controlled), was he threatened with fines and imprisonment? Why, if someone is doing nothing wrong, would a gag order be issued to restrain that person's free speech? It is because someone doesn't want that person to go public. So they issue threats to control that person, so the child can be used as a test subject without any repercussions.

While they claimed child abuse in Justina's family, none could be proven, and their other daughter who had been diagnosed with the same medical condition has been doing well with the treatments that she has been receiving. When all of this came out, I was all over the internet looking for any data to back up the child abuse claims. I found no real evidence to support the accusations. And the fact that the general public didn't provide more of an outcry on this situation only encouraged me to start speaking up about all the wrongs in our country today.

As Americans, we watch other countries and are quick to judge how they treat their citizens, but we don't use the same assessment on ourselves. For example, during the 2014 Winter Olympics in Russia, a protest rock band that calls themselves "Pussy Riot" came out with videos about the oppression in their country. They were arrested and beaten, but they came back out to show that is not enough to stop them. We read about it in the news and felt bad for them. Yet, our own First Amendment rights have been taken away in many subtle ways, such as limiting free speech to "free speech zones," and people are beaten by corrupt police and given gag orders, but typical Americans don't think twice about these things. Americans seem to have a "blind spot" to see that we have become the same oppressed people that we watch on television, except to us, the oppression only *seems* to exist in other countries. We look at the Egyptian riots, and think *how terrible*, but don't consider "Occupy Wall Street" or "Tea Party" protests. What about how our "Law Enforcement" (who are civil servants you know) frequently treat the American people with excessive and abusive force? The Rodney King fiasco in 1992 was just a forerunner of what has been occurring on a regular basis since.

In addition, many YouTube videos documenting abuse are

regularly blocked or removed which is a way to censor and trample on our free speech rights. Proposed internet laws such as Stop Online Piracy Act (SOPA), Protect Intellectual Property Act (PIPA), Anti-Counterfeiting Trade Agreement (ACTA), the Trans-Pacific Partnership Agreement (TPP), and potentially "Net Neutrality" all threaten free speech on the internet. We might not have had the internet or YouTube in communist Poland, but we were silenced in much the same way. Regardless, we found ways around the oppression, and took risks to get the message out, just as the alternative news media does now.

Why should the alternative news media take risks to get important messages out to warn the rest of us, when most Americans are intentionally distracted by meaningless images caught in headlines or on television? Most Americans see nothing wrong with what is going on in our society, and ignore any signs of possible threats. They agree that all these laws need to be made in order to protect them, not realizing that slowly, every liberty and right they ever had is being systematically stripped away by people they have never heard of.

They never question why the National Defense Authorization Act (NDAA) of 2012, which allows the indefinite detention of Americans, had to be signed on New Year's Eve,[129-130] while most Americans are celebrating the start of a new year. What president signs bills on New Year's Eve? What does he have to hide? Why he must do it in secrecy, when no one will notice? All the while, the president's comments regarding the indefinite detention of American citizens on American soil state the he will not authorize it; but his comments never state that it is not only illegal, but unconstitutional. Instead, he implies that he already has that authority, but that his intentions are not to use it,[131] at least not right now. How reassuring. And what about the next president?

But instead of noticing, the American people are pacified with their cheap trinkets, their cell phones that spy on them, and social networks that keep them preoccupied: their "bread and circuses," so they don't do real things like step outside and look at the sky or talk to their neighbors.

Much earlier I discussed how the Federal Government is using funding to try to get control over a variety of local and state institutions such as police and schools. One important question to ask is, "Why?" Why is the Federal Government doing these things? The answers to that question are actually woven throughout this book. However, another very important question to ask is: "Where are they getting the money to do all these things?" The answer to that is taxes (mostly federal income taxes), borrowing more national debt (which all Americans become obligated like slaves to pay back), and perhaps most importantly, the Federal Reserve "printing" (or digitizing) currency out of nothing, which causes inflation and lowers the purchasing power of all Americans' income and savings. So in effect, the Federal Government is using our own money, the product of our own labor, as a weapon against us. By using that money to infiltrate and take over our local institutions of police and education through what amounts to bribery, they exert pressure to push through their own agendas.

After the 2008 financial crisis, I couldn't understand why people didn't focus more attention on the major role that the Federal Reserve has played in bringing the US economy to the brink of disaster, particularly once it started engaging in large scale money printing known as "Quantitative Easing" or "QE." If you or I were to start printing currency and putting it into circulation, it would be called "counterfeiting," and we would be called "criminals" and put in prison. However, if the chairman of the Federal Reserve, such as Ben Bernanke (or now, Janet Yellen), does the very same thing, it is called "monetary stimulus" or "quantitative easing," he (or she) is called a "genius," and rather than prison, that person is put on the cover of *Time* magazine.[132]

The Federal Reserve, which controls the country's money supply, is not a typical government agency but rather a hybrid between an independent government agency and a privately-owned consortium or trade group. It has the power to set certain interest rates, which ultimately affects all interest rates and inflation, among other things. These in turn affect other factors like unemployment, and how much those Federal Reserve notes known as "dollars" that sit in your wallet are actually worth.[133] The people who must earn and use those Federal Reserve Notes (99.99% of Americans) have absolutely no say in monetary policy. Instead, small groups of people known as the Federal Reserve Board of Governors and the Federal Open Market Committee are given the green light to do as they see fit.[134]

Most people are accustomed to receiving payment in the form of dollars, then taking those dollars to stores and buying essentials such as food. It is through gradualism that most people don't understand what a dollar even is, or more importantly, what it is not, nor where it came from. When one delves into the research, it becomes evident that the dollar is now indeed a fiat fiction printed from thin air, backed by nothing: it is nothing more than a simple accounting trick.[135] From 1792 until 1971, the US Dollar was backed by something of actual tangible value: gold and/or silver. This is no longer the case.[136-137]

With that said, I can't understand why people don't demand an audit of the Federal Reserve's activities. In an era where it is widely accepted that "money is power," to hand over nearly infinite power in the form of the ability to create a nearly infinite amount of (alleged) "money" out of literally nothing, to an institution that is wholly unaccountable to the American people, is absolutely insane, if not treasonous.

Double standards and special privilege abound, particularly when you realize that the member banks of this consortium or trade group, known as Federal Reserve member banks, are permitted to borrow this freshly created currency at a greatly discounted interest rate from the Federal Reserve's "discount window," which you and I cannot do. Because those banks get first access to that newly created money, they receive the greatest benefit. Member banks can then lend that money, at whatever market rate they choose, to businesses, individuals, or can even buy US Treasury bonds. Most of the money that banks lend out is not actually from deposits, but from money created from nothing, either from the Federal Reserve discount window or via the process of fractional reserve banking. Fractional reserve banking, in summary, means that banks can lend out large percentages of depositors' money to someone else, while still counting the money as belonging to the depositor. This is like "double accounting" of the money, and in the process, new money is created out of nothing. For example, I deposit $100 in the bank and you borrow $90 from the bank, but I still have my $100. So $90 was created out of nothing, and instead of there only existing $100, now $190 exists. Now add to that: the $90 that you borrowed is deposited into your account, and now that bank has an additional $90 and can now lend out $80 of that, while you still keep the $90. And that process just keeps going and going. It's all a very interesting accounting or bookkeeping fairy tail.[138]

It would take far too many pages to go into the corrupt details of the US monetary system, or the nefarious origins of the Federal Reserve and all the sordid activities it has conducted since. For those who wish to learn more about the fraudulent nature of our current monetary system, I recommend reading the report *Modern Money Mechanics* published by none other than the Federal Reserve Bank of Chicago.[139] For those who wish to learn more about the history of the Federal Reserve, I recommend reading *The Creature from Jekyll Island* by G. Edward Griffin.

Along the same line as the Federal Reserve, I couldn't begin to understand why there were not more serious investigations into some of the big Wall Street investment banks like Goldman Sachs, JP Morgan Chase, and Citibank, after the 2008 financial crisis.

On a related topic, I do think it is important to clarify that I have nothing against people having wealth per se. *If* they earned it honestly and morally, they should be able to keep what they have earned. We shouldn't be asking if someone has more wealth or less wealth. We should be asking the question of *how someone got the wealth they have* and if they earned it honestly and morally or if they acquired it fraudulently. I would categorize most entrepreneurs, small business owners, and middle class working families among the former group. In the context of an honest system and approach to creating wealth, there is nothing wrong with someone being wealthy. In such a scenario, what that wealth indicates is that person served other people in a valuable way; in a way that others were willing to freely exchange something of value for what that person or company provided.

I most certainly *do* have a problem with the significant number of people who have become wealthy by *stealing* from the American people. I would consider most politicians and Wall Street bankers fitting in that category. In a dishonest system, wealth becomes evil or immoral when people have become wealthy by acquiring that wealth through theft or fraud, and that is to a great degree the point to which our economic system has degraded today. There is now so much corruption and so many perverse incentives, right up into the heart of our monetary, financial, banking, legal, and governmental systems, that a large number of people have become wealthy through fraud, theft, and corruption. Unfortunately that has caused many people to think that being wealthy *in itself* is somehow inherently immoral. That seems to me as an incorrect understanding of what being wealthy *should* mean, even if it is sometimes accurate in what wealth *does* mean in the world as it is today.

As an outsider to American culture I've observed that individuals tend to make generalizations about businesses, government, and people as either being generally "bad" or generally "good." But it strikes me that Ayn Rand had it correct in her book *Atlas Shrugged* in that there are clearly both honest, principled business people, and corrupt conniving business people. I find it unfortunate that people tend to not be more discerning in how they look at things like businesses, economics, and politics.

The solution to these problems is not to tear everyone down to a level of equal poverty through more government theft and redistribution. Stealing from people who honestly produce things of value and giving it to people who are not being productive does not solve anything. Two wrongs don't make a right. If you want to save a person from a deadly parasitic infection, you don't shoot the patient in the chest, you precisely exterminate the infection.

The real solution to these problems is to end the financial fraud, the special privilege, and the political corruption and oppression that are being used by megalomaniacal elitist con artists to steal from the majority of honest, productive people to acquire unearned disproportionate wealth. That theft, fraud, and corruption is systemic in America today. Solving this problem could even potentially include stripping the wealth from those who have acquired it immorally through theft, fraud, and corruption, after being found guilty via a trial, of course. Eliminating the Federal Reserve and the special privilege the Wall Street banks receive is an essential starting point. Without correcting the monetary and banking system as a high priority the rest of the problems will be intractable to deal with. A starting point for this is proper financial investigation into and audits of the Federal Reserve, the Wall Street banks, and most federal and state-level politicians.

Similarly, after the profound information was released by Edward Snowden and Glenn Greenwald about the massive scale on which the NSA was (and is) spying on the American public, why was there not a major investigation or at least public outcry for an investigation into the NSA and their fundamental violations of Americans' Constitutional rights? Had the American public fallen asleep at the wheel that badly? Had Americans all become sheep, passively willing to accept anything, including being led to slaughter?

While each of these examples by itself may not seem to be an overwhelming problem, when taken as a whole, repeated patterns of behavior demonstrate that there *is* a *very* significant problem with corruption and abuse of power by a majority of Federal agencies. While corruption or abuses of power are often excused as just bad individuals, repeated patterns of abuse indicate not a problem with individuals but a problem with the entire system. People may also argue that because they don't drink raw milk or use supplements, or because they haven't yet had difficulty with the IRS or EPA, or don't mind the Federal Reserve creating money from nothing, and don't mind being spied upon by the NSA because they're "not doing anything wrong," that these problems do not affect them. But when you have a systematic pattern of abuses such as this, it will inevitably, eventually, affect *everyone*. The history of corrupt and abusive governments, including the communist Polish government, tells us that this is true.

When you start to analyze everything, you start to see a different picture than what you are told, based on what you are not told. When you really start to think for yourself and not let someone else insert an opinion in place of your own, you see the picture from the outside and you see that it's painted all wrong. Everything is upside down and turned on its head, philosophically, morally, practically, and functionally. You finally see that corrupt, tyrannical government doesn't have to be limited to communism, socialism, fascism, or whatever label you want to put on it. You start to see that things are heading in a very bad and very dangerous direction.

However, it's not all bad. People like me are still speaking up, for now. I feel duty and obligation as an American and a Pole to teach that freedom is not permanent unless you are actively seeking to keep it so, even though I risk being pointed at and referred to as "Oh, you're one of them." I still get up and speak what is true, and I still do my best to open the minds of the people who may just listen to what I have to say. Frankly, I don't care if the NSA hears me say it, because unlike Poland, this is different. While it might not affect the NSA employees now, it will in the future when the house comes crashing down, and no one, not even the most favored politicians will be safe. I know this from my experience in Poland, as history always seems to rhyme.

And I am not alone. The alternative news media is huge and is growing in their messages. Although I find news radio to be questionable at times, those hosts too have helped in spreading the message that freedom just might be at stake here. There are so many "liberty" and "prepper" websites I can no longer keep up, and so on. The mainstream news media can keep on ignoring real issues, continue heading into irrelevancy, and continue making perfectly rational and reasonable people sound crazy. But there are now too many of us "kooks" to back down at this point and sit back and say, "It's okay, it doesn't affect me, so I'm not going to worry about it." If the journalists in the alternative media are crazy, then why do the mainstream media shills care what the alternative media says if it's not true?

If the threat that I have described is valid, it will eventually affect all of us. In my personal hypothesis, I think that an economic collapse in the US is not only likely to happen, but is inevitable based on the direction we are headed. It used to be that people worked until they died and it was a huge accomplishment to become self sufficient by owning land that one could use to produce food, and extended family members would often help. Instead, the goal today is to buy a large house, with a small lot and a patch of grass, and invest your hard earned money in a retirement account where you get a monthly retirement check. This is based on a functioning real economy and financial markets. When the value of the dollar crashes, and/or the stock and bond markets crash, and/or Social Security no longer provides for people, most Americans will be caught very unprepared. They will have to go back to work and/or lower their standards of living. This is not what I want to see happen, but unless people make major changes, this is what will happen.

Yet rather than change their attitudes to more realistic economic approaches, people will cry out that government needs to "do something" for their retirement checks. This entire fiat-based monetary system will not work in the long run because it's a figment of the American imagination. It's an unsustainable Ponzi scheme with pretty window dressing. Debt can not grow and compound indefinitely, but this current monetary and financial system requires exactly that to keep from imploding. But as long as the people believe it to be true, it will stay mostly afloat in the short term, until one of two things happens. Either the system won't be able to support itself anymore such that we have a major economic collapse, and we are getting close to that point, or the people will figure out the scam on their own, and they will withdraw from the system, resulting in an economic collapse. Whichever way leads to collapse doesn't really matter, because there will be a collapse regardless. When the collapse finally does occur, it's the perfect opportunity for government politicians and bureaucrats to stampede in, make promises they don't intend to keep (or know they can't keep), and take total control of the population by any means necessary, just like the Soviets did in pre-communist Poland.

I would like to conclude here with some very sobering statistics, before going on to more positive and constructive topics in the next chapter. I researched the data and history of what the number one cause of death was during the twentieth century (other than age-related pathologies). I was expecting that it was perhaps from war, or possibly infectious disease, or that crime related violence might be on the list. I was shocked to discover that the number one killer of humans of the 20th twentieth century (other than age-related pathologies) was actually democide.[140]

Democide is defined by professor Rudolph.J. Rummel of the University of Hawaii Political Science department as, "The murder of any person or people by their own government, including genocide, politicide, and mass murder."[141] Examples of this during the twentieth century include Stalin's Soviet Union, Mao's communist China, and Hitler's Nazi Germany. There are also many other examples throughout history.[142]

To some this topic may seem out of place here. But I assure you it has a great deal of relevance to the topics at hand. If one follows the trends to their logical conclusions, tyrannical governments historically always end up murdering their own citizens, in one way or another, and often in significant numbers. My family and I have seen this firsthand in Poland. If you see this happen even once, you will never assume it cannot happen again. Don't live in normalcy bias induced denial. Instead, take constructive steps to make sure this type of atrocity does not ever happen again. Recall from the introduction that I hope this book can be a self-defeating prophecy. That is the subject of the next chapter.

Lesson 9a: Just because something "bad" has been around all your life, doesn't mean it's right or legal, or that you shouldn't question its existence.

Lesson 9b: Just because something "good" has been around all your life, doesn't mean that it will continue to be around without people being vigilant to keep it so.

"America will never be destroyed from the outside. If we falter and lose our freedoms, it will be because we destroyed ourselves."
-Abraham Lincoln

INTERLUDE: HOW EVIL TRICKS GOOD PEOPLE INTO SUPPORTING IT

The following has been reprinted with the permission of the publisher, Casey Research.[1-2]

The Only Thing Necessary for Evil to Triumph Is...

A Free Man's Perspective, by Paul Rosenberg

I'm betting that most of my readers can complete this phrase. The problem is, it isn't quite true. Edmund Burke, its supposed source, was a good man, but that doesn't make the saying true.

Here's the complete passage, in the form most of us know:

> "The only thing necessary for evil to triumph is for good men to do nothing."

Yes, there is a time when good men and women must stand up for what's right, even when it involves risk, but that moment comes only after evil has already been well established and is powerfully on the move.

Fighting evil may be an essential thing, but it isn't the *first* problem—it matters only after thousands or millions of mistakes have already been made. And if those first mistakes had not been made, great fights against evil wouldn't be necessary.

Where Evil Comes From

Let's begin with a crucial point: **Evil is inherently weak.**

Here's why that's true:

Evil does not produce. It must take advantage of healthy and effective life (AKA good men and women) if it's to succeed. Evil, by its nature, is wasteful and destructive: It breaks and kills and disrupts, but it does not produce and invent. Evil requires the production of the good in order to do its deeds.

- How much territory could Caesar have conquered on his own?

- How many people could Joe Stalin have killed with no one to take his orders?

- How many people could Mao have starved to death without obedient middlemen?

- *With* duteous followers, however, evil rulers killed some 260 million people in the 20th century.

The truth is that evil survives by tricking the good into doing its will. Without thousands of basically decent people confused enough to obey, evil would fail quickly. [Emphasis added]

The great tragedy of our era is the extent to which evil has been successful in convincing people to service it. Good people having yielded their wills, arm evil, accommodate evil, and acquiesce to its actions.

Hannah Arendt summarized it this way:

> "The sad truth is that most evil is done by people who never make up their minds to be good or evil."

People end up supporting evil because they don't want to make up their minds at all. They want to avoid criticism and vulnerability, so they hold to the middle of the pack and avoid all risk.

These people wouldn't initiate murders by themselves, but in the name of duty, loyalty, unity, and/or the greater good, they cooperate with evil and give it their strength. But each plays a small part—*none of them stretches so far that they'd have to contemplate the final effects of their actions.*

In the 20th century, however, the actions of such people led directly to the murders of 260 million people. And they did this precisely by *avoiding* decisions... by merely obeying.

Sins of Obedience

People think of murder, lying, and robbery as sins, but none of those has nearly the death toll of obedience. Basically decent men and women obey agents of evil for very mundane reasons. The process often goes like this:

1. Being confused and intimidated, they look for the center of the pack.

2. They try not to make waves.

3. They learn that they can avoid making waves best if they adopt the perspectives of their overlords. So they run the overlords' slogans through their minds as a default program.

In the end, these people *don't* make up their minds. Rather, they take on the minds of their overlords and do *their* will.

And so, the vast majority of evil done on Earth traces back to minds and wills that have been abandoned to fear and laid on the Altar of Obedience.

So...

This is what the famous quote should say:

The only thing necessary for evil to triumph is for good men to obey.

We should be painting *that* saying on our walls.

CHAPTER 10: OPTIONS: FIGHT, FLIGHT, OR ACT OUTSIDE THE BOX

"Freedom is not won by merely overthrowing a tyrannical ruler or an oppressive regime. That is usually only the prelude to a new tyranny, a new oppression."

-Jonathan Sacks

"I just don't believe that when people are being unjustly oppressed that they should let someone else set rules for them by which they can come out from under that oppression."

-Malcolm X

Almost thirty years ago, I had no choice but to go with my mother, who, if she wanted to be with my father, had to leave Poland, as my father was not allowed to return. The decision was essentially made for me, although we would have gone in a heartbeat anyway even without the disappearance incident. Now it's different, because there are no more places to go where freedom reigns. There are no other countries that hold the values and principles that this country once did. You *almost* have to stay and fight, because the alternatives are limited, and are not really much better. Back then, America was a supposed beacon of freedom. People had somewhere they could go: America. Now there are few places a human can go to escape tyranny and oppression because just about every country has become tyrannical. Look at Edward Snowden, who barely found asylum in Russia, which used to be completely totalitarian.

My husband and I have often considered and even planned for leaving America to immigrate to another country or become a PT (Perpetual Traveler or Permanent Tourist). The options are few, as there are few places that are not oppressed, and/or under strict government regulations. Freedoms are rapidly eroding everywhere. Despite my open mindedness to leaving the US, I don't want to. I consider myself an American. I am a US citizen. I think the Constitution is one of the most brilliant governing documents in history and needs to be recognized for what it is. No other country has such a Constitution. Regardless if it is been shredded to pieces in practice over the last few decades, it is still there, waiting to be taken up again. I want to believe that one day, we Americans will stand up to the special interest and government tyrants and fight to take our country back.

Having been in a position where I've left a country, I'm not afraid to do it again, should the time come. The oppressed world I left back then in Poland is the world that the US is becoming today. But at the same time, I don't want to leave America behind. I love this country, and I respect the Constitution, as should all other Americans. To me, leaving the country may just be running away from one set of problems, only to end up with a different set, and putting oneself in a more difficult situation than necessary.

The biggest problem with leaving the country is that the tyranny, corruption, and political rot that exists in the US is occurring in most other countries across the world as well. Eventually, you run out of countries. Freedom, civil rights, and property rights as core values are not the norm in most places, and in practice, that now also includes the US. There seem to be few "good" countries. Most of them seem to be afflicted with various degrees of territorial gangsters that people inaccurately call "government." I just don't see Mars as being habitable soon enough to run away to, so I choose to stay on Earth.

With that said, I fully understand and respect the decision of flight instead of fight, and expatriating to another country. Many people have written that America is an idea and not just a place. While that may be true, it is only true if we make it so. The way to do that, should you choose to expatriate, is to spread the values and ideals of liberty that America was founded on. Values are not spread by violence, as the Federal Government attempts to do, but by living by those values, and by persuading others of their merit. As Americans, that is what we should all strive to do, whether we choose to stay and try to rebuild those values, or whether we choose to leave and spread those values abroad.

I suppose if you're still reading and have gotten this far, then either you're one of those that must finish every book you start, or you are somewhere on the same page as those of us who advocate liberty and the Constitution, and you are looking for strategies and methods to correct or outwit the oppression that is upon us. I do not claim to have all the answers, but I will offer lessons that I've learned and lessons that the Poles who worked for Solidarity taught. My analysis may seem harsh, but realize that I have already performed my research and comparisons and feel justified in stating openly that America is very much becoming tyrannical. At this point it is just a matter of placing the last few bricks in the wall to finish the job before enough people notice and react to what is happening.

For those who choose to stay, there are many things to consider. When people think of affecting political change the first method they usually think of is to accomplish it through the political process by "voting the bums out." This is understandable, but because people commonly think this way, I think it is necessary to address that thought process. Unfortunately, the political system at the federal and state levels are so corrupt and so broken that trying to work within such a controlled system is, in my opinion, a futile approach and a waste of precious time and resources. In general, I do not have high hopes for trying to accomplish much through the political system as it currently exists. Getting elected to federal or state political positions is a very expensive project and thus would be more likely to either be unsuccessful against status quo special interests with deep pockets, or worse, would possibly be co-opted by bankrolling or buying out opposition campaigns. Such campaigns would then end up becoming nothing more than "controlled opposition" — or opposition in appearance only and not in substance. If my personal story of voting in America didn't convince you that elections are rigged, I recommend you watch the documentaries "*Hacking Democracy*" and "*Unprecedented.*"

Politics at the local level is a different story. There are too many county and local governments for them to all be controlled by special interests and megalomaniacs with money. So running for local legislative positions may actually offer some utility by using those positions to nullify unconstitutional federal and state laws, and by eliminating oppressive land use laws. I hope there are still good people who are willing to run for local office, with term limits of course. I hope liberty-minded people still turn out to vote for them, to remove from local office any puppets who have sold out our country. This approach is also applicable to county Sheriff's offices, not just purely political offices.

Liberty-minded people have been working for some time to try to correct the problems through the political process, with only limited success, as only a few truly upstanding people have been elected to positions where they are able to actually make any difference. Unfortunately, that's just not enough. To correct things through the political system at this point would require the cavalry to come in, and for that to happen it would at a minimum require fixing the voting system so it's not rigged. Therefore, we can either futilely continue trying to win by putting good people in office, or awaken to the fact that voting is rigged and we have to find other means to take our country back. As mentioned earlier, *it is much harder to get out from under oppression than it is to prevent it in the first place.* I hope it never comes to the point where we have to hang for supposed "treason." But because our voting system is rigged via various methods including electronic voting, we will ultimately have to use approaches beyond the ballot box to succeed in correcting the problems.

At this time, we, the US citizens, are not short on resources, nor are we short on other people that are of like mind. We are, for the time being at least, short on courage, and deficient in our understanding of applicable strategies. However, I think that will change as more and more people demonstrate they are aware of the seriousness of what's going on around them, and as less and less people are willing to tolerate the destruction of their rights and freedoms.

I do not plan to acquiesce without a fight. I plan to seize my freedoms back. Just as there are lessons to be learned about what it is like to live under communist rule, so too are there lessons about how to outcompete a system that has been developed to oppress you. If the Poles could do it with limited resources and technology, we can definitely do it better with the current resources and technology at our fingertips. It's just a matter of developing effective strategies and tactics, and organizing when necessary.

When dealing with crisis scenarios, the options are often framed as "fight or flight," implying that one must either engage in combative rebellion, or run away. But in reality, those are not the only options. There are many other ways one can subtly or covertly "fight" tyrants. I cover a variety of strategies for increasing your freedom later. For now I just want to highlight a few key points.

Engaging in combative rebellion is often less effective than other approaches, and in my opinion should only be utilized as a last resort. One reason is that if you ultimately want to succeed, it is important to maintain public support, as Solidarity did. In order to do that you have to maintain the moral high ground. Otherwise you will just be labeled a "terrorist" and disappeared, and the public will support that instead of your efforts.

One approach to freedom is simply by living your life freely, as you want to, and by carefully and selectively ignoring "laws" that you find abhorrent. If enough people simply ignore unjust laws, they become unenforceable and therefore in practice null and void. It is like a highway where the "legal" speed limit is 55mph, but everyone drives 75mph. It is impossible to ticket everyone.

Another way is to stop providing financial resources to your oppressors that they use against you. For example, if you don't want to have your tax dollars used to fund all the "wars against you" then do whatever you can to arrange your affairs to minimize paying taxes.

While withdrawing support from oppressors is indeed a good start, that doesn't necessarily complete the process. If you remove a negative, even if you succeed, you are merely left with the absence of that negative. *You have nothing positive with which to replace it.* So an even better approach is to *create positives, or work on creating what you do want, rather than eliminating what you don't want.* This is the difference between saying "I'm going to lose fat" (a negative) and "I'm going to develop fitness" (a positive). In the latter case you have what you want, rather than merely avoiding what you don't want. An outstanding book on how to think and problem solve in this manner is *The Path of Least Resistance* by Robert Fritz.

This could be called the "build a better model" strategy: outcompete them in terms of the useful services that they actually do provide. For example, if the local police are problematic, either retrain them so they do the job properly, or if that is not an option, create your own community security or neighborhood watch, and eliminate the need for the local police. If you don't want to support the banking and monetary system, create a different system based on barter, precious metals, Bitcoin, or whatever works for your community; but drop out of the financial system that is abusing and oppressing you. If you think that big-agribusiness "food" is undesirable poison, then grow your own, and/or support local farmers markets and Community Supported Agriculture (CSAs).

There is an additional risk to consider in eliminating an oppressive system before having alternatives to replace it: it creates a vacuum that can allow different tyrannical people come into power. This ultimately solves nothing, as it merely trades one oppressor for another. It doesn't truly build freedom.

If you eliminate the need for existing oppressive institutions by building something better, the elitists will primarily have two options: either they will fade away into irrelevancy, or more likely they will try to destroy your alternatives through force or subversion. If they try to do so through force, it becomes clear who the tyrant is, and it becomes justifiable to use force to defend yourselves, while still maintaining the moral high ground and public support. If they try to undermine your positive alternatives covertly through subversion, you will be faced with the task of removing their influence and spreading the truth about their activities. For example, this might involve removing agent provocateurs and spreading the truth about them far and wide. In either case, success will neither be quick nor easy. *But it is both possible and necessary.*

My husband will argue that to the average person, the difference between communism and socialism is paper thin, and between socialism and fascism is non-existent. Whether you prefer to describe it as communist tyranny or fascist tyranny makes little difference as the current circumstances really comprise the worst of both.

Statist approaches like socialism and communism largely start from the premise that people will mostly not be corrupt or incompetent. More problematically, other than the ballot box, they do not have a system of checks and balances to prevent or correct corruption and incompetence. As political history teaches us, and as any superficial evaluation of US politicians will reveal, the ballot box is not a very reliable method for correcting these problems.

In theory, statist systems also do not allow you to stop supporting the state if it becomes corrupt and incompetent, because participation is forced through coercion and violence. Unlike institutions based on *free choice*, participation is *not voluntary*. If people's relationship with government was a "romance," government would be that physically abusive stalker you just can't get rid of when you try to end the relationship. Talk about "breaking up is hard to do!" Sure, as mentioned earlier, you can "vote with your feet" and move somewhere else. But what if *all* governments are corrupt and/or incompetent? The world seems to be largely infected with corrupt and incompetent statists.

Free markets assume that people have the potential to be corrupt or incompetent. However, when free markets exist, there are inherently many checks and balances on organizations within that framework. If a business is corrupt or incompetent, people can go elsewhere and the business will cease to exist. Or, if there are no good alternatives, people are free to start their own businesses, non-profits, or cooperatives. In these cases, activities are all conducted on a *voluntary* basis. Businesses don't have the ability to *force* people to use their products or services, unless they get the state to force that, such as in the case of health insurance in the Affordable Care Act. But government politicians and "terrocrats" (short for terrorist bureaucrats) tend to get violently aggressive if you announce that you are no longer going to conduct "business" with them, and that you are starting your own competing government. Like mafias, governments like to have a monopoly on extortion.

Just as there are checks and balances on organizations in a free market, the Founding Fathers also wrote the Constitution and the Bill of Rights to include its own system of checks and balances to try to prevent people in government positions from succeeding in acts of corruption and abuse of power. The separation of powers between the branches of government was one check on the abuse of power. The separation between Federal and State governments was another check. An independent judiciary was a check. Giving Congress the power of the purse and the power to declare war were checks. The Bill of Rights was a check. And as mentioned, Jury Nullification was a check. Yet over time, all of these checks on the abuse of power have been gradually and systematically circumvented. The problem now is that government and big businesses are intertwined which encourages and locks in a type of crony corporatist corruption and oppression, such as the Wall Street banks, who should have been allowed to fail long ago.

In the end these are all just labels; the truth of the matter is that our liberties and rights are in great jeopardy, and we must do something to keep them from being completely wiped out. Placing a label on the problem does not create a solution.

Much has been written on what made Polish Solidarity work. How do you get so many people to actively work for the same cause? And how many people do you really need to affect change? There are a lot of opinions I agree with, and many I disagree with. I think one of the main things that historians agree upon is that the perceived need for change was widespread among the Polish people. The Poles wanted change, they didn't like their living conditions and knew there was a better way. They had gotten to a point where everything Polish was taken from them, they were hungry, and they worked long hours, and saw no future for their children. It was commonly believed that if you wanted to have a career, you lived under the tyranny placed upon you, but if you wanted to be free, you had to give up your career.[1] This resulted in many Poles continuing to work under the oppression in hopes of at least having a means to buy food. Thus, many Poles stayed on the fence.

Then the Pope's visit to Poland occurred and he presented his speech on freedom. This was a "tipping point" event because of the number of Poles that turned out to see the Pope. The official censored papers tried to hide how many people turned out for the event, but the ploy failed. The people saw how many of them there actually were. This is similar to how Ron Paul and the liberty movement on the internet have shown us all how many like-minded people there actually are in the US. The Pope's support for the values of freedom truly brought those on the fence to come to terms that things needed change, and they joined either the Solidarity movement, or one of the other groups that held similar principles. With the Pope, additional common ground was found, even among people who were not Catholic.

After the Pope's speech, the Solidarity movement grew by leaps and bounds. People felt connected: they felt a responsibility to their God and to their Country, and they felt a responsibility to each other. The large numbers of people who cooperated to go on strike in order for the government to respond resulted in the Soviet elites to act out desperate measures such as martial law and sending the Polish army against the people.

Lech Wałęsa gained popularity because he was truly there for the people. He was a union leader that never sold out. But he was also just a regular guy, an electrician who worked long hours for little pay. He was like everyone else. It just so happened that he (along with many others) helped Solidarity come to fruition, but not without paying a high price. He served time in jail, and refused to pick up his Nobel Peace Prize without his colleagues (at that time he feared he would not be able to return to Poland if he left). Most importantly, he never bought into the bribes that were offered him. He stayed true to the people and his principles and values. It's also important to note that while Wałęsa seems to get credit for the Solidarity movement, he is far from a lone wolf on the matter. He was among ten thousand Solidarity leaders that were arrested when martial law occurred; hardly a single-man project. I'm not sure why he gets all the credit. I have learned in life that the people who do most of the behind the scenes hard work are often never recognized.

That's a key as well: willing to be a person who takes risks and chances, and makes things happen, but accepts that s/he may never get credit for doing so. The humbleness of the working Poles to allow one person to take credit, in order to have a leader, is astounding.

We have to be aware of our motivations for why we do things. Are we doing something for fame? For recognition? For fortune? Or are we working toward a shared goal (liberty), with shared values (freedom, Constitution, civil rights, property rights), where different people contribute in their own unique way? One lesson from Solidarity is that there is greater strength from a large number of people where the focus is on a shared set of values, rather than on one lone "cult of personality" individual.

There was one point in time that Wałęsa lost a great deal of credibility. He decided to call an end to the strikes on his own, rather than consulting with other Solidarity members. He ended a key strike, which resulted in a turning point for Solidarity. He was accused of wanting to be king, and his poor decision broke down Solidarity.[2] This allowed a window of opportunity for the Polish government to succeed in applying the divide and conquer strategy. This allowed their propaganda to have some success in making Solidarity look bad in the eyes of the people.[3] And to a degree it worked: Solidarity lost much of their cohesiveness and was not the same after that.

There are several ways that a small number of people can control a very large number of people through manipulation. The methods that I have mentioned so far include strategies like instilling complacency, gradualism, divide and conquer, and fear and intimidation. One method I have not mentioned is the Problem, Reaction, Solution approach, also known as the "Hegelian Dialectic." This approach basically involves a government agency, a corporation, or a front group, covertly creating an artificial problem, to which the public will then adversely react and demand that the government "do something" to solve the problem that an institution itself created. The public's outcry is the Reaction. Finally, a premeditated and desired "Solution" will be implemented to satisfy the public. But the "solution" is typically one that benefits whatever institution created the initial problem in the first place. As President Obama's former chief of staff Rahm Emanuel has been quoted as saying: "Never let a serious crisis go to waste."[4] These scenarios never really benefit the people, only the elitist insiders, and almost always involve the general public to relinquish more freedoms, more rights, and/or more money.

A good analogy here is a flock of sheep where the sheep think they are being protected by a shepherd, but in reality are being "protected" by a wolf impersonating a shepherd. The sheep are not worried about the world beyond their fenced safe zone because they think their shepherd cares for their safety. But in reality they are being preyed upon. The wolf then periodically causes a sheep to "disappear" to frighten the flock, and the flock submits to the wolf's demands that more funding is needed for more shepherd staff to protect the herd. False flag events are one form of this, but they are not the only form.

Similar to the Bydgoszcz incident in Poland, it is becoming increasingly likely that intentionally created and unnecessary internal conflict could be used against us in America. With several recent conflicts in the news between local police and the communities they serve (Ferguson, NYC, Baltimore, etc.), it is entirely possible or even likely that violence could break out on a scale that could be used to justify federal intervention and even martial law on a localized scale. Americans need to learn the lesson from the Poles at Bydgoszcz that they could be intentionally being provoked to violence to justify a much worse crackdown. Americans also need to realize that turning to violence in such a manner could be falling right into a trap set by those instigating the situation. Finally, Americans need to realize that if they are going to win the struggle for liberty and rights nationwide, they need to maintain the moral high ground and maintain the upper hand in public relations. In order to accomplish these two goals, violence must either not be used at all, or it must remain strictly as a defensive posture, with the government being seen as the aggressor. This was how Solidarity maintained the moral high ground in Poland, and the rest of the Polish people took note.

If you pay attention to ongoing current events in politics it becomes easy to spot when these various techniques of manipulation and propaganda are being used against the public to achieve a desired public opinion. This is the dark side of public relations as was originally invented by Edward Bernays,[5] as discussed in his book *Propaganda*.[6] To get an idea of Bernays' perspective, one only has to read quotes from his book: "The conscious and intelligent manipulation of the organized habits and opinions of the masses is an important element in democratic society. Those who manipulate this unseen mechanism of society constitute an invisible government which is the true ruling power of our country. We are governed, our minds are molded, our tastes formed, our ideas suggested, largely by men we have never heard of."[7] The US government and some US corporations use some or all of these techniques today. The Polish government used all of these tactics, but perhaps the most important was *compliance*.

As the attitude goes, *"So what if they are watching me, I'm not doing anything wrong."* That is compliance. To comply with unjust actions *is to accept them*, and it is to risk that when things finally change enough so they *do* affect you, it will be too late to take action. Again, this is the frog being boiled. I fear that waiting until tyranny directly affects you is the wrong line of thinking. The Jews who stepped on the trains towards the concentration camps complied, and that got them imprisoned, beaten, tortured, and killed. These people had literally done nothing wrong, other than being born into a certain religion. Those of Jewish heritage harmed no one; they had no ill intent. They were responsible, they worked hard, they took their jobs seriously, and they were still exterminated. Learn from those who would try to teach you history. Don't comply. Don't be obedient sheep lacking independent thinking. Despite what you have been taught or what you think, the government is not there to help you, and neither are many major corporations, particularly Wall Street banks.

My words alone are unlikely to bring people together enough to prevent the disaster that is unfolding before us. However, I will leave you with some suggestions of how people can work to affect positive change into the future. Several of these are additional lessons that can be learned from studying the Polish Solidarity movement. The rest are based on psychological principles, strategies that are known to be effective at accomplishing political change, or are important principles for living in freedom.

As a generalization, the most effective solutions to problems are not "top down" solutions provided by some magical leader or "guru" who is far removed from the actual problem and from the people who are the most affected by the situation. Top down hierarchical structures, are slow, dumb, and demoralizing. "Bottom up" solutions proposed by those who are closest to the problem, therefore the most impacted, and who can have the most impact, are usually the best. Free societies tend to have much more bottom up problem solving, while oppressed societies tend to have much more top down problem solving. It is no coincidence then that free societies on average tend to function better and are more prosperous. In our current situation, there is not going to be one, or even a few, top down solutions, charismatic leaders, or gurus that are going to solve the problem. This actually provides a strategic advantage because large hierarchical "command and control" organizations like governments and large corporations don't match up well against a distributed and networked people. Bureaucratic institutions simply move to slowly and clumsily. Just as Solidarity was a distributed, bottom up solution, so too will we have to operate in order to effectively restore or rebuild freedom in our country. Keep that idea in mind as a background context for the rest of these suggestions. Remember, "Only slaves need masters."

1. Learn about and develop self empowerment. If you want to restore freedom, or even simply live life freely, the reality is you are going to have to operate outside your comfort zone, and ultimately expand your comfort zone. That is what developing your self empowerment is all about. One of the biggest obstacles that I have observed in people who want to live in and expand freedom is a general feeling of helplessness. To a certain extent this is understandable because our current environment is fairly disempowering to individuals. Helplessness can be a trap. If you feel helpless you also tend to feel helpless *about* your helplessness. So this has to be a starting point for everyone. If you think you are helpless, you will accomplish nothing. If you develop self empowerment, you can accomplish almost anything. There are many approaches to become a more self empowered individual. One of the most basic of these is to learn about the psychology of self empowerment.

The psychologist Martin Seligman of the University of Pennsylvania conducted research and developed a theory that he termed "learned helplessness." He also wrote an excellent book called *Learned Optimism* which has some very effective tools for overcoming helplessness and increasing individual empowerment. Many people who feel helpless have "learned" from certain experiences that they can not control their lives. So they need to retrain the way they think. The details are a bit too lengthy to include here. But I recommend people investigate and consider this for themselves if you or someone you know needs to overcome a feeling of helplessness.

Another way to become more self empowered is to become more consciously self aware, and to become more aware of the choices you make and your decision making processes. Greater self awareness allows us to protect ourselves from unwanted outside influences such as government and corporate propaganda. As Timothy Leary wrote in *Neuropolitics:* "Brainwashing is happening to all of us all of the time. Knowledge of brain function is our only protection against it. The solutions to our predicament are neurological. We must assume responsibility for our nervous systems. Our robothood can remain static if we endlessly repeat the imprints of infancy to adolescence, or it can be drastically altered by brainwashers without our consent, or we can take control of our nervous systems. *If we **don't** assume this personal responsibility, somebody else will; if we **do** take over the control board, we can each be any person we want to be.* [italics added]." Two good books for developing greater self awareness are *The Evolution of Consciousness* by Robert Ornstein, and *Choices: Discover your 100 Most Important Life Choices* by Shad Helmstetter. Note that even if your religious views cause you to reject the idea of evolution, you can still gain many insights about the human mind and behavior if you read Ornstein's book with an open mind. Two good books for improving decision making are *Decision Power* by Harvey Kaye and *The Confident Decision Maker* by Roger Dawson. Realize that everything you do is a choice, and your level of awareness about the choices you make is the difference between living based on animal instinct, living based on social programming like a robot, or living based on true free will like a self-actualizing human being. Learning about Abraham Maslow's self actualizing psychology and hierarchy of needs can also help you improve your self-empowerment and decision-making processes.[8-9] Maslow's hierarchy of needs is even a useful tool for thinking about preparedness.

Just because people often exhibit robot-like or zombie-like behavior doesn't mean that is desirable. In fact, if we want to restore, rebuild and maintain a free society, we should encourage people to become as conscious as possible, and to make decisions based on their own freely chosen values, rather than based on government, corporate, or cultural programming.

An additional way to become more empowered is to develop your critical thinking skills to help cut through the propaganda. True critical thinking, psychological independence, and how to achieve freedom from manipulation, are not taught in any formal institutions; not in schools, the media, or by the government. They can't, for a simple reason: if they taught you how to recognize their attempts to control you, they'd lose that control. Two good books for improving your thinking skills are de Bono's Thinking Course by Edward de Bono and Brain Power by Karl Albrechet. Improving your thinking skills will both help you to improve your problem solving ability, as well as improve your "bovine excrement" filter, and may help you earn more and/or improve your ability to work with others.

Through the process of developing your thinking, determine what your true values and principles are. People who do not know their own values are easy to manipulate. Remember this old saying: "People who do not stand for something will fall for anything." Also recall from the interlude that people who do not make conscious choices about their own values are easily tricked into serving those with nefarious intents.

Improving your communication skills can be empowering and can also provide benefits in working with others. Effective communication can sometimes be the difference between success and failure.

One more way to become more empowered is to educate yourself about topics like the philosophy of freedom, individual rights, and jury nullification, etc. Become as informed and educated as possible about the true facts of the current economic circumstances and political reality, and share that information with others.

Equally important to becoming more psychologically or intellectually empowered is to become as self reliant and logistically self sufficient as possible. There are many ways to do this, including: storing food, water, and fuel, producing your own food, learning and developing personal defense skills, producing your own off grid power with solar, wind or hydro, and moving to a more sustainable, private, and secure location. As mentioned previously, also consider home schooling your own children, or create private true community based schools. There are many resources available on the internet to learn more about all of these topics, as well as other topics, that can help you to become more independent from an increasingly controlled and oppressive political and economic system.

One very important thing that you can do to become more self empowered that helps both psychologically and logistically is to take charge of your own health and fitness. Work toward becoming as healthy and fit as possible through nutrition, exercise, supplementation, stress management, and sleep. There are many obvious benefits to this, but there are also many not so obvious advantages. If you can avoid becoming sick, you can avoid the politically-controlled medical care system and much of the associated expense. In the near future, it is likely that Americans will be facing both limited healthcare services and some very difficult and challenging times. The more healthy and fit you are, the more resilient you will be and the easier it will be for you to succeed in that environment. There is also ample scientific evidence that good health, exercise, fitness, and quality nutrition improve brain function and help to support clear thinking and emotional stability.

All of the above can also be shared with other people. Collaborate with people you know regarding teaching of information about self-empowerment, preparedness or health and fitness. In an effort to save time and be more efficient, each member can pick some material to study and explain the most valuable points to others. There is obviously a large number of resources available on these subjects, both online and hard copy. As you advance your critical thinking skills you will also be able to improve the *quality* of the information you consume. Note that most mainstream information that people are exposed to on a regular basis is of relatively low quality.

2. Find common values and/or common ground with others, and ideally, develop a shared vision or shared goals

Within the Solidarity movement, there were several shared, common ground values, and there was a collection of events that brought people together. First, there was the common denominator belief that the status quo of so called "socialism" wasn't working, and people wanted freedom. Then there were events that occurred that galvanized people against the government, such as the murder of college opposition members and shipyard workers. Those events led to the mass strikes when the opposition groups were not even allowed to honor those that died on the anniversaries of those events. The movement had already been strong at that point, but people feared job loss, arrests, and other repercussions, so up to that point many chose not to get involved out of fear. Then the Pope came to Poland and openly objected to the communist regime. This brought a lot of people off the fence and into action. When the government instituted martial law and attempted to stop the Solidarity movement via the arrest of ten thousand leaders, new leaders came forward and continued the movement. The common denominator was the human desire for freedom.

I hope we don't have to wait for a large number of protestors like the "Occupy Wall Street" or "Tea Party" members to be murdered by the US government before people take action in greater numbers. We have recently witnessed the militarized police and the DHS use tear gas, flash bang grenades, rubber bullets, sound cannons, and armored personnel carriers against various protest groups. Contrary to popular American government public relations, it CAN happen here. The US Federal Government does have a history of violent civil rights abuses of its citizens, including shooting peacefully protesting American Veterans,[10] corralling innocent Japanese-Americans into internment camps using force,[11] shooting college student protestors,[12] and shooting and killing innocent people by biased federal agents over court clerical errors and inaccurate hearsay reports.[13] There are certainly many more examples, including against African-American civil rights protestors, like the questionable circumstances surrounding the death of Martin Luther King, Jr.[14]

Americans, due to our religious diversity, don't have a Pope to bring us all together as the Poles did. I choose not to include religion here only because as a country, we come from so many different religious backgrounds that I think it would be very difficult to find common ground on that issue alone among Americans, other than freedom of religion itself.

However, we do have the documents that our Founding Fathers left us (Declaration of Independence, Constitution, Bill of Rights, and the Federalist Papers), and the philosophy and principles of personal liberty, individual rights (civil rights and property rights), and equal justice before the law. Many people would also add the non-aggression principle, which basically means that it is not acceptable for anyone (government included) to use violence or force against others, except in defense against violent or forceful criminal acts. Finally, some people would also include the principle of contract law, which simply means that you do what you say or promise you will do; your word is your bond. These few basic ideas allow us to have a common ground foundation from which we can rebuild. And yes, I do mean *rebuild*, as America is in the last stages of falling apart, or being torn apart.

We do have a current common denominator in the US, and that is the Constitution and the philosophy of liberty and the maxim "live and let live." So a starting point would be to actually follow the Constitution and Bill of Rights and not sell out to special interests. Contrary to what some presstitutes and politicians claim, the Constitution that was left to us by the Founding Fathers of this country is hardly outdated. As stated earlier, it's one of the most brilliant governing documents that has ever been written when it comes to human rights and freedoms. It needs to be revived, re-taught, and respected.

The philosophy of liberty is also a common denominator among those who live in the US. Although not recognized by many, it has for most been a way of life here in the US for over two centuries. The philosophy of liberty also needs to be revived, re-taught, and lived on a daily basis. The true intent and meaning of the philosophy of liberty has become so distorted and forgotten by a majority of Americans today that we need to truly reexamine, re-teach, and re-apply it. If the majority of Americans truly did this, the current circumstances in this country would be much, much, different than what they are now. Based on my observations, many Americans have become either so ignorant or so confused or brainwashed that they actually believe that we still live in a "free" country. If one simply takes the red pill and opens one's eyes outside of the matrix of the mainstream media, it becomes apparent that nothing could be further from the truth. But for some people it might take seeing (more) innocent, peaceful protestors shot right in front of their eyes to realize this. Let us all hope that is not the case.

I can't say that the principles of the Constitution and liberty will bring the whole country together, but I do think that they are two things that few true Americans would argue against. The Constitution, while often re-written in textbooks, is available in original form. While some will debate interpretation, if one reads it with the spirit of liberty from tyranny in mind (as the Founding Fathers wrote it), most will grasp the insights and conclusions that the Founders intended.

This also means that petty differences need to be put aside. Of course it is likely that people will always have certain differences of opinion on certain issues. But without certain core values or principles, a country or a civilization cannot survive. People cannot disagree on almost everything and insist on *forcing* their own values onto everyone else and continue to have a functioning and peaceful society. Rather, trying to use *force* to get everyone on the same page is a recipe for societal collapse, and is one of the contributing reasons the US is in its current state. Fortunately, as discussed previously, I believe many of these differences are contrived by those who benefit from the strategy of divide and concur. I believe most Americans *could* agree on a basic core set of values and principles – if they were allowed to do so without special interest interference. Everyone has a right to live their life how they want, as long as their lifestyle does not harm anyone else. No one should have force used against them unless they are harming someone else. People should be free to be who they want, so long as they stay in the line with the principle of *live and let live*.

3. Non compliance; withdraw support from any oppressive institution or organization

The interesting paradox about state oppression in a society that values freedom is that the more control the elitists try to get, the more people will rebel. Like trying to grasp flowing water with an iron fist, most of it slips away to continue on its own path. People find loopholes and workarounds or just invent new ways to make progress possible. Every time the control apparatus shuts a door or closes a loophole, people find and exploit two more doors, and two more loopholes. This is because a free people will not accept being controlled. They will struggle to live freely, and often they will succeed. The first key is for people to recognize they can seize their freedom, regardless of what the state apparatus does. Despite the excessive number of surveillance cameras popping up in cities large and small all across the country,[15-16] state oppression is neither omnipotent nor omniscient (yet). It is not some magical force from the sky that can catch every act of disobedience. And those gaps between the fingers of the iron fist allow non-compliant individuals to slip through regularly.

On those occasions when people do get caught and prosecuted for "non-crimes," that is when jury nullification and activist legal assistance come into play.

Many people, when they think about non-compliance or civil disobedience, may think of large-scale activities like what Gandhi and Martin Luther King, Jr. practiced. Those are good methods too, but they create single, large, easy targets to crush. So that is not exactly what I have in mind. What I have in mind is more along the line of individual non-compliance, with some similarity to what Henry David Thoreau advocated. It is much more difficult for the state to crush ten thousand individual acts of disobedience than it is one protest march with ten thousand participants.

When I think of non-compliance, the first example that always pops into my mind is my mother bartering our American sent items for goods to survive, which was very illegal at the time — especially when she used American dollars to purchase things. It is this type of non-compliance that frees individuals from the oppression placed upon them. My mother didn't recognize such laws as moral, and therefore, she did not follow them.

Another example that often comes to mind is from the book *The Modern Survival Manual: Surviving the Economic Collapse* by Fernando (FerFAL) Aguirre. In this book, FerFAL describes how he survived the economic collapse in Argentina, and in one of the stories he described how roadblocks were erected in an effort to extort money from innocent drivers. In other words, in order to pass through, you had to pay the corrupt official a fee. FerFAL disagreed with this practice, and rather than paying the fee, he would just drive through the roadblock by following another car and wouldn't stop. He also would not make eye contact with the so called "official," and would just keep on going.[17] This is a form of non-compliance by not recognizing the corrupt official as having any legitimate authority over him. Immoral behaviors are immoral, and making them a "law" doesn't make them any less immoral.

In Poland, non-compliance was practiced in many forms,

including using the underground economy for purchasing much needed items, dropping the career and finding work outside of government paid jobs, publishing underground newspapers (that was a big one), and many other methods. There were those who stocked up on typewriters and ribbons along with paper and money when they saw that martial law was coming.[18] This was a good thing because as at one point typewriters were required to be registered as well.[19] Can you imagine if all of a sudden you were required to register your printer because the government feared you might have an independent newspaper sometime in the future?

We are actually almost facing a similar situation today where there have been many proposed government regulations such as SOPA, PIPA, and the Trans-Pacific Partnership that could have a chilling effect on internet journalism. The jury is still out on whether "Net Neutrality" regulations will have a positive or negative affect on internet journalism and freedom of speech. I suspect the latter.

The most important form of non-compliance in Poland was the support of strikes. The farmers, who refused to sell food at undercut government-set prices[20], instead brought food and *donated* it to the factory and mine strikers.[21]

While we don't have roadblocks yet, there are other ways to practice non-compliance. For instance, you could rebel against using your physical address for everything. After all, if you are not a criminal on probation, why does the government need to know where you live? In communist Poland, if you wanted ration cards, you had to register where you lived. This translated into: if you wanted to eat, you had to tell the government where you physically resided. This information was later used against Solidarity members by having the equivalent of SWAT teams showing up door-to-door of the leaders of Solidarity to arrest them. There is a parallel here in the US, and that is the requirement to provide your physical address in order to be able to get a driver's license, or how people are required to provide their home address to purchase a firearm through licensed dealer, or when RealID becomes fully implemented. This information would certainly make it easier for the police if door-to-door gun confiscation was ever enacted.

Another approach to ditch the oppressive system relates to your children's education. I am skeptical that government-run schools offer the best solution to education, and my life experiences have shown me that services provided by government (any government) usually tend to be of higher cost and lower quality than those provided privately. In this context, "privately" could mean home schooling, it could mean truly locally organized and run non-profit community schools, or it could mean for-profit private schools. Voucher systems could also play a role in some of these scenarios. Individuals and local communities need freedom and flexibility in order to provide quality education, as no two communities or individuals are identical. I strongly believe that centralized "one size fits all" approaches are definitely *not* the solution for providing quality education. Yet centralized "one size fits all" methods are exactly where we are headed with education in the US. Importantly, because "education" (in the form of indoctrination and conformity/obedience training) can cause as much harm as it can good, it *must* be guarded carefully by an attentive public. This is why I am a strong advocate of *local* oversight by parents, teachers, and other local community members. It would be much more difficult to corrupt school systems in three thousand individual counties or communities than it would be to corrupt a single national (or global) education standard, as was done in communist Poland, and as many people argue has happened in the US with the recent Common Core standards.

So if you don't like what your school is teaching your children or how they are being indoctrinated, take them out of school and home school them, or find an alternative school such as a Montessori school. Better yet, create your own local community of teachers and home school children in groups based on your own shared values. This serves two purposes. One, it removes your child from being exposed to things you had no idea was being taught in some schools, and two, it allows you to withdraw support from an oppressive government system. No time, you say? Well, let me break it to you gently: I was taught by our "wonderful" public education system, and it taught me to dislike who I was, and it also taught me to disconnect from my parents because they weren't "Americanized." So either find time, or your child will be brainwashed and might just eventually turn against you. The Nazi government used this very tactic to get children to spy on their own parents. Maybe one day little Johnny will report you to the IRS for that bit of income you "forgot" to report. You'll correct them after school, you say? How can you compete with eight hours a day of indoctrination with a weekend of softball?

No matter what the subject, find ways around the corrupt and oppressive system. There are many ways to circumvent oppression in a non-compliant manner, without directly confronting the state, and without supporting big businesses. Here are some additional random examples.

Conduct as much of your business or financial transactions as you can in cash. This has several benefits. First, it can be a means to escape paying more taxes, and thus you will be partially cutting off their funding. That's an astute way to begin to creatively and nonviolently disengage from the endless cycle of oppression. Don't pay for your own enslavement. Withdraw your financial support from the corrupt system. Second, it increases your privacy. Third, it actually improves your financial security as digital "money" in the bank can be frozen or confiscated at any time. This may become increasingly difficult in the future as we move to a "cashless society." Making this practice more difficult is probably one of the reasons *for* the great push for the cashless society. In which case there is always precious metals and barter. Who wants their worthless green paper anyway?

Instead of paying for products or services with politically-controlled counterfeit "dollars," pay with precious metals, or barter your goods, services, or time with others. Start a local barter network. If you can trade services or goods directly, it's best to forego the paper trail. If money doesn't change hands, you can avoid all kinds of problems with the government. Barter has become a natural response to the tax collector.

Instead of keeping money at risk in the bank at zero or negative net interest rates, in a 401(k) or IRA, or in manipulated stock markets, pay off debts, buy tangible supplies and equipment, buy land, or buy precious metals. Anything in a bank or financial account can easily be stolen by bankers or seized by government or forced into US Treasury bonds. This also obviously applies to government retirement accounts like Social Security or government pensions. Some people recommend crypto-currencies like Bitcoin as an alternative, but I am not yet convinced of the long term viability of these. Anything digital can easily disappear. In times like these, if you don't physically take possession, you don't own it.

Realize that if you have a lot of debt, either to a bank such as a mortgage or credit cards, or to the Federal Government in the form of student loans, you can also be easily oppressed by the debt collectors. This is actually one method of financial or economic warfare being used against the American public: making people debt slaves. Fake or counterfeit currency ("dollars") are created out of nothing and loaned out, and because of the way the banking and loans are set up, it is very difficult to ever become free of that debt. If possible, avoid the trap; don't support this process of financial indentured servitude. If you are already in such a situation, find a way out. Eliminating debts defeats a method that can be used to enslave and oppress you. There are different ways to eliminate debt, from simply paying them off, to filing bankruptcy, to repudiation. I will leave it up to the reader to decide what the "right" thing to do is. Whatever your approach, it is important to understand that, as explained previously, the banking and monetary systems are rigged against individuals, and in favor of big banks and the Federal Government.

If you want to build on your land, but are having difficulty with local permits, find out what the minimum square footage is for required said permit, and build smaller than that. So what if you have ten different buildings, each only ten-by-twenty feet? (That's still two thousand square feet!) At least then you can have the structures. Alternately, use several movable structures, such as travel trailers, to live in and use a "toy hauler" for a garage. Or, just build without the permits. My experience is that bureaucrats will eventually go away if they don't think you will be an easy or compliant target.

Don't participate in social networks that compromise your privacy. Reduce your digital footprint. Giving Facebook your whole life story is the same as giving it to the NSA. This also applies to smart phones or other digital gadgets (HDTVs?) used to spy on you.

Use encryption and other software tools to improve your online privacy. The Tor anonymity network is one example of a privacy-enhancing software tool. But realize that none of these will be foolproof against someone who is highly determined and has a significant amount of resources to crack such measures at their disposal.

Boycott companies that work to oppress you or are in bed with the government to do so. One example is to not do business with any of the big Wall Street banks, but there are many others that would fall under this category. Remember: many of the same people who own the puppet politicians and pull their strings are the same people who own many of the major businesses or corporations. It is a multi-pronged approach to tyranny.

Once things start to really break down in the US due to whatever causes — whether it is an economic collapse, another war, a pandemic, or simply political oppression and total lack of respect for the

Constitution by those who swore to uphold it — the more the general public will find ways to be non-compliant over laws that just can't be justified. When civilization stops functioning because of unreasonable laws, people *will* become non-compliant toward those laws out of pure necessity. Determine which laws are rational, moral, and justifiable in your community, and don't allow the bureaucrats exceed that by one iota; they have an annoying habit of trying to do so. For example, in the small town near where I live, pretty much everyone ignores building permits, and outside of increased property taxes there have been almost no consequences to that.

If you don't like "breaking" laws or circumventing them, then get involved in changing them on the local level. Don't just accept rules placed upon you that don't make any sense and have no rational or moral justification. Get involved in your community, and if you don't like something, such as glyphosate being sprayed on your county road, do something about it.

But don't sit back and do nothing; *to do nothing is to accept the oppression.*

4. Create positive alternatives to the oppressive system so people don't have to depend on it. Ultimately, outcompete the existing structures with something better.

Stop begging or expecting the government to take care of everything. If you want a better world, go make it happen. Compared to the rigged political process or the slow process of mass education, the work of outcompeting the state through innovation is a promising strategy. Consider the example of the US Post Office. It has not been privatized or eliminated, but it has fallen into disuse and irrelevancy, thanks to the creation of better alternative ways of communicating. While working on this approach, keep in mind that voluntary relationships outcompete coerced ones, and openness and transparency defeat concealment and deceit.

"Inventions ... have done far more to overpower oppression than every volume of political thought ever written." –Doug Casey

Start a true free market business, which are alternately known as "private market" or "black market" or "underground" options. This doesn't mean you should do something truly illegal; it just means that you may not quite be following all the insane and oppressive regulations and taxes. Undermine the control apparatus with a million acts of entrepreneurship, and make a living, or supplement your income, in the process.

Learn a trade or a skill. Apply your skills or interests to produce something or provide a service of value. This not only withdraws your support from a corrupt system, it creates positive alternatives that will also make you and your local community more independent and resilient. By either starting or supporting small businesses that share values of liberty, you eliminate support to large corporations who may be working against your values or interests. Your imagination is your only limit here. Even if you don't make this a full time gig, it will still allow you to independently earn extra income, or at least use for yourself the products or services you can produce.

Since it is highly likely that in the near future the US economy will have a significant economic/financial/currency crash, it is important to realize that products and services that may be in demand now may not be in the future. Your financial adviser or insurance sales business will have no place in a world without a functioning financial system. You will have to be able to do something real. The opposite of that is also potentially true. The products and services that may be in demand in a post-crash economy may not make for good business models in the current environment. A small scale US-based manufacturing business may struggle now while the imports are flowing from China. But if trade is cut off for whatever reason, that business could turn into a gold mine. Thus, it is a good idea to hedge your bets with more than one type of product, service, or business model, or develop a business model that will work in both pre and post-economic crash environments.

I won't provide suggestions for pre-crash business models because that is a book (at least) unto itself. However, if you have the proper training or skills, one field that would be a good model both before and after any economic crash is healthcare, but not using the typical "in the system" model. Provide health services for cash, outside of the insurance and government system.

After the crash, people are going to need essentials that may not be as readily available as they are now. Examples for after the crash include: food production (gardening/livestock), food preservation, building construction, plumbing/electrician, furniture/woodworking, welding, auto repair, other repair services (appliance, computers, other electronics), gunsmithing and ammunition production/reloading, biodiesel, home made ethanol, sew custom clothes, make soap and personal care products, build web sites or program software (assuming the internet is still up, these will still be needed), grow herbs and sell nutritional/medicinal supplements, teach classes.

As mentioned earlier, creating alternative education and schooling solutions will be another opportunity. Since our public schools have largely been taken over by the Federal Government for brainwashing purposes, it is important that we create superior alternatives.

One idea that I think has been largely overlooked, and which I think could become vital, is small scale manufacturing using a combination of small machine shops and 3D printing. Much of the US large scale manufacturing has been shipped overseas, but that does not mean the need for manufacturing goes away. If China refuses to accept US dollars, or cuts off trade for military or political reasons, people in the US are going to be in a world of hurt regarding manufactured goods. 3D printers, computers, and design software are all coming down significantly in price. Yet unless you get expensive CNC machining equipment, it is not quite ready to work with metal materials (at least at the time of this writing). This will possibly change eventually. But for now, we still need machinists and machine shops, welders, and CNC equipment. I see two current options for providing this. First, there are still many small businesses with this capacity in the US. Second, there are a growing number of "maker spaces" available throughout the US that allow you to either rent or use production equipment freely. Local, small-scale fabrication facilities like these could become critical infrastructure in the future I see likely coming to the US.

Another possibility is to stock up on alternative energy production equipment with the intent of starting your own "power company" if there is ever a "grid down" type of situation.

Create community-based security, outside of the police system if you need to, but involve the local Sheriff's office if they abide by the Constitution. Oath Keepers have resources to help with this. As Solidarity learned, if you can resolve problems in your local community without the police, it eliminates the excuse for the police to come in to your community to harass people. This also reduces the influence of the Federal Government on your local community. Don't limit this to community security either. Take responsibility and make plans for the security of yourself and your own family, should help not arrive quickly enough.

Create an alternative, truthful free press. This was a major component of Solidarity. There are already many, many alternative media websites that provide this However, what if the internet becomes censored or is shut down? People will still need to have a way to spread news and information, communicate, and to advertise products and services.

In areas where fires are a frequent problem, such as many forested rural locales, consider joining a volunteer fire department. You can often also learn valuable skills this way, such as EMT or Paramedic training. If there is no volunteer fire department, see if your local professional fire crew will let you volunteer.

If you have the appropriate knowledge, skills, or background, provide legal services to liberty-minded business owners and activists. In my opinion, it is best to minimize contact with the state as much as possible, but there will be times when it is unavoidable. Being able to get legal assistance from someone who is philosophically sympathetic will certainly be valuable. This only holds true so long as the current legal system continues to exist.

Along a similar line as legal assistance, bypass the corrupted court system to create and use private arbitration and private escrow services for contracts. This is a great way to avoid government interference or involvement.

Create alternative financial systems based on sound money and financial practices. This could not only involve barter and using alternative money like precious metals, but it could also involve direct lending from an individual or group for projects within their own community by people who actually care about the outcome, rather than merely extracting money and power.

For certain activities it may be necessary to set up "safe homes" and "floating offices." These were common practices among Solidarity in communist Poland, particularly for people operating the free press. The state doesn't like being outcompeted by better, more honest services. So for activities that can't easily be moved, you may have to operate covertly (safe houses) to remain, well, safe. Alternately, for those activities that can be moved around, it would be a good idea to do so. It is harder to catch that which is regularly on the move.

Whatever your circumstance, you have to become independent of the government by becoming as self sufficient as possible. As long as you are *dependent* on any government service or assistance, even disability checks, you are dependent on said government, and therefore that government has some control over you.

I understand that some people have disabilities that prevent them from working a full time job. For such people, I'm not suggesting getting a full-time job. Instead, I am suggesting to find a way to earn your own income outside of government assistance. I feel safe in saying that any government assistance may not always be there to rely on. So

if you are physically disabled, that doesn't mean your mind is disabled too, or vice-versa. Here in America, we are taught to treat certain conditions such as (non-violent) schizophrenia, autism, wheelchair-bound, blind, deaf, and the like, as disabling rather than as an individual with different abilities or skills. What we have failed is to recognize that these individuals are perfectly capable of contributing to society. The hard part is figuring out how. What we should do instead is treat these individuals as contributors to society by accepting their talents and not giving them disability-related labels. A great example is Temple Grandin. She was born autistic in a world where autism was very much misunderstood. Despite how her mother was treated by the supposed "medical professionals" of that time, she never treated Temple as a child with disabilities. Sure, she took her to special schools, but she also sent her to a college and pushed her to find her calling. Temple Grandin's college research led her to the development of a different and more humane practice for raising cattle. She also has a website for helping other people with autism find their calling.[22] While she still holds the autistic label, in her case, that label is crucial to her contribution to society. While she may be less capable than a "normal" person in certain aspects, her abilities in other areas far exceed most "normal" people, and that is something to truly appreciate.

I include schizophrenia because not all schizophrenic individuals are incapable of functioning in society. Unfortunately, what we usually hear in the media about such individuals is that they are violent. But there are plenty of individuals who have "personality disorders" that function fine in society. It's when we start to label them that it becomes a problem. The same goes for people who are wheelchair-bound, deaf, or blind, or have other disabilities.

If you are a person with such a disability, find your niche. Find a way that you can be self reliant. I realize that's not practical advice for everyone, but for many it is, particularly those who receive government assistance but do not have any disabilities.

So your goal should be to become independent of government. Find a way to earn a living; learn a trade, teach yourself some skills, take a college course, and learn something that will be valued and always needed. But don't simply think and act with the present in mind. Think about and act based on what the future might hold, particularly after a major economic crash.

If you learn to weld, stock up on all the tools and supplies you will need and learn how to improvise if you don't have all the right materials. If you learn to be a plumber, again, stock up on common supplies, and learn to be creative in working with limited resources. If you learn to hunt or raise livestock, then learn to butcher and process the meat yourself rather than hiring someone else to do it for you. If you learn to garden, learn how to make your own nutritious soil from compost and manure and avoid using store bought products. Learn, learn, and learn. Then take it to the next level, and learn some more. Heck, you might as well learn how to re-invent paper newsletters, because if the internet becomes controlled, we might be at a loss on how to communicate *real* news otherwise. In a worst case scenario, maybe even learn how to use an old fashioned type writer (if you can find one). A computer and printer would be more efficient, but some typewriters don't require electricity, which would come in handy if the power is out. Alternately develop plans to create private patchwork computer networks using technology like WiFi and "Darknet" approaches like private IP addresses.[23] The opportunities are endless; you just have to find what works for you.

Just remember, as long as you are dependent on government, then government has control over you. That is what happened in Poland with politicians who needed that paycheck, and the special benefits they received. Likewise for the police, who were just trying to feed their families. This was also true for the Polish military, who never before attacked their own citizens, but as a means to feed their kids they had to do as ordered. Self sufficiency is a key step toward independence from a tyrannical or oppressive government.

This isn't to say that you can't work a normal eight-to-five job if you please. You can still live parallel to the system. As stated by a former regime supporter who was affected by the attacks of 1968 on Czechoslovakia: "We started to act like free people. If you wanted to live in such a way, you had to give up any kind of career. So we crossed the barrier of being dissidents. *We became people who lived freely in a totalitarian society.* That was not yet opposition. After leaving prison, those who could, finished their studies; we worked in factories or whatever. But we lived parallel to the system."[24]

5. Be creative; find other ways to beat the oppressive system

The Polish organization KOR, which I mentioned earlier, is a very inspiring organization. It printed books that were outlawed, such as George Orwell's writings. It printed news that no other "legal" paper would. They had their own printing shop, and used the money they raised from selling their printed material (and generous donations they received) to pay for their operations, and to help those who were unfairly treated when arrested. They worked with lawyers to help workers who had been beaten, and they educated the public about issues that were illegal to discuss, such as ideas of freedom.

KOR was given bad press by the censored media on a regular basis, but they didn't let that deter them. They stuck to their principles, and continued working for a better Poland. I already see many organizations in the US that have the same principles. One example is the Innocence Project, which concentrates on using DNA evidence to exonerate wrongfully convicted people. This organization gets little attention and little funding, but is a strong organization that has helped many families. As the famous quote by Margaret Mead states: "Never doubt that a small group of thoughtful, committed citizens can change the world; indeed, it's the only thing that ever has."

There was another huge organization in Poland that I have not discussed much so far, because frankly, I know little about it. But in doing my research and talking with my relatives about what made Solidarity successful, and an online search of Polish history, I found out about "The Orange Alternative," which was apparently an artistic movement that was popular with the college crowd and used freedom of expression to protest.[25] Apparently this Orange Alternative group used absurd artistic methods to humiliate the government: "Orange Alternative participants looked for spots on city walls where the regime had painted over anti-Communist graffiti, in order to paint humorous images of dwarves on these spots. They could not be arrested by the police for opposition to the Communist regime without the authorities becoming a laughingstock over their alarm at painted dwarves on city streets." There was ultimately the "Revolution of Dwarves" in 1988, where over ten thousand people wearing orange dwarf hats marched through the city of Wrocław. The government didn't know how to respond.[26] One of the most effective ways to belittle the power of tyrants is to laugh at them.

You cannot ignore the most important contributing factor to the survival of Solidarity: the independent un-censored newspapers. There were many, and many people (especially women) risked their livelihoods in an effort to get real news out.

The ability to dispense accurate news will play a key role in the future of America as well. While right now it is simple with the internet and the click of a button to get news of any sort, as mentioned earlier, this might not be possible if the internet is ever restricted or disabled. The alternative media leaders of Poland, when they heard rumors of martial law coming, had the forethought to stock up on crucial supplies such as typewriter ribbons and paper[27] along with contact information of various sources who would help bring the news and deliver the news. Such news was delivered on foot from home to home as transportation was shut down during martial law. One of the major papers went so far as to have a team memorize all the important names and addresses of contacts so that there would be no written evidence, which would allow the officials discover their sources.[28] Such actions can not be dismissed as anything but legendary.

This does not mean that the previous actions of generations before us are the right actions for us now. So far in our current time, it seems we keep repeating the same approaches, because that's all we have been able come up with. We keep trying to change laws that are immoral only to lose due to voting fraud. We continue electing politicians even though we know they are outright lying to and betraying us. We continue to pay taxes, even though that very same money is then later used as a weapon against us. But what if a different approach was tried?

What if we could circumvent the system and build a better, different, and honest system? People would contribute once they saw how effective this new approach would be. We would no longer be perpetually stuck with the status quo circumstances that have been demonstrated over and over as corrupt and dysfunctional. People would naturally withdraw support from the corrupt, broken system if effective alternatives existed, particularly if they were gaining public support. Rather than continue being in a controlled box trying to take control from within, we act outside the box and create a new system that makes the old system and its corruption obsolete.

6. Don't blindly accept propaganda; research and fact check to find the truth

Tyrants typically use multiple approaches to oppress people. These include:

1. Disinformation, propaganda, fear, and psychological warfare through the abuse of language.

2. Financial and economic warfare.

3. Health warfare. Starvation, malnourishment, contaminated water and

food, limiting access to health care, or providing "healthcare" that is not really helpful. Sick people are more compliant and less able to disobey or fight back.

4. Physical violence of force (police/military raids, martial law, and the police state).

They usually use them in this order because it is more efficient and cost-effective to persuade and brainwash people into enslaving themselves than it is implement a police state with physical force. If people will sheepishly cooperate with every dictate, no matter how absurd, why bother going to any more trouble? Likewise, it is easier and more beneficial to turn the populace into financial or economic dependents than it is to implement a police state. It is far more profitable to turn people into debt slaves than it is to have to pay for maintaining martial law. Neither psychological independence, nor financial independence, nor logistical independence can be permitted by tyrants, because they make people more free. Physical force is a last resort for tyrants. It is expensive and messy, and tends to stir up as much resistance as it suppresses. It also tends to expose the tyrants for who they really are, which is usually sociopaths. It is much easier to hide behind disinformation and covert financial oppression than it is to hide behind the barrel of a gun.

For individuals to live in freedom, all of these situations must be avoided or overcome. In many cases, physical resistance (or at least physical independence) becomes necessary, and economic resources are typically needed to a certain degree. However, the first step to freedom is always overcoming the psychological and intellectual hurdles used to control and manipulate people. A big part of that is understanding how language can be used both to manipulate people, and to set their minds free.

Language can be tricky. Sometimes people have different meanings for various words. Different people will illicit different emotions for certain words such as feminist, anarchist, liberal, progressive, prepper, globalism, and so on. We had that problem in Poland. There are often different meanings from one culture to another — internationalism, leftist politics, feminism, collaboration — these were all identified with communism leadership, which was totalitarian.[29] When Shana Penn was interviewing the Polish Women who ran the underground press during martial law, she experienced the same language bloc when interviewing these women. They responded adversely to questions such as "Did you think of yourself as a leader?" To these women, leadership meant power.[30] Although that wasn't the question that Shana Penn was asking, because of her choice of words the response was poor, and rather than fight over identity/position, these women humbly did the job that needed to be done, as there was no time to worry about status/position.[31]

In this case, the women who fought so strongly for a common goal of freedom and liberty ended up trading full store shelves for less freedom. Not only did they lose many of their civil rights after communism fell, but to speak out against the problem often meant being called an ideologist, which in those days, was a code word for "communist." This was, of course, one of the greater insults to the liberty-minded people of the time.[32] Another important factor to remember is that language can have many different translations.

Such language confusion, or outright abuse, is pervasive even today in America with the words I mentioned above.

Here are some different interpretations:

Feminist: "Women should rule the world!" vs. "Women should be treated equally."

Anarchist: "There are no rules, there will be chaos!" vs. "There are no *rulers*, and it is in people's best interest to cooperate and resolve disputes civilly."

Liberal: "About what?"

Progressive: "Where are we going?"

Prepper: "A paranoid hoarder." vs. "Someone who makes logical preparations for potential adverse conditions."

Globalism: "The theory that multiple nations or the entire world should be so interconnected and interdependent that there is no localized self sufficiency and there are multiple points of failure, thus ensuring the greatest societal fragility possible – and all ultimately controlled in a "top down" manner by a small number of well connected elitists. Contrast with localism: "smaller communities that are organized on a the basis of a "bottom up" approach rather than a "top down" approach, and which are largely self sufficient and, therefore far more protected and insulated from any adverse events, whether economic, political, natural disaster, etc.

We will all find our own definitions for these types of words somewhere in the sea of language. What is important is that individuals clarify their meanings for words, so people can communicate effectively and honestly, without making assumptions, and without misrepresenting intentions via language abuse.

Government politicians and bureaucrats on the other hand, are very proficient at abusing language with the intention of deceiving. Some of the most exotic linguistic manipulation and abuse is used in defense of government, especially in supposed "democratic" societies. How else could they make masters appear as servants? But sometimes the camouflage is so comical it reveals, rather than conceals. For example, under the Affordable Care Act, you are "asked" for a "contribution" rather than being "required" to pay a "tax". Only linguistic camouflage can disguise "taxes"[33-34] collected at the point of a gun - into "user fees" or "contributions." Power lives behind the walls of euphemism. To quote Lewis Carroll's *Through the Looking Glass*:

> 'When *I* use a word,' Humpty Dumpty said, in rather a scornful tone, 'it means just what I choose it to mean — neither more

nor less.'

'The question is,' said Alice, 'whether you *can* make words mean so many different things.'

'The question is,' said Humpty Dumpty, *'which is to be master — that's all.'*

Lewis Carroll certainly understood how the elites of his time abused language for the benefit of their own power, and their tactics have only been refined since. I am not aware of any euphemisms for robberies or muggings. No one has the nerve to make them appear as anything other than what they are. But abusing language with twisted semantics and euphemisms is central to the government enterprise. You see, we ordinary folks can't be trusted with the simple truth of simple language. Complicated legalese must be used instead. So who does that complicated legalese benefit? Politicians and lawyers; certainly not average people. The first tool that tyrants use to enslave people is language.

Here is the way it works: the media or politicians spew information and mention certain words, and we associate those words with some particular contrivance, rather than the real thing. Before you judge someone based on the terminology they use, fact-check the words to make sure you have *their* definitions correct. Meanings are not in words, meanings come from the people who use them. Even various types of dictionaries can define words differently; legal dictionaries and lawyers are notorious for doing this.

Interestingly, when the controlled Polish media was seriously pushing the agenda to make Solidarity look bad, one of the things they said was that Solidarity was against KOR. KOR, which stands for workers' defense committee, was an underground organization and press intended to aid families that were affected by the 1976 arrests.[35] Lech Wałęsa worked very closely with this organization for many years. And since Wałęsa co-founded Solidarity, it would seem strange that all of a sudden Solidarity was against KOR. Yet, many people fell for such lies. As I learned a long time ago, "Show me the data" and "Cui bono" ("who benefits") are the two questions you should be asking in situations where you're not sure who the "good" guy is and who the "bad" guy is.

As Lech Wałęsa had written, "The newspaper prattle was intended to hide the thousands of idle factories and the people in them, full of rebellion and hope. This propaganda had still one more, very characteristic aim: it was to persuade people that those disruptions of work and irregularities were caused not by the workers, nor even by specific people, but by "the work force", anonymous and impersonal." In other words, the propagandized media framed the opposition in the most-dis-empowering way possible, as those in power typically do. Wałęsa further referred to the role of a worker as a tool, and tools do not strike, implying that ordinary workers held no power against the system. When in all reality, millions of workers were breaking down the barriers placed upon them and yelling for a strike, something the powers tried to suppress.[36]

Another example from Poland where fear and disinformation was used was the day prior to the ruling deciding Solidarity's legal status. Last minute efforts were made to influence the legal ruling through propaganda. The communist government claimed that Polish and Soviet troops had been performing joint exercises over the prior several days. There was increased media attention on the issue, including film clips of the exercises, in an effort to influence the vote outcome. However, closer analysis of the films showed that the exercises were done in summer weather based on the uniforms worn by the troops and the presence of leaves on the trees. Yet at that time it was winter in Poland, and thus the fear mongering was discredited.[37] This story provides a good example of the type of propaganda that can be used to scare people into acquiescing or subordinating themselves to the powers that be, and potentially vote on an issues in a way they didn't intend to or agree with.

It is useful to point out that in Poland during the 1980s everyone knew that everything on TV and in the official newspapers was a lie. It was a natural tendency to believe nothing from the official sources. If anything, the people knew it was the opposite, and so they knew that if the official media said something was good, then it was bad, and if the media said something was bad, then it was really good. It got to the point where the people didn't know if something was really true or not, such as when the civil rights movement occurred in America.[38] This is quite different from the US at present where a majority of Americans still naively believe that what is reported in the mainstream "news" actually accurately represents what is really happening.

Another important angle to consider is that disinformation can come in many forms. When the *original* Black Panther organization in the US was trying to fight the oppression of African Americans in the 1960s, disinformation pamphlets were released by the FBI and possibly the police, in an effort to make the Black Panthers appear as though their goal was to *instigate* violence against police, when in reality their position was to *defend* themselves against police violence and oppression. That reputation for violence was then promoted and exaggerated as propaganda intended to confuse the public and discredit the organization. Ultimately it worked in making many people believe that the Black Panthers were primarily a violent organization rather than a political one, and that reputation still persists today.[39-40] This is not dissimilar to how so-called "patriot" groups today are often characterized by the media with a broad brush as all being racist or "white supremacist," when in reality this is the rare and unfortunate exception rather than the norm.

I use these examples not because I necessarily agree or disagree with these particular political perspectives, but rather to point out that sometimes it is extremely difficult to know who is lying and who is not. Sometimes it is easier to become disillusioned about determining what the facts truly are. Discerning or determining the truth is often a difficult journey for which I have no easy answers. The only real answer is to hold an unwavering commitment to finding the truth, even if it may conflict with what you originally believed.

A different tactic of propaganda occurred when the Solidarity miners locked themselves in the mines (a dangerous risk) during one of their strikes. The Polish government was so desperate to try to get them to come out that they first offered perks to end the strikes,[41] but it was a no go. So instead, they used tactics of fake stories of ill family members, wives having gone into labor, and even had women impersonators beg on the radio for the miners (mostly men) to come out. But the miners figured out it was all a lie because there were "tells," or signs of fabrications. For example, there were no ill family members, or because one of the "wives" in labor was supposed to be the wife of a miner who wasn't even married.[42] Oops.

About two months prior to martial law in Poland, Jaruzelski ordered to extend the Polish military conscription period (Poles were required to serve two years in the military) by two months, with data analysis implying that the turnover in troops during martial law wouldn't work out very well. The troops were disbursed over rural areas where the Solidarity presence wasn't as strong, and the military was more respected. However, just a couple weeks prior to martial law, the government had recalled these groups, and disbursed similar but larger group in the forty-nine provincial capitals. The number of troops varied by city size, but the explanation for this was, "The groups would include specialists in medical support, supply, communications, and other technical areas to help people prepare for the hardships of winter. The troops were tasked with insuring the efficient utilization of local resources, including the provision of fuels, electric power, transportation, and health services."[43] This was quite a way to convince the people that the military was on their side while disbursing the military throughout the country, which was really a strategic placement of troops prior to the announcement of martial law. The description of the justification of the disbursement of military members also sounds eerily similar to US Presidential Executive Order 13603 which in a nutshell claims the President has the authority to take control over all sources of food, water, medication, energy, and transportation, to "allocate resources" as the President and his cabinet members see fit. [44-45] Of course this is all described as being for the purpose of "national defense preparedness" but nowhere in the document does it state that these powers are limited to national defense or national emergencies.

During this time, Solidarity was also weakened by disinformation in the controlled media, taking comments of union members out of context, implying that union members were madman. It was described as "the most coordinated and vitriolic media campaign ever against Solidarity."[46]

Food was also used as a weapon against the people. While Solidarity was blamed for the food shortages, it was exposed that the food warehouses (which were controlled by the government) were actually full of food,[47] which was rotting away as the people starved.

There are other ways for those in power to control an individual's actions by disinformation. In December of 1970, due to large price increases and the witness of nomenklatura receiving special benefits while the rest of the people starved, the Polish workers responded with work stoppages and public demonstrations throughout the country. This was before they learned the important lesson that open public demonstrations allowed for government agent provocateurs to disrupt the demonstrations. During such public demonstrations the police would deploy provocateurs in an effort to discredit demonstrators.[48] This allowed justification for the regime to "meet violence with violence" and the police and army were ordered in to shoot workers.[49] However, the government found that the Poles were true to their heritage, and a Pole doesn't usually kill a Pole. Much of the military resisted orders to shoot, and instead offered gas masks to the workers, and discarded their rifles into the waters.[50] The modern equivalent to this in America would be if large numbers of the active US military joined Oath Keepers, pledged not to infringe on Americans right to peaceably assemble, and then were ordered to shoot protesters, and instead of doing so, stood down and allowed the protest to continue.

In response to the Polish soldiers' conciliatory actions toward the protestors, the Polish government brought in soldiers from outside of the area and drove them around in locked trucks so they had no idea what was going on other than seeing tanks on the streets. These soldiers were sleep deprived and cold, were not allowed to make contact with the people, and were tricked into believing that they were shooting at Germans instead of Poles. So they shot. Some soldiers did make contact with the civilian targets, and realized what was going on. At that point they refused orders again, even though they were threatened with being court-martialed.[51] Regardless, the damage was already done.

This is where understanding that the US Constitution supersedes the Uniform Code of Military Justice (UCMJ) is extremely important. The UCMJ are laws for the military, which are authorized according to the Constitution, therefore the Constitution supersedes the UCMJ. The idea of being court-martialed is scary to most active duty military personnel. If such threats are used against our military as they were in Poland, it will be crucial for our military to understand that because the Constitution supersedes the UCMJ, they can not be convicted for adhering to the Constitution. If anything, they can be convicted for following unethical orders and harming innocent people. This is exactly what happened to Nazi officers at the Nuremberg trials, which resulted in the creation of the International Criminal Court.[52]

Finally on this topic, when evaluating information or propaganda, just remember the two most important questions you should be asking: where's the data, and who benefits? The answers to these questions will usually lead you to who stated the information, and what their true intent was.

7. To the degree possible, have the support of a number of people, and be organized

The first part of this section provides some insights and suggestions on how to operate if you do have the support of a large number of relatively organized people, as did the Solidarity movement in Poland. However, what if you don't have a large organization to provide support? Do not get discouraged; that scenario will be covered later in this section.

While there are certain advantages to having a large number of organized supporters, there can also be disadvantages. Similarly, there can be certain circumstances where working in smaller, decentralized, disconnected groups can offer several advantages as well. Which strategy is more appropriate at any given time will depend the specific circumstances and goals of the time.

There were many reasons that strikes were threatened in Poland between 1980 and the end of 1981. During this time was when Solidarity had gained legal (though mostly unrecognized) status. As mentioned before, the only power the Poles had against their government was strikes. But the strikes in those times were not like the strikes we know in America. Rather, the workers would pack extra clothes, sleeping bags, and food. The workers would lock themselves in the shipyards, the mines, the steel factories, the very buildings were things were produced, and they refused to work. The government couldn't bring in temporary employees to keep the workflow going, and that's how the strikes were effective.

The reason the workers moved the strikes indoors was because

318

they learned from Polish history. Previously, when the Poles went on strike in the streets, it resulted in mass beatings, people getting shot, and easy identification of protesters, which resulted in more arrests.[53] People realized that protesting in the streets allowed for provocateurs to come in and cause riots which only led to the beatings and deaths. It was safer to strike from inside the workplace, where they could lock themselves in. However, this tactic may prove more difficult for Americans to implement, as not many things are still made in America today. That is OK; we have a number of other approaches that we can employ, according to each individual's circumstance.

The reasons for the Polish strikes were important as well. Food price hikes were a common reason, but so were the unjust firings of employees, and the demands for the release of arrested political activists. Specifically, two activists, Jan Norzniak and Piotr Sapiello who were sentenced to five years. A strike was organized demanding their release, and also included ending harassment of the accused, along with other demands.[54] It started with a flyer that said "Today Narozniak, tomorrow Wałęsa, and the day after tomorrow – you."[55] The two activists were released seven days after their arrest.[56] This was only effective because the strikers agreed on their demands and stayed consistent.

I want to mention other important leaders in the Solidarity movement. I've written about Lech Wałęsa and the Pope, but not about Anna Walentynowicz. She is one that has received little credit for her contribution to the movement. It was her employment termination that led to the strikes in August of 1980. She was a welder and then a crane operator, who turned in her supervisor for a dishonest act, but rather than have the supervisor punished, she lost her job.[57] Another source states that she was fired due to trying to promote a memorial for the protesters killed in the 1970 strikes.[58-59] Regardless of the reason for her termination, the strike occurred and the other workers demanded that she be hired back. Anna wasn't just some random shipyard worker. She was very much appreciated by her fellow co-workers, as she was always one that was fighting for what was right, despite the fact that she might get fired. Many Poles will say that without her, Wałęsa would have never gained such popularity.

Another approach that Solidarity employed was the use of women in the movement. Thanks to stereotypes, women were often able to get away with a little bit more in hiding from surveillance. This may seem sexist to some, but let's be real. If batting your eye lashes at a guard gets you through a security checkpoint with an illegal gun, and on the other side lurks danger that you can't escape without a gun, would you not bat your eyelashes at the lonely security guard? I'm not saying this was what Anna Walentynowicz did. Actually, my research shows quite the opposite. However, many women did accept their beauty as a way to win the struggle, by dressing up in high heels with makeup, or by using their pregnancy as a way to conceal newspapers intended for distribution. Even the elder women were experts at duping the police into thinking it's just an innocent old lady with a hat and walking stick that you would never perform a body search on.[60] These women should also receive credit for their acts of courage. In reality, most women during that time that were involved in politics lived double lives and used the stereotype camouflage to their advantage. Dirty diapers were less likely to be searched, neither were washing machines, ovens and other nooks and crannies that would be considered women's domesticity.[61] It was a very common belief that women just didn't have time for politics due to their domestic responsibilities.[62]

According to the book Solidarity's Secret: The women who defeated Communism in Poland by Shana Penn, the Polish "national secret" was the women. When martial law was ordered in 1981, over ten thousand activists were arrested, only ten percent of which were women. History shows this was because the communist government paid little attention to the women, and therefore they were considered less likely to be involved in the Solidarity movement. This allowed seven women to continue the Solidarity organization underground after the martial law arrests of December of 1981, and to write the main underground newspaper, which was a major contributor to Solidarity's continuity. This was especially critical since much of the Solidarity leadership, Wałęsa included, were arrested, and these seven women ran their underground news articles using names of Solidarity leaders that they protected in hiding. While the ZOMO and secret police searched for these few remaining male activists, the women who did all the work were able to operate unnoticed, as they snuck in typewriters, ink, and moved from place to place to evade capture. This is an example of how the "floating offices" that were mentioned earlier were used.

The continued Solidarity resistance after martial law was in place ultimately led to Jaruzelski's downfall. He thought his problems were men like Wałęsa, and did not believe that women had any power.[63] Thus these seven women played a huge role in keeping the movement going. It was to their advantage that they looked like ordinary Polish women, and did not seem like a threat, as no one saw these women as organizers of an illegal organization. Few people know that it was these seven women who immediately got together and came up with a plan to find the few male Solidarity leaders who eluded arrest and put them into hiding. They then proceeded to continue to print the real news via an underground newspaper using the men in hiding as the supposed voice. They continued this underground charade for almost a decade.[64] These seven women kept Solidarity alive during the most devastating hit on the organization.

These women did not accomplish this without hardships. They often had to send their children to live with extended family and had to give up on any chance of a career or education. They had to constantly move and live among strangers that were willing to take them in. These women also gave up most recognition within the movement for several reasons, one of which was the fact that they were women. More importantly, they avoided the spotlight of recognition to maintain their secret positions of running the Solidarity union underground, while martial law was in effect. None of these women received the appropriate credit they should have, and yet, they were "The National Secret."[65] These women humbly know the crucial role they played in helping to bring down communism in Poland.

While I doubt that history would repeat itself in the sense of women being disregarded as unlikely leaders of an illegal organization, there is something to be said about being a member of a group where you will more likely be overlooked as someone who would potentially be considered a "threat."

When the ten thousand Solidarity leaders were arrested, the principles and beliefs of freedom and prosperity lived on through others, who took over the organization when it lacked leaders. Whether it was women or men, Solidarity kept going, even if it had to be very much underground. This is important, because a strong organization is one that doesn't need the same people to lead it. Organizations based on shared principles, values, and vision can continue even if the leadership changes. When Solidarity's "leaders" were arrested, the communist regime had expected, counted on, and planned for the Solidarity movement to fall apart. But because Solidarity's founding principles were strong and ingrained in the population, new leaders took charge and the movement continued. This is a very important concept, and I believe it to be one of the most important aspects that kept Solidarity going, even if it had to be run from the underground. American liberty activists should strive to incorporate this idea into their thinking and planning.

For any political resistance movement, going underground isn't necessarily bad. If nothing else, it gives the opposition a false sense of security of the movement being wiped out. Such movements can use this advantageously, and only come out strong when a decisive victory can be achieved. The only benefit to working in public during a time when you will be arrested and imprisoned is if you want to make a martyr of yourself to rally public opinion. Otherwise, working underground allows much more freedom to accomplish tangible goals. History teaches that when you are working towards freedom under an oppressive regime, sometimes you have to remain anonymous and underground in order to continue working for that freedom.

With so many people part of a large group like Solidarity, a certain degree of organization become necessary. Depending on the intended strategy and the circumstances of the time, the degree of organization varied from highly connected, to only very loosely connected. When Solidarity members noted that the regime was taking its time in the implementation of the Gdansk agreement (which would make Solidarity an official trade union), they organized a one hour symbolic "warning strike" as a protest. But what was key here was that a single central location had organized a simultaneous strike throughout the entire country.[66] That was no easy task I can assure you. But it told the powers that be how serious and organized the laborers of Poland could be. This further led to strikes being taken seriously by the regime, which was a strategy card well played by the Poles, when they noted that the regime attempted to insert language in the Gdansk agreement that was not initially agreed upon.

Thus the Solidarity movement through organization was able to strike back against the regime. They organized strikes, including a large number of Solidarity members (between 35 and 90 percent of the workforce, depending on which statistics you read) not reporting for work on assigned Saturdays. This occurred after they refused to accept a revised schedule of working two Saturdays a month instead of the promised five day work week, even though they were threatened with not getting paid if they did not come to work.[67] These were demonstrations of strength shown to the regime that the people could not be controlled with threats.

A further demonstration of strength was of the Poles coming together from different groups, such as the laborers and the farmers. This was evidenced by the laborers demands for the inclusion of an independent farmers' union which was initially denied by the Polish Supreme Court as it was ruled that farmers were "self-employed".[68] When a "day of Solidarity" with the farmers was decided for January 28, negotiations between the government and farmers began the next day.[69] But only because the Solidarity leaders organized well, communicated well, and the other workers followed their lead, that these strikes worked so effectively.

This all eventually led to martial law. To me, martial law was and is a desperate last ditch effort to maintain control of a people that will not be controlled, which meant the strikes were becoming effective in overcoming the government oppression. Jaruzelski could not get the Poles under control. Jaruzelski referred to the action of martial as the lesser of two evils, meaning that he had to get the Poles back under the control of the extended Soviet regime, or there would have been an attack on Poland by the Soviet military. Jaruzelski knew that without the threat of a Soviet invasion, he could not count on the Polish military in any crackdown, as there was a strong national tradition that Poles wouldn't shoot Poles. Therefore he was able to use this false choice to convince the military and police to accept martial law as the lesser of two evils.[70] What the Polish security forces failed to consider is that supporting the lesser of two evils is still supporting evil. This is a common tactic used by tyrants: create a limiting false choice between two bad options to justify choosing a bad option, rather than opening up options to a scenario that would actually benefit the people rather than controlling them.

Solidarity members alone did not bring down communism in Poland, even though they did play a key role. By the late 1980s, additional groups had formed by people from different generations who had new ideas. That doesn't mean that Solidarity didn't play a large role, as it was the spark that started so many other great organizations. Just as Lech Wałęsa should not get to take sole credit for Solidarity, Solidarity should not get to take sole credit for defeating an oppressive regime. It was the combination of everyone involved, including the independent newspapers that carried real truthful news. But organization of large numbers of people was the underlying factor.

One important organizational lesson is, if a large number of people are involved in such a movement or in any community in general, the community must have the capability to police itself. If you want to get tyrants out of your community, you need to be able to maintain and restore order on your own so that there is no reason for the gestapo to show up.[71] For example, one of the things that the Solidarity workers did was institute a voluntary ban on alcohol during any strikes, and anyone caught drinking would be banned from Solidarity. This allowed members to stay clear headed, and helped prevent internal conflicts. It was the community governing themselves in order to reduce potential conflict that would create a reason for the gestapo to intervene.

Another extremely important point is that, while organizing a large number of people into a political movement can create certain strengths, such as what Solidarity eventually achieved, doing so can also create certain weaknesses. Depending on the circumstances of the time and the desired strategy, these weaknesses may outweigh any advantages gained. One of these weaknesses is that large organizations create large targets for tyrants to attack. Large organizations can also create single points of failure or defeat, particularly if not managed or organized well. If military strategists have learned anything from guerilla organizations it is that it is much more difficult to stamp out many small independent resistance groups (or "leaderless resistance") than it is to eliminate one large one. Smaller independent groups can also operate flexibly, but when the circumstances call for it, can also operate in cooperation with other small groups to create a temporary larger organization. The type of strategy used by Solidarity would today be characterized by US military analysts as a mostly non-violent type of "fourth-generation warfare" which includes the use of public opinion within its venue.[72] Many historians tend to write about Solidarity as though it was one monolithic movement. But drilling down into the historical details finds that this is not necessarily the case. In many cases, workers from individual factories, individual economic sectors, individual newspapers, or even individual cities, worked completely independently of the rest of Solidarity. Yet when widespread cooperation was called for, they made it happen.

So, with that said, if you do not find the idea of joining a large movement or organization appealing to you, or that starting and leading one is something you may not be interested in, you have options and alternative approaches you can take. Here is a brief list of some things that you can (and should) do without becoming part of any large political movement:

First, as mentioned previously, become as self sufficient or self reliant as possible, both financially and logistically. People who do not depend as much on a job, or the larger "system" benefit from having greater resilience against whatever political or economic turmoil might arise, and are more difficult to oppress. Good resources for learning how to become more independent can be found on the internet (there are too many to list here), and also other print publications.

Next, network with like-minded people. This does not necessarily mean you have to organize in any formal way. But what it does do to us is open up channels by which people can later organize, either formally or informally, should the need arise. This is actually how

Solidarity got its start.

Finally, there are actually many individual activities that one can engage in to increase personal freedom and circumvent tyranny. There are actually too many to list them all here. However an excellent resource to start with is the book *The Freedom Outlaw's Handbook* by Claife Wolfe. I can't recommend this book highly enough, as many of the individual steps I would recommend are discussed in this book, and it contains many more that I had not thought of.

"When freedom is illegal, criminals make laws, and outlaws make freedom."

- Claire Wolfe

Finally, perhaps the most important thing to remember when working to free yourself from an oppressive regime is to not be awed by it. What little such a regime actually accomplishes is almost always due to the voluntary participation or compliance of its own citizens. Those who don't want to help tyrants in oppressing themselves and their fellow citizens can often become extensively non-supportive and non-compliant before anyone in government even notices, let alone takes action.

8. Know when to go public and when to stay underground (have good timing), and have patience because you may be in for a long battle.

After the ten thousand Solidarity leaders were arrested and imprisoned, the Solidarity movement continued via underground newspapers. It was almost a decade before Poland could declare itself a free country, and in that decade, many people gave up their lives to achieve that goal. To publish newspapers that told the truth, to be part of an opposition movement in whatever capacity they could contribute.

In 1986, many political prisoners were freed in a general amnesty, which resulted in many people going public with their opposition to the communist government. Those who were released under amnesty also wanted others to go public as a demonstration of support for freedom. They argued that even people who had never been arrested and were still operating in the underground should go public. However those who were still working in the underground wanted to continue with that way of life for fear of getting caught. After all, they had not been granted amnesty. Advocates of these two different approaches never did come to an agreement, so both proceeded in their own way.

In this case there was no clear cut answer as to which approach was better. Freeing Poland from the iron grip of tyranny required a combination of both above ground activity and underground resistance. It may even be another false choice to argue that only one strategy or the other is the right approach. One lesson that could be taken away from this is that it may be better for a single individual or group to operate either publicly, or in the underground, but not both, particularly if it involves high profile public activity. Such high profile public visibility makes one an obvious target, so the group or individual is better off having no behind the scenes hidden operations for which they could be prosecuted. Conversely, underground resistance needs to remain as low profile as possible, so any public activity that could draw attention is most likely not desirable. Solidarity teaches us that changing circumstances can require changing strategies, from public to underground or from underground to public, the strategies needed can change. It's knowing when to do so that can be tricky.

In the summer of 1988, Joanna Szczesna, who ran one of the underground newspapers, cut her vacation short when she heard of fresh strikes breaking out among the workers, as she realized that the strikers would need support via truth told in the media. But because all her staff was on vacation too, she was left on her own to do all the interviewing, writing, editing, and printing. Because she was on her own, she decided she had no choice but to give out her own phone number to the interviewees, something she had never done before because she knew her phones were tapped. But she decided that getting the news out at this critical time was more important and worth getting caught. Her place was raided several weeks later, but Joanna was not arrested, probably because the government was already attempting to work with the Solidarity movement via Wałęsa, in hopes of getting the workers to return to work.[73]

I mention this particular example because this event was very big at the time, and if Joanna wanted to print the news, she had to take risks to make it happen without any staff. In the end it was a well timed risk, as this was the final event that sparked the protests of food price increases from every group new and old.

There were many strategic gambits that Solidarity members took to make their movement successful. The article below states it best, and I could never paraphrase what is being said. I apologize for the long quote, but it is well worth it:

[All italics added for emphasis.]

> "Solidarity members' actions cannot be analyzed independently from the phenomenon of the Solidarity movement itself. The power of Solidarity as a mass resistance movement derived from an intangible fabric of civic capital created by a thick web of human interactions and underground activities and institutions whose purpose was to free the society from the control of the government.
> This generated forces no less powerful or important for waging civil resistance and its eventual success than the impact of specific strategies and tactics. Solidarity was not merely an opposition movement, it was, to paraphrase Vaclav Havel, *a collective experience of living within the truth*. Solidarity was an extraordinary mobilization of citizens from all walks of life united in protest against living in a communist lie. Solidarity was a massive societal polity organized independently outside the

realm of the state that encompassed a number of historical, cultural, philosophical and human experiences. As such it was a socializing force that promoted behavioral attitudes based on mutual responsibility, solidarism, assistance, trust, loyalty; *a teaching force that offered lessons in decentralized modes of self-organizing* and participatory democratic governance; *an empowering force that endorsed egalitarianism, individualism, and independence; and finally, a nonviolent force* with its strict nonviolent discipline and belief in the greater effectiveness of nonviolent actions over other means of a political contestation.

In the 1980s, Solidarity drew on a rich palette of nonviolent tactics that included, among others, protests; leaflets; flags; vigils; symbolic funerals; catholic masses; protest painting; parades; marches; slow-downs; strikes; hunger strikes; "Polish strikes" in the mine shafts; underground socio-cultural institutions: radio, music, films, satire, humor; over 400 underground magazines with millions of copies distributed, including literature on how to scheme, strike, and protest; *alternative education and libraries*; *a dense network of alternative teaching* in social science and humanities; commemorations of forbidden anniversaries; and internationalization of Solidarity's struggle".[74]

There will never be a lone wolf that can take credit for freeing a country from oppression. Even Mohandas "Mahatma" Gandhi had a legion of supporters who made Indian independence happen. Just as Gandhi can not take such credit as he had a lot of support, neither can Lech Wałęsa who also had many key supporters. If you're motivation for your actions is to receive credit in the end, then forget it; celebrity status is not a sustainable motivator for being a liberty activist. Living in freedom is, and is its own reward. In the end, everyone, including each individual person whose name could never be included in every book, contributed to the success of their campaigns.

Learn from both the mistakes and successes of history. Expand upon the successes, and develop strategies to prevent repeating the same mistakes. Not only can you learn from people like Martin Luther

King Jr., Gandhi, and others, but with new tactics including the internet, you can learn to be even more successful. The best teachers have students who surpass them.

With that said, don't expect large victories to be mentioned in the media. Successes will always be intentionally ignored by the mainstream news in the hope that they can prevent fueling the next groups or actions. If anything, expect the stories to be skewed and mis-representative. Disinformation and ridicule will be used to make activists look bad to the masses, no matter how noble their actions or goals. Sometimes, you just have to keep the victories to yourself, and know in your heart, that you are doing the right thing. In fact this reminds me of the saying by Gandhi: "First they ignore you, then they laugh at you, then they fight you, then you win."

A final lesson about timing is to be prepared for your own success. You don't want to find yourself in a position like Solidarity did during the first "free" elections.

In his book The Magic Lantern, The Revolution of 89, Timothy Garton Ash wrote about what he witnessed himself by being in Poland at the time of the first free vote. He wrote about how the first free presidential election was rigged, by those Solidarity members who now held seats, but not rigged towards Solidarity members, but rather towards making sure that Jaruzelski won. Jaruzelski only won by one mere vote, and only because several members abstained from voting, and seven members of parliament cast invalid votes deliberately. This may seem counterintuitive, and of course the Solidarity supporters were angry. The reason for this rigged vote was due to the fact that the Solidarity group was unprepared to deal with the economic problems of Poland, including the empty store shelves, the price hikes, and value of the zloty. The new parliament felt only Jaruzelski could deal with these issues, claiming the next election would be an honest one. [75]

The lesson here is if you are contending for a leadership role via politics, then you better be ready to assume that role if you actually succeed in making a breakthrough in that way.

9. Always stick with your principles and maintain the moral high ground

(More simply put: don't sell out and don't support sell outs.)

This point is not as easy to accomplish as it sounds. One of the major contributing factors to those who chose to oppress the Polish people by force, such as the "glina" and the Polish military, was not that they were evil, but because they too were hungry. They too had families they needed to feed, and they too wanted things that most could not afford or to which they did not have access.

Each individual was in a "fight for his soul." People who challenged the regime were often bribed or brought into the nomenklatura circle. The regime knew that the police and military were the last line of defense.[76] When you know you can become exempt from arrest and prosecution by simply being in the inner circle[77], it is hard not to sell out. This is also how the communist government got Solidarity members to "snitch" on others: they were intimidated with the threat of severe prosecution if they failed to submit, and were offered amnesty if they complied.

It is easy to say, "I would never sell out." But until you have actually gone for weeks without being able to get food, without medical care, without basic needs met, you don't really know where your breaking point is. No one does. In fact, the only people that do are those who have lived through oppressive regimes like the Poles, or lived through being a prisoner of war, or lived through true poverty.

Just as my mother participated in the underground economy using her American dollars in Poland, so would every other person who determines that a certain laws are immoral. So will any individual who can justify in his or her mind that a certain action is right, because they must feed their child, or even themselves. This is not to say that all people will break the law for purely selfish reasons, but that different people have different breaking points, and different people will find different ways to justify actions to themselves.

This is why it is important to be on the watch for, and refuse to support, those who are willing to compromise their principles (and yours) for special privilege, bribes, or a little temporary comfort. Such people are not necessarily evil, they are just weak. As Stewart Emery has written, *"Weakness corrupts and absolute weakness corrupts absolutely."* Such people will justify their compromises in their own minds. And once you lend support or understanding to an individual for selling out in such a way (or doing so yourself), you are solidifying their personal justification. So while we can't stop people from accepting bribes in exchange for acquiescing in many ways to the establishment powers that be, you can stop the spread of such actions by not supporting them.

Yes, I'm aware: easier said than done. But that's all the more reason for everyone to become prepared for any emergency, and not have to worry about being held hostage for, and bribed with, basic necessities.

10. Recognize when an organization no longer represents your values

Things change, people change, and ideals change. Holding on to something because it has always been there for you is sometimes easier than knowing when to let that go and move on to something that better fits you. Kind of like a favorite sweater from your favorite Grandma, that no longer fits, has too many loose threads from being in the dryer too much, and the color is so faded you can't quite remember what color it originally was.

Everything changes, and so do great organizations. Solidarity was a patient group of people that striked peacefully by locking themselves inside the shipyards and factories where they could not be arrested for striking. It was a strategy that always worked to some degree. But this did not fare well for the next generation, and the one after that, as they struggled with different hardships. To some of them, it wasn't practical to be patiently waiting for the government to come around and offer just a remnant of the demands only to go back to how it used to be.

So they created different organizations, different newspapers, different ways to bring people together, and different ways to build freedom and prosperity. Some Solidarity members chose to drop their Solidarity membership and join new groups, and some joined both. Not one of those organizations was solely responsible for the events that helped to bring down communism, and leaving one organization to join another was merely a way for people to find their niche.

Right now here in the US there are so many groups working to restore liberty, and so many independent alternative media sources, that I personally find it difficult to keep track. But at the same time, I like having options, as I can choose my favorite news sources and follow those. Occasionally taking a glimpse at some of the others, and every now and then deciding that my favorite alternative media source is no longer, and I find a new one.

This is as it will be with the future of America as different pro-liberty movements rise up in liberty against the tyranny, the options will be many for people to choose, should they choose to be part of any of them at all.

It's important to keep the idea in the back of your mind that you're not going to stay with an organization forever.

For example, in Shana Penn's book Solidarity's Secret, she

discusses how the women were able to use their "minority" status as a way to beat the system. However, when it came to the "round table discussions" between Solidarity and the communist government, the women were not invited, and only one made it into office in the end. My understanding is that the Roman Catholic Church was heavily involved at this point in helping to run the new Polish Government. So when re-election came, Wałęsa was not re-elected, as he had become too influenced by the church. Because the church had influenced the new Polish government to begin to take women's rights away,[78] women voted to make yet another change. This is not to say that these women were no longer religious, they just found the church no longer aligned with their rights simply because they were women.

While this is a difficult topic for some, it is also okay to walk away from your church and find a new one, if you find that the church you attended no longer aligns with your spirituality, your views, or you find it corrupt. During communist Poland, different churches were found to go different ways. Some were corrupt and in bed with the communist government, and some were on the side of Solidarity. Out of one hundred and fifty priests, reports state that only twenty could not be bribed or blackmailed.[79] In 2005, newspapers printed excerpts revealing many high-ranking church officials who collaborated during communist rule. The Polish Church finally requested an investigation to learn of everyone else that might have collaborated.[80] More collaborations with secret services were noted, and in January of 2007 a newly-appointed Archbishop of Warsaw along with a Reverend in Krakow, resigned their position after their secret service collaborations were revealed.

I will conclude this point with this: The lesson learned is that if people are not very careful, it is very easy for an organization or a political movement to be co-opted by people with ulterior motives or interests – people that you would not support if you knew their true agenda. Such people are not ally's but more likely adversaries in disguise, or are at least misguided, and they will attempt to misdirect your organization or movement for their own ends, not yours. In more recent history this occurred with several of the "Arab Spring" movements that were trying to replace oppressive governments. When you are working to overcome an oppressive regime, you have to be very careful to not end up removing certain tyrants only to replace them with others. Instead, you have to create systems or institutions that uphold true principles of liberty; that will stay true to those principles and not become subverted or mis-directed into a different form of tyranny. This is the approach that the US Founding Fathers attempted, and their efforts were fairly successful – at least for a period of time (the details of that timing are debatable).

11. Never give up and don't ever lose hope

There were many Poles who essentially accepted their fate as it was, and justified to themselves that it could be worse. Thus they chose not to join Solidarity (or other organizations that formed during martial law). Perhaps they didn't want to take the risk as they were a single parent, or they felt their job was descent and their basic needs were met. Whatever their reason, they did not make an effort to make their lives better, or freer. This isn't to say that they gave up on everything, but that they did give up hope that their lives and their country could be better.

An important point to realize is that even though the Solidarity movement wasn't recognized as an official union until 1980, Wałęsa had encouraged workers to strike since the early 1970s. Solidarity was an organization that took over a decade to evolve to the point were they could actually achieve what they set out to accomplish. During this time Wałęsa was surveyed at least as much and probably more than my family. He was interrogated on several occasions. He lost jobs due to his involvement. But yet he kept going, just as many other ordinary Poles did. Solidarity didn't happen overnight.

It took another decade of underground activities of printing illegal newspapers and people organizing and preparing. Often, the writers of the illegal newspapers were taking huge risks to publish, without even knowing if they were making any difference.[81] Timothy Garton Ash had an experience that illustrates an important point. While visiting the Lenin Shipyard (the birthplace of Solidarity as he called it) sometime in 1988, he made a comment about the lack of toilet paper after forty years of socialism. In response to him wishing the workers luck with the strikes, "maybe in thirty years [they would have toilet paper]" was their response.[82] This exemplifies that real change doesn't happen overnight; times may be extremely difficult, if not brutal. But that's no reason to give up, because things can also sometimes change more quickly than you can imagine, as those very workers were having free elections just two years later.

"The biggest success of the government was not that it arrested people and destroyed organizations, but that it killed hope." This was a statement made by activist Lech Budrewicz during an interview with Jack Bloom, at a time when exhaustion hit in 1986 and people were losing hope, especially after another prominent Solidarity leader was reported captured.[83] Maintaining hope for a liberty movement is a key function of any organization, network, or activity. Keeping that spirit of hope alive, is an essential and necessary function of that kind of movement. That doesn't mean that results will happen overnight, or that accomplishing goals will be easy. Chances are there will be plenty of hardship for everyone, and potentially for extended periods of time. This is why maintaining that hope is essential: outcompeting oppressive tyrants and regimes can take years.

In June of 1989, the first real free elections occurred in Poland. The people voted by crossing out the undesired candidates, referred to as a blunder of the party-coalition. There were many first time voters, or so the party claimed. Because to admit that many people had voted before, would be an embarrassment to the government officials, as everyone knew there were never free elections prior to that day. Solidarity won, communism lost, by a landslide. There was only one communist Member of Parliament that was not defeated.[84]

Despite some initial dishonest voting by the new, mostly Solidarity filled parliament, Wałęsa was eventually voted in to be Poland's president in 1990. Although he is famous for saying "I don't want to, but I've got no choice," he was truly voted for by the people. Yes, it took years, it took jail time, and it took all the hardships you could possibly imagine. But the people of Poland kept at it, each individual kept going, and eventually, the people of Poland won. It's a good thing they never gave up hope.

I will conclude with this:

There is a popular film called "The International." Somehow this movie ended up my rental list. Although I don't know how it got there, I am very glad it did. Maybe someone from the freedom-minded hacktivist group Anonymous[85] hacked into my Netflix account. Anyway, there is a very important lesson in this movie. Towards the end, the main protagonist character is following one of the criminal bankers across the rooftops of some city (I don't recall where, but that's irrelevant). The banker is running scared, suspecting it is a hired criminal assassin chasing him. Wanting to know for certain who this person is chasing him, he stops and faces his pursuer. Upon discovering that the person chasing him is an ordinary investigative law enforcement minion who follows all the rules placed upon him, the criminal banker no longer shows fear. Why? Because the banker understood that minions follow the very laws utilized to suppress them. The banker was confident that the minion would not harm him; that the minion was too obedient to his training, which did not allow him to harm anyone outside of the "justice" system – except in self defense. The criminal banker is proven wrong; everyone has their limits.

As long as the oligarchs and elitists believe that we the people will play by the rules they have created to chain us for their own benefit, they will never fear we the people. I do want say that I do not condone any truly illegal behavior that harm innocent people or violates their Natural Rights. But at the same time I do not believe in mindlessly obeying arbitrary, immoral, tyrannical, and/or absurd laws that are designed by people in power to enslave the rest of us for their own benefit. And I absolutely do claim the right to live freely.

Lesson 10: There are many ways to beat the oppression being forced upon you. The keys are to act outside the box that your oppressors have built around you, and to figure out what your skills are, what your friends' skills are, and how to put them all to best use to live free lives.

"You never change things by fighting the existing reality. To change something, build a new model that makes the existing model obsolete."

-R. Buckminster Fuller

"We are free not because we claim freedom, but because we practice it."

-William Faulkner

AFTERWORD

"A Dark Age is not just a period in which people no longer know how to do things. The real key is that people no longer remember that certain things can be done at all."

-Jerry Pournelle

On April 10, 2010, almost the entire Polish government was killed in a plane crash in Russia. A total of ninety-six people were killed, including then President Lech Kaczyński and his spouse. Others killed included former president Ryszard Kacaorowski, the Chief of the Polish General Staff, several military officers, the national bank governor, the deputy foreign minister, and eighteen members of the Polish parliament. In addition, several relatives of victims of the Katyn massacre were killed.[1] Ironically, the plane was on its way to the seventieth anniversary of the Katyn massacre, which involved the murder of twenty-two thousand Polish army officers by the Soviets. This historical tragedy was ordered by Lavrentiy Beria and Joseph Stalin.[2] It was a very sad and symbolic day for Poland and the Polish people.

My husband didn't understand why I was glued to the internet reading about what happened. The claim was that it was an accident in icy conditions, but I believe nothing anymore. They stated that a full and transparent investigation would be conducted, and the public would be informed, but the results of the investigation are questionable to me.

Then, in June/July of 2010, the happy people of Poland didn't vote in the former President's twin brother. I am disconnected from current Polish politics, but I am doubtful of the story I heard on the mainstream news media, and my personal experience with voting in free America has resulted in a justified mistrust of any voting process.

No one's freedom is safe — not ours, and not that of the Poles. We must always fight for truth, we must always study history, and most importantly, we must never allow the divide and conquer strategy to get the better of people, no matter where they are from, what their background, or what language they speak.

This is what growing up in Poland under a communist regime has taught me.

However, my history does not define who I am. I define myself though the choices that I make, just as everyone else defines themselves by the choices they make throughout their lives. It does not matter what circumstances someone is born into: race, religion, culture, or social status. People cannot choose or change what circumstances they are born into. What is important is the choices we make as adults, because people *do* have control over those.

I should not be judged for something I was not involved in, but feel free to judge me for who I am now, and for what I write now. I may have disavowed my culture in the past for lack of understanding, but the choices I make now make me the person that I am, regardless of my past. Regardless of the actions of our parents, what defines me, you, and everyone else is the actions we take as adults. What is most relevant is that we are human, and we treat each other humanely.

Part of what helped me become who I am is that I did experience shortages, I did experience martial law, and I did experience the disappearing of someone. At six years old that might not seem like a lot, but what happens to you at a young age will influence your beliefs for the rest of your life.

One of the things that I learned from growing up in a society that had to be changed just for people to be able to live, is that you can't wait for someone else to fix things for you. Because of this, I do not suffer from the "bystander effect." I will be the first to pull over if I see someone broken down on the road. I will be the first to call 911 if I see an event that would require such. And I am one of those people that will not sit idly by and wait for someone else to come forward and save the United States Constitution and all of our Natural Rights.

I hope I have at least opened your mind to the idea that your freedoms may be in jeopardy, and that you not only need to maintain a watchful eye, but to take action to make sure our freedoms are never taken from us. As Thomas Jefferson wrote, "Eternal vigilance is the price of liberty." If not that, then I hope you at least ask the questions of "Where's the data?" and "Who benefits?"

I'm living by the principles that this country was founded on, and that makes me an American.

School is out; no more lessons. Time to address the real world we are facing.

"I have always been and will be an enemy of communism, but I love all people."

-Lech Wałęsa

AFTERWORD

DELETED SCENES

There were topics which I thought were either important, interesting, or entertaining enough to include in this book, but I could not find an appropriate place for them in the main body. So I have included them here in the Appendix. If you were watching this as a movie on DVD you could consider these the "Deleted Scenes" or "Bonus Features."

On the topic of feminism in Poland under communism:

While the women of the west were burning bras in the 1960s, the Eastern Bloc women were working long hours without breaks in hopes to be able to afford a bra.[1]

On the topic of preparing for martial law:

Solidarity members had been expecting martial law for some time, so they devised the secret signal of hanging a polish flag in their window to warn others when they first learned that it had been implemented. Liberty activists might want to consider some similar signaling mechanism, like hanging a Gadsden flag upside down in their window.

On the topic of formal education and media perpetuating labels that divide people:

I had a Hispanic/Latina college friend who grew up in Honduras and legally immigrated to the US say to me: "I didn't know I was a minority until I was taught that in school."

On the topic of philosophy in the modern world:

As a civilization, particularly in America, we seem to have almost completely abandoned philosophy as useful tool in solving real world problems. Average people tend to regard the subject as a painful waste of time that is detached from reality and has no practical application to every day life. Yet, nothing could be further from the truth. Philosophy not only asks and tries to answer questions about the nature and proper role of "government" and politics, but it also asks and tries to answer the question of how a person should live, which is a question we all face. With so much change, both technological as well as political and economic, this is one of the questions that people need to consider and answer for themselves the most.

All great thinkers throughout history had a certain philosophy in mind when making their great contributions. The fact that practical philosophy is not something that people think much about is partly a failure of philosophers. But I believe this state of affairs has also been intentionally created by those who would prefer Americans to be ignorant. Ignorance by Americans about the subjects of philosophy, and particularly economics, is quite beneficial to those who take advantage of that ignorance. For example, if you don't understand real economics and how our current monetary and banking system works, you won't understand how you are being defrauded by that system. Yet our education and culture tend to make people find these subjects boring and irrelevant, when in reality they have major impacts on people's lives. One of the steps to restoring or rebuilding freedom is to shift the public's perspective on these topics to one that acknowledges the important role these topics play in our every day lives.

On the topic of cooperation versus competition:

I have noticed a recent trend: people have been debating the merits of cooperation versus competition in the context of economic and political discourse. I find this to be a positive thing because people are actually discussing this idea. However, I have observed that the discussion has gone a bit off-track because it has been framed as an "either or" debate, when it should be framed as a question of "When is cooperation good or bad and when is competition good or bad?" After all, there can be both "good" and "bad" competition and both "good" and "bad" cooperation. Some examples would be helpful here.

An example of good cooperation would be if a few biotech companies who happen to be working on similar medical conditions agree to share intellectual resources under an agreed upon contract that stipulates certain financial compensation should they discover and bring products to market. These individual companies may not have the resources independently to produce results, but as a team they would be able to cure a terrible disease. This is a win-win-win situation: the shareholders and employees of all the companies win because they bring a product to market that they would otherwise not be able to accomplish independently, and people suffering from the disease get a better (or any) treatment. Yet if the different companies did not work together it would be lose-lose-lose, as the shareholders and employees would not benefit from a discovery that did not happen, and neither would potential patients/customers. Another example of win-win cooperation in action is open source software development such as the Linux and FreeBSD operating systems.

An example of bad cooperation would be collusion between different companies for the purpose of price fixing. Let's say that there are only four companies that make widgets, and let's also say that the investment required to make widgets is high so that creates a barrier of entry to other companies. Let's say that while these companies are competing, it drives the price to twenty dollars per widget. Now if those five companies cooperate instead, they may collude and all agree to fix the price by charging one hundred dollars for widgets. This is certainly not desirable, except for perhaps the four companies. This is what economists call an "oligopoly," and it is the reason for anti-trust, anti-collusion, and pro-competition laws.

Similarly, competition can be good if different companies or individuals create better products, or offer better service or a better price, in order to gain customers. This is a benefit for the customers, and may be a benefit to the most successful companies or individuals, but can certainly be bad for unsuccessful competitors. Yet this is the "creative destruction" by which inefficient activities are weeded out.

There can also be bad competition. For example, if several companies are competing for customers based on price alone for a product of equivalent quality, unethical managers could be driven to reduce the quality of the item to reduce the cost, while claiming the product is really the same quality (misrepresentation). This is clearly a lose-lose scenario and is also clearly dishonest and fraud. But just like cooperation, competition can drive bad behavior as well as good behavior. Incentives almost always matter, and we need to keep that in mind when thinking about how we want to do things.

What is perhaps missed in the debate about competition and cooperation, and which I think is very important to point out is, in the greater context of freedom in a society, individuals or businesses can either choose to compete or choose to cooperate. If a bunch of hackers choose to cooperate to write open source software, great. If a business chooses to write proprietary software and compete with an open source group, that is great too. (Hint: you don't need copyright law for intellectual property to exist. You only need contract law, which is where copyright originated.) If some people choose to operate a for-profit commercial farm, great. If some other group decides to develop a communal farm where produce is shared rather than sold, that is great too. People should have the freedom to choose what they do, and not be *forced* into one ideology or pattern. We are all different and unique individual human beings. It is up to us all to decide as individuals when cooperation will produce better results and when competition will produce a better outcome. There is no "one right way" or "one size fits" all that is will work for everyone or all the time. But there are certainly "wrong" ways, and those include force, coercion, fraud, and lies.

Freedom allows people to live in a manner that suits their own needs or desires. Freedom also allows people to conduct voluntary "scientific" social experiments where we all get to learn and discover what works and what doesn't. This was actually one of the reasons or ideas (but definitely not the only or primary reason) the Founding Fathers had behind having multiple states: to have multiple experiments in freedom. The diversity of approaches would provide feedback as to what worked and what didn't. Unfortunately, political homogenization and loss of freedom has largely caused a loss of that diversity.

So if you think you have a better way to do things, great. Do it. Prove it. Convince the world it is better through example, by living it. But it is terribly immoral to use violence, and the force of the state, to mandate that people do things a certain way, unless to do otherwise would mean that people were being literally harmed or their rights (civil or property) are being infringed.

Unfortunately, as a society, that is the point to which we have degraded. Many groups or individuals think they know the "one true way" things should be done, and set out to go about making it so for everyone, via the force of the state. In the end, this only backfires. Forcing people in this way only creates animosity, resentment, and ultimately, war. Remember: divide and conquer is a proven strategy. So is freedom.

On the topic of solutions:

I don't claim to have "all the answers" or "the one true way," but I do have some of the answers.

If you allow people to be free, without state or corporate oppression, they will ultimately take care of themselves and prosper.

Responsibility and freedom go hand in hand and you can not have one without the other. Wanting freedom without responsibility is the immature mindset of a teenager. Taking away people's freedom breeds irresponsibility, because in an oppressed environment people aren't "allowed" to do things for themselves. But giving people freedom forces them to become more responsible. As I've written previously, irresponsibility in the context of freedom is a self-correcting problem, as people have to face the consequences of their choices and actions. Statists often argue that people are too irresponsible to trust with freedom. The solution to get people to be responsible is to give them more freedom, not less. If people are empowered by being unshackled from oppression, they will be able to accomplish more, including taking care of themselves.

To the extent that people are disempowered, they become proportionally more helpless to accomplish anything, including helping themselves or others. Freedom empowers people, and government bureaucracy and regulation disempower people.

Maturity empowers people, and immaturity disempowes people. Yet our current culture and political atmosphere demonstrate and promote immaturity at every opportunity. If we want to live in a free society it would be *extremely* helpful if people — particularly people in the public spotlight — would start acting like grown ups.

Knowledge empowers people, and ignorance disempowers people. And no one says education has to be formal. No one says individuals can't educate themselves.

Similarly, information and transparency empower people. They allow people to make good decisions. Lack of information and lack of transparency disempower people and cause them to make poor decisions. If nothing else, *this* of all things needs to be corrected. *Our civilization is drowning in a sea of lies. The truth and transparency alone would go a long way to addressing the current problems.* A quote about truth:

One
basic
truth can
be used as
a foundation for
a mountain of lies,
and if we dig down deep
enough in the mountain of lies,
and bring out that truth, to set it
on top of the mountain of lies; the entire
mountain of lies will crumble under the weight of
that one truth, and there is nothing more devastating to a
structure of lies than the revelation of the truth upon which
the structure of lies was built, because the shock waves of the
revelation of the truth reverberate, and continue to
follow, awakening even those
people who had no
desire to be
awakened
to the
truth.

- Delamar Duverus

"I heartily accept the motto, — 'That government is best which governs least;" and I should like to see it acted up to more rapidly and systematically. Carried out, it finally amounts to this, which I also believe, — 'That government is best which governs not at all;' and when men are prepared for it, that will be the kind of government which they will have. Government is at best but an expedient; but most governments are usually, and all governments are sometimes, inexpedient." [2]

—Thoreau, Civil Disobedience

REFERENCES:

Introduction:

[1]Self-defeating prophecy - Wikipedia, the free encyclopedia. 2015. *Self-defeating prophecy - Wikipedia, the free encyclopedia.* [ONLINE] Available at: http://en.wikipedia.org/wiki/Self-defeating_prophecy. [Accessed 16 March 2015].

Chapter 1:

[1] Frédéric Bastiat - Wikiquote. 2014. *Frédéric Bastiat - Wikiquote.* [ONLINE] Available at: http://en.wikiquote.org/wiki/Fr%C3%A9d%C3%A9ric_Bastiat. [Accessed 27 December 2014].

[2] The Road to Serfdom - Wikipedia, the free encyclopedia. 2014. *The Road to Serfdom - Wikipedia, the free encyclopedia.* [ONLINE] Available at: http://en.wikipedia.org/wiki/The_Road_to_Serfdom. [Accessed 27 December 2014].

[3] 2014. [ONLINE] Available at: http://www.columbia.edu/cu/ece/research/intermarium/vol14/Gasztold-Sen.pdf. [Accessed 11 November 2014]. P. 9.

[4] Overview of gun laws by nation - Wikipedia, the free encyclopedia. 2015. *Overview of gun laws by nation - Wikipedia, the free encyclopedia.* [ONLINE] Available at: http://en.wikipedia.org/wiki/Overview_of_gun_laws_by_nation#Poland. [Accessed 01 January 2015].

[5] Robert W. Harris, 1975. American Heritage DICTIONARY of the English Language NEW COLLEGE Edition PLAIN EDGE. Edition. Houghton Mifflin. P. 802. Print.

[6] Polish legislative election, 1947 - Wikipedia, the free encyclopedia. 2014. *Polish legislative election, 1947 - Wikipedia, the free encyclopedia.* [ONLINE] Available at: http://en.wikipedia.org/wiki/Polish_legislative_elections,_1947.

[Accessed 25 November 2013].

[7] History of Poland (1945–89) - Wikipedia, the free encyclopedia. 2014. *History of Poland (1945–89) - Wikipedia, the free encyclopedia.* [ONLINE] Available at: http://en.wikipedia.org/wiki/History_of_Poland_%281945%E2%80%9389%29. [Accessed 25 November 2013].

[8] Ash, Timothy. *The Polish Revolution: Solidarity.* 3rd ed. New Haven: Yale UP, 2002. P. 7. Print.

[9] Polish legislative election, 1947 - Wikipedia, the free encyclopedia. 2014. *Polish legislative election, 1947 - Wikipedia, the free encyclopedia.* [ONLINE] Available at: http://en.wikipedia.org/wiki/Polish_legislative_elections,_1947. [Accessed 25 November 2013].

[10] Ash, Timothy. *The Polish Revolution: Solidarity.* 3rd ed. New Haven: Yale UP, 2002. P. 12. Print.

[11] Władysław Gomułka - Wikipedia, the free encyclopedia. 2014. *Władysław Gomułka - Wikipedia, the free encyclopedia.* [ONLINE] Available at: http://en.wikipedia.org/wiki/W%C5%82adys%C5%82aw_Gomu%C5%82ka. [Accessed 18 November 2014].

[12] Bloom, Jack M. *Seeing through the Eyes of the Polish Revolution: Solidarity and the Struggle against Communism in Poland.* Chicago: Haymarket, 2014. P. 64. Print.

[13] Ibid., 65.

[14] History of Poland (1945–89) - Wikipedia, the free encyclopedia. 2014. *History of Poland (1945–89) - Wikipedia, the free encyclopedia.* [ONLINE] Available at: http://en.wikipedia.org/wiki/History_of_Poland_%281945%E2%80%9389%29. [Accessed 25 November 2013].

[15] Poland pays off communist debt - Thenews.pl: News from Poland. 2014. *Poland pays off communist debt - Thenews.pl: News from Poland.* [ONLINE] Available at: http://www.thenews.pl/1/12/Artykul/116918,Poland-pays-off-communist-debt. [Accessed 11 November 2013].

[16] Bloom, Jack M. *Seeing through the Eyes of the Polish Revolution: Solidarity and the Struggle against Communism in Poland.* Chicago: Haymarket, 2014. P. 27. Print.

[17]Poland - The Economy. 2014. *Poland - The Economy*. [ONLINE] Available at: http://countrystudies.us/poland/47.htm. [Accessed 11 November 2013].

[18]Ash, Timothy. *The Polish Revolution: Solidarity*. 3rd ed. New Haven: Yale UP, 2002. P. 116. Print.

[19]PEASANTS VS. STATE IN POLAND - NYTimes.com. 2014. *PEASANTS VS. STATE IN POLAND - NYTimes.com*. [ONLINE] Available at: http://www.nytimes.com/1981/10/10/business/peasants-vs-state-in-poland.html. [Accessed 11 November 2013]

[20] Solidarity (Polish trade union) - Wikipedia, the free encyclopedia. 2014. *Solidarity (Polish trade union) - Wikipedia, the free encyclopedia*. [ONLINE] Available at: http://en.wikipedia.org/wiki/Solidarnosc. [Accessed 11 November 2013].

[21] Ash, Timothy. *The Polish Revolution: Solidarity*. 3rd ed. New Haven: Yale UP, 2002. P. 84. Print.

[22]Solidarity (Polish trade union) - Wikipedia, the free encyclopedia. 2014. *Solidarity (Polish trade union) - Wikipedia, the free encyclopedia*. [ONLINE] Available at: http://en.wikipedia.org/wiki/Solidarity_%28Polish_trade_union%29. [Accessed 11 November 2013].

[23] Bloom, Jack M. *Seeing through the Eyes of the Polish Revolution: Solidarity and the Struggle against Communism in Poland*. Chicago: Haymarket, 2014. Print. P. 14.

[24] Ash, Timothy. "Introduction." *The Polish Revolution: Solidarity*. 3rd ed. New Haven: Yale UP, 2002. Print.

[25] Ibid., 79.

[26] MacEachin, Douglas J. *US Intelligence and the Polish Crisis 1980-1981*. Washington, D.C.: Center for the Study of Intelligence, 2000. Print. p.15. Print.

[27]Ash, Timothy. *The Polish Revolution: Solidarity*. 3rd ed. New Haven: Yale UP, 2002. P. 100. Print.

[28]Ash, Timothy. *The Polish Revolution: Solidarity*. 3rd ed. New Haven: Yale UP, 2002. P. 98. Print.

[29]Antoni Dudek, Dzieje dziesię ciomilionowej. (1980 - 1981) [in:] Droga

doniepodległości Solidarność 1980 – 2005, collective work, Warsaw 2005, p. 25.

[30]2014. [ONLINE] Available at: http://www.columbia.edu/cu/ece/research/intermarium/vol14/Gasztold-Sen.pdf. [Accessed 11 November 2014]. p. 5.

[31]2014. [ONLINE] Available at: http://www.columbia.edu/cu/ece/research/intermarium/vol14/Gasztold-Sen.pdf. [Accessed 11 November 2014].

Chapter 2:

[1] Ash, Timothy. *The Polish Revolution: Solidarity*. 3rd ed. New Haven: Yale UP, 2002. P. 114. Print.

[2] Ibid., 115.

[3] Bloom, Jack M. *Seeing through the Eyes of the Polish Revolution: Solidarity and the Struggle against Communism in Poland*. Chicago: Haymarket, 2014. P.263. Print.

[4] Rationing - Wikipedia, the free encyclopedia. 2014. *Rationing - Wikipedia, the free encyclopedia*. [ONLINE] Available at: http://en.wikipedia.org/wiki/Rationing. [Accessed 28 December 2013].

[5] Rationing - Wikipedia, the free encyclopedia. 2014. *Rationing - Wikipedia, the free encyclopedia*. [ONLINE] Available at: http://en.wikipedia.org/wiki/Rationing. [Accessed 28 December 2013].

[6]Ash, Timothy. The Polish Revolution: Solidarity. 3rd ed. New Haven: Yale UP, 2002. P. 194. Print. P.

[7]Bloom, Jack M. *Seeing through the Eyes of the Polish Revolution: Solidarity and the Struggle against Communism in Poland*. Chicago: Haymarket, 2014. P. 203. Print.

[8] ZOMO - Wikipedia, the free encyclopedia. 2015. *ZOMO - Wikipedia, the free encyclopedia*. [ONLINE] Available at: http://en.wikipedia.org/wiki/ZOMO. [Accessed 03 January 2015].

[9] Solidarity (Polish trade union) - Wikipedia, the free encyclopedia. 2014. *Solidarity (Polish trade union) - Wikipedia, the free encyclopedia*. [ONLINE] Available at:

http://en.wikipedia.org/wiki/Solidarity_%28Polish_trade_union%29. [Accessed 11 November 2013].

[10] Ash, Timothy. *The Polish Revolution: Solidarity.* 3rd ed. New Haven: Yale UP, 2002. P. 156. Print.

[11] Ibid., 195-196.

[12] Animal Farm - Wikipedia, the free encyclopedia. 2015. *Animal Farm - Wikipedia, the free encyclopedia.* [ONLINE] Available at: http://en.wikipedia.org/wiki/Animal_Farm. [Accessed 27 December 2014].

[13] Ash, Timothy. *The Polish Revolution: Solidarity.* 3rd ed. New Haven: Yale UP, 2002. P. 9. Print.

[14] Ibid., 24.

[15] Ibid., 18.

[16] Ibid.

[17] Dye, Thomas R. "Interest Groups: Getting Their Share and More." *Politics in America.* 7th ed. Upper Saddle River, N.J.: Pearson Prentice Hall, 2007. Print.

[18] Here's Why There Will Be No Criminal Charges In The MF Global Case. 2015. *Here's Why There Will Be No Criminal Charges In The MF Global Case.* [ONLINE] Available at: http://www.huffingtonpost.com/2013/06/28/criminal-charges-mf-global_n_3516652.html. [Accessed 3 January 2015].

[19] Corzine's Crime of the Century | National Review Online. 2015. *Corzine's Crime of the Century | National Review Online.* [ONLINE] Available at: http://www.nationalreview.com/articles/339811/corzine-s-crime-century-bruce-bialosky. [Accessed 13 January 2015].

[20] Operation Fast and Furious Fast Facts - CNN.com. 2015. *Operation Fast and Furious Fast Facts - CNN.com.* [ONLINE] Available at: http://www.cnn.com/2013/08/27/world/americas/operation-fast-and-furious-fast-facts/. [Accessed 3 January 2015].

[21] ATF gunwalking scandal - Wikipedia, the free encyclopedia. 2015. *ATF gunwalking scandal - Wikipedia, the free encyclopedia.* [ONLINE] Available at: http://en.wikipedia.org/wiki/ATF_gunwalking_scandal. [Accessed 3 January 2015].

[22] MacEachin, Douglas J. *US Intelligence and the Polish Crisis 1980-1981.* Washington, D.C.: Center for the Study of Intelligence, 2000. P. 144. Print.

[23] Penn, Shana. *Solidarity's Secret: The Women Who Defeated Communism in Poland.* Ann Arbor: U of Michigan, 2005. 37. Print.

[24] Tischner, Jo. "From the Translators." *The Spirit of Solidarity.* 2nd ed. San Francisco: Harper & Row, 1984. Print.

[25] Karta - strona główna. 2014. *Karta - strona główna.* [ONLINE] Available at: http://www.karta.org.pl. [Accessed 28 December 2013].

[26] President Obama Inauguration Cost $170 Million - ABC News. 2015. *President Obama Inauguration Cost $170 Million - ABC News.* [ONLINE] Available at: http://abcnews.go.com/Business/Inauguration/president-obama-inauguration-cost-170-million/story?id=6665946. [Accessed 3 January 2015].

[27] Bam's inauguration is most expensive ever - NY Daily News. 2015. *Bam's inauguration is most expensive ever - NY Daily News.* [ONLINE] Available at: http://www.nydailynews.com/news/politics/obama-inauguration-expensive-160-million-article-1.421186. [Accessed 3 January 2015].

[28] Consumer Price Index. 2004. *Consumer Price Index.* [ONLINE] Available at: http://www.shadowstats.com/article/consumer_price_index [Accessed 4 January 2015].

[29] Consumer Price Index. 2012. *Consumer Price Index.* [ONLINE] Available at: http://www.shadowstats.com/article/archived-438-inflation-measurement. [Accessed 4 January 2015].

[30] Why you should be skeptical about the government's national unemployment rate | Deseret News National. 2015. *Why you should be skeptical about the government's national unemployment rate | Deseret News National.* [ONLINE] Available at: http://national.deseretnews.com/article/2516/Why-you-should-be-skeptical-about-the-governments-national-unemployment-rate.html. [Accessed 26 January 2015].

[31] The Official Unemployment Rate Is Wrong, Says Guy Who Used To Calculate It. 2015. *The Official Unemployment Rate Is Wrong, Says Guy Who Used to Calculate It.* [ONLINE] Available at: http://www.huffingtonpost.com/2013/07/19/unemployment-rate-wrong_n_3619152.html. [Accessed 26 January 2015].

[32] MacEachin, Douglas J. US Intelligence and the Polish Crisis 1980-1981. Washington, D.C.: Center for the Study of Intelligence, 2000. Print.

[33] 2014. [ONLINE] Available at: http://www.columbia.edu/cu/ece/research/intermarium/vol14/Gasztold-Sen.pdf. [Accessed 11 November 2014]. P. 6.

[34] Ash, Timothy. The Polish Revolution: Solidarity. 3rd ed. New Haven: Yale UP, 2002. P. 163. Print.

[35] 2014. [ONLINE] Available at: http://www.columbia.edu/cu/ece/research/intermarium/vol14/Gasztold-Sen.pdf. [Accessed 11 November 2014]. P. 11.

[36] 2014. [ONLINE] Available at: http://www.columbia.edu/cu/ece/research/intermarium/vol14/Gasztold-Sen.pdf. [Accessed 11 November 2014]. P. 13.

[37] 2014. [ONLINE] Available at: http://www.columbia.edu/cu/ece/research/intermarium/vol14/Gasztold-Sen.pdf. [Accessed 20 October 2014].

[38] US Intelligence and the Polish Crisis 1980-1981 — Central Intelligence Agency. 2014. *US Intelligence and the Polish Crisis 1980-1981 — Central Intelligence Agency.* [ONLINE] Available at: https://www.cia.gov/library/center-for-the-study-of-intelligence/csi-publications/books-and-monographs/us-intelligence-and-the-polish-crisis-1980-1981/index.htm. [Accessed 20 October 2014].

[39] MacEachin, Douglas J. "Caught off Guard." US Intelligence and the Polish Crisis 1980-1981. Washington, D.C.: Center for the Study of Intelligence, 2000. P. 179. Print.

[40] MacEachin, Douglas J. "Caught off Guard." *US Intelligence and the Polish Crisis 1980-1981.* Washington, D.C.: Center for the Study of Intelligence, 2000. P. 180. Print.

[41] MacEachin, Douglas J. "Jaruzelski Takes the Government Reins." *US Intelligence and the Polish Crisis 1980-1981.* Washington, D.C.: Center for the Study of Intelligence, 2000. P. 90. Print.

[42] Ash, Timothy. "Introduction." *The Polish Revolution: Solidarity.* 3rd ed. New Haven: Yale UP, 2002. P. 19-20. Print.

⁴³ 1993. *Economic Vulnerability in International Relations: East- West Trade, Investment, and Finance (Paperback) by Crawford, Beverly published by Columbia University Press*. Edition. Columbia University Press. P. 189-196. Print.

⁴⁴ MacEachin, Douglas J. "The Burgeoning Confrontation." US Intelligence and the Polish Crisis 1980-1981. Washington, D.C.: Center for the Study of Intelligence, 2000. P. 10. Print.

⁴⁵ Gold standard - Wikipedia, the free encyclopedia. 2015. *Gold standard - Wikipedia, the free encyclopedia*. [ONLINE] Available at: http://en.wikipedia.org/wiki/Gold_standard. [Accessed 21 March 2015].

⁴⁶ Nixon Shock - Wikipedia, the free encyclopedia. 2015. *Nixon Shock - Wikipedia, the free encyclopedia*. [ONLINE] Available at: http://en.wikipedia.org/wiki/Nixon_Shock. [Accessed 21 March 2015].

⁴⁷ Standard and SGS Alternate CPI Measures - Part I. 2015. *Standard and SGS Alternate CPI Measures - Part I*. [ONLINE] Available at: http://www.shadowstats.com/article/cpi-measures. [Accessed 02 May 2015].

⁴⁸ Alternate Inflation Charts. 2015. *Alternate Inflation Charts*. [ONLINE] Available at: http://www.shadowstats.com/alternate_data/inflation-charts. [Accessed 02 May 2015].

⁴⁹ Normalcy bias - Wikipedia, the free encyclopedia. 2015. *Normalcy bias - Wikipedia, the free encyclopedia*. [ONLINE] Available at: http://en.wikipedia.org/wiki/Normalcy_bias. [Accessed 26 January 2015].

⁵⁰ The dollar's 70-year dominance is coming to an end - Telegraph. 2015. *The dollar's 70-year dominance is coming to an end - Telegraph*. [ONLINE] Available at: http://www.telegraph.co.uk/finance/comment/liamhalligan/10978178/The-dollars-70-year-dominance-is-coming-to-an-end.html. [Accessed 26 January 2015].

⁵¹ With Dollar Demise in Focus, Beijing Pushes "New World Order". 2015. *With Dollar Demise in Focus, Beijing Pushes "New World Order"*. [ONLINE] Available at: http://www.thenewamerican.com/economy/economics/item/16748-with-dollar-demise-in-focus-beijing-pushes-new-world-order. [Accessed 02 May 2015].

⁵² Is your money safe at the bank? An economist says 'no' and withdraws his | Making Sen$e | PBS NewsHour. 2015. *Is your money safe at the bank? An economist says 'no' and withdraws his | Making Sen$e | PBS NewsHour*.

[ONLINE] Available at: http://www.pbs.org/newshour/making-sense/is-your-money-safe-at-the-bank-an-economist-says-no-and-withdraws-his/. [Accessed 26 January 2015].

53 US Deposits in Perspective: $25 Billion in Insurance, $9,283 Billion in Deposits; $297,514 Billion in Derivatives | Zero Hedge. 2015. *US Deposits in Perspective: $25 Billion in Insurance, $9,283 Billion in Deposits; $297,514 Billion in Derivatives | Zero Hedge.* [ONLINE] Available at: http://www.zerohedge.com/news/2013-03-19/us-deposits-perspective-25-billion-insurance-9283-billion-deposits-297514-billion-de. [Accessed 26 January 2015].

54 A Bank Holiday [ushistory.org]. 2014. *A Bank Holiday [ushistory.org].* [ONLINE] Available at: http://www.ushistory.org/us/49a.asp. [Accessed 1 November 2014].

Chapter 3:

1 Bloom, Jack M. *Seeing through the Eyes of the Polish Revolution: Solidarity and the Struggle against Communism in Poland.* Chicago: Haymarket, 2014. Print. P. 20.

2 Ash, Timothy. *The Polish Revolution: Solidarity.* 3rd ed. New Haven: Yale UP, 2002. Print. p. 30.

3 New York City soft drink size limit - Wikipedia, the free encyclopedia. 2015. *New York City soft drink size limit - Wikipedia, the free encyclopedia.* [ONLINE] Available at: http://en.wikipedia.org/wiki/New_York_City_soft_drink_size_limit. [Accessed 4 January 2015].

4 . 2015. . [ONLINE] Available at: http://www.gpo.gov/fdsys/pkg/BILLS-111hr3590enr/pdf/BILLS-111hr3590enr.pdf. [Accessed 4 January 2015].

5 Nancy Pelosi - Wikiquote. 2015. *Nancy Pelosi - Wikiquote.* [ONLINE] Available at: http://en.wikiquote.org/wiki/Nancy_Pelosi. [Accessed 22 February 2015].

6 Pelosi: "We Have to Pass the Bill So That You Can Find Out What Is In It" - YouTube. 2015. *Pelosi: "We Have to Pass the Bill So That You Can Find Out What Is In It" - YouTube.* [ONLINE] Available at: https://www.youtube.com/watch?v=hV-05TLiiLU. [Accessed 22 February 2015].

7 2015. . [ONLINE] Available at: http://www.gpo.gov/fdsys/pkg/BILLS-

111hr3590enr/pdf/BILLS-111hr3590enr.pdf. [Accessed 4 January 2015]. SEC 1101.

[8] 2015. . [ONLINE] Available at: http://www.gpo.gov/fdsys/pkg/BILLS-111hr3590enr/pdf/BILLS-111hr3590enr.pdf. [Accessed 16 January 2015]. SEC 4205

[9] 2015. . [ONLINE] Available at: http://www.gpo.gov/fdsys/pkg/BILLS-111hr3590enr/pdf/BILLS-111hr3590enr.pdf. [Accessed 16 January 2015]. SEC 5101.

[10] 2015. . [ONLINE] Available at: http://www.gpo.gov/fdsys/pkg/BILLS-111hr3590enr/pdf/BILLS-111hr3590enr.pdf. [Accessed 4 January 2015]. SEC 1555.

[11] VA deaths covered up to make statistics look better, whistle-blower says - CNN.com. 2015. *VA deaths covered up to make statistics look better, whistle-blower says - CNN.com.* [ONLINE] Available at: http://www.cnn.com/2014/06/23/us/phoenix-va-deaths-new-allegations/. [Accessed 22 February 2015].

[12] Veterans Health Administration scandal of 2014 - Wikipedia, the free encyclopedia. 2015. *Veterans Health Administration scandal of 2014 - Wikipedia, the free encyclopedia.* [ONLINE] Available at: http://en.wikipedia.org/wiki/Veterans_Health_Administration_scandal_of_2014. [Accessed 21 February 2015].

Chapter 4:

[1] Tischner, Jo. "Solidarity of Consciences." *The Spirit of Solidarity.* 2nd ed. San Francisco: Harper & Row, 1984. Print. P. 3.

[2] Back Door for "Real" ID - EPautos. 2015. *Back Door for "Real" ID - EPautos.* [ONLINE] Available at: http://ericpetersautos.com/2015/03/06/back-door-for-real-id/. [Accessed 18 March 2015].

Chapter 5:

[1] Natural Rights and the Founding Fathers – The Virginians. *Natural Rights and the Founding Fathers – The Virginians.* 2015. [ONLINE] Available at: http://scholarlycommons.law.wlu.edu/cgi/viewcontent.cgi?article=3506&context=wlulr. [Accessed 22 February 2015].

[2] Natural law - Wikipedia, the free encyclopedia. 2015. *Natural law - Wikipedia, the free encyclopedia.* [ONLINE] Available at:

http://en.wikipedia.org/wiki/Natural_law. [Accessed 22 February 2015].

[3] First Amendment to the United States Constitution - Wikipedia, the free encyclopedia. 2015. *First Amendment to the United States Constitution - Wikipedia, the free encyclopedia.* [ONLINE] Available at: http://en.wikipedia.org/wiki/First_Amendment_to_the_United_States_Constituti on. [Accessed 22 February 2015].

[4] Second Amendment to the United States Constitution - Wikiquote. 2015. *Second Amendment to the United States Constitution - Wikiquote.* [ONLINE] Available at: http://en.wikiquote.org/wiki/Second_Amendment_to_the_United_States_Constit ution. [Accessed 22 February 2015].

[5] First Amendment to the United States Constitution - Wikipedia, the free encyclopedia. 2015. *First Amendment to the United States Constitution - Wikipedia, the free encyclopedia.* [ONLINE] Available at: http://en.wikipedia.org/wiki/First_Amendment_to_the_United_States_Constituti on. [Accessed 22 February 2015].

[6] Property Rights and Free Markets: Economic Principles of America's Founders. 2015. *Property Rights and Free Markets: Economic Principles of America's Founders.* [ONLINE] Available at: http://www.heritage.org/research/reports/2010/08/the-economic-principles-of-america-s-founders-property-rights-free-markets-and-sound-money. [Accessed 22 February 2015].

[7] Fifth Amendment to the United States Constitution - Wikipedia, the free encyclopedia. 2015. *Fifth Amendment to the United States Constitution - Wikipedia, the free encyclopedia.* [ONLINE] Available at: http://en.wikipedia.org/wiki/Fifth_Amendment_to_the_United_States_Constituti on#.22Just_compensation.22. [Accessed 22 February 2015].

[8] The Primacy of Property Rights and the American Founding: The Freeman: Foundation for Economic Education. 2015. *The Primacy of Property Rights and the American Founding: The Freeman: Foundation for Economic Education.* [ONLINE] Available at: http://fee.org/freeman/detail/the-primacy-of-property-rights-and-the-american-founding. [Accessed 22 February 2015].

[9] Coulson, Andrew J. *Market Education: The Unknown History.* Bowling Green, OH: Social Philosophy & Policy Center; 1999. 27. Print.

[10] Penn, Shana. *Solidarity's Secret: The Women Who Defeated Communism in Poland.* Ann Arbor: U of Michigan, 2005. 37. Print.

[11] Mondale, Sarah. *School, the Story of American Public Education*. Boston: Beacon, 2001. 11 Print.

[12] Ibid., 12.

[13] Ibid., 15-16.

[14] Ibid., 21-22.

[15] Ibid., 38.

[16] Ibid., 57.

[17] Ibid., 58.

[18] A Brief History of Education in America. *A Brief History of Education in America.* 2014. [ONLINE] Available at: http://www.cblpi.org/ftp/School%20Choice/EdHistory.pdf. [Accessed 29 November 2014].

[19] Mondale, Sarah. *School, the Story of American Public Education*. Boston: Beacon, 2001. Print. P. 21-22.

[20] Coulson, Andrew J. *Market Education: The Unknown History*. Bowling Green, OH: Social Philosophy & Policy Center; 1999. 49. Print.

[21] Ibid., 46-51.

[22] Ibid., 55.

[23] Ibid., 56.

[24] Kendall, John S. *Understanding Common Core State Standards*. Alexandria, VA: ASCD, 2011. 1. Print.

[25] Kendall, John S. *Understanding Common Core State Standards*. Alexandria, VA: ASCD, 2011. 1. Print.

[26] Common Core and UN Agenda 21: Mass Producing Green Global Serfs. 2015. *Common Core and UN Agenda 21: Mass Producing Green Global Serfs.* [ONLINE] Available at: http://www.thenewamerican.com/culture/education/item/17930-common-core-and-un-agenda-21-mass-producing-green-global-serfs. [Accessed 02 May 2015].

[27] Education for Sustainable Development Toolkit. *Education for Sustainable Development Toolkit.* 2015. [ONLINE] Available at: http://unesdoc.unesco.org/images/0015/001524/152453eo.pdf. [Accessed 02 May 2015].

[28] Pattison, Darcy. "Chapter 1." *What Is Common Core?* Little Rock, Arkansas: Mims House, 2013. Print.

[29] Beck, Glenn. *Conform: Exposing the Truth about Common Core and Public Education.* New York: Threshol Editions, 2014. 104. Print.

[30] Kendall, John S. *Understanding Common Core State Standards.* Alexandria, VA: ASCD, 2011. 41. Print.

[31] Beck, Glenn. *Conform: Exposing the Truth about Common Core and Public Education.* New York: Threshol Editions, 2014. 105. Print.

[32] Ibid., 107.

[33] Pattison, Darcy. "Chapter 1." *What Is Common Core?* Little Rock, Arkansas: Mims House, 2013. Print.

[34] Beck, Glenn. *Conform: Exposing the Truth about Common Core and Public Education.* New York: Threshol Editions, 2014. 108. Print.

[35] Ibid., 109.

[36] Jasper, Kathleen, *ConversationED*: Free chapter emailed on 11/21/14 (book is not published at the time of this writing).

[37] Pattison, Darcy. "Chapter 1." *What Is Common Core?* Little Rock, Arkansas: Mims House, 2013. Print.

[38] Pattison, Darcy. "Chapter 1." *What Is Common Core?* Little Rock, Arkansas: Mims House, 2013. Print.

[39] Coulson, Andrew J. *Market Education: The Unknown History.* Bowling Green, OH: Social Philosophy & Policy Center; 1999. 8. Print.

Chapter 6:

[1] Post-9/11 Changes By the U.S. Government | Infoplease.com. 2014. Post-9/11 Changes by the U.S.

Government | Infoplease.com. [ONLINE] Available at: http://www.infoplease.com/us/history/911-anniversary-government-changes.html. [Accessed 20 December 2014].

[2] 2015. [ONLINE] Available at: https://www.dhs.gov/xlibrary/assets/hr_5005_enr.pdf. [Accessed 22 February 2015].

[3] 2015. [ONLINE] Available at: https://www.du.edu/korbel/hrhw/researchdigest/terror/patriotact.pdf. [Accessed 22 February 2015].

[4] 2015. [ONLINE] Available at: http: //www.fas.org/sgp/crs/misc/RL31724.pdf. [Accessed 22 February 2015].

[5] Chart: How 9/11 Changed the Law | Mother Jones. 2014. Chart: How 9/11 Changed the Law | Mother Jones. [ONLINE] Available at: http://www.motherjones.com/politics/2011/09/law-changes-from-9-11. [Accessed 20 December 2014].

[6] Bill Text - 112th Congress (2011-2012) - THOMAS (Library of Congress). 2015. *Bill Text - 112th Congress (2011-2012) - THOMAS (Library of Congress).* [ONLINE] Available at: http://thomas.loc.gov/cgi-bin/query/z?c112:H.R.1540: [Accessed 22 February 2015].

[7] The Problem with the National Defense Authorization Act - Forbes. 2015. *The Problem with the National Defense Authorization Act - Forbes.* [ONLINE] Available at: http://www.forbes.com/sites/erikkain/2011/12/05/the-national-defense-authorization-act-is-the-greatest-threat-to-civil-liberties-americans-face/. [Accessed 22 February 2015].

[8] 1033 program - Wikipedia, the free encyclopedia. 2015. *1033 program - Wikipedia, the free encyclopedia.* [ONLINE] Available at: http://en.wikipedia.org/wiki/1033_program. [Accessed 22 February 2015].

[9] Militarization of police more widespread than previously thought, especially in small towns | The Daily Sheeple. 2015. *Militarization of police more widespread than previously thought, especially in small towns | The Daily Sheeple.* [ONLINE] Available at: http://www.thedailysheeple.com/militarization-of-police-more-widespread-than-previously-thought-especially-in-small-towns_082013. [Accessed 22 February 2015].

[10] Milgram experiment - Wikipedia, the free encyclopedia. 2015. *Milgram experiment - Wikipedia, the free encyclopedia.* [ONLINE] Available at: http://en.wikipedia.org/wiki/Milgram_experiment. [Accessed 22 February

2015].

[11] Reichstag fire - Wikipedia, the free encyclopedia. 2014. Reichstag fire - Wikipedia, the free encyclopedia. [ONLINE] Available at: http://en.wikipedia.org/wiki/Reichstag_fire. [Accessed 20 December 2014]. and The Reichstag Fire and the Enabling Act of March 23, 1933 | Britannica Blog. 2014. The Reichstag Fire and the Enabling Act of March 23, 1933 | Britannica Blog. [ONLINE] Available at: http://www.britannica.com/blogs/2007/03/the-reichstag-fire-and-the-enabling-act/. [Accessed 20 December 2014].

[12] A Brief History of False Flag Terror : The Corbett Report. 2015. *A Brief History of False Flag Terror : The Corbett Report*. [ONLINE] Available at: https://www.corbettreport.com/a-brief-history-of-false-flag-terror/. [Accessed 03 May 2015].

[13] False flag - Wikipedia, the free encyclopedia. 2014. False flag - Wikipedia, the free encyclopedia. [ONLINE] Available at: http://en.wikipedia.org/wiki/False_flag. [Accessed 20 December 2014].

[14] Ash, Timothy. "The Ides of March." *The Polish Revolution: Solidarity*. 3rd ed. New Haven: Yale UP, 2002. 158-174. Print.

[15] MacEachin, Douglas J. *US Intelligence and the Polish Crisis 1980-1981*. Washington, D.C.: Center for the Study of Intelligence, 2000. 96-101. Print.

[16] Report of the Joint Inquiry Into The Terrorist Attacks of September 11, 2001 – By the House Permanent Select Committee On Intelligence and the Senate Select Committee On Intelligence. 2015. [ONLINE] Available at: https://www.fas.org/irp/congress/2002_rpt/911rept.pdf. [Accessed 22 February 2015].

[17] Why Did U.S. Intelligence Fail September 11th? | Looking For Answers | FRONTLINE | PBS. 2015. *Why Did U.S. Intelligence Fail September 11th? | Looking For Answers | FRONTLINE | PBS*. [ONLINE] Available at: http://www.pbs.org/wgbh/pages/frontline/shows/terrorism/fail/. [Accessed 22 February 2015].

[18] 10 companies profiting the most from war. 2015. *10 companies profiting the most from war*. [ONLINE] Available at: http://www.usatoday.com/story/money/business/2013/03/10/10-companies-profiting-most-from-war/1970997/. [Accessed 16 March 2015].

[19] Big Defense Contractors' Profits Defy Budget Alarms. 2015. *Big Defense Contractors' Profits Defy Budget Alarms*. [ONLINE] Available at: http://www.newsmax.com/Finance/StreetTalk/defense-contractor-profits-

Budget/2013/07/24/id/516840/. [Accessed 16 March 2015].

[20] U.S. Constitution Under Siege over Libya, Taxes, Health Care - TIME. 2014. U.S. Constitution Under Siege over Libya, Taxes, Health Care - TIME. [ONLINE] Available at: http://content.time.com/time/nation/article/0,8599,2079445,00.html. [Accessed 20 December 2014].

Chapter 7:

[1] Nancy Pelosi - Wikiquote. 2015. *Nancy Pelosi - Wikiquote.* [ONLINE] Available at: http://en.wikiquote.org/wiki/Nancy_Pelosi. [Accessed 22 February 2015].

[2] Pelosi: "We Have to Pass the Bill So That You Can Find Out What Is In It" - YouTube. 2015. *Pelosi: "We Have to Pass the Bill So That You Can Find Out What Is In It" - YouTube.* [ONLINE] Available at: https://www.youtube.com/watch?v=hV-05TLiiLU. [Accessed 22 February 2015].

[3] Bloom, Jack M. *Seeing through the Eyes of the Polish Revolution: Solidarity and the Struggle against Communism in Poland.* Chicago: Haymarket, 2014. 195. Print.

[4] Ibid., 193.

[5] Wedge issue - Wikipedia, the free encyclopedia. 2015. *Wedge issue - Wikipedia, the free encyclopedia.* [ONLINE] Available at: http://en.wikipedia.org/wiki/Wedge_issue. [Accessed 22 February 2015].

[6] Bloom, Jack M. *Seeing through the Eyes of the Polish Revolution: Solidarity and the Struggle against Communism in Poland.* Chicago: Haymarket, 2014. 183. Print.

[7] Ibid.,184.

[8] Ibid., 187.

[9] Ibid., 191.

[10] Penn, Shana. *Solidarity's Secret: The Women Who Defeated Communism in Poland.* Ann Arbor: U of Michigan, 2005. 236. Print.

11 Bloom, Jack M. *Seeing through the Eyes of the Polish Revolution: Solidarity and the Struggle against Communism in Poland.* Chicago: Haymarket, 2014. 283. Print.

12 Is Your Local Police Department Using Pictures of Pregnant Women and Children for Target Practice? - Hit & Run : Reason.com. 2015. *Is Your Local Police Department Using Pictures of Pregnant Women and Children for Target Practice? - Hit & Run : Reason.com.* [ONLINE] Available at: http://reason.com/blog/2013/02/19/is-your-local-police-department-using-pi. [Accessed 03 May 2015].

13 Bloom, Jack M. *Seeing through the Eyes of the Polish Revolution: Solidarity and the Struggle against Communism in Poland.* Chicago: Haymarket, 2014. Print. P. 86.

14 Ibid., 85.

15 2015. [ONLINE] Available at: http://oathkeepers.org/oktester/declaration-of-orders-we-will-not-obey/. [Accessed 22 February 2015].

16 2015. [ONLINE] Available at: http://oathkeepers.org/oktester/10-orders-we-will-not-obey/. [Accessed 22 February 2015].

17 Normalcy bias - Wikipedia, the free encyclopedia. 2014. Normalcy bias - Wikipedia, the free encyclopedia. [ONLINE] Available at: http://en.wikipedia.org/wiki/Normalcy_bias. [Accessed 21 December 2014].

18 Bloom, Jack M. *Seeing through the Eyes of the Polish Revolution: Solidarity and the Struggle against Communism in Poland.* Chicago: Haymarket, 2014. 284. Print.

19 Ibid., 283.

20 1033 program - Wikipedia, the free encyclopedia. 2015. *1033 program - Wikipedia, the free encyclopedia.* [ONLINE] Available at: http://en.wikipedia.org/wiki/1033_program. [Accessed 22 February 2015].

21 The Pentagon gave nearly half a billion dollars of military gear to local law enforcement last year - The Washington Post. 2015. *The Pentagon gave nearly half a billion dollars of military gear to local law enforcement last year - The Washington Post.* [ONLINE] Available at: http://www.washingtonpost.com/blogs/wonkblog/wp/2014/08/14/the-pentagon-gave-nearly-half-a-billion-dollars-of-military-gear-to-local-law-enforcement-

last-year/. [Accessed 22 February 2015].

[22] Posse Comitatus Act - Wikipedia, the free encyclopedia. 2015. *Posse Comitatus Act - Wikipedia, the free encyclopedia.* [ONLINE] Available at: http://en.wikipedia.org/wiki/Posse_Comitatus_Act#Recent_legislative_events. [Accessed 22 February 2015]

[23] The Invisible Battle Over Posse Comitatus | Center for American Progress. 2015. *The Invisible Battle Over Posse Comitatus | Center for American Progress.* [ONLINE] Available at: https://www.americanprogress.org/issues/media/news/2008/10/23/5081/think-again-the-invisible-battle-over-posse-comitatus/. [Accessed 22 February 2015].

[24] Review: Federal Support for Local Law Enforcement Equipment Acquisition. 2014. *Review: Federal Support for Local Law Enforcement Equipment Acquisition.* [ONLINE] Available at: http://www.whitehouse.gov/sites/default/files/docs/federal_support_for_local_law_enforcement_equipment_acquisition.pdf [Accessed 22 February 2015].

[25] Was Watertown's Door-to-Door Search for Bombing Suspects a Violation of the Fourth Amendment? | Video | TheBlaze.com. 2015. *Was Watertown's Door-to-Door Search for Bombing Suspects a Violation of the Fourth Amendment? | Video | TheBlaze.com.* [ONLINE] Available at: http://www.theblaze.com/stories/2013/04/23/ready-how-watertown-door-to-door-search-for-bombing-suspects-did-not-violate-the-fourth-amendment/. [Accessed 22 February 2015].

[26] Your Town - Boston.com. 2015. *Your Town - Boston.com.* [ONLINE] Available at: http://www.boston.com/yourtown/news/watertown/2013/11/lawyers_to_speak_about_unconstitutional_watertown_home_searc.html. [Accessed 22 February 2015].

[27] Kerry signs UN arms treaty, senators threaten to block it | Fox News. 2015. *Kerry signs UN arms treaty, senators threaten to block it | Fox News.* [ONLINE] Available at: http://www.foxnews.com/politics/2013/09/25/kerry-signs-un-arms-treaty-senators-threaten-to-block-it/. [Accessed 22 February 2015].

[28] Dangers of U.N. Arms Trade Treaty Begin to Surface. 2015. *Dangers of U.N. Arms Trade Treaty Begin to Surface.* [ONLINE] Available at: http://www.heritage.org/research/reports/2014/01/dangers-of-un-arms-trade-treaty-begin-to-surface. [Accessed 22 February 2015].

[29] Codex Alimentarius - Wikipedia, the free encyclopedia. 2015. *Codex*

Alimentarius - Wikipedia, the free encyclopedia. [ONLINE] Available at: https://en.wikipedia.org/wiki/Codex_Alimentarius. [Accessed 20 March 2015].

[30] What the Supreme Court ruled on health care 'tax' - CNN.com. 2015. *What the Supreme Court ruled on health care 'tax' - CNN.com.* [ONLINE] Available at: http://www.cnn.com/2012/07/05/politics/scotus-health-care-tax/. [Accessed 22 February 2015].

[31] Affordable Care Act Tax Provisions. 2015. *Affordable Care Act Tax Provisions.* [ONLINE] Available at: http://www.irs.gov/Affordable-Care-Act/Affordable-Care-Act-Tax-Provisions. [Accessed 22 February 2015].

[32] The Requirement to Buy Coverage Under the Affordable Care Act | The Henry J. Kaiser Family Foundation. 2015. *The Requirement to Buy Coverage Under the Affordable Care Act | The Henry J. Kaiser Family Foundation.* [ONLINE] Available at: http://kff.org/infographic/the-requirement-to-buy-coverage-under-the-affordable-care-act/. [Accessed 22 February 2015].

[33] National Defense Authorization Act for Fiscal Year 2012 - Wikipedia, the free encyclopedia. 2015. *National Defense Authorization Act for Fiscal Year 2012 - Wikipedia, the free encyclopedia.* [ONLINE] Available at: http://en.wikipedia.org/wiki/National_Defense_Authorization_Act_for_Fiscal_Year_2012. [Accessed 22 February 2015].

[34] NDAA Sections 1021 and 1022: Scary Potential | Tenth Amendment Center. 2015. *NDAA Sections 1021 and 1022: Scary Potential | Tenth Amendment Center.* [ONLINE] Available at: http://tenthamendmentcenter.com/2012/02/06/ndaa-sections-1021-and-1022-scary-potential/. [Accessed 22 February 2015].

Chapter 8:

[1] Who Owns What on Television? - Neatorama. 2014. Who Owns What on Television? - Neatorama. [ONLINE] Available at: http://www.neatorama.com/2008/07/07/who-owns-what-on-television/. [Accessed 22 December 2014].

[2] FCC's Review of the Broadcast Ownership Rules | FCC.gov. 2014. FCC's Review of the Broadcast Ownership Rules | FCC.gov. [ONLINE] Available at: http://www.fcc.gov/guides/review-broadcast-ownership-rules. [Accessed 22 December 2014].

[3] GOP convention cut short | Las Vegas Review-Journal. 2014. GOP convention cut short | Las Vegas Review-Journal. [ONLINE] Available at:

http://www.reviewjournal.com/news/elections/gop-convention-cut-short. [Accessed 28 April 2008].

[4] MacEachin, Douglas J. *US Intelligence and the Polish Crisis 1980-1981.* Washington, D.C.: Center for the Study of Intelligence, 2000. 126-127. Print.

[5] Missouri Information Analysis Center - Wikipedia, the free encyclopedia. 2014. Missouri Information Analysis Center - Wikipedia, the free encyclopedia. [ONLINE] Available at: http://en.wikipedia.org/wiki/Missouri_Information_Analysis_Center. [Accessed 22 December 2014].

[6] MacEachin, Douglas J. *US Intelligence and the Polish Crisis 1980-1981.* Washington, D.C.: Center for the Study of Intelligence, 2000. 35. Print.

[7] Activist Post: CIA Flashback: "We'll Know Our Disinformation Program Is Complete When Everything the American Public Believes Is False.". 2015. *Activist Post: CIA Flashback: "We'll Know Our Disinformation Program Is Complete When Everything the American Public Believes Is False.".* [ONLINE] Available at: http://www.activistpost.com/2015/01/cia-flashback-well-know-our.html. [Accessed 21 March 2015].

[8] 2015. [ONLINE] Available at: https://www.nolanchart.com/article3588-ron-pauls-delegate-wars-iii-html. [Accessed 22 February 2015].

[9] The 2008 Republican National Convention: A perfect farce. 2015. *The 2008 Republican National Convention: A perfect farce.* [ONLINE] Available at: http://proliberty.com/observer/20080910.htm. [Accessed 22 February 2015].

[10] Ron Paul supporters walk out of GOP convention - Los Angeles Times. 2015. *Ron Paul supporters walk out of GOP convention - Los Angeles Times.* [ONLINE] Available at: http://articles.latimes.com/2012/aug/28/news/la-pn-ron-paul-supporters-walk-out-of-gop-convention-20120828. [Accessed 22 February 2015].

[11] Rule 15 Ron Paul RNC Vote - Rule 15 and the Great RNC Screwing of Ron Paul. 2015. *Rule 15 Ron Paul RNC Vote - Rule 15 and the Great RNC Screwing of Ron Paul.* [ONLINE] Available at: http://www.esquire.com/news-politics/politics/a15545/rule-15-ron-paul-rnc-12152380/. [Accessed 22 February 2015].

[12] Bloom, Jack M. *Seeing through the Eyes of the Polish Revolution: Solidarity and the Struggle against Communism in Poland.* Chicago: Haymarket, 2014. 69.

Print.

[13] Penn, Shana. *Solidarity's Secret: The Women Who Defeated Communism in Poland.* Ann Arbor: U of Michigan, 2005. 177. Print.

[14] Ash, Timothy. *The Magic Lantern: The Revolution of '89 Witnessed in Warsaw, Budapest, Berlin, and Prague.* New York: Random House, 1990. 132. Print.

[15] Bloom, Jack M. *Seeing through the Eyes of the Polish Revolution: Solidarity and the Struggle against Communism in Poland.* Chicago: Haymarket, 2014. 219. Print.

Chapter 9:

[1] Polish underground press - Wikipedia, the free encyclopedia. 2014. Polish underground press - Wikipedia, the free encyclopedia. [ONLINE] Available at: http://en.wikipedia.org/wiki/Polish_underground_press. [Accessed 22 December 2014].

[2] Penn, Shana. *Solidarity's Secret: The Women Who Defeated Communism in Poland.* Ann Arbor: U of Michigan, 2005. 11. Print.

[3] Penn, Shana. *Solidarity's Secret: The Women Who Defeated Communism in Poland.* Ann Arbor: U of Michigan, 2005. 176. Print.

[4] IU students to print underground newspaper in one-of-a-kind course with legendary Polish journalist: IU News Room: Indiana University. 2014. IU students to print underground newspaper in one-of-a-kind course with legendary Polish journalist: IU News Room: Indiana University. [ONLINE] Available at: http://newsinfo.iu.edu/news-archive/15808.html. [Accessed 22 December 2014].

[5] Edward Snowden - Wikipedia, the free encyclopedia. 2015. *Edward Snowden - Wikipedia, the free encyclopedia.* [ONLINE] Available at: http://en.wikipedia.org/wiki/Edward_Snowden. [Accessed 07 March 2015].

[6] Silverglate, Harvey A. Three Felonies a Day: How the Feds Target the Innocent. New York: Encounter, 2009. Print.

[7] You May Think You Have Nothing to Hide ... But You Are Still Breaking Laws Which Government Spying Could Discover and Use Against You Washington's Blog. [ONLINE] Available at:

http://www.washingtonsblog.com/2013/10/you-break-the-law-every-day-without-even-knowing-it.html. [Accessed 22 December 2014].

[8] 2015. [ONLINE] Available at: http://constitution.org/abus/le/miac-strategic-report.pdf. [Accessed 05 March 2015].

[9] 'Fusion Centers' Expand Criteria to Identify Militia Members | Fox News. 2015. *'Fusion Centers' Expand Criteria to Identify Militia Members | Fox News.* [ONLINE] Available at: http://www.foxnews.com/politics/2009/03/23/fusion-centers-expand-criteria-identify-militia-members/. [Accessed 05 March 2015].

[10] Missouri Information Analysis Center - Wikipedia, the free encyclopedia. 2015. *Missouri Information Analysis Center - Wikipedia, the free encyclopedia.* [ONLINE] Available at: http://en.wikipedia.org/wiki/Missouri_Information_Analysis_Center. [Accessed 08 March 2015].

[11] Wedge issue - Wikipedia, the free encyclopedia. 2015. *Wedge issue - Wikipedia, the free encyclopedia.* [ONLINE] Available at: http://en.wikipedia.org/wiki/Wedge_issue. [Accessed 13 March 2015].

[12] Wolf, Naomi. *The End of America: Letter of Warning to a Young Patriot.* White River Junction, Vt.: Chelsea Green Pub., 2007. Print.

[13] Reporters Without Borders. 2015. *Reporters Without Borders.* [ONLINE] Available at: http://rsf.org/index2014/en-index2014.php#. [Accessed 05 March 2015].

[14] U.S. Plunges to #46 in World Press Freedom Index, Below Romania and Just Above Haiti | Liberty Blitzkrieg. 2015. *U.S. Plunges to #46 in World Press Freedom Index, Below Romania and Just Above Haiti | Liberty Blitzkrieg.* [ONLINE] Available at: http://libertyblitzkrieg.com/2014/02/12/u-s-plunges-to-46-in-world-press-freedom-index-below-romania-and-just-above-haiti/. [Accessed 05 March 2015].

[15] Cooper, Jeff. *The Art of the Rifle.* Boulder, Colo.: Paladin, 1997. P. 2. Print.

[16] Gun Facts | Gun Control, Guns and Crime Prevention. 2015. *Gun Facts | Gun Control, Guns and Crime Prevention.* [ONLINE] Available at: http://www.gunfacts.info/gun-control-myths/guns-and-crime-prevention/. [Accessed 05 March 2015].

[17] Gun Facts | Gun Control and Crime. 2015. *Gun Facts | Gun Control and Crime.* [ONLINE] Available at: http://www.gunfacts.info/gun-control-myths/crime-and-guns/. [Accessed 05 March 2015].

[18] Gun Facts | Gun Control and Crime. 2015. *Gun Facts | Gun Control and Crime*. [ONLINE] Available at: http://www.gunfacts.info/gun-control-myths/crime-and-guns/. [Accessed 05 March 2015].

[19] Guns and Self Defense | Cato Institute. 2015. *Guns and Self Defense | Cato Institute*. [ONLINE] Available at: http://www.cato.org/guns-and-self-defense. [Accessed 05 March 2015].

[20] Defensive gun use - Wikipedia, the free encyclopedia. 2015. *Defensive gun use - Wikipedia, the free encyclopedia*. [ONLINE] Available at: http://en.wikipedia.org/wiki/Defensive_gun_use. [Accessed 05 March 2015].

[21] CDC Study: Use of Firearms for Self-Defense is 'Important Crime Deterrent' | CNS News. 2015. *CDC Study: Use of Firearms for Self-Defense is 'Important Crime Deterrent' | CNS News*. [ONLINE] Available at: http://www.cnsnews.com/news/article/cdc-study-use-firearms-self-defense-important-crime-deterrent. [Accessed 05 March 2015].

[22] Chile's Gun-Control Lesson for Americans - The Future of Freedom Foundation. 2015. *Chile's Gun-Control Lesson for Americans - The Future of Freedom Foundation*. [ONLINE] Available at: http://fff.org/explore-freedom/article/chiles-gun-control-lesson-for-americans/. [Accessed 18 March 2015].

[23] Understanding the Fear of Self-Defense and Revolution. 2015. *Understanding The Fear Of Self-Defense and Revolution*. [ONLINE] Available at: http://alt-market.com/articles/2506-understanding-the-fear-of-self-defense-and-revolution. [Accessed 14 February 2015].

[24] Duncan, Alastair. *Gandhi Selected Writings*. Newburyport: Dover Publications, 2012. 65. Print.

[25] The bad joke called 'the FISA court' shows how a 'drone court' would work | Glenn Greenwald | Comment is free | The Guardian. 2015. *The bad joke called 'the FISA court' shows how a 'drone court' would work | Glenn Greenwald | Comment is free | The Guardian*. [ONLINE] Available at: http://www.theguardian.com/commentisfree/2013/may/03/fisa-court-rubber-stamp-drones. [Accessed 05 March 2015].

[26] An International Perspective on FISA: No Protections, Little Oversight | Electronic Frontier Foundation. 2015. *An International Perspective on FISA: No Protections, Little Oversight | Electronic Frontier Foundation*. [ONLINE] Available at: https://www.eff.org/deeplinks/2013/06/modern-foreign-surveillance-legal-perspective. [Accessed 05 March 2015].

[27] The FISA Court's Problems Run Deep, and More Than Tinkering is Required | American Civil Liberties Union. 2015. *The FISA Court's Problems Run Deep, and More Than Tinkering is Required | American Civil Liberties Union.* [ONLINE] Available at: https://www.aclu.org/blog/national-security-technology-and-liberty/fisa-courts-problems-run-deep-and-more-tinkering. [Accessed 05 March 2015].

[28] Support Oversight of the Secret FISA Court | American Civil Liberties Union. 2015. *Support Oversight of the Secret FISA Court | American Civil Liberties Union.* [ONLINE] Available at: https://www.aclu.org/support-oversight-secret-fisa-court. [Accessed 05 March 2015].

[29] FISA Court Decision Upholding Surveillance Is a Joke | The New Republic. 2015. *FISA Court Decision Upholding Surveillance Is a Joke | The New Republic.* [ONLINE] Available at: http://www.newrepublic.com/article/114853/fisa-court-decision-upholding-surveillance-joke. [Accessed 05 March 2015].

[30] The bad joke called 'the FISA court' shows how a 'drone court' would work | Glenn Greenwald | Comment is free | The Guardian. 2015. *The bad joke called 'the FISA court' shows how a 'drone court' would work | Glenn Greenwald | Comment is free | The Guardian.* [ONLINE] Available at: http://www.theguardian.com/commentisfree/2013/may/03/fisa-court-rubber-stamp-drones. [Accessed 05 March 2015].

[31] Racketeer Influenced and Corrupt Organizations Act - Wikipedia, the free encyclopedia. 2015. *Racketeer Influenced and Corrupt Organizations Act - Wikipedia, the free encyclopedia.* [ONLINE] Available at: http://en.wikipedia.org/wiki/Racketeer_Influenced_and_Corrupt_Organizations_Act. [Accessed 08 March 2015].

[32] The continuing outrage that is civil asset forfeiture - The Washington Post. 2015. *The continuing outrage that is civil asset forfeiture - The Washington Post.* [ONLINE] Available at: http://www.washingtonpost.com/news/the-watch/wp/2014/07/24/the-continuing-outrage-that-is-civil-asset-forfeiture/. [Accessed 08 March 2015].

[33] Taken - The New Yorker. 2015. *Taken - The New Yorker.* [ONLINE] Available at: http://www.newyorker.com/magazine/2013/08/12/taken. [Accessed 05 March 2015].

[34] Asset Forfeiture – How Cops Continue to Steal Americans' Hard Earned Cash with Zero Repercussions | Liberty Blitzkrieg. 2015. *Asset Forfeiture – How Cops Continue to Steal Americans' Hard Earned Cash with Zero Repercussions*

| *Liberty Blitzkrieg.* [ONLINE] Available at: http://libertyblitzkrieg.com/2014/07/28/asset-forfeiture-how-cops-continue-to-steal-americans-hard-earned-cash-with-zero-repercussions/. [Accessed 05 March 2015].

35 How Police Are Stealing Millions from Innocent Americans. 2015. *How Police Are Stealing Millions from Innocent Americans.* [ONLINE] Available at: http://www.theblot.com/police-stealing-millions-innocent-americans-7725549. [Accessed 08 March 2015].The Forfeiture Racket - Reason.com. 2015. *The Forfeiture Racket - Reason.com.* [ONLINE] Available at: http://reason.com/archives/2010/01/26/the-forfeiture-racket. [Accessed 05 March 2015].

36 Suspicious activity report - Wikipedia, the free encyclopedia. 2015. *Suspicious activity report - Wikipedia, the free encyclopedia.* [ONLINE] Available at: http://en.wikipedia.org/wiki/Suspicious_activity_report. [Accessed 22 March 2015].

37 Before the Income Tax. 2015. *Before the Income Tax.* [ONLINE] Available at: http://www.thenewamerican.com/culture/history/item/14268-before-the-income-tax. [Accessed 13 March 2015].

38 100 Years Old And Still Killing Us: America Was Much Better Off Before The Income Tax. 2015. *100 Years Old And Still Killing Us: America Was Much Better Off Before The Income Tax.* [ONLINE] Available at: http://theeconomiccollapseblog.com/archives/100-years-old-and-still-killing-us-america-was-much-better-off-before-the-income-tax. [Accessed 13 March 2015].

39 IRS targeting controversy - Wikipedia, the free encyclopedia. 2015. *IRS targeting controversy - Wikipedia, the free encyclopedia.* [ONLINE] Available at: http://en.wikipedia.org/wiki/IRS_targeting_controversy. [Accessed 08 March 2015].

40 Obama administration won't release IRS targeting documents | TheHill. 2015. *Obama administration won't release IRS targeting documents | TheHill.* [ONLINE] Available at: http://thehill.com/business-a-lobbying/232249-feds-wont-release-irs-targeting-documents. [Accessed 08 March 2015].

41 List of countries by incarceration rate - Wikipedia, the free encyclopedia. 2015. *List of countries by incarceration rate - Wikipedia, the free encyclopedia.* [ONLINE] Available at: http://en.wikipedia.org/wiki/List_of_countries_by_incarceration_rate#United_States. [Accessed 08 March 2015].

[42] U.S. prison population dwarfs that of other nations - The New York Times. 2015. *U.S. prison population dwarfs that of other nations - The New York Times.* [ONLINE] Available at: http://www.nytimes.com/2008/04/23/world/americas/23iht-23prison.12253738.html?pagewanted=all&_r=1&. [Accessed 08 March 2015].

[43] Incarceration in the United States - Wikipedia, the free encyclopedia. 2015. *Incarceration in the United States - Wikipedia, the free encyclopedia.* [ONLINE] Available at: http://en.wikipedia.org/wiki/Incarceration_in_the_United_States. [Accessed 07 March 2015].

[44] Victimless Crime Constitutes 86% of The Federal Prison Population | Libertarian News. 2015. *Victimless Crime Constitutes 86% of The Federal Prison Population | Libertarian News.* [ONLINE] Available at: https://www.libertariannews.org/2011/09/29/victimless-crime-constitutes-86-of-the-american-prison-population/. [Accessed 07 March 2015].

[45] Why We Need Prison Reform: Victimless Crimes Are 86% of the Federal Prison Population - Mic. 2015. *Why We Need Prison Reform: Victimless Crimes Are 86% of the Federal Prison Population - Mic.* [ONLINE] Available at: http://mic.com/articles/8558/why-we-need-prison-reform-victimless-crimes-are-86-of-the-federal-prison-population. [Accessed 08 March 2015].

[46] Overcrowded Prisons Are Forcing the Government to Think About Victimless Crime | The Free Thought Project. 2015. *Overcrowded Prisons Are Forcing the Government to Think About Victimless Crime | The Free Thought Project.* [ONLINE] Available at: http://thefreethoughtproject.com/overcrowded-prisons-forcing-government-victimless-crime/. [Accessed 08 March 2015].

[47] Geithner -Secretary of the Treasury Despite Tax Evasion. 2015. *Geithner - Secretary of the Treasury Despite Tax Evasion.* [ONLINE] Available at: http://www.shortnews.com/start.cfm?id=76569. [Accessed 08 March 2015].

[48] Wesley Snipes - Wikipedia, the free encyclopedia. 2015. *Wesley Snipes - Wikipedia, the free encyclopedia.* [ONLINE] Available at: http://en.wikipedia.org/wiki/Wesley_Snipes. [Accessed 08 March 2015].

[49] Jon Corzine - Wikipedia, the free encyclopedia. 2015. *Jon Corzine - Wikipedia, the free encyclopedia.* [ONLINE] Available at: http://en.wikipedia.org/wiki/Jon_Corzine. [Accessed 08 March 2015].

[50] Former MF Global CEO Jon Corzine Is Really Sorry But Wants His Notes Back - Business Insider. 2015. *Former MF Global CEO Jon Corzine Is Really Sorry But Wants His Notes Back - Business Insider.* [ONLINE] Available at:

http://www.businessinsider.com/the-best-of-corzines-statement-2011-12.
[Accessed 13 March 2015].

[51] Here's Why There Will Be No Criminal Charges In The MF Global Case.
2015. *Here's Why There Will Be No Criminal Charges In The MF Global Case.*
[ONLINE] Available at: http://www.huffingtonpost.com/2013/06/28/criminal-charges-mf-global_n_3516652.html. [Accessed 13 March 2015].

[52] Bernard Madoff - Wikipedia, the free encyclopedia. 2015. *Bernard Madoff -
Wikipedia, the free encyclopedia.* [ONLINE] Available at:
http://en.wikipedia.org/wiki/Bernard_Madoff. [Accessed 08 March 2015].

[53] Congress Quickly And Quietly Rolls Back Insider Trading Rules For Itself |
Techdirt. 2015. *Congress Quickly And Quietly Rolls Back Insider Trading Rules
For Itself | Techdirt.* [ONLINE] Available at:
https://www.techdirt.com/articles/20130416/08344222725/congress-quickly-quietly-rolls-back-insider-trading-rules-itself.shtml. [Accessed 08 March 2015].

[54] Private prison - Wikipedia, the free encyclopedia. 2015. *Private prison -
Wikipedia, the free encyclopedia.* [ONLINE] Available at:
http://en.wikipedia.org/wiki/Private_prison. [Accessed 08 March 2015].

[55] Prison–industrial complex - Wikipedia, the free encyclopedia. 2015. *Prison–
industrial complex - Wikipedia, the free encyclopedia.* [ONLINE] Available at:
http://en.wikipedia.org/wiki/Prison%E2%80%93industrial_complex. [Accessed
08 March 2015].

[56] Private Prisons | American Civil Liberties Union. 2015. *Private Prisons |
American Civil Liberties Union.* [ONLINE] Available at:
https://www.aclu.org/prisoners-rights/private-prisons. [Accessed 08 March
2015].

[57] Prison Labor is Industry's "Best Kept Secret in Outsourcing" and What Has
Killed Your Job. 2015. *Prison Labor is Industry's "Best Kept Secret in
Outsourcing" and What Has Killed Your Job.* [ONLINE] Available at:
http://www.shtfplan.com/headline-news/prison-labor-is-industrys-best-kept-secret-in-outsourcing-and-what-has-killed-your-job_04202015. [Accessed 03
May 2015].

[58] The Prison Industry in the United States: Big Business or a New Form of
Slavery? | Global Research. 2015. *The Prison Industry in the United States: Big
Business or a New Form of Slavery? | Global Research.* [ONLINE] Available
at: http://www.globalresearch.ca/the-prison-industry-in-the-united-states-big-business-or-a-new-form-of-slavery/8289. [Accessed 08 March 2015].

[59] Jury nullification - Wikipedia, the free encyclopedia. 2015. *Jury nullification - Wikipedia, the free encyclopedia.* [ONLINE] Available at: http://en.wikipedia.org/wiki/Jury_nullification. [Accessed 08 March 2015].

[60] Jury Nullification | Fully Informed Jury Association. 2015. *Jury Nullification | Fully Informed Jury Association.* [ONLINE] Available at: http://fija.org/. [Accessed 22 March 2015].

[61] Obama to Force Americans to Buy Government Bonds? 2015. *Obama to Force Americans to Buy Government Bonds?* [ONLINE] Available at: http://www.thenewamerican.com/usnews/politics/item/17508-obama-to-force-americans-to-buy-government-bonds. [Accessed 08 March 2015].

[62] National Seniors Council. 2015. *National Seniors Council.* [ONLINE] Available at: http://www.nationalseniorscouncil.org/index.php?option=com_content&view=article&id=89%3Aobama-begins-push-for-new-national-retirement-system&catid=34%3Asocial-security&Itemid=62. [Accessed 22 March 2015].

[63] New Rules: Cyprus-style Bail-ins to Take Deposits and Pensions | Ellen Brown. 2015. *New Rules: Cyprus-style Bail-ins to Take Deposits and Pensions | Ellen Brown.* [ONLINE] Available at: http://www.huffingtonpost.com/ellen-brown/new-g20-bailin-rules-now-_b_6244394.html. [Accessed 22 March 2015].

[64] The Cyprus Bank 'Bail-In' Is Another Crony Bankster Scam - Forbes. 2015. *The Cyprus Bank 'Bail-In' Is Another Crony Bankster Scam - Forbes.* [ONLINE] Available at: http://www.forbes.com/sites/nathanlewis/2013/05/03/the-cyprus-bank-bail-in-is-another-crony-bankster-scam/. [Accessed 22 March 2015].

[65] Polish Pension Funds Seized by Government – Who is Next? | Armstrong Economics. 2015. *Polish Pension Funds Seized by Government – Who is Next? | Armstrong Economics.* [ONLINE] Available at: http://armstrongeconomics.com/2014/11/18/polish-pension-funds-seized-by-government-who-is-next/. [Accessed 22 March 2015].

[66] Poland's Piggish Pols--They're Not Alone - Forbes. 2015. *Poland's Piggish Pols--They're Not Alone - Forbes.* [ONLINE] Available at: http://www.forbes.com/sites/steveforbes/2013/09/17/polands-piggish-pols-theyre-not-alone/. [Accessed 22 March 2015].

[67] Now Obama wants your 401(k). 2015. *Now Obama wants your 401(k).* [ONLINE] Available at: http://www.wnd.com/2012/11/now-obama-wants-your-401k/. [Accessed 22 March 2015].

[68] McCormick, James M. *American Foreign Policy and Process*. 4th ed. Belmont, CA: Thomson/Wadsworth, 2005. 107. Print.

[69] Political power grows out of the barrel of a gun - Wikipedia, the free encyclopedia. 2015. *Political power grows out of the barrel of a gun - Wikipedia, the free encyclopedia.* [ONLINE] Available at: http://en.wikipedia.org/wiki/Political_power_grows_out_of_the_barrel_of_a_gun. [Accessed 08 March 2015].

[70] Farmers, ranchers oppose EPA water grab | Human Events. 2015. *Farmers, ranchers oppose EPA water grab | Human Events.* [ONLINE] Available at: http://humanevents.com/2014/08/15/farmers-ranchers-oppose-epa-water-grab/. [Accessed 08 March 2015].

[71] FedGov Moves To Seize Water Rights From 100,000 Montanans: "All Surface Water And Wells". 2015. *FedGov Moves To Seize Water Rights From 100,000 Montanans: "All Surface Water And Wells".* [ONLINE] Available at: http://www.shtfplan.com/headline-news/fedgov-moves-to-seize-water-rights-from-100000-montanans-all-surface-water-and-wells_03182015. [Accessed 04 May 2015].

[72] Feds Push For Total Control of Property Rights: "Government is Named as the Owner of ALL the Water". 2015. *Feds Push For Total Control of Property Rights: "Government is Named as the Owner of ALL the Water".* [ONLINE] Available at: http://www.shtfplan.com/headline-news/feds-push-for-total-control-of-property-rights-government-is-named-as-the-owner-of-all-the-water_04162015. [Accessed 04 May 2015].

[73] How the EPA separates landowners from their properties | The PPJ Gazette. 2015. *How the EPA separates landowners from their properties | The PPJ Gazette.* [ONLINE] Available at: http://ppjg.me/2014/08/26/how-the-epa-separates-landowners-from-their-properties/. [Accessed 08 March 2015].

[74] Counties Claim EPA is Destroying Agriculture - Farm Futures. 2015. *Counties Claim EPA is Destroying Agriculture - Farm Futures.* [ONLINE] Available at: http://farmfutures.com/blogs-counties-claim-epa-destroying-agriculture-8527. [Accessed 08 March 2015].

[75] Man Faces $75,000-A-Day in EPA Fines for Building Pond on His Land | Off the Grid News. 2015. *Man Faces $75,000-A-Day in EPA Fines for Building Pond on His Land | Off the Grid News.* [ONLINE] Available at: http://www.offthegridnews.com/current-events/rancher-faces-75000-a-day-fine-for-building-pond-on-his-land/. [Accessed 08 March 2015].

[76] Oregon Man Sentenced to 30 Days in Jail -- for Collecting Rainwater on His Property | CNS News. 2015. *Oregon Man Sentenced to 30 Days in Jail -- for Collecting Rainwater on His Property | CNS News.* [ONLINE] Available at: http://cnsnews.com/news/article/oregon-man-sentenced-30-days-jail-collecting-rainwater-his-property. [Accessed 08 March 2015].

[77] Blueprint for water 'control'? Pol says EPA made secret maps for new regulatory push | Fox News. 2015. *Blueprint for water 'control'? Pol says EPA made secret maps for new regulatory push | Fox News.* [ONLINE] Available at: http://www.foxnews.com/politics/2014/08/27/blueprint-for-water-control-pol-says-epa-secretly-created-maps-for-new/. [Accessed 08 March 2015].

[78] Obama Plays Water-Guzzling Desert Golf Courses Amid California Drought. 2015. *Obama Plays Water-Guzzling Desert Golf Courses Amid California Drought.* [ONLINE] Available at: http://time.com/7853/obama-golfs-water-guzzling-desert-courses-amid-the-drought/. [Accessed 08 March 2015].

[79] Justices side with WSU in golf course water-use case - Washington Times. 2015. *Justices side with WSU in golf course water-use case - Washington Times.* [ONLINE] Available at: http://www.washingtontimes.com/news/2015/feb/12/justices-side-with-wsu-in-golf-course-water-use-ca/?page=all. [Accessed 08 March 2015].

[80] Summary of the Clean Water Act | Laws & Regulations | US EPA. 2015. *Summary of the Clean Water Act | Laws & Regulations | US EPA.* [ONLINE] Available at: http://www2.epa.gov/laws-regulations/summary-clean-water-act. [Accessed 08 March 2015].

[81] Documents Related to the Proposed Definition of "Waters of the United States" Under the Clean Water Act | Clean Water Rule | US EPA. 2015. *Documents Related to the Proposed Definition of "Waters of the United States" Under the Clean Water Act | Clean Water Rule | US EPA.* [ONLINE] Available at: http://www2.epa.gov/cleanwaterrule/documents-related-proposed-definition-waters-united-states-under-clean-water-act. [Accessed 08 March 2015].

[82] 'Biggest land grab in the history of the world'. 2015. *'Biggest land grab in the history of the world'.* [ONLINE] Available at: http://www.wnd.com/2014/04/biggest-land-grab-in-the-history-of-the-world/. [Accessed 08 March 2015].

[83] UPDATE Powder Keg: Cliven Bundy Supporters Openly Warn Feds To Stand Down In 3 Million Acre Land Grab | Alternative. 2014. UPDATE Powder Keg: Cliven Bundy Supporters Openly Warn Feds To Stand Down In 3 Million Acre Land Grab | Alternative. [ONLINE] Available at: http://beforeitsnews.com/alternative/2014/10/powder-keg-cliven-bundy-

supporters-openly-warn-feds-to-stand-down-in-3-million-acre-land-grab-
3053462.html. [Accessed 22 December 2014].

84 Bundy standoff - Wikipedia, the free encyclopedia. 2014. Bundy standoff -
Wikipedia, the free encyclopedia. [ONLINE] Available at:
http://en.wikipedia.org/wiki/Bundy_standoff. [Accessed 22 December 2014].

85 BLM won't back up claim rancher Cliven Bundy owes $1 million |
OregonLive.com. 2014. BLM won't back up claim rancher Cliven Bundy owes
$1 million | OregonLive.com. [ONLINE] Available at:
http://www.oregonlive.com/pacific-northwest-
news/index.ssf/2014/07/blm_wont_back_up_claim_rancher.html. [Accessed 22
December 2014].

86 Bundy Hoax Exposed: Full Video of Cliven Bundy's Non-Racist, Pro-Black,
Pro-Mexican, Anti-Government Remarks | Alternative. 2014. Bundy Hoax
Exposed: Full Video of Cliven Bundy's Non-Racist, Pro-Black, Pro-Mexican,
Anti-Government Remarks | Alternative. [ONLINE] Available at:
http://beforeitsnews.com/alternative/2014/04/bundy-hoax-exposed-full-video-
of-cliven-bundys-non-racist-pro-black-pro-mexican-anti-government-remarks-
2944710.html. [Accessed 22 December 2014].

87 Article One of the United States Constitution - Wikipedia, the free
encyclopedia. 2014. Article One of the United States Constitution - Wikipedia,
the free encyclopedia. [ONLINE] Available at:
http://en.wikipedia.org/wiki/Article_One_of_the_United_States_Constitution.
[Accessed 22 December 2014].

88 Article Four of the United States Constitution - Wikipedia, the free
encyclopedia. 2014. Article Four of the United States Constitution - Wikipedia,
the free encyclopedia. [ONLINE] Available at:
http://en.wikipedia.org/wiki/Article_Four_of_the_United_States_Constitution.
[Accessed 22 December 2014].

89 Agenda 21 - Wikipedia, the free encyclopedia. 2015. *Agenda 21 - Wikipedia,
the free encyclopedia.* [ONLINE] Available at:
http://en.wikipedia.org/wiki/Agenda_21. [Accessed 08 March 2015].

90 Articles: UN Agenda 21 - Coming to a Neighborhood near You. 2015.
Articles: UN Agenda 21 - Coming to a Neighborhood near You. [ONLINE]
Available at:
http://www.americanthinker.com/articles/2009/10/un_agenda_21_coming_to_a_
neigh.html. [Accessed 08 March 2015].

91 Articles: UN Agenda 21 - Coming to a Neighborhood near You. 2015.

Articles: UN Agenda 21 - Coming to a Neighborhood near You. [ONLINE]
Available at:
http://www.americanthinker.com/articles/2009/10/un_agenda_21_coming_to_a_
neigh.html. [Accessed 08 March 2015].

[92] What Is Agenda 21? After Watching This, You May Not Want to Know |
Video | TheBlaze.com. 2015. *What Is Agenda 21? After Watching This, You
May Not Want to Know | Video | TheBlaze.com.* [ONLINE] Available at:
http://www.theblaze.com/stories/2012/11/19/what-is-agenda-21-after-watching-
this-you-may-not-want-to-know/. [Accessed 07 March 2015].

[93] DEMOCRATS AGAINST U. N. AGENDA 21 - OK, So what is Agenda 21?
And why should I care? Part 1. 2015. *DEMOCRATS AGAINST U. N.
AGENDA 21 - OK, So what is Agenda 21? And why should I care? Part 1.*
[ONLINE] Available at: http://www.democratsagainstunagenda21.com/.
[Accessed 08 March 2015].

[94] Here We Stand, At The Twilight's Last Gleaming: "All Private Property
Rights In The U.S. To Be Strategically Usurped". 2015. *Here We Stand, At The
Twilight's Last Gleaming: "All Private Property Rights In The U.S. To Be
Strategically Usurped".* [ONLINE] Available at:
http://www.shtfplan.com/headline-news/here-we-stand-at-the-twilights-last-
gleaming-all-private-property-rights-in-the-u-s-to-be-strategically-
usurped_04282015. [Accessed 04 May 2015].

[95] Particulate Matter | Air & Radiation | US EPA. 2015. *Particulate Matter | Air
& Radiation | US EPA.* [ONLINE] Available at:
http://www.epa.gov/particles/index.html. [Accessed 08 March 2015].

[96] The EPA's Half-Baked Wood Stove Regulation - US News. 2015. *The EPA's
Half-Baked Wood Stove Regulation - US News.* [ONLINE] Available at:
http://www.usnews.com/opinion/economic-intelligence/2014/05/27/the-epas-
half-baked-wood-stove-regulation. [Accessed 07 March 2015].

[97] Federal Noxious Weed Act of 1974 - Wikipedia, the free encyclopedia. 2015.
Federal Noxious Weed Act of 1974 - Wikipedia, the free encyclopedia.
[ONLINE] Available at:
http://en.wikipedia.org/wiki/Federal_Noxious_Weed_Act_of_1974. [Accessed
08 March 2015].

[98] Glyphosate poisoning. - PubMed - NCBI. 2015. *Glyphosate poisoning. -
PubMed - NCBI.* [ONLINE] Available at:
http://www.ncbi.nlm.nih.gov/pubmed/15862083. [Accessed 08 March 2015].

[99] Glyphosate induces human breast cancer cells growth via estrogen re... -

PubMed - NCBI. 2015. *Glyphosate induces human breast cancer cells growth via estrogen re... - PubMed - NCBI.* [ONLINE] Available at: http://www.ncbi.nlm.nih.gov/pubmed/23756170. [Accessed 08 March 2015].

[100]Glyphosate-based herbicides are toxic and endocrine disruptors in h... - PubMed - NCBI. 2015. *Glyphosate-based herbicides are toxic and endocrine disruptors in h... - PubMed - NCBI.* [ONLINE] Available at: http://www.ncbi.nlm.nih.gov/pubmed/19539684. [Accessed 08 March 2015].

[101]Glyphosate formulations induce apoptosis and necrosis in human umbi... - PubMed - NCBI. 2015. *Glyphosate formulations induce apoptosis and necrosis in human umbi... - PubMed - NCBI.* [ONLINE] Available at: http://www.ncbi.nlm.nih.gov/pubmed/19105591. [Accessed 08 March 2015].

[102]A glyphosate-based herbicide induces necrosis and apoptosis in matu... - PubMed - NCBI. 2015. *A glyphosate-based herbicide induces necrosis and apoptosis in matu... - PubMed - NCBI.* [ONLINE] Available at: http://www.ncbi.nlm.nih.gov/pubmed/22200534. [Accessed 08 March 2015].

[103]Roundup disrupts male reproductive functions by triggering calcium-... - PubMed - NCBI. 2015. *Roundup disrupts male reproductive functions by triggering calcium-... - PubMed - NCBI.* [ONLINE] Available at: http://www.ncbi.nlm.nih.gov/pubmed/23820267. [Accessed 08 March 2015].

[104]Cytotoxic and DNA-damaging properties of glyphosate and Roundup in ... - PubMed - NCBI. 2015. *Cytotoxic and DNA-damaging properties of glyphosate and Roundup in ... - PubMed - NCBI.* [ONLINE] Available at: http://www.ncbi.nlm.nih.gov/pubmed/22331240. [Accessed 08 March 2015].

[105]Monsanto Weedkiller Is 'Probably Carcinogenic,' WHO Says - Bloomberg Business. 2015. *Monsanto Weedkiller Is 'Probably Carcinogenic,' WHO Says - Bloomberg Business.* [ONLINE] Available at: http://www.bloomberg.com/news/articles/2015-03-20/who-classifies-monsanto-s-glyphosate-as-probably-carcinogenic-. [Accessed 21 March 2015].

[106]Roundup weedkiller 'probably' causes cancer, says WHO study | Environment | The Guardian. 2015. *Roundup weedkiller 'probably' causes cancer, says WHO study | Environment | The Guardian.* [ONLINE] Available at: http://www.theguardian.com/environment/2015/mar/21/roundup-cancer-who-glyphosate-. [Accessed 21 March 2015].

[107]Nestle Continues To Bottle Water In Drought-Crippled California. 2015. *Nestle Continues To Bottle Water In Drought-Crippled California.* [ONLINE] Available at: http://www.mintpressnews.com/nestle-continues-to-bottle-water-in-drought-crippled-california/194026/. [Accessed 03 May 2015].

[108]Codex Alimentarius : Rated Rx. 2015. *Codex Alimentarius : Rated Rx.* [ONLINE] Available at: http://www.thepeoplesvoice.org/TPV3/Voices.php/2011/06/08/codex-alimentarius-rated-rx. [Accessed 22 March 2015].

[109]FDA views your supplements in the same light as synthetic food preservatives. 2015. *FDA views your supplements in the same light as synthetic food preservatives.* [ONLINE] Available at: http://www.lef.org/featured-articles/2011/7/FDA-views-supplements-as-synthetic-food-preservatives/Page-01. [Accessed 08 March 2015].

[110]The Rise of Tyranny | WholeFoods Magazine. 2015. *The Rise of Tyranny | WholeFoods Magazine.* [ONLINE] Available at: http://www.wholefoodsmagazine.com/columns/vitamin-connection/rise-tyranny. [Accessed 08 March 2015].

[111]Codex Alimentarius - Wikipedia, the free encyclopedia. 2015. *Codex Alimentarius - Wikipedia, the free encyclopedia.* [ONLINE] Available at: http://en.wikipedia.org/wiki/Codex_Alimentarius. [Accessed 22 March 2015].

[112]Codex Alimentarius: Population Control under the Guise of Consumer Protection - NaturalNews.com. 2015. *Codex Alimentarius: Population Control under the Guise of Consumer Protection - NaturalNews.com.* [ONLINE] Available at: http://www.naturalnews.com/024128_CODEX_food_health.html#. [Accessed 22 March 2015].

[113] Codex Alimentarius: An Introduction to Soft Kill Eugenics | The Organic Prepper. 2015. *Codex Alimentarius: An Introduction to Soft Kill Eugenics | The Organic Prepper.* [ONLINE] Available at: http://www.theorganicprepper.ca/codex-alimentarius-an-introduction-to-soft-kill-eugenics-2-12102012. [Accessed 22 March 2015].

[114]War on Health: The FDA's Cult of Tyranny by Gary Null. 2015. *War on Health: The FDA's Cult of Tyranny by Gary Null.* [ONLINE] Available at: http://articles.mercola.com/sites/articles/archive/2012/08/18/war-on-health.aspx. [Accessed 08 March 2015].

[115] Senate bill 3767 seeks to put dietary supplement makers in prison for ten years (for telling the truth) - NaturalNews.com. 2015. *Senate bill 3767 seeks to put dietary supplement makers in prison for ten years (for telling the truth) - NaturalNews.com.* [ONLINE] Available at: http://www.naturalnews.com/029828_Senate_bill_3767_dietary_supplements.html. [Accessed 08 March 2015].

116 SWAT Team Shaking Down the Family Dairy Farm - Jeff Carter - Townhall Finance Conservative Columnists and Financial Commentary - Page 1. 2015. *SWAT Team Shaking Down the Family Dairy Farm - Jeff Carter - Townhall Finance Conservative Columnists and Financial Commentary - Page 1.* [ONLINE] Available at: http://finance.townhall.com/columnists/jeffcarter/2011/08/30/swat_team_shaking_down_the_family_dairy_farm. [Accessed 08 March 2015].

117 Raw Milk Raid on Amish Farmer Highlights Stupid FDA Tactics - Hit & Run: Reason.com. 2015. *Raw Milk Raid on Amish Farmer Highlights Stupid FDA Tactics - Hit & Run: Reason.com.* [ONLINE] Available at: http://reason.com/blog/2011/05/16/raw-milk-raid-on-amish-farmer. [Accessed 08 March 2015].

118 USDA Doesn't Need Submachine GunsAction Alert. 2015. *USDA Doesn't Need Submachine GunsAction Alert.* [ONLINE] Available at: http://www.farmtoconsumer.org/news_wp/?p=16769. [Accessed 08 March 2015].

119 US Postal Service Joins in Federal Ammo Purchases. 2015. *US Postal Service Joins in Federal Ammo Purchases.* [ONLINE] Available at: http://www.newsmax.com/Newsfront/USPS-ammo-purchase-federal/2014/04/14/id/565541/. [Accessed 22 March 2015].

120Why are federal agencies arming themselves?. 2015. *Why are federal agencies arming themselves?.* [ONLINE] Available at: http://www.onenewsnow.com/politics-govt/2014/05/20/why-are-federal-agencies-arming-themselves#.VUaNifC3uoU. [Accessed 03 May 2015].

121Is Opting Out of Processed Food the New Eating Disorder? | The Organic Prepper. 2015. *Is Opting Out of Processed Food the New Eating Disorder? | The Organic Prepper.* [ONLINE] Available at: http://www.theorganicprepper.ca/is-opting-out-of-processed-food-the-new-eating-disorder-03032015. [Accessed 08 March 2015].

122Is Opting Out of Processed Food the New Eating Disorder? | The Organic Prepper. 2015. *Is Opting Out of Processed Food the New Eating Disorder? | The Organic Prepper.* [ONLINE] Available at: http://www.theorganicprepper.ca/is-opting-out-of-processed-food-the-new-eating-disorder-03032015. [Accessed 08 March 2015].

123Compelling Peer Reviewed Scientific Studies | GMO Free PA. 2014. Compelling Peer Reviewed Scientific Studies | GMO Free PA. [ONLINE] Available at: http://www.gmofreepa.org/compelling-peer-reviewed-studies/#.VJgqvAABOM. [Accessed 22 December 2014].

[124]Justina Pelletier's legal nightmare should frighten all parents | Fox News. 2015. *Justina Pelletier's legal nightmare should frighten all parents | Fox News.* [ONLINE] Available at: http://www.foxnews.com/opinion/2014/06/17/justina-pelletier-legal-nightmare-should-frighten-all-parents/. [Accessed 08 March 2015].

[125]Justina Pelletier | TheBlaze.com. 2014. Justina Pelletier | TheBlaze.com. [ONLINE] Available at: http://www.theblaze.com/news/justina-pelletier/. [Accessed 22 December 2014].

[126]Justina Pelletier heads home after judge ends state custody - Metro - The Boston Globe. 2014. Justina Pelletier heads home after judge ends state custody - Metro - The Boston Globe. [ONLINE] Available at: http://www.bostonglobe.com/metro/2014/06/17/judge-orders-custody-justina-pelletier-returned-parents/mDWtuGURNawSuObO0pDX4J/story.html. [Accessed 22 December 2014].

[127] Justina Pelletier says 'no one should go through' her ordeal | Fox News. 2015. *Justina Pelletier says 'no one should go through' her ordeal | Fox News.* [ONLINE] Available at: http://www.foxnews.com/us/2014/06/28/justina-pelletier-says-no-one-should-go-through-her-ordeal/. [Accessed 08 March 2015].

[128] Justina Pelletier heads home after judge ends state custody - Metro - The Boston Globe. 2015. *Justina Pelletier heads home after judge ends state custody - Metro - The Boston Globe.* [ONLINE] Available at: http://www.bostonglobe.com/metro/2014/06/17/judge-orders-custody-justina-pelletier-returned-parents/mDWtuGURNawSuObO0pDX4J/story.html. [Accessed 08 March 2015].

[129] Obama Rings in the New Year By Signing Bill Allowing Indefinite Detention of Americans Washington's Blog. 2015. *Obama Rings in the New Year By Signing Bill Allowing Indefinite Detention of Americans Washington's Blog.* [ONLINE] Available at: http://www.washingtonsblog.com/2012/01/obama-rings-in-the-new-year-by-signing-bill-allowing-indefinite-detention-of-americans.html. [Accessed 08 March 2015].

[130] Forum Post: NDAA 2012: Obama Uses New Year's Eve As Cover To Usher In Fourth Reich Amerika | OccupyWallSt.org. 2015. *Forum Post: NDAA 2012: Obama Uses New Year's Eve As Cover To Usher In Fourth Reich Amerika | OccupyWallSt.org.* [ONLINE] Available at: http://occupywallst.org/forum/ndaa-2012-obama-uses-new-years-eve-as-cover-to-ush/. [Accessed 08 March 2015].

131 Obama Signs Controversial Defense Bill on New Year's Eve | Mother Jones. 2015. *Obama Signs Controversial Defense Bill on New Year's Eve | Mother Jones*. [ONLINE] Available at: http://www.motherjones.com/mojo/2012/01/obama-signs-controversial-defense-bill-new-years-eve. [Accessed 08 March 2015].

132 2015. [ONLINE] Available at: http://img.timeinc.net/time/magazine/archive/covers/2009/1101091228_400.jpg. [Accessed 08 March 2015].

133 Ben Bernanke - Person of the Year 2009 - TIME. 2015. *Ben Bernanke - Person of the Year 2009 - TIME*. [ONLINE] Available at: http://content.time.com/time/specials/packages/article/0,28804,1946375_194725 1_1947520,00.html. [Accessed 08 March 2015].

134 Federal Reserve System - Wikipedia, the free encyclopedia. 2015. *Federal Reserve System - Wikipedia, the free encyclopedia*. [ONLINE] Available at: http://en.wikipedia.org/wiki/Federal_Reserve_System. [Accessed 22 March 2015].

135 "That Couldn't Possibly Be True": The Startling Truth about the US Dollar | Casey Research. 2015. *"That Couldn't Possibly Be True": The Startling Truth about the US Dollar | Casey Research*. [ONLINE] Available at: http://www.caseyresearch.com/cdd/that-couldnt-possibly-be-true-the-startling-truth-about-the-us-dollar. [Accessed 08 March 2015].

136 Gold standard - Wikipedia, the free encyclopedia. 2015. *Gold standard - Wikipedia, the free encyclopedia*. [ONLINE] Available at: http://en.wikipedia.org/wiki/Gold_standard. [Accessed 22 March 2015].

137 Nixon Shock - Wikipedia, the free encyclopedia. 2015. *Nixon Shock - Wikipedia, the free encyclopedia*. [ONLINE] Available at: http://en.wikipedia.org/wiki/Nixon_Shock. [Accessed 22 March 2015].

138 Fractional-reserve banking - Wikipedia, the free encyclopedia. 2015. *Fractional-reserve banking - Wikipedia, the free encyclopedia*. [ONLINE] Available at: http://en.wikipedia.org/wiki/Fractional-reserve_banking. [Accessed 22 March 2015].

139 Modern Money Mechanics. *Modern Money Mechanics*. 2015. [ONLINE] Available at: http://upload.wikimedia.org/wikipedia/commons/4/4a/Modern_Money_Mechanics.pdf. [Accessed 08 March 2015].

140 DEATH BY GOVERNMENT: GENOCIDE AND MASS MURDER. 2015.

DEATH BY GOVERNMENT: GENOCIDE AND MASS MURDER. [ONLINE]
Available at: https://www.hawaii.edu/powerkills/NOTE1.HTM. [Accessed 08
March 2015].

[141] Democide - Wikipedia, the free encyclopedia. 2015. *Democide - Wikipedia,
the free encyclopedia.* [ONLINE] Available at:
http://en.wikipedia.org/wiki/Democide. [Accessed 01 January 2015].

[142] DEATH BY GOVERNMENT: GENOCIDE AND MASS MURDER. 2015.
DEATH BY GOVERNMENT: GENOCIDE AND MASS MURDER. [ONLINE]
Available at: https://www.hawaii.edu/powerkills/NOTE1.HTM. [Accessed 08
March 2015].

Interlude:

[1] The Only Thing Necessary for Evil to Triumph Is… | Casey Research. 2015.
The Only Thing Necessary for Evil to Triumph Is… | Casey Research.
[ONLINE] Available at: http://www.caseyresearch.com/cdd/the-only-thing-
necessary-for-evil-to-triumph-is. [Accessed 07 March 2015].

[2] Freeman's Perspective - See the world as it really is. 2015. *Freeman's
Perspective - See the world as it really is.* [ONLINE] Available at:
http://www.freemansperspective.com/. [Accessed 07 March 2015].

Chapter 10:

[1] Bloom, Jack M. *Seeing through the Eyes of the Polish Revolution: Solidarity
and the Struggle against Communism in Poland.* Chicago: Haymarket, 2014.
77. Print.

[2] Ibid., 229-231.

[3] Ibid., 233.

[4] In Crisis, Opportunity for Obama - WSJ . 2015. *In Crisis, Opportunity for
Obama - WSJ .* [ONLINE] Available at:
http://www.wsj.com/articles/SB122721278056345271. [Accessed 03 April
2015].

[5] Edward Bernays - Wikipedia, the free encyclopedia. 2015. *Edward Bernays -
Wikipedia, the free encyclopedia.* [ONLINE] Available at:
http://en.wikipedia.org/wiki/Edward_Bernays. [Accessed 09 March 2015].

[6] Propaganda (book) - Wikipedia, the free encyclopedia. 2015. *Propaganda

(book) - Wikipedia, the free encyclopedia. [ONLINE] Available at: http://en.wikipedia.org/wiki/Propaganda_%28book%29. [Accessed 09 March 2015].

[7] Bernays, Edward L. *The Verdict of Public Opinion on Propaganda.* New York: Universal Trade Syndicate, 1927. 7. Print.

[8] Self-actualization - Wikipedia, the free encyclopedia. 2015. *Self-actualization - Wikipedia, the free encyclopedia.* [ONLINE] Available at: http://en.wikipedia.org/wiki/Self-actualization#Maslow.27s_characteristics_of_self-actualizers. [Accessed 24 March 2015].

[9] Abraham Maslow - Wikipedia, the free encyclopedia. 2015. *Abraham Maslow - Wikipedia, the free encyclopedia.* [ONLINE] Available at: http://en.wikipedia.org/wiki/Abraham_Maslow#Hierarchy_of_needs. [Accessed 24 March 2015].

[10] Bonus Army - Wikipedia, the free encyclopedia. 2015. *Bonus Army - Wikipedia, the free encyclopedia.* [ONLINE] Available at: http://en.wikipedia.org/wiki/Bonus_Army. [Accessed 09 March 2015].

[11] Internment of Japanese Americans - Wikipedia, the free encyclopedia. 2015. *Internment of Japanese Americans - Wikipedia, the free encyclopedia.* [ONLINE] Available at: http://en.wikipedia.org/wiki/Internment_of_Japanese_Americans. [Accessed 09 March 2015].

[12] Kent State shootings - Wikipedia, the free encyclopedia. 2015. *Kent State shootings - Wikipedia, the free encyclopedia.* [ONLINE] Available at: http://en.wikipedia.org/wiki/Kent_State_shootings. [Accessed 09 March 2015].

[13] Ruby Ridge - Wikipedia, the free encyclopedia. 2015. *Ruby Ridge - Wikipedia, the free encyclopedia.* [ONLINE] Available at: http://en.wikipedia.org/wiki/Ruby_Ridge. [Accessed 09 March 2015].

[14] Assassination of Martin Luther King Jr. - Wikipedia, the free encyclopedia. 2015. *Assassination of Martin Luther King Jr. - Wikipedia, the free encyclopedia.* [ONLINE] Available at: http: //en.wikipedia.org/wiki/Assassination_of_Martin_Luther_King_Jr. [Accessed 24 March 2015].

[15] US doles out millions for street cameras - The Boston Globe. 2015. *US doles out millions for street cameras - The Boston Globe.* [ONLINE] Available at: http://www.boston.com/news/nation/articles/2007/08/12/us_doles_out_millions_

for_street_cameras/?page=full. [Accessed 26 March 2015].

[16] How many surveillance cameras are there in Manhattan? 2015. *How many surveillance cameras are there in Manhattan?* [ONLINE] Available at: http://www.slate.com/articles/news_and_politics/explainer/2010/05/big_apple_i s_watching_you.html. [Accessed 26 March 2015].

[17] Fernando "Ferfal" Aguirre, 2009. *The Modern Survival Manual: Surviving the Economic Collapse.* 1st Edition. Fernando Aguirre. Print.

[18] Penn, Shana. *Solidarity's Secret: The Women Who Defeated Communism in Poland.* Ann Arbor: U of Michigan, 2005. 104. Print

[19] Bloom, Jack M. *Seeing through the Eyes of the Polish Revolution: Solidarity and the Struggle against Communism in Poland.* Chicago: Haymarket, 2014. 104. Print.

[20] Ash, Timothy. *The Polish Revolution: Solidarity.* 3rd ed. New Haven: Yale UP, 2002. 126. Print.

[21] Bloom, Jack M. *Seeing through the Eyes of the Polish Revolution: Solidarity and the Struggle against Communism in Poland.* Chicago: Haymarket, 2014. 7. Print.

[22] Welcome to Temple Grandin's Official Autism Website. 2014. Welcome to Temple Grandin's Official Autism Website. [ONLINE] Available at: http://www.templegrandin.com/. [Accessed 22 December 2014].

[23] Darknet (overlay network) - Wikipedia, the free encyclopedia. 2015. *Darknet (overlay network) - Wikipedia, the free encyclopedia.* [ONLINE] Available at: http://en.wikipedia.org/wiki/Darknet_%28overlay_network%29. [Accessed 26 March 2015].

[24] Bloom, Jack M. *Seeing through the Eyes of the Polish Revolution: Solidarity and the Struggle against Communism in Poland.* Chicago: Haymarket, 2014. 77. Print.

[25] Orange Alternative - Wikipedia, the free encyclopedia. 2015. *Orange Alternative - Wikipedia, the free encyclopedia.* [ONLINE] Available at: http://en.wikipedia.org/wiki/Orange_Alternative. [Accessed 09 March 2015].

[26] Solidarity, Pope John Paul II, and the Orange Alternative: Bringing Down Communism in Poland | Tavaana Case Study. 2014. Solidarity, Pope John Paul II, and the Orange Alternative: Bringing Down Communism in Poland | Tavaana

Case Study. [ONLINE] Available at: https://tavaana.org/en/content/Solidarity-pope-john-paul-ii-and-orange-alternative-bringing-down-communism-poland-0. [Accessed 22 December 2014].

[27] Penn, Shana. *Solidarity's Secret: The Women Who Defeated Communism in Poland.* Ann Arbor: U of Michigan, 2005. 104. Print

[28] Ibid., 160.

[29] Ibid., 233.

[30] Ibid.

[31] Ibid., 236.

[32] Ibid., 304.

[33] Contribution Requirements | Affordable Care Act Health Coverage Guide. 2015. *Contribution Requirements | Affordable Care Act Health Coverage Guide.* [ONLINE] Available at: http://healthcoverageguide.org/reference-guide/laws-and-rights/contribution-requirements/. [Accessed 24 March 2015].

[34] ObamaCare Employer Mandate. 2015. *ObamaCare Employer Mandate.* [ONLINE] Available at: http://obamacarefacts.com/obamacare-employer-mandate/. [Accessed 24 March 2015].

[35] Workers' Defence Committee - Wikipedia, the free encyclopedia. 2014. Workers' Defence Committee - Wikipedia, the free encyclopedia. [ONLINE] Available at: http://en.wikipedia.org/wiki/Workers%27_Defence_Committee. [Accessed 22 December 2014].

[36] Tischner, Jo. "Afterword by Lech Wałęsa." *The Spirit of Solidarity.* 2nd ed. San Francisco: Harper & Row, 1984. Print.

[37] MacEachin, Douglas J. *US Intelligence and the Polish Crisis 1980-1981.* Washington, D.C.: Center for the Study of Intelligence, 2000. 23. Print.

[38] Bloom, Jack M. *Seeing through the Eyes of the Polish Revolution: Solidarity and the Struggle against Communism in Poland.* Chicago: Haymarket, 2014. 389. Print.

[39] The Forbidden History of the Black Panther Party - Politics - Utne Reader. 2015. *The Forbidden History of the Black Panther Party - Politics - Utne*

Reader. [ONLINE] Available at: http://www.utne.com/politics/black-panther-party-ze0z1303zwar.aspx. [Accessed 26 March 2015].

[40] Black Panther Party - Wikipedia, the free encyclopedia. 2015. *Black Panther Party - Wikipedia, the free encyclopedia.* [ONLINE] Available at: http://en.wikipedia.org/wiki/Black_Panther_Party. [Accessed 26 March 2015].

[41] Bloom, Jack M. *Seeing through the Eyes of the Polish Revolution: Solidarity and the Struggle against Communism in Poland.* Chicago: Haymarket, 2014. 315. Print.

[42] Ibid., 316.

[43] MacEachin, Douglas J. *US Intelligence and the Polish Crisis 1980-1981.* Washington, D.C.: Center for the Study of Intelligence, 2000. 171. Print.

[44] Executive Order -- National Defense Resources Preparedness | The White House. 2015. *Executiv Order -- National Defense Resources Preparedness | The White House.* [ONLINE] Available at: http://www.whitehouse.gov/the-press-office/2012/03/16/executive-order-national-defense-resources- preparedness. [Accessed 16 March 2015].

[45] Obama's Plan to Seize Control of Our Economy and Our Lives - Forbes. 2015. *Obama's Plan To   Seize Control Of Our Economy And Our Lives - Forbes.* [ONLINE] Available at: http://www.forbes.com/sites/jimpowell/2012/04/29/obamas-plan-to-seize-control-of-our-economy-and-our-lives/. [Accessed 16 March 2015].

[46] MacEachin, Douglas J. *US Intelligence and the Polish Crisis 1980-1981.* Washington, D.C.: Center for the Study of Intelligence, 2000. 176-177. Print.

[47] Ibid., 220.

[48] Ibid., 83.

[49] Ibid.

[50] Ibid., 85.

[51] Ibid., 86.

[52] Nuremberg trials - Wikipedia, the free encyclopedia. 2015. *Nuremberg trials - Wikipedia, the free encyclopedia.* [ONLINE] Available at:

http://en.wikipedia.org/wiki/Nuremberg_trials. [Accessed 26 March 2015].

[53] Bloom, Jack M. *Seeing through the Eyes of the Polish Revolution: Solidarity and the Struggle against Communism in Poland.* Chicago: Haymarket, 2014. 28-29. Print.

[54] Ash, Timothy. *The Polish Revolution: Solidarity.* 3rd ed. New Haven: Yale UP, 2002. 96. Print.

[55] Ibid., 97

[56] Ibid., 98.

[57] Anna Walentynowicz - Wikipedia, the free encyclopedia. 2014. Anna Walentynowicz - Wikipedia, the free encyclopedia. [ONLINE] Available at: http://en.wikipedia.org/wiki/Anna_Walentynowicz. [Accessed 22 December 2014].

[58] Ash, Timothy. *The Polish Revolution: Solidarity.* 3rd ed. New Haven: Yale UP, 2002. 4. Print.

[59] MacEachin, Douglas J. *US Intelligence and the Polish Crisis 1980-1981.* Washington, D.C.: Center for the Study of Intelligence, 2000. 4. Print.

[60] Penn, Shana. *Solidarity's Secret: The Women Who Defeated Communism in Poland.* Ann Arbor: U of Michigan, 2005. 183. Print.

[61] Ibid., 181.

[62] Ibid., 182.

[63] Ibid., 188.

[64] Ibid., *Introduction.*

[65] Ibid.

[66] MacEachin, Douglas J. *US Intelligence and the Polish Crisis 1980-1981.* Washington, D.C.: Center for the Study of Intelligence, 2000. 17-18. Print.

[67] Ibid., 73.

[68] Ibid., 70-74.

⁶⁹ Ibid., 74.

⁷⁰ Ibid., 56.

⁷¹ Bloom, Jack M. *Seeing through the Eyes of the Polish Revolution: Solidarity and the Struggle against Communism in Poland.* Chicago: Haymarket, 2014. 91. Print.

⁷² Fourth-generation warfare - Wikipedia, the free encyclopedia. 2015. *Fourth-generation warfare - Wikipedia, the free encyclopedia.* [ONLINE] Available at: http://en.wikipedia.org/wiki/Fourth-generation_warfare. [Accessed 16 March 2015].

⁷³ Penn, Shana. *Solidarity's Secret: The Women Who Defeated Communism in Poland.* Ann Arbor: U of Michigan, 2005. 266-268. Print.

⁷⁴ Movements and Campaigns. 2014. Movements and Campaigns. [ONLINE] Available at: http://www.nonviolent-conflict.org/index.php/movements-and-campaigns/movements-and-campaigns-summaries?sobi2Task=sobi2Details&sobi2Id=8. [Accessed 22 December 2014].

⁷⁵ Ash, Timothy. *The Magic Lantern: The Revolution of '89 Witnessed in Warsaw,Budapest, Berlin, and Prague.* New York: Random House, 1990. 38-39. Print.

⁷⁶ MacEachin, Douglas J. *US Intelligence and the Polish Crisis 1980-1981.* Washington, D.C.: Center for the Study of Intelligence, 2000. 22. Print.

⁷⁷ Ibid., 21.

⁷⁸ Penn, Shana. "Chapter 10." *Solidarity's Secret: The Women Who Defeated Communism in Poland.* Ann Arbor: U of Michigan, 2005. Print.

⁷⁹ Bloom, Jack M. *Seeing through the Eyes of the Polish Revolution: Solidarity and the Struggle against Communism in Poland.* Chicago: Haymarket, 2014. 134. Print.

⁸⁰ Ibid., 135.

⁸¹ Ibid., 129.

⁸² Ash, Timothy. _The Magic Lantern: The Revolution of '89 Witnessed in Warsaw, Budapest, Berlin, and Prague.* New York: Random House, 1990. 16. Print.

[83] Bloom, Jack M. *Seeing through the Eyes of the Polish Revolution: Solidarity and the Struggle against Communism in Poland.* Chicago: Haymarket, 2014. 360- 361. Print.

[84] Ash, Timothy. *The Magic Lantern: The Revolution of '89 Witnessed in Warsaw, Budapest, Berlin, and Prague.* New York: Random House, 1990. 27-31. Print.

[85] Anonymous (group) - Wikipedia, the free encyclopedia. 2015. *Anonymous (group) - Wikipedia, the free encyclopedia.* [ONLINE] Available at: http://en.wikipedia.org/wiki/Anonymous_%28group%29. [Accessed 28 March 2015].

Afterword:

[1] 2010 Polish Air Force Tu-154 crash - Wikipedia, the free encyclopedia. 2014. 2010 Polish Air Force Tu-154 crash - Wikipedia, the free encyclopedia. [ONLINE] Available at: http://en.wikipedia.org/wiki/2010_Polish_Air_Force_Tu-154_crash. [Accessed 22 December 2014].

[2] Katyn massacre - Wikipedia, the free encyclopedia. 2015. *Katyn massacre - Wikipedia, the free encyclopedia.* [ONLINE] Available at: http://en.wikipedia.org/wiki/Katyn_massacre. [Accessed 28 March 2015].

Deleted Scenes:

[1] Penn, Shana. *Solidarity's Secret: The Women Who Defeated Communism in Poland.* Ann Arbor: U of Michigan, 2005. 76. Print.

[2] Thoreau, Henry David (1849). *Civil Disobedience.* first paragraph.

Made in the USA
Middletown, DE
15 June 2023

32673278R00229